AWAKE IN THE DARK

AWAKE IN THE DARK

An Anthology of American Film Criticism, 1915 to the Present

EDITED BY DAVID DENBY

VINTAGE BOOKS

A DIVISION OF RANDOM HOUSE / NEW YORK

A VINTAGE BOOKS ORIGINAL, May 1977

FIRST EDITION

 Published in the United States by Random House, Inc., New York, and simultaneously in Canada by Random House of Canada Limited, Toronto.

Library of Congress Cataloging in Publication Data

Main entry under title:

Awake in the dark.

1. Moving-picture criticism—United States.
2. Moving-pictures—Addresses, essays, lectures.
I. Denby, David.
PN1995.A86 791.43'0973 76-62494
ISBN 0-394-72194-2 pbk.

Manufactured in the United States of America

Grateful acknowledgment is made to the following for permission to reprint previously published material:

The Dial Press: "The Passion of Anna" by John Simon. Reprinted from *Movies Into Film: Film Criticism 1967–1970* by John Simon. Copyright © 1971 by John Simon.

E.P. Dutton & Co., Inc.: "Toward a Theory of Film History" by Andrew Sarris. Reprinted from *The American Cinema* by Andrew Sarris. Copyright © 1968 by Andrew Sarris.

Manny Farber: "Preston Sturges: Success in the Movies" by Manny Farber. Originally published in *City Lights,* 1954; "The Decline of the Actor" by Manny Farber, excerpted from "The Fading Movie Star," which was published in *Commentary,* 1963. Reprinted by permission of the author.

Farrar, Straus & Giroux, Inc.: "The Imagination of Disaster" by Susan Sontag. Reprinted from *Against Interpretation* by Susan Sontag. Copyright © 1965, 1966 by Susan Sontag.

The Film Society of Lincoln Center: "Notes on Film Noir" by Paul Schrader. Reprinted from *Film Comment,* Vol. 8, No. 1, Spring, 1972. Copyright © 1972 by Film Comment Publishing Corporation.

Grosset & Dunlap, Inc.: Selections from "David Wark Griffith," "Comedy's Greatest Era," "Undirectable Director," and "Short Reviews," totaling 39 pages from *Agee on Film,* Volume 1 by James Agee. Copyright © 1958 by The James Agee Trust.

Harper & Row Publishers, Inc.: "La Notte-February 26, 1962" by Stanley Kauffmann. Reprinted from *A World of Film* by Stanley Kauffmann. Copyright © 1962 by Stanley Kauffmann.

ACKNOWLEDGMENTS

I am indebted to my friends Gail Winston (of Random House), Sanford Schwartz and Paul Warshow for editorial advice and criticism during the preparation of this volume.

CONTENTS

INTRODUCTION

It is a well-known truth, or should be, that any anthologist entirely consistent in his criteria will wind up with a dead book on his hands. In compiling this anthology of American film criticism I did an elaborate juggling act, including certain writers who met a given criterion while excluding others who met the same criterion but disappointed in one way or another. My intentions were to suggest the depth and variety of American film criticism with selections from all periods of movie history after 1915 (the time when film criticism begins to get interesting), and to put together a book of good prose that could stand on the shelf next to comparable volumes of literary, dramatic, art, dance or music criticism. Most film critics would probably shudder at the phrase *belles lettres* (they might prefer *lettres sauvages*), but I suppose they must accept the consequences of respectability. Film criticism has established itself as a minor branch of literature.

It may not be self-evident that a book of good writing on movies must inevitably be a book of *journalism.* Despite the considerable celebrity of the American journalist-critics, one still needs to assert that their work is the essential American literature on film. They generally write about film history better than the film historians, about film aesthetics better than the aestheticians. This should not always be true: The American universities, if they do not succumb to certain obscurantist methodologies imported from the Fifth and Sixth arrondissements of Paris, may yet produce a group of scholar-critics to compare with Lionel Trilling, R. P. Blackmur, Kenneth Burke, F.O. Matthiessen, et al.* However, it is certainly true of the situation so far. With the exception of Erwin Panofsky's classic essay "Style and Medium in the Motion Pictures" (reprinted here) and Hugo Munsterberg's *The Photoplay: A Psychological Study* (1916), there isn't much academic writing on film that's exciting to read. There may be two practical reasons for this: Until recently, archival facilities were less than adequate, and scholars who wrote about film could not secure tenure at a major American university. In defense of my exclusivity, I cite the reader's pleasure. I was determined to print nothing solemn or bland or jargon-ridden, and also nothing

*I am not forgetting the film critic Andrew Sarris, who is a tenured professor at Columbia University. Sarris first made his reputation as a journalist.

written in that ghastly loosened-tie, feet-up-on-desk style of arch condescension that academic writers on film often affect when trying to relax.

The writers included here had to be lucid, aggressive, immersed in the subject; they had to "put their blood," as Toscanini once described his attitude toward conducting. No slummers or summer vacationers would be allowed in these sacred precincts. This meant leaving out a great number of famous and distinguished authors. It seems that nearly everyone in twentieth-century American literature has written about film at one time or another (like pornography, film criticism appears to exert a peculiar fascination for writers), and for the most part these occasional efforts have been bad. There seems to be a widespread notion that film criticism is too important to be left to film critics. In the first three decades of film history, when film criticism was far less developed than it is now and movies were widely seen as leading to the destruction (or alternately to the salvation) of the entire republic, it was not uncommon for a distinguished man of letters to launch boldly into print with an article in praise of Chaplin or Eisenstein or Murnau, follow this up with a lyrical celebration of the "potential" of the film medium combined with a slashing attack on Hollywood "commercialism," only to discover after one or two more articles that the entire field had been covered and there was nothing further to be said.

It is of course precisely at this point that serious film criticism begins. I have omitted all these distinguished visitors and occasional commentators, whether they were hostile scolds (Randolph Bourne, Theodore Dreiser, H. L. Mencken, George Jean Nathan, Stark Young, Lincoln Kirstein, Edmund Wilson, Paul Goodman, Diana Trilling, Philip Roth, James Baldwin, et al.) or genial well-wishers (William Dean Howells, Carl Sandburg, Mark Van Doren, Henry Miller, Delmore Schwartz, et al.). Neither the despair and lively malice of the first group nor the hopeful yea-saying of the second has produced much of lasting value on movies, and I suspect that these men and women, so astute in most respects, would be among the first to admit it. I have also omitted the work of Saul Bellow and Norman Mailer, both of whose occasional writings on movies display a breath-taking and finally defeating mixture of brilliant insight, dressed-up commonplaces, and sheer bad judgment. (Most of these writers certainly could have become great film critics if they had tried; my point is only that they weren't, in the long run, very interested in movies and refused to approach the task of writing about them with a decent amount of humility.)

My contributors are either working critics or those intellectuals writing occasionally on movies who have given themselves to the medium in a totally uncondescending way. But how to choose among so many potential contributors? I wanted to give an informal overview of American film criticism without printing anything that was *solely* of historical value. Everything here is still alive today—most of the movies have stood the test of time, the writing still vibrates. In a book of living writing, I felt that I could not print the critics of the twenties who lamented the American cinema's lack of "refinement"; or the technological utopians of the early thirties who, fired up by the recently imported classics of the Soviet cinema and the writings of Sergei Eisenstein, confidently expected that "montage" methods would lead to the psychological, moral, and political regeneration of the movies; or, at a more popular level of Marxism, those "progressive" critics of the middle and late thirties who scorned the superior Hollywood comedies, musicals, and gangster movies of the time, only to celebrate the "maturity" of a medium which produced *Winterset* and *The Life of Emile Zola.* I could not print special pleaders of any sort who exploited the authority of critical language in order to attract reluctant moviegoers to unpopular genres (such as "underground" films or documentaries); or print anyone who cared more for theories of film than for particular movies, styles or actors—not in a book of good writing, anyway. Having compiled this list of prejudices, I hasten to add that I omitted dozens of pieces as good, or almost as good, as the ones printed. But it's useless to apologize: an anthologist must choose.

As many have noted, the American journalist-critics are in an enviable position: They have *readers* (particularly in recent years). Their influence on box-office receipts is small and functions only in special cases (foreign films and small-budget or "independent" American films), but they have a serious effect on reputations, and they are the prime stimulant to good talk about movies, the give-and-take among constant moviegoers which is so much part of the fun—both the serious fun and the frivolous fun. And lately they've been doing something else. In a famous diatribe against the cult of literary criticism in the early fifties ("The Age of Criticism"), Randall Jarrell remarked, "One occasionally encounters intellectual couples for whom some critic has taken the place of the minister they no longer have." I submit that in recent years one is likely to encounter intellectual couples for whom Kael or Sarris or Simon or Haskell has taken the place of the Wilson or Trilling they no longer have. (I don't mean that the movie critics are as profound as Wilson or Trilling, only that their significance for readers is similar.) Increasingly, they are expected to arbitrate manners and morals. One goes to them, as one goes to the best literary critics, for "style and wit and sermons [Jarrell again], informal essays, aesthetics, purple passages, confessions, aphorisms, wisdom—a thousand things."

Needless to say, critics writing on weekly or even monthly deadlines cannot satisfy all these demands, and readers frequently become disgusted with them. Like most public figures in America, movie critics are buffeted by alternating waves of admiration and revulsion. In recent years, it frequently has been said that the critics want to be media stars; that they have an insatiable need to dominate public opinion or seduce public approval; that their bouts of squabbling are tiresome and unilluminating—mere personal quarrels masked as conflicts of principle; that they spend too much time dramatizing themselves and not enough time reviewing the movie at hand; that when they finally get around to the movie they don't stick to the point but bring in "irrelevant" sociological or political speculations; and so on.

Some of this may be true as description of individual performances, but it doesn't add up to much. There's a certain amount of jealousy in these attacks (they generally come from dramatic or literary critics) and more than a little priggishness. Of course critics dramatize themselves—that's partly what makes them exciting as writers. Something like a "star system" operates in criticism—is that so terrible? Criticism never really matters, never carries much weight, until one writer sticks with it, week after week, month after month, book after book, and establishes a kind of communion with readers. And after the plays or novels or movies have faded from view the relationship with readers remains. We don't continue to read Bernard Shaw's music criticism because we're interested in the opera singers of the eighteen-nineties. Edmund Wilson certainly did not commit any of the sins listed above—that grand-seignorial manner he perfected at the age of thirty and sustained for over forty years was a demand for respect, not affection—yet readers returned to him over and over because Wilson, in his own person and through the medium of his magisterial prose, embodied with such openly theatrical force the *figure* of a literary critic. Readers wanted to read *Wilson,* as well as his discussion of a new book or reflection on an old one, and they stayed with him even after his interest in contemporary writing declined and he became cranky and haughty. For years, his self-dramatization attracted readers, and he used his influence to create interest in the writing that mattered to him. Indeed, if interest in literary and dramatic criticism has declined somewhat recently, it may be because few critics of first-rate ability have the energy or courage to write as frequently as Wilson or Alfred Kazin or Stark Young or Eric Bentley or Robert Brustein all did in their days as journalists. Perhaps these genres could use a few "stars."

Jarrell was writing out of a very real fear that people were reading literary criticism *instead* of poetry and fiction. But this is hardly a problem in a mass medium like movies; critics rarely discourage moviegoers from seeing a given film. Unlike theater critics, whose word can close a show, movie critics enjoy a situation of relative powerlessness, which frees them to cultivate their personal pleasures and vices. Of course, if that's all they do, they aren't much good. In any fine piece of criticism, the "personality" of the critic recedes (Jarrell wanted it to disappear, but that's impossible) and becomes a secondary medium through which the movie is recreated for the reader.

There exists a second, more serious complaint against American film journalism. From time to time we have heard that American criticism is congenitally shallow and intellectually feeble—that it lacks an "intellectual center." According to this analysis, a critic working without a theory or system, or at least a sustained and explicit set of assumptions, must inevitably carry himself and his readers into a swamp of "mere sensibility" or, even more contemptible, "mere impressionism."

It's tempting just to quote T.S. Eliot's famous remark about criticism, "The only method is to be very intelligent," and leave it at that, but I don't suppose this will do. Putting aside the evaluation of American criticism in these complaints, we can admit a partial truth here. Compared with French or German writing on film, American film criticism is strikingly anti-theoretical, empirical, descriptive, pragmatic, local, and spontaneous. We are concerned more with getting the surface right—the way a film looks or feels, the contours of a director's style, an actor's stance or gesture—than with analyzing in detail the subtext of sociopolitical meanings in a film, or with evaluating it according to some platonic ideal of cinema. We describe more, interpret less.

Even Robert Warshow, who has often been described as a "sociological" critic, never attempted to sustain a general theoretical framework from one piece to the next. His understanding of the relations between art and society was only one of the many kinds of intelligence that Warshow brought to bear on movies. And the same is true of the best "sociological" critics who followed Warshow—Pauline Kael, for instance, who is occasionally a superb sociologist of taste as well as a fine aesthetic critic. Andrew Sarris is widely known for his Americanization of the *auteur* theory; but as Sarris readily admits, the theory is principally an attitude toward film history, and not a method to be applied to the evaluation of every new film.

In general, the Americans have been heavily influenced by the Anglo-American literary tradition of "moral criticism." An aestheticized moral imagination is absolutely necessary in the evaluation of movies, a commercially corrupt art form, whose products often enter into the most intricate and duplicitous relations with reality. Nearly all the good American film critics have been moralists, though they've done their best to disguise it.

This divergence in critical temperament is hardly an accident; fully developed national traditions in philosophy and pedagogy stand behind it. Yet Americans have no reason to feel defensive about their own traditions; although European criticism may at times appear rather formidable, we should not conclude that American informality is a product of intellectual laziness. "Getting the surface right" requires first-rate descriptive abilities; working without a critical system requires independence of mind, rhetorical ingenuity, and—invaluable for a critic—a good-humored sense of proportion about the importance of the object at hand and the work one is doing. The American critics, despite the allegedly monstrous egotism of the group as individuals, have consciously cultivated a certain modesty of attitude, a refusal of *authority.* They have been loath to construct a law out of their personal impressions.

Many of them would say that they have been modest by necessity. Film is an art form with an industrial base, intimately connected to the economy and banking systems, the social and political morale, of individual countries; it combines many of the older arts (theater, photography, fiction, music) and requires the collaboration of dozens of artists, craftsmen, and businessmen; it is simultaneously realism and dream, reportage and myth, narrative and image. To assimilate all these variables into a unified theoretical model would probably be impossible; and even if it were possible, the model would be so bulky that anyone using it would feel like a nature-lover crossing a meadow in a Rolls-Royce. Most of us prefer to go on foot —we see more and have a better time. Indeed, the critic is in desperate need of all the mobility he can get. Even if he writes only occasionally, he's forced to confront a bewildering variety of cultural products, and he would be crazy not to value his freedom to place each movie in whatever context suits his purpose. Like the western hero, the American critic travels light and moves on when the action gets stale.

But to say that eclecticism has been the dominant mode among American critics is not the same as saying that their work is a mere chaos of assertion or that they have been hostile to general ideas or to methods of interpretation. This book is bursting with different notions on how to look at and evaluate films, debates over movie history and style, and complex but uncodified notations on myth, society, gesture. I have organized it in sections that suggest some of the major traditions of criticism and lines of personal influence, yet, as the reader will see, none of the writers here could be mistaken for any other. Synthesizing like mad, jumping from one level of discourse to another, the American critic has tried to be Renaissance man and hipster at the same time; what emerges from the intellectual disorder of his profession is the charm of a highly charged, utterly personal voice—the Whitmanesque rapture of Vachel Lindsay, the tough-guy sentience of Manny Farber, the alternately grave and savage eloquence of James Agee.

The reader may wonder why any of this needs defending or why I insist on clinging to such archaic and homely terms as "sensibility" or "personal voice." The answer is that the kind of good writing found in this book is coming under increasing attack (in the terms that I suggested earlier) in university film courses, and is in danger of being replaced by the new methodologies—structuralism and semiology—that now dominate serious film discourse in France and, increasingly, in England. This is not the place for discussion of either of these "sciences." However, as a frequent teacher of undergraduate film courses, I cannot resist wondering what effect this sort of study will have on the students who undertake it. Although it's not really their own fault, American students of the mid-seventies are likely to have enjoyed a narrower personal experience of the arts (including movies) than students of twenty or thirty years ago. The college teacher usually cannot take it for granted that more than a few eyes will light up if he mentions *Bleak House* or *Tristan und Isolde* in passing, or even that students have seen many movie classics beyond the Groucho-Garbo-Gable-Bogie stand-bys. Therefore if he is going to render a genuine service, the film teacher should at least try to open as many doors as possible, relating the film at hand to work in the other arts, to other films earlier and later in film history, and in general using his hold on the students' attention to reduce their panic and inertia before the seeming inaccessibility of culture.

In light of this, I despair at the thought of students being asked (now or in the near future) to swallow such indigestibles as a 120-page dissection, complete with graphs, charts, equations, vectors, and God knows what else, of one of the most charming films ever made, *North by Northwest.* The jargon in this kind of article is a nightmare come true and beyond parody; forcing undergraduates to spend weeks mastering this mumbo-jumbo for the purpose of studying two or at most three films seems a kind of outrage. And I think the likely effect of such study will be to discourage all but the most curious and tough-minded students from taking any serious intellectual interest in movies in the future.

Film study needs a wider, not a narrower, focus. There's no reason, in fact, why it should not involve a joyous summing-up of everything one has known or felt. And the same is true of criticism. The writers in this volume, seeking only a personal rather than a formal discipline, give the impression of intellectual good health: It shows in their excitability, their eagerness to dazzle and entertain. They are people who have found the right tone, which is always a problem in writing about popular art forms.

The early film critics, for instance, were largely baffled by what they saw. Before about 1914 there was very little writing that we would now recognize as criticism; most reviews consisted either of blandly inert summations of plot and character or vaporous rhapsodizing on the "reality" of the images. Anguished attacks on the movies as mass perverter were met by equally excited prophecies of democratic enlightenment; meanwhile, few were willing to look closely at what was happening on the screen. Movies were considered the poor sister of the arts—a disreputable, lowbrow entertainment for workers and immigrants—and movie criticism was the poor sister of journalism. Some of the critics even used pseudonyms to cover their shame (the same thing was to happen fifty years later in television criticism).

Of course, while the critics were still clearing their throats, Porter and Griffith and Sennett (just to name the native talents) were inventing the art of film. In a sense, it was Chaplin who created film criticism, perhaps because his combination of slapstick and pathos was a recognizable art form—mime. However, when Chaplin was not on screen and intellectuals could not recognize the art in movies so easily, they remained in deep trouble. What, after all, was the right attitude to take? When reviewing a book of poetry or an exhibition of paintings one could apply the highest standards of criticism, as measured by previous achievements in these arts. But a mass industrial form that connected with so large an audience presented new problems. Shouldn't movies and the movie audience be elevated to the level of theater? Or was there possibly something hard to describe in those whirling comedies and childish melodramas, something poetic, wildly beautiful—not art exactly but a devastating new form of *energy?* For the poet Vachel Lindsay movies were a glorious new democratic art form whose primary characteristic was *spectacle.* Neither mechanically realistic nor stagelike, the movie image was a "mural painting from which flashes of lightning come."

But Lindsay was more a lyric celebrant than a critic. The first modern film critic in this country was undoubtedly the late Gilbert Seldes. By "modern" I mean a writer who embraced the medium without illusions or disdain and who consequently settled into that tone of fond exasperation which we recognize as the sound of a movie critic. Here, for instance (from the chapter of *The Seven Lively Arts* that I have included), is Seldes in 1923, complaining about the possible replacement of slapstick comedy by the "sophisticated" contemporary melodramas of Cecil B. De Mille:

> . . . the tradition of gentility, the hope of being "refined," has touched the grotesque comedy; its directors have heard abuse and sly remarks about custard pies so long that they have begun to believe in them, and the madness which is a monstrous sanity in the movie comedy is likely to die out. The moving picture is being prettified; the manufacturers and exhibitors are growing more and more pretentious, and the riot of slap-stick seems out of place in a "presentation" which begins with the overture to *Tannhäuser,*

and includes a baritone from the imperial opera house in Warsaw singing *Indian Love Lyrics* in front of an art curtain.

Now there's nothing spectacular about this, but I can't help thinking that readers who came across it in the early twenties must have thought, "*That's* the way a movie critic should sound." Once writers like Seldes began to acknowledge the complex kinds of pleasure they got from the seeming crudity of the images on screen, the problem of writing about movies became one of talent, not of attitude. Indeed, out of the meeting of intellectuals and mass medium would come a new tone in American letters. Many of the best movie critics would take the formal discourse of criticism and joyously drive it *down,* introducing puns, jokes, slang, obscenities, patter—anything for greater speed and temperament, anything to capture in prose the multiplicity of sensations that the movies offered. If the critic has become something of a celebrity in recent years, part of the reason may be that an increasing number of people realize that to write well about movies is very, very hard.

November, 1976

AWAKE IN THE DARK

IN DEFENSE OF A POPULAR NEW ART FORM

In the beginning, the movies were rude, the audience was rude, and movie art developed in an atmosphere of exhilarating freedom. But the movies' freedom was constantly being threatened, not only by commercial pressure to lower standards, but by well-meaning (and sometimes not so well-meaning) people who discerned in the movies' extraordinary popularity with working-class and immigrant audiences a threat to social stability, established standards of behavior, and older cultural values. For years the movies were hounded both by the vestigial forces of Puritanism (which claimed their greatest victory in prohibition) and by spokesmen for class interests fearful of the movies' effect on the huge urban audience. Eager to turn the movies into an instrument of popular refinement, these spokesmen—certain critics, social commentators, would-be censors in church and civic organizations, and also a minority of people working in the film business itself—would have been appalled by the notion that the movies' "vulgarity" was the source of their strength and possibly the source of their art, too. In their attempt to bring the medium under social control, the uplifters turned automatically to the dying tradition of gentility (social and aesthetic) for ammunition. In response, some of the best early critics (Gilbert Seldes in particular) carried H. L. Mencken's struggle against the genteel tradition into the arena of popular culture.

Moral and social disapproval of movies has persisted in a variety of forms until the present day, and so has the effort of certain critics to preserve movies from false notions of the good. Purists of the rough, wise philistines (but not really philistines at all), these critics have celebrated the movies' ability to transform the crude materials of popular imagination into vigorous and at times complex works of art.

In this chapter from his 1915 volume, *The Art of the Moving Picture,* the poet Vachel Lindsay admits that the silent film was ill-suited to bring out the intensities and ironies of an Ibsen play; instead, Lindsay praises the movies' genius as spectacle and dramatic tableaux—what he called, in a kind of rapture, *splendor.* The evocative power of Lindsay's rapid-fire sentences, the high spirits and obvious fellowship with the audience, remains exciting even after six decades. Writing only seven years later, Gilbert Seldes was afraid that movies were already succumbing to a kind of vulgar, fashionable "sophistication," against which he posed the vigorous crudity of slapstick comedy. For Seldes, the spirit of slapstick ("Fantasy is liberated, imagination is still riotous and healthy") was capable of producing a revolution in the arts.

In Seldes's piece, and also in Erwin Panofsky's magnificent essay, "Style and Medium in the Motion Pictures," one senses an implicit hostility to the legitimate theater, with its bourgeois rituals of dressing up and elaborate sociability, and its unexciting, middlebrow productions. In their statements of aesthetic preference there's an element of social bravado, of going against class expectations. Panofsky, of course, was not a journalist but one of the great art historians of the century, and his essay remains exciting, in part, because it's clearly a declaration of forbidden love; one gathers that in Panofsky's circle at Princeton love for the movies was not readily admitted. Even more surprising, it is not the art film that Panofsky praises, but the ordinary narrative cinema—the central tradition of movies; and it is not the finer feelings he sees as the source of the movies' strength, but the emotions of conventional folk art—a primitive sense of justice and decorum, sentimentality, mild sadism and pornography, slapstick humor. Whether Panofsky would have extended his approval of movies into the sixties and seventies, when the sadism and pornography were no longer so mild and the primitive sense of justice had become a nihilistic fantasy of revenge, remains an unsettling question for anyone trying to sustain faith in the ultimate beneficence of a mass art form and its audience.

Strictly speaking, his essay is a work of aesthetics, but critics have been borrowing or debating his ideas for years, and I did not see how I could possibly exclude the piece. One critic who practiced Panofsky's realist aesthetic was Otis Ferguson, who wrote about movies mainly for *The New Republic* in the thirties and early forties. (Ferguson, an enlistee in the merchant marine, was killed in 1943 when his ship was bombed in the Bay of Salerno.) In his essay, "Life Goes to the Pictures," while admitting that "there is everywhere in pictures a tendency to fakery and Dick Powell," Ferguson praises the American cinema for allowing a considerable degree of workaday reality to break through the artifice. As portraits of workingmen, Ferguson preferred the Warner Brothers melodrama *Black Fury* to G. W. Pabst's *Kameradschaft* (which he admired, too) because the American film, less consciously formulated as art, was more successful at involving the audience in the lives of its characters.

It's eternally to Ferguson's credit that he never allowed his populist ethos to degenerate into the dreary righteousness endemic among leftist writers of the thirties. Indeed, Ferguson could be wickedly funny, and Alfred Kazin has compared his informal, loose-limbed, melancholy wit to the sound of good jazz. But Kazin also gives the impression (in his memoir *Starting Out in the Thirties*) that Ferguson was almost exclusively a wise guy, hostile to all art except jazz. Actually, Ferguson's occasional jeering at European "art films" (see the final section of this book) and at the bohemian audience that appreciated these films all too readily was a serious attempt to distinguish between mere artiness and genuine art, which Ferguson celebrated as warmly as anyone else when he found it. In this regard, Ferguson was a direct influence on Pauline Kael, a much greater critic.

Ferguson was perhaps the first critic of note to insist on the value of the American genre film—musicals, comedies, and action films of all sorts. His appreciation of action films was taken up by Manny Farber, who wrote for *The New Republic* (and many other places) in the forties and after. If Raymond Chandler had been a movie critic, he might have sounded a little like Manny Farber. Farber introduced a note of suave brutality and knowingness—the lowlife poetry of big-city moviegoing—into American film criticism, most famously in this essay of 1957, "Underground Films." By "underground" Farber did not mean the independent avant-garde cinema (later known as "underground movies"), but the fast, unpretentious male action films of the thirties and forties turned out by directors (Hawks, Wellman, Walsh, et al.) working "anonymously" in the backlot corner of some vast studio on pulp material assumed to be hopelessly banal. Unpressured by studio demands for "prestige" filmmaking, these men were "able to spring the leanest, shrewdest, sprightliest notes from material that looks like junk . . . The important thing is not so much the banal-seeming journeys to nowhere that make up the stories, but the tunneling that goes on inside the classic Western-gangster incidents and stock hoodlum-dogface-cowboy types." Farber has always championed "minor" rather than "major" directors, "termite art" (i.e., the artist working industriously in a small area of perception, avoiding "statements") rather than "white elephant art." Farber, who is also a painter, writes about the visual design of movies better than anyone else; his evocative notations on directorial style in seemingly lowbrow genres remains a striking anticipation of Andrew Sarris's American formulation of the *auteur* theory (see Section III). In recent years Farber's interests have shifted to the work of the American avant-garde (Michael Snow in particular) and the younger European stylists (Godard, Fassbinder) who have adapted American genres and moods to their own expressive needs.

Farber's opposite number in many ways was James Agee, who wrote for the *Nation* and *Time* in the forties. In his obituary for D. W. Griffith, Agee celebrates a great intuitive movie poet who was at the same time a man with "no remarkable power of intellect, or delicateness of soul; no subtlety; little restraint; little if any 'taste' . . ." In other words, a typical movie director of genius. So many of the most creative directors have been close to charlatanism at times (think of Eisenstein, Welles, Ford, Fellini, Bergman) that it's hard not to credit a degree of intellectual humbug as an essential source of their strength as artists. If Griffith had been a man of taste and reason, he would never have embarked on such outrageous projects as *The Birth of a Nation* and *Intolerance*.

Agee himself possessed considerable "intellect" and "subtlety," so part of the drama of this piece derives from the confrontation of a highly sensitive writer with the glorious crudity of the movies. While many writers on movies are reduced to stammering by the ambivalence of their feelings, Agee was at his most passionate and brilliant in moments of judicious appraisal. On the one hand, a fierce idealizing eloquence; on the other, a shrewd, absolutely accurate summing up of intellectual and artistic shortcomings. How did he do it? In part, this man was blessed with a special sweetness of temperment, a form of grace that shines on only a few writers in any age. And it's possible that Agee had the best ear for prose rhythm, for balance and euphony and dramatic surprise in the long sentence, of any American writer since Henry James. At the least, we can say he's the only American movie critic who could write a swelling line of praise without making a damn fool of himself.

The section concludes with Pauline Kael's famous first review for *The New Yorker,* a 9,000-word analysis of *Bonnie and Clyde.* Like Solti or Bernstein bounding out of the wings to conduct before a full house, this critic's appearances have often assumed the character of a dramatic event. When Kael began writing regularly for *The New Yorker,* the function of a weekly critic seemed to shift from coverage to *performance.* The review printed here was the first of her pieces to have a large immediate effect on opinion. At the time of its release (1967), *Bonnie and Clyde* shocked a great many people with its volatile mixture of gentleness and violence; Kael's defense of an artist's right to use violence in certain circumstances (an example of "moral criticism" at its most useful and daring) helped to dissolve the confusions surrounding this movie and the whole issue of violence; it may also have set the stage for the wide-scale critical appreciation of such key American movies of the seventies as *The Godfather, Chinatown,* and *Taxi Driver.* For the hundredth time, movie art was returning to its roots in pulp fiction and newspaper headlines. For better or worse, gentility was finally dead.—*Ed.*

THIRTY DIFFERENCES BETWEEN THE PHOTOPLAYS AND THE STAGE (1915)

By Vachel Lindsay

The stage is dependent upon three lines of tradition: first, that of Greece and Rome that came down through the French. Second, the English style, ripened from the miracle play and the Shakespearian stage. And third, the Ibsen precedent from Norway, now so firmly established it is classic. These methods are obscured by the commercialized dramas, but they are behind them all. Let us discuss for illustration the Ibsen tradition.

Ibsen is generally the vitriolic foe of pageant. He must be read aloud. He stands for the spoken word, for the iron power of life that may be concentrated in a phrase like the "All or nothing" of Brand. Though *Peer Gynt* has its spectacular side, Ibsen generally comes in through the ear alone. He can be acted in essentials from end to end with one table and four chairs in any parlor. The alleged punch with which the "movie" culminates has occurred three or ten years before the Ibsen curtain goes up. At the close of every act of the dramas of this Norwegian one might inscribe on the curtain "This the magnificent moving picture cannot achieve." Likewise after every successful film described in this book could be inscribed "This the trenchant Ibsen cannot do."

But a photoplay of *Ghosts* came to our town. The humor of the prospect was the sort too deep for tears. My pastor and I reread the William Archer translation that we might be alert for every antithesis. Together we went to the services. Since then the film has been furiously denounced by the literati. Floyd Dell's discriminating assault upon it is quoted in *Current Opinion,* October, 1915, and Margaret Anderson prints a denunciation of it in a recent number of *The Little Review.* But it is not such a bad film in itself. It is not Ibsen. It should be advertised "The Iniquities of the Fathers, an American drama of Eugenics, in a Palatial Setting."

Henry Walthall as Alving, afterward as his son, shows the men much as Ibsen outlines their characters. Of course the only way to be Ibsen is to be so precisely. In the new plot all is open as the day. The world is welcome, and generally present when the man or his son go forth to see the elephant and hear the owl. Provincial hypocrisy is not implied. But Ibsen can scarcely exist without an atmosphere of secrecy for his human volcanoes to burst through in the end.

Mary Alden as Mrs. Alving shows in her intelligent and sensitive countenance that she has a conception of that character. She does not always have the chance to act the woman written in her face, the tart, thinking, handsome creature that Ibsen prefers. Nigel Debrullier looks the buttoned-up Pastor Manders, even to caricature. But the crawling, bootlicking carpenter, Jacob Engstrand, is changed into a respectable, guileless man with an income. And his wife and daughter are helpless, conventional, upper-class rabbits. They do not remind one of the saucy originals.

The original Ibsen drama is the result of mixing up five particular characters through three acts. There is not a situation but would go to pieces if one personality were altered. Here are two, sadly tampered with: Engstrand and his daughter. Here is the mother, who is only referred to in Ibsen. Here is the elder Alving, who disappears before the original play starts. So the twenty great Ibsen situations in the stage production are gone. One new crisis has an Ibsen irony and psychic tension. The boy is taken with the dreaded intermittent pains in the back of his head. He is painting the order that is to make him famous: the King's portrait. While the room empties of people he writhes on the floor. If this were all, it would have been one more moving picture failure to put through a tragic scene. But the thing is reiterated in tableau-symbol. He is looking sideways in terror. A hairy arm with clutching demon claws comes thrusting in toward the back of his neck. He writhes in deadly fear. The audience is appalled for him.

This visible clutch of heredity is the nearest equivalent that is offered for the whispered refrain: "Ghosts," in the original masterpiece. This hand should also be reiterated as a refrain, three times at least, before this tableau, each time more dreadful and threatening. It appears but the once, and has no chance to become a part of the accepted hieroglyphics of the piece, as it should be, to realize its full power.

The father's previous sins have been acted out. The boy's consequent struggle with the malady has been traced step by step, so the play should end here. It would then be a rough equivalent of the Ibsen irony in a contrary medium. Instead of that, it wanders on through paraphrases of scraps of the play, sometimes literal, then quite alien, on to the alleged motion picture punch, when the Doctor is the god from the machine. There is no doctor on the stage in the original *Ghosts.* But there is a physician in *The Doll's House,* a scientific, quietly moving oracle, crisp, Spartan, sophisticated.

Is this photoplay physician such a one? The boy and his half-sister are in their wedding clothes in the big church. Pastor Manders is saying the ceremony. The audience and building are indeed showy. The doctor charges up the aisle at the moment people are told to speak or forever hold their peace. He has tact. He simply breaks up the marriage right there. He does not tell the guests why. But he takes the wedding party into the pastor's study and there blazes at the bride and groom the long-suppressed truth that they are brother and sister. Always an orotund man, he has the Chautauqua manner indeed in this exigency.

He brings to one's mind the tearful book, much loved in childhood, *Parted at the Altar,* or *Why Was it Thus?* And four able actors have the task of telling the audience by facial expression only, that they have been struck by moral lightning. They stand in a row, facing the people, endeavoring to make the crisis of an alleged Ibsen play out of a crashing melodrama.

The final death of young Alving is depicted with an approximation of Ibsen's mood. But the only ways to suggest such feelings in silence, do not convey them in full to the audience, but merely narrate them. Wherever in *Ghosts* we have quiet voices that are like the slow drip of hydrochloric acid, in the photoplay we have no quiet gestures that will do trenchant work. Instead there are endless writhings and rushings about, done with a deal of skill, but destructive of the last remnants of Ibsen.

Up past the point of the clutching hand this film is the prime example for study for the person who would know once for all the differences between the photoplays and the stage dramas. Along with it might be classed Mrs. Fiske's decorative moving picture *Tess,* in which there is every determination to convey the original Mrs. Fiske illusion without her voice and breathing presence. To people who know her well it is a surprisingly good tintype of our beloved friend, for the family album. The relentless Thomas Hardy is nowhere to be found. There are two moments of dramatic life set among many of delicious pictorial quality: when Tess baptizes her child, and when she smooths its little grave with a wavering hand. But in the stage version the dramatic poignancy begins with the going up of the curtain, and lasts till it descends.

The prime example of complete failure is Sarah Bernhardt's *Camille.* It is indeed a tintype of the consumptive heroine, with every group entire, and taken at full length. Much space is occupied by the floor and the overhead portions of the stage setting. It lasts as long as would the spoken performance, and wherever there is a dialogue we must imagine said conversation if we can. It might be compared to watching Camille from the top gallery through smoked glass, with one's ears stopped with cotton.

It would be well for the beginning student to find some way to see the first two of these three, or some other attempts to revamp the classic, for instance Mrs. Fiske's painstaking reproduction of *Vanity Fair,* bearing in mind the list of differences which this chapter now furnishes.

There is no denying that many stage managers who have taken up photoplays are struggling with the Shakespearian French and Norwegian traditions in the new medium. Many of the moving pictures discussed in this book are rewritten stage dramas, and one, *Judith of Bethulia,* is a pronounced success. But in order to be real photoplays the stage dramas must be overhauled indeed, turned inside out and upside down. The successful motion picture expresses itself through mechanical devices that are being evolved every hour. Upon those many new bits of machinery are founded novel methods of combination in another field of logic, not dramatic logic, but tableau logic. But the old-line managers, taking up photoplays, begin by making curious miniatures of stage presentations. They try to have most things as before. Later they take on the moving picture technique in a superficial way, but they, and the host of talented actors in the prime of life and Broadway success, retain the dramatic state of mind.

It is a principle of criticism the world over that the distinctions between the arts must be clearly marked, even by those who afterwards mix those arts. Take, for instance, the perpetual quarrel between the artists and the half-educated about literary painting. Whistler fought that battle in England. He tried to beat it into the head of John Bull that a painting is one thing, a mere illustration for a story another thing. But the novice is always stubborn. To him Hindu and

Arabic are both foreign languages, therefore just alike. The book illustration may be said to come in through the ear, by reading the title aloud in imagination. And the other is effective with no title at all. The scenario writer who will study to the bottom of the matter in Whistler's *Gentle Art of Making Enemies* will be equipped to welcome the distinction between the old-fashioned stage, where the word rules, and the photoplay, where splendor and ritual are all. It is not the same distinction, but a kindred one.

But let us consider the details of the matter. The stage has its exits and entrances at the side and back. The standard photoplays have their exits and entrances across the imaginary footlight line, even in the most stirring mob and battle scenes. In *Judith of Bethulia,* though the people seem to be coming from everywhere and going everywhere, when we watch close, we see that the individuals enter at the near right-hand corner and exit at the near left-hand corner, or enter at the near left-hand corner and exit at the near right-hand corner.

Consider the devices whereby the stage actor holds the audience as he goes out at the side and back. He sighs, gestures, howls, and strides. With what studious preparation he ripens his quietness, if he goes out that way. In the new contraption, the moving picture, the hero or villain in exit strides past the nose of the camera, growing much bigger than a human being, marching toward us as though he would step on our heads, disappearing when largest. There is an explosive power about the mildest motion picture exit, be the actor skillful or the reverse. The people left in the scene are pygmies compared with each disappearing cyclops. Likewise, when the actor enters again, his mechanical importance is overwhelming. Therefore, for his first entrance the motion picture star does not require the preparations that are made on the stage. The support does not need to warm the spectators to the problem, then talk them into surrender.

When the veteran stage-producer as a beginning photoplay producer tries to give us a dialogue in the motion pictures, he makes it so dull no one follows. He does not realize that his camera-born opportunity to magnify persons and things instantly, to interweave them as actors on one level, to alternate scenes at the slightest whim, are the big substitutes for dialogue. By alternating scenes rapidly, flash after flash: cottage, field, mountain-top, field, mountain-top, cottage, we have a conversation between three places rather than three persons. By alternating the picture of a man and the check he is forging, we have his soliloquy. When two people talk to each other, it is by lifting and lowering objects rather than their voices. The collector presents a bill: the adventurer shows him the door. The boy plucks a rose: the girl accepts it. Moving objects, not moving lips, make the words of the photoplay.

The old-fashioned stage producer, feeling he is getting nowhere, but still helpless, puts the climax of some puzzling lip-debate, often the climax of the whole film, as a sentence on the screen. Sentences should be used to show changes of time and place and a few such elementary matters before the episode is fully started. The climax of a motion picture scene cannot be one word or fifty words. The crisis must be an action sharper than any that has gone before in organic union with a tableau more beautiful than any that has preceded: the breaking of the tenth wave upon the sand. Such remnants of pantomimic dialogue as remain in the main chase of the photoplay film are but guide-posts in the race toward the goal. They should not be elaborate toll-gates of plot, to be laboriously lifted and lowered while the horses stop, mid-career.

The Venus of Milo, that comes directly to the soul through the silence, requires no quotation from Keats to explain her, though Keats is the equivalent in verse. Her setting in the great French museum is enough. We do not know that her name is Venus. She is thought by many to be another statue of Victory. We may some day evolve scenarios that will require nothing more than a title thrown upon the screen at the beginning, they come to the eye so perfectly. This is not the only possible sort, but the self-imposed limitation in certain films might give them a charm akin to that of the "Songs without Words."

The stage audience is a unit of three hundred or a thousand. In the beginning of the first act there is much moving about and extra talk on the part of the actors, to hold the crowd while it is settling down, and enable the latecomer to be in his seat before the vital part of the story starts. If he appears later, he is glared at. In the motion picture art gallery, on the other hand, the audience is around two hundred, and these are not a unit, and the only crime is to obstruct the line of vision. The high-school girls can do a moderate amount of giggling without breaking the spell. There is no spell, in the stage sense, to break. People can climb over each other's knees to get in or out. If the picture is political, they murmur war-cries to one another. If the film suggests what some of the neighbors have been doing, they can regale each other with the richest sewing society report.

Then people in the motion picture audience total about two hundred, any time, but they come in groups of two or three at no specified hour. The newcomers do not, as in Vaudeville, make themselves part of a jocular army. Strictly as individuals they judge the panorama. If they disapprove, there is grumbling under their breath, but no hissing. I have never heard an audience in a photoplay theater clap its hands even when the house was bursting with people. Yet they often see the film through twice. When they have had enough, they stroll home. They manifest their favorable verdict by sending some other member of the family to "see the picture." If the people so delegated are likewise satisfied, they may ask the man at the door if he is going to bring it back. That is the moving picture kind of cheering.

It was a theatrical sin when the old-fashioned stage actor was rendered unimportant by his scenery. But the motion picture actor is but the mood of the mob or the landscape or the department store behind him, reduced to a single hieroglyphic.

The stage-interior is large. The motion-picture interior is small. The stage out-of-door scene is at best artificial and little and is generally at rest, or its movement is tainted with artificiality. The waves dash, but not dashingly, the water flows, but not flowingly. The motion picture out-of-door scene is as big as the universe. And only pictures of the Sahara are without magnificent motion.

The photoplay is as far from the stage on the one hand as it is from the novel on the other. Its nearest analogy in literature is, perhaps, the short story, or the lyric poem. The key-words of the stage are *passion* and *character;* of the photoplay, *splendor* and *speed.* The stage in its greatest power deals with pity for some one especially unfortunate, with whom we grow well acquainted; with some private revenge against some particular despoiler; traces the beginning and culmination of joy based on the gratification of some preference, or love for some person, whose charm is all his own. The drama is concerned with the slow, inevitable approaches to these intensities. On the other hand, the motion picture, though often appearing to deal with these things, as a matter of fact uses substitutes, many of which have been listed. But to review: its first substitute is the excitement of speed-mania stretched on the framework of an obvious plot. Or it deals with delicate informal anecdote as the short story does, or fairy legerdemain, or patriotic banners, or great surging mobs of the proletariat, or big scenic outlooks, or miraculous beings made visible. And the further it gets from Euripides, Ibsen, Shakespeare, or Molière—the more it becomes like a mural painting from which flashes of lightning come—the more it realizes its genius. Men like Gordon Craig and Granville Barker are almost wasting their genius on the theatre. The Splendor Photoplays are the great outlet for their type of imagination.

The typical stage performance is from two hours and a half upward. The movie show generally lasts five reels, that is, an hour and forty minutes. And it should last but three reels, that is, an hour. Edgar Allan Poe said there was no such thing as a long poem. There is certainly no such thing as a long moving picture masterpiece.

The stage-production depends most largely upon the power of the actors, the movie show upon the genius of the producer. The performers and the dumb objects are on equal terms in his paint-buckets. The star-system is bad for the stage because the minor parts are smothered and the situations distorted to give the favorite an orbit. It is bad for the motion pictures because it obscures the producer. While the leading actor is entitled to his glory, as are all the actors, their mannerisms should not overshadow the latest inspirations of the creator of the films.

The display of the name of the corporation is no substitute for giving the glory to the producer. An artistic photoplay is not the result of a military efficiency system. It is not a factory-made staple article, but the product of the creative force of one soul, the flowering of a spirit that has the habit of perpetually renewing itself.

Once I saw Mary Fuller in a classic. It was the life and death of Mary Queen of Scots. Not only was the tense, fidgety, over-American Mary Fuller transformed into a being who was a poppy and a tiger-lily and a snow-queen and a rose, but she and her company, including Marc Macdermott, radiated the old Scotch patriotism. They made the picture a memorial. It reminded one of Maurice Hewlett's novel *The Queen's Quair.* Evidently all the actors were fused by some noble managerial mood.

There can be no doubt that so able a group have evolved many good films that have escaped me. But though I did go again and again, never did I see them act with the same deliberation and distinction, and I laid the difference to a change in the state of mind of the producer. Even baseball players must have managers. A team cannot pick itself, or it surely would. And this rule may apply to the stage. But by comparison to motion picture performers, stage-actors are their own managers, for they have an approximate notion of how they look in the eye of the audience, which is but the human eye. They can hear and gauge their own voices. They have the same ears as their listeners. But the picture producer holds to his eyes the seven-leagued demon spy-glass called the kinetoscope, as the audience will do later. The actors have not the least notion of their appearance. Also the words in the motion picture are not things whose force the actor can guage. The book under the table is one word, the dog behind the chair is another, the window curtain flying in the breeze is another.

This chapter has implied that the performers were but paint on the canvas. They are both paint and models. They are models in the sense that the young Ellen Terry was the inspiration for Watts's Sir Galahad. They resemble the persons in private life who furnish the basis for novels. Dickens's mother was the original of Mrs. Nickleby. His father entered into Wilkins Micawber. But these people are not perpetually thrust upon us as Mr. and Mrs. Dickens. We are glad to find them in the Dickens biographies. When the stories begin, it is Micawber and Mrs. Nickleby we want, and the Charles Dickens atmosphere.

The photoplays of the future will be written from the foundations for the films. The soundest actors, photographers, and producers will be those who emphasize the points wherein the photoplay is unique. What is adapted to complete expression in one art generally secures but half expression in another. The supreme photoplay will give us things that have been but half expressed in all other mediums allied to it.

Once this principle is grasped there is every reason why the same people who have interested themselves in the advanced experimental drama should take hold of the super-photoplay. The good citizens who can most easily grasp the distinction should be there to perpetuate the higher welfare of these institutions side by side. This parallel development should come, if for no other reason, because the two arts are still roughly classed together by the public. The elect cannot teach the public what the drama is till they show them precisely what the photoplay is and is not. Just as the university has departments of both History and English teaching in amity, each one illuminating the work of the other, so these two forms should live in each other's sight in fine and friendly contrast. At present they are in blind and jealous warfare.

THE KEYSTONE THE BUILDERS REJECTED

By Gilbert Seldes (1923)

For fifteen years there has existed in the United States, and in the United States alone, a form of entertainment which, seemingly without sources in the past, restored to us a kind of laughter almost unheard in modern times. It came into being by accident; it had no pretensions to art. For ten years or more it added an element of cheerful madness to the lives of millions and was despised and rejected by people of culture and intelligence. Suddenly—suddenly as it appeared to them—a great genius arose and the people of culture conceded that in his case, but in his case alone, art existed in slap-stick comedy; they did not remove their *non expedit* from the form itself.

Perhaps only those of us who care for the rest know how good Charlie is. Perhaps only the inexpressive multitudes who have laughed and not wondered why they laughed can know how fine slap-stick is. For myself, I have had no greater entertainment than these dear and preposterous comedies, and all I can do is remember. The long, dark, narrow passage set out with uncomfortable chairs; the sharp almond odors, the sense of uncertainty, and the questionable piano; and then upon the screen, in a drab gray and white, jiggling insecurely, something strange and wonderful occurred. It was mingled with dull and stupid things; but it had a fire, a driving energy of its own—and it was funny! Against all our inhibitions and habits it played games with men and women; it made them ridiculous and mad; it seemed to have no connexion with the logic of human events, trusting to an undecipherable logic of its own. A few scholars found the commedia dell'arte living again; a few artists saw that the galvanic gestures and movements were creating fresh lines and interesting angles. And a nation cared for them intensely until the remorseless hostility of the genteel began to corrupt the purity of slap-stick. That is where we are now: too early to write an epitaph —late enough to pay a tribute.

Lest the year 1914 should be not otherwise distinguished in history, it may be recorded that it was then, or a year earlier, or possibly a year later, that the turning point came in the history of the American moving picture. The first of the great mergers arrived—an event not unforeseen in itself, a "logical development" the press agents called it—seeming to establish the picture as a definitely accepted form of entertainment. It was a moment when a good critic might have foretold the course of the moving picture during the next decade, for at that time the Triangle of Fine Arts (D. W. Griffith), Kay-Bee (Thomas H. Ince), and Keystone (Mack Sennett) was formed. Two of these names were already known, and of the two one was to become, for a time, the most notable name in the profession; the third was hidden behind the obscure symbol of the Keystone; it represented one who had acted in, and was now directing, the most despised, and by all odds the most interesting, films produced in America. Mr. Griffith was already entered on that road which has since ruined him as a director; he was producing *Intolerance,* and, if I may borrow a phrase from the Shuberts, his personal supervision was not always given to the Triangle–Fine Arts releases; Mr. Ince was presently to meditate upon the possibility of joining the word "super" to the word "spectacle," thus creating the word "super-spectacle"; and Mr. Sennett—by a process of exclusion one always arrives at Mr. Sennett. He is the Keystone the builders rejected.

I know nothing more doleful as a subject of conversation than the social-economics of the moving picture; what was remarkable about the Triangle was not its new method of distribution, its new hold on the timid exhibitor, or its capacity for making or losing fortunes. The thing to note is that the two "serious" producers, and the hard-headed business men who invested money in their efforts, thought it well to associate with themselves the best producer of vulgar slap-stick comedy. More than that, they combined in a peculiar ratio for the scheme provided that there was to be released each week either a Fine Arts or an Ince picture; and that with each of these was to be shown a Keystone comedy. So that those who were perpetually being caught in the rain, or missing the eleven-o'clock from Philadelphia to New York, saw twice as many Keystone comedies as (a) Fine Arts or (b) Kay-Bee releases. The recent all-hailing of Mr. Chaplin as an artist because of his work in *The Kid,* the bright young reputations of Harold Lloyd and Buster Keaton, indicate that most critics of the moving picture caught the train and missed the shower. They certainly missed the comedies; for the Fine Arts and Ince pictures were in their time the best pictures produced; and the Keystone comedies were consistently and almost without exception better.

This is not the place to discuss the shortcomings of the feature film; for the moment, let the dreadful opulent gentility of a Cecil De Mille production serve only to sharpen the saucy gaiety of the comic, the dullness of a Universal set off the revelry of slap-stick. There is one serious point which a good critic (Aristotle, for example) would have discovered when he regarded the screen as long ago as 1914 and became aware of the superiority of the comic films. He would have seen at once while Mr. Griffith and Mr. Ince were both developing the technique of the moving picture, they were exploiting their discoveries with materials equally or better suited to another medium: the stage or the dime novel or whatever. Whereas Mr. Sennett was already so enamored of his craft that he was doing with the instruments of the moving picture precisely those things which were best suited to it—those things which could not be done with any instrument but the camera, and could appear nowhere if not on the screen.

This does not mean that nothing but slap-stick comedy is proper to the cinema; it means only that everything in slap-stick *is* cinematographic; and since perceiving a delicate adjustment of means to end, or a proper relation between method and material, is a source of pleasure, Mr. Sennett's developments were more capable of pleasing the judicious than those of either of his two fellow-workers. The highly logical humanist critic of the films could have foreseen in 1914 —without the decade of trial and error which has intervened—what we see now: that the one field in which the picture would most notably declare itself a failure would be that of the drama (Elinor Glyn–Cecil De Mille–Gilbert Parker, in short). Without a moment's hesitation he would have put his finger on those two elements in the cinema which, being theoretically sound, had a chance of practical success: the spectacle (including the spectacular melodrama) and the grotesque comedy. Several years later he would have added one word more, that grotesque tragedy might conceivably succeed. For it is not only the fun in the Keystones which makes them successful: it is the method of presentation.

The rightness of the spectacle film is implicit in its name: the screen is a place on which things can be *seen,* and so long as a film depends upon the eye it is right for the screen—and whether it is right in any other regard depends upon taste and judgment and skill. Omit as irrelevant the news reels, animated cartoons, educational and travel films—all of them good; omit equally those printed jokes and clippings from the *Literary Digest* which are at once the greatest trial *and* error of the screen. What remains? The feature film and *The Cabinet of Dr Caligari.* This—the only film of high fantasy I have ever seen—is the seeming exception which proves the rule, since it owes its success to the skillfully concealed exploitation of the materials and technique of the spectacle and of the comic film, and not to the dramatic quality of its story. The studio settings in distortion represent the spectacle; they are variations of scenery or "location"; the chase over the roofs is a psychological parallel to the Keystone cops; and the weak moment of this superb picture is that in which the moving picture always fails, in the double revelation at the end, like that of *Seven Keys to Baldpate,* representing "drama."

No. The drama film is almost always wrong, the slap-stick almost always right; and it is divinely just that the one great figure of the screen should have risen out of the Keystone studios. He came too early; Chaplin spoiled nearly everything else for us, and he is always used by those who dislike slap-stick to prove their case. Their case, regrettably, is in a fair way to be proved, for slap-stick is in danger. The hypothetical critic mentioned above has not yet occurred; Mr. Bushnell Diamond, the best actual critic of the movies, is without sympathy for Mack Sennett and calls him a Bourbon, in the sense of one who forgets nothing and learns less. What Mr. Sennett has needed long since is encouragement and criticism; and stupid newspaper critics (who write half-columns about a new Gloria Swanson picture and add "the comedy which ends the bill is *Down in the Sewer*") have left slap-stick wholly without direction.[1] At the

[1]Except that supplied by the professional journals—often excellent.

same time the tradition of gentility, the hope of being "refined," has touched the grotesque comedy; its directors have heard abuse and sly remarks about custard pies so long that they have begun to believe in them, and the madness which is a monstrous sanity in the movie comedy is likely to die out. The moving picture is being prettified; the manufacturers and exhibitors are growing more and more pretentious, and the riot of slap-stick seems out of place in a "presentation" which begins with the overture to *Tannhäuser,* and includes a baritone from the imperial opera house in Warsaw singing *Indian Love Lyrics* in front of an art curtain. In Paris there are one or two Chaplin films visible nearly every day; in New York the Rialto Theatre alone seems to make a habit of Chaplin revivals and of putting its comic feature in the electric sign. The Capitol, the largest and rapidly becoming the most genteel, of moving picture palaces (but who ever heard of an opera palace?) frequently announces a programme of seven or eight items without a comedy among them; and you have to go to squalid streets and disreputable neighborhoods if you want to see Chaplin regularly. He could ask for no finer tribute, to be sure; but it is not much to our credit that the greatest mimic of our time has no theatre named after him, that it was in Berlin, not in Chicago or New York, that the first Chaplin festival took place, and that *Tillie's Punctured Romance,* a film intensely important in his development, was last billed in a converted auction room on the lower East Side of New York, where Broadway would find it vulgar.

There were always elements in the Keystone which jeopardized its future—it lacked variety, it was often dull, its lapses of taste were serious. (I transfer the name of Keystone to the genre of which it was the most notable example; it was for long, and may still be, superior to most of the others.) But, while there is still time, its miraculously good qualities can be caught and possibly preserved. The ideal comedy of Mack Sennett is a fairly standardized article; too much so, perhaps, but the elements are sound. They include a simple, usually preposterous plot, frequently a burlesque of a serious play; more important are the characters, grotesque in bulk, form, or make-up; and, finally, the events which have as little connexion with the plot as, say, a clog dance in a musical comedy. In the early days of the Keystone, it is said, the plot was almost nonexistent in advance, and developed out of the set and the props. The one which was called, in revival, *The Pile Driver,* must have been such a film, for its plot is that two men meet a pretty girl near a river and they find a huge mallet. It is a film full of impromptus—not very brilliant ones, as a matter of fact—in which Sennett and Chaplin and Mabel Normand each occasionally give flashes of their qualities. A few years later you see the same thing when the trick of working up a film from the material in hand has become second nature. *His Night Out* presents Ben Turpin and Charlie Chaplin as equal comedians: two men on a drinking party, stumbling into a luxurious hotel, reverting automatically to the saloon from which they have been thrown, mutually assisting and hindering each other in a serious effort to do something they cannot define, but which they feel to be of cosmic importance. Later, one finds a more sophisticated kind of comic. *Bright Eyes* has to do with a gawky young man, reputed rich, received into a wealthy family, engaged to the daughter, denounced as an impostor, reduced to the kitchen, flirting there with the maid, restored to favour, and, nobly refusing the daughter's hand, marrying the maid. Here Ben Turpin had good moments, but much of the gaiety of the film depended upon Chester Conklin (or one who much resembles him) as another servant in the house, bundling himself up in furs like Peary in the Arctic, bidding farewell at an imaginary outpost of civilization, and striding into a huge refrigerator, to bring back a ham before the adoring eyes of the cook.

The comic film is by nature adventurous and romantic, and I think what endears it to us is that the adventure is picaresque and the romance wholly unsentimental—that is, both are pushed to the edge of burlesque. For the romance you have a love affair, frequently running parallel to a parody of itself. The hero is marked by peculiarities of his own: the Chaplin feet, the Hank Mann bangs and somber eyes, the Turpin squint, the Arbuckle bulk; against these oddities and absurdities plays the serene, idle beauty of a simple girl (Edna Purviance or Mabel Normand in her lovely early days), and only on occasions a comic in her own right like Louise Fazenda or Polly Moran. In some five hundred slap-stick comedies I do not remember one single moment of sentimentality; and it seems to me that every look and gesture of false chivalry and exaggerated devotion has been parodied there. The characteristic moment, after all, is when the comedy is ended, and just as the hero is about to kiss the heroine he winks broadly and ironically at the spectators. Our whole tradition of love is destroyed and outraged in these careless comedies; so also our tradition of heroism. And since the moving picture, quite naturally, began by importing the whole baggage of the romantic and sentimental novel and theater, the moving-picture comedy has at last arrived at burlesquing its silly-serious half-sister. Two years before *Merton of the Movies* appeared, Mack Sennett, with the help of Ben Turpin's divinely crossed eyes, had consummated a burlesque of Messrs Griffith, Ince, and Lubitsch, in *A Small Town Idol,* far more destructively, be it said, than Chaplin in his *Carmen,* and with a vaster fun than *Merton.*

Everything incongruous and inconsequent has its place in the unrolling of the comic film: love and masquerade and treachery; coincidence and disguise; heroism and knavishness; all are distorted, burlesqued, exaggerated. And—here the camera enters—all are presented at an impossible rate; the culmination is in the inevitable struggle and the conventional pursuit, where trick photography enters and you see the immortal Keystone cops in their flivver, mowing down hundreds of telegraph poles without abating their speed, dashing through houses or losing their wheels and continuing, blown to bits and reassembled in midair; locomotives running wild, yet never destroying the cars they so miraculously send spinning before them; airplanes and submarines in and out of their elements—everything capable of motion set into motion; and at the height of the revel, the true catastrophe, the solution of the preposterous and forgotten drama, with the lovers united under the canopy of smashed motor cars, or the gay feet of Mr. Chaplin gently twinkling down the irised street.

And all of this is done *with the camera, through action* presented to the eye. The secret of distortion is in the camera, and the secret of pace in the projector. Regard them for a moment, regard the slap-stick as every moment explains itself, and then go to the picture palace and spend one-third of your time reading the flamboyancies of C. Gardner Sullivan and another third watching the contortions of a famous actress as she "registers" an emotion which action and photography should present directly, and you will see why the comic film is superior. There is virtually no registering in the comedy, there is no senseless pantomime, and the titles are succinct and few. In *Bright Eyes,* as the marriage of convenience is about to take place, the mother sweeps in with these words, "Faint quick—he's dead broke." An absurd letter or telegram is introduced to set the play going; the rest is literally silence.

What I have said about Chaplin regards him as a typical slap-stick comedian. The form would have succeeded without him and he has passed beyond the form entirely. The other practitioners of the art come out of his shadow, and some of them are excellent. What makes Chaplin great is that he has irony and pity, he knows that you must not have the one without the other; he has both piety and wit. Next to him, for his work in *His Bread and Butter* and a few other films, stands Hank Mann, who translates the childlike gravity of Chaplin into a frightened innocence, a serious endeavor to understand the world which seems always hostile to him. He was trained, I have been told, as a tragic actor on the East Side of New York, and he seems always stricken with the cruelty and madness of an existence in which he alone is logical and sane. If he, walking backward to get a last glimpse of his beloved (after "A Waiter's Farewell," as the caption has it), steps on the running board of a motor instead of a street car, he is willing to pay the usual fare and let bygones be bygones. His black bangs almost meet his eyes, and his eyes are mournful and piteous; his gesture is slow and rounded; a few of the ends of the world have come upon his head and the eyelids are a little weary. He is the Wandering Jew misdirected into comic life by an unscrupulous fate.

His most notable opposite is Harold Lloyd, a man of no tenderness, of no philosophy, the embodiment of American cheek and indefatigable energy. His movements are all direct, straight; the shortest distance between two points he will traverse impudently and persistently, even if he is knocked down at the end of each trip; there is no poetry in him, his whole utterance being epigrammatic, without overtone or image. Yet once, at least, he too stepped into that lunatic Arcadia to which his spirit is alien; not in *Grandma's Boy,* which might just as well have been done by Charles Ray, but in *A Sailor-made Man.* Here the old frenzy fell upon him, the weakling won by guile, and instead of fighting one man he laid out a mob from behind; something excessive, topsy-turvy, riotous at last occurred in his ordered existence. He is funny; but he has no vulgarity; he is smart. He amuses me without making me laugh, and I figure him as a step toward gentility.

Ben Turpin has progressed, fortunately without taking that step. In *Bright Eyes* he was mildly absurd; in *His Night Out,* with Chaplin, he was tremendously funny; and what he learned there of the lesson of the master he imported into his private masterpiece, *A Small Town Idol.* Like Chaplin, he disarms you and endears himself; unlike him, and often to Turpin's advantage, he knows how to be ridiculous. One always sees Chaplin's impersonations as they see themselves. Is he a count or a pretender, or an English gentleman, or a policeman, or a tramp, the character is completely embodied; Chaplin never makes fun of himself. The process of identification is complete and, apart from the interest and the fun of the action, your chief pleasure is in awaiting the inevitable denunciation. Ben Turpin, who has only a talent for Chaplin's genius, makes the most of it and lets you see through him. His exaggerations do more than reveal—they betray, and above all they betray the fact that Turpin is aware of the absurdities of his characters; you see them objectively, and through him you see through them.

When he returns home as the Wild West screen hero, and his own picture is shown before those who so recently had despised him, his deprecating gesture before the screen on which his exploits are being shown is so broad, so simple-silly, that it is more than a description of himself as he thinks it is, and lets us perceive his absurdity. He is exactly a zany.

Three other buffoons of the old Keystone days retain their capacity to be amusing: the galvanic, jack-in-the-box, Al St John; Mack Swain, and Chester Conklin; they are exactly as they were ten years ago, and one fancies they will never be great. The difficult person to be sure about is Buster Keaton, who came to the pictures from vaudeville, and has carried into his new medium his greatest asset, an enormous, incorruptible gravity. He never smiles, they say, and I have sat through some of his pictures—*The Boat,* for one—without seeing any reason why he should. It was a long mechanical contrivance with hardly any humour, and was considered a masterpiece; while *The Paleface,* in which Keaton played an entomologist captured by Indians, passed unnoticed. It had nearly everything a comic needs, and there were certain movements *en masse,* certain crossings of the lines of action, which were quite perfect. Keaton's intense preoccupation and his hard sense of personality are excellent. In *Cops* he took a purely Keystone subject and multiplied and magnified it to its last degree of development: thousands of policemen rushed down one street; equal thousands rushed up another; and before them fled this small, serious figure, bent on self-justification, caught in a series of absurd accidents, wholly law-abiding, a little distracted. I do not think one will soon forget the exquisite close of that picture: the whole police force forming a phalanx, hurled as one body into the courtyard of the station—and then the little figure which, having been trapped within, seems doomed to arrest, coming out, itself accoutred in uniform, and quietly, quietly locking the huge doors behind it. It, yes; for by that time Keaton has become wholly impersonal. So affecting Larry Semon has never been; nor Clyde Cook; and behind them, but *longo intervallo,* come the misguided creatures who make the kind of slap-stick which most people think Sennett makes. I am sure there are other good comedians; but I am not trying to make a catalogue. No one, in any case, has been able to impose himself as these few have; and most of the others are so near in method and manner to these that they require nothing fresh to be said of them.

It seemed for a moment, in 1922, that if a confessed murderer were set free by a jury, he or she went into the movies; but if a moving-picture actor was declared innocent, he was barred from the screen. The justice of this I cannot discuss; yet a protest can be made against the aethetically high-minded who said that the real reason for barring the films of "Fatty" Arbuckle was their vulgarity and their dullness. For "Fatty" had gone over to a comedy more refined than slap-stick long before 1922; and in 1914 he was neither stupid nor dull. Once indeed, in *Fatty and Mabel Adrift* (Mabel being Miss Normand) he came near to the best of slap-stick, and the same picture was as photography and printing, for sepia seascapes and light and shade, a superior thing entirely. The fatuous, ingratiating smile was innocent then, in all conscience, and as for vulgarity . . .

Let us, before we go to the heart of that question, look for a moment at the comedy which was always set against the slap-stick to condemn the custard-pie school of fun—the comedy of which the best practitioners were indisputably Mr. and Mrs. Sidney Drew. In them there was nothing offensive, except an enervating dullness. They pretended to be pleasant episodes in our common life, the life of courtship and marriage; they accepted all our conventions; and they were one and all exactly the sort of thing which the junior class at high school acted when money was needed to buy a new set of erasers for Miss Struther's course in mechanical drawing. The husband stayed out late at night or was seen kissing a stenographer; the wife had trouble with a maid or was extravagant at the best shops; occasionally arrived an ingenuity, such as the romantic attachment of the wife to anniversaries contrasted with her husband's negligence —I seem to recall that to cure her he brought her a gift one day in memory of Washington's birthday. These things were little stories, not even smoking-room stories; they were acted entirely in the technique of the amateur stage; they were incredibly genteel, in the milieu where "When Baby Came" is genteel; neither in matter nor in manner did they employ what the camera and the projector had to give. And, apart from the agreeable manners of Mr. and Mrs. Sidney Drew, nothing made them successful except the corrupt desire, on the part of the spectators, to be refined.

Nothing of the sort operated in the far better (feature film) comedies which Douglas Fairbanks made when he was with Fine Arts. To suit his physique, they were almost all adventurous; they were always entertaining. *Flirting With Fate*[1] presented a young man who had decided to die and gave "Automatic Joe," a gunman, his last fifty dollars to "bump him off" unexpectedly. Once the agreement was made, the tide of fortune turned for the young man, and, desiring earnestly to live, he felt the paid hand of the assassin always upon his shoulder. At the same time the gunman had reformed; his one object was to return the unearned fifty dollars. And the cross-purposes, the chase and flight, were within short distance of high farce. The comedies of Charles Ray were also unpretentious, and also used the camera. These and others were always perfectly decent; but none of them was refined.

And there, essentially, we are back at slap-stick; for the refined comedy was pretentious, and what is pretentious is vulgar in any definition of the word; while slap-stick never pretended to be anything but itself and could be disgusting or tasteless or dull, but it could not be vulgar. I consider vulgar the thing which offends against the canons of taste accepted by honest people, not by imitative people, not by snobs. It is equally bad taste, presumably, to throw custard pies and to commit adultery; but it is not bad taste to speak of these things. What is intolerable only is the pretense, and it was against pretentiousness, that the slap-stick comedy had its hardest fight. It showed a man sitting down on a lighted gas stove, and it did not hesitate to disclose the underwear charred at the buttocks which were the logical consequence of the action. There was never the slightest suggestion of sexual indecency, or of moral turpitude, in the Keystones; there was a fuller and freer use of gesture—gesture with all parts of the human frame—than we are accustomed to. The laughter they evoked was broad and long; it was thoracic, abdomi-

[1]Scenario by the adroit Anita Loos.

nal; it shook us because it was really the earth trembling beneath our feet. The animal frankness and health of these pictures constituted the ground of their offense. And something more.

For the Keystone offended our sense of security in dull and business-like lives. Few of us imagined ourselves in the frenzy of action which they set before us; none of us remained unmoved at the freedom of fancy, the wildness of imagination, the roaring, destructive, careless energy which it set loose. It was an ecstasy of comic life, and in our unecstatic lives we fled from it to polite comedy, telling ourselves that what we had seen was ugly and displeasing. Often it was. I am stating the case for slap-stick, but I do not wish to make myself responsible for the millions of feet of stupidity and ugliness which have been released as comic films. I have seen Ham and Bud and the imitators of Charlie Chaplin; I have seen an egg splattered over a man's face with such a degree of nauseous ugliness that it seemed I could never see a comic again. But as like as not, on the same bill was the James Young screen version of *The Devil* with George Arliss, or Geraldine Farrar in *Carmen,* or the *"Affairs of Anatol."* And when people who have seen these "artistic" films, or the barber-shop scene in a Hitchcock revue or Eddie Cantor in a dentist's chair, exclaim (falsely) that moving-picture comedians do nothing but throw pies, I am moved to wonder what on earth they are expected to throw. They are using the eternal materials of their art, precisely as Aristophanes used them and Rabelais, with already far too many concessions to a debased and cowardly and artificial taste. At the two extremes simple and sophisticated people have looked directly at the slap-stick screen and loved it for itself alone; in between are the people who can see nothing without the lorgnettes of prejudice provided by fashion and gentility. The simple ones discovered and prospered the slap-stick screen long before the sophisticated were aware of its existence; they took it for what it was and cared nothing for the fact that it was made by inartistic people and shown in reeking rooms for a nickel. For long the poison of culture was powerless to enter; but not long enough.

I feel moderately certain that the slap-stick comedy is a good thing for America to have; yet, being neither an apostle of pagan joy nor a reformer, I have to put my plea for slap-stick on personal grounds. It has given me immeasurable entertainment and I would like to see it saved; I would like to see a bit more of its impromptus, its unpremeditated laughter; I would like to do something to banish the bleak refinement which is setting in upon it.

Seven years ago, in an imaginary conversation, I made Mr. David Wark Griffith announced that he would produce *Helen of Troy,* and I made him defend the Keystone comedy. It seemed to me then as now that there is nothing incongruous in these subjects; properly made, they would be equally unrefined, but *Helen of Troy,* being in the grand manner, would be called "artistic." Mr. Griffith has not made *Helen of Troy,* and the pre-eminent right to make it has passed from his hands. The Keystone, with its variations, needs still an authoritative defender and an authoritative critic. It is one of the few places where the genteel tradition does not operate, where fantasy is liberated, where imagination is still riotous and healthy. In its economy and precision are two qualities of artistic presentation; it uses still everything commonest and simplest and nearest to hand; in terror of gentility, it has refrained from using the broad farces of literature—Aristophanes and Rabelais and Molière—as material; it could become happily sophisticated, without being cultured. But there is no fault inherent in its nature, and its virtues are exceptional. For us to appreciate slap-stick may require a revolution in our way of looking at the arts; having taken thought on how we now look at the arts, I suggest that the revolution is not entirely undesirable.

STYLE AND MEDIUM IN THE MOTION PICTURES (1934; • revised 1947)

By Erwin Panofsky

Film art is the only art the development of which men now living have witnessed from the very beginnings; and this development is all the more interesting as it took place under conditions contrary to precedent. It was not an artistic urge that gave rise to the discovery and gradual perfection of a new technique; it was a technical invention that gave rise to the discovery and gradual perfection of a new art.

From this we understand two fundamental facts. First, that the primordial basis of the enjoyment of moving pictures was not an objective interest in a specific subject matter, much less an aesthetic interest in the formal presentation of subject matter, but the sheer delight in the fact that things seemed to move, no matter what things they were. Second, that films—first exhibited in "kinetoscopes," viz., cinematographic peep shows, but projectable to a screen since as early as 1894—are, originally, a product of genuine folk art (whereas, as a rule, folk art derives from what is known as "higher art"). At the very beginning of things we find the simple recordings of movements: galloping horses, railroad trains, fire engines, sporting events, street scenes. And when it had come to the making of narrative films these were produced by photographers who were anything but "producers" or "directors," performed by people who were anything but actors, and enjoyed by people who would have been much offended had anyone called them "art lovers."

The casts of these archaic films were usually collected in a "café" where unemployed supers or ordinary citizens possessed of a suitable exterior were wont to assemble at a given hour. An enterprising photographer would walk in, hire four or five convenient characters and make the picture while carefully instructing them what to do: "Now, you pretend to hit this lady over the head"; and (to the lady): "And you pretend to fall down in a heap." Productions like these were shown, together with those purely factual recordings of "movement for movement's sake," in a few small and dingy cinemas mostly frequented by the "lower classes" and a sprinkling of youngsters in quest of adventure (about 1905, I happen to remember, there was only one obscure and faintly disreputable *kino* in the whole city of Berlin, bearing, for some unfathomable reason, the English name of "The Meeting Room"). Small wonder that the "better classes," when they slowly began to venture into these early picture theaters, did so, not by way of seeking normal and possibly serious entertainment, but with that characteristic sensation of self-conscious condescension with which we may plunge, in gay company, into the folkloristic depths of Coney Island or a European kermis; even a few years ago it was the regulation attitude of the socially or intellectually prominent that one could confess to enjoying such austerely educational films as *The Sex Life of the Starfish* or films with "beautiful scenery," but never to a serious liking for narratives.

Today there is no denying that narrative films are not only "art" —not often good art, to be sure, but this applies to other media as well—but also, besides architecture, cartooning and "commercial design," the only visual art entirely alive. The "movies" have re-established that dynamic contact between art production and art consumption which, for reasons too complex to be considered here, is sorely attenuated, if not entirely interrupted, in many other fields of artistic endeavor. Whether we like it or not, it is the movies that mold, more than any other single force, the opinions, the taste, the language, the dress, the behavior, and even the physical appearance of a public comprising more than 60 percent of the population of the earth. If all the serious lyrical poets, composers, painters and sculptors were forced by law to stop their activities, a rather small fraction of the general public would become aware of the fact and a still smaller fraction would seriously regret it. If the same thing were to happen with the movies the social consequences would be catastrophic.

In the beginning, then, there were the straight recordings of movement no matter what moved, viz., the prehistoric ancestors of our "documentaries"; and, soon after, the early narratives, viz., the prehistoric ancestors of our "feature films." The craving for a narrative element could be satisfied only by borrowing from older arts, and one should expect that the natural thing would have been to borrow from the theater, a theater play being apparently the *genus proximum* to a narrative film in that it consists of a narrative enacted by persons that move. But in reality the imitation of stage performances was a comparatively late and thoroughly frustrated development. What happened at the start was a very different thing. Instead of imitating a theatrical performance already endowed with a certain amount of motion, the earliest films added movement to works of art originally stationary, so that the dazzling technical invention might achieve a triumph of its own without intruding upon the sphere of higher culture. The living language, which is always right, has endorsed this sensible choice when it still speaks of a "moving picture" or, simply, a "picture," instead of accepting the pretentious and fundamentally erroneous "screen play."

The stationary works enlivened in the earliest movies were indeed pictures: bad nineteenth-century paintings and postcards (or waxworks à la Madame Tussaud's), supplemented by the comic strips—a most important root of cinematic art—and the subject matter of popular songs, pulp magazines and dime novels; and the films descending from this ancestry appealed directly and very intensely to a folk-art mentality. They gratified—often simultaneously—first, a primitive sense of justice and decorum when virtue and industry were rewarded while vice and laziness were punished; second, plain sentimentality when "the think trickle of a fictive love interest" took its course "through somewhat serpentine channels," or when Father, dear Father returned from the saloon to find his child dying of diphtheria; third, a primordial instinct for bloodshed and cruelty when Andreas Hofer faced the firing squad, or when (in a film of 1893–94) the head of Mary Queen of Scots actually came off; fourth, a taste for mild pornography (I remember with great pleasure a French film of *ca.* 1900 wherein a seemingly but not really well-rounded lady as well as a seemingly but not really slender one were shown changing to bathing suits—an honest, straightforward *porcheria* much less objectionable than the now extinct Betty Boop films and, I am sorry to say, some of the more recent Walt Disney productions); and, finally, that crude sense of humor, graphically described as "slapstick," which feeds upon the sadistic and the pornographic instinct, either singly or in combination.

Not until as late as *ca.* 1905 was a film adaptation of *Faust* ventured upon (cast still "unknown," characteristically enough), and not until 1911 did Sarah Bernhardt lend her prestige to an unbelievably funny film tragedy, *Queen Elizabeth of England.* These films represent the first conscious attempt at transplanting the movies from the folk art level to that of "real art"; but they also bear witness to the fact that this commendable goal could not be reached in so simple a manner. It was soon realized that the imitation of a theater performance with a set stage, fixed entries and exits, and distinctly literary ambitions is the one thing the film must avoid.

The legitimate paths of evolution were opened, not by running away from the folk-art character of the primitive film but by developing it within the limits of its own possibilities. Those primordial archetypes of film productions on the folk art level—success or retribution, sentiment, sensation, pornography, and crude humor—could blossom forth into genuine history, tragedy and romance, crime and adventure, and comedy, as soon as it was realized that they could be transfigured—not by an artificial injection of literary values but by the exploitation of the unique and specific possibilities of the new medium. Significantly, the beginnings of this legitimate development antedate the attempts at endowing the film with higher values of a foreign order (the crucial period being the years from 1902 to *ca.* 1905), and the decisive steps were taken by people who were laymen or outsiders from the viewpoint of the serious stage.

These unique and specific possibilities can be defined as *dynamization of space* and, accordingly, *spatialization of time.* This statement is self-evident to the point of triviality but it belongs to that kind of truths which, just because of their triviality, are easily forgotten or neglected.

In a theater, space is static, that is, the space represented on the stage, as well as the spatial relation of the beholder to the spectacle, is unalterably fixed. The spectator cannot leave his seat, and the setting of the stage cannot change, during one act (except for such incidentals as rising moons or gathering clouds and such illegitimate reborrowings from the film as turning wings or gliding backdrops). But, in return for this restriction, the theater has the advantage that time, the medium of emotion and thought conveyable by speech, is free and independent of anything that may happen in visible space. Hamlet may deliver his famous monologue lying on a couch in the middle distance, doing nothing and only dimly discernible to the spectator and listener, and yet by his mere words enthrall him with a feeling of intensest emotional action.

With the movies the situation is reversed. Here, too, the spectator occupies a fixed seat, but only physically, not as the subject of an aesthetic experience. Aesthetically, he is in permanent motion as his eye identifies itself with the lens of the camera, which permanently shifts in distance and direction. And as movable as the spectator is, as movable is, for the same reason, the space presented to him. Not only bodies move in space, but space itself does, approaching, receding, turning, dissolving and recrystallizing as it appears through the controlled locomotion and focusing of the camera and through the cutting and editing of the various shots—not to mention such special effects as visions, transformations, disappearances, slow-motion and fast-motion shots, reversals and trick films. This opens up a world of possibilities of which the stage can never dream. Quite apart from such photographic tricks as the participation of disembodied spirits in the action of the *Topper* series, or the more effective wonders wrought by Roland Young in *The Man Who Could Work Miracles,* there is, on the purely factual level, an untold wealth of themes as inaccessible to the "legitimate" stage as a fog or a snowstorm is to the sculptor; all sorts of violent elemental phenomena and, conversely, events too microscopic to be visible under normal conditions (such as the life-saving injection with the serum flown in at the very last moment, or the fatal bite of the yellow-fever mosquito); full-scale battle scenes; all kinds of operations, not only in the surgical sense but also in the sense of any actual construction, destruction or experimentation, as in *Louis Pasteur* or *Madame Curie;* a really grand party, moving through many rooms of a mansion or a palace. Features like these, even the mere shifting of the scene from one place to another by means of a car perilously negotiating heavy traffic or a motorboat steered through a nocturnal harbor, will not only always retain their primitive cinematic appeal but also remain enormously effective as a means of stirring the emotions and creating suspense. In addition, the movies have the power, entirely denied to the theater, to convey psychological experiences by directly projecting their content to the screen, substituting, as it were, the eye of the beholder for the consciousness of the character (as when the imaginings and hallucinations of the drunkard in the otherwise overrated *Lost Weekend* appear as stark realities instead of being described by mere words). But any attempt to convey thought and feelings exclusively, or even primarily, by speech leaves us with a feeling of embarrassment, boredom, or both.

What I mean by thoughts and feelings "conveyed exclusively, or even primarily, by speech" is simply this: Contrary to naïve expectation, the invention of the sound track in 1928 has been unable to change the basic fact that a moving picture, even when it has learned to talk, remains a picture that moves and does not convert itself into a piece of writing that is enacted. Its substance remains a series of visual sequences held together by an uninterrupted flow of movement in space (except, of course, for such checks and pauses as have the same compositional value as a rest in music), and not a sustained study in human character and destiny transmitted by effective, let alone "beautiful," diction. I cannot remember a more misleading statement about the movies than Mr. Eric Russell Bentley's in the spring number of the *Kenyon Review,* 1945: "The potentialities of the talking screen differ from those of the silent screen in adding the dimension of dialogue—which could be poetry." I would suggest: "The potentialities of the talking screen differ from those of the silent screen in integrating visible movement with dialogue which, therefore, had better not be poetry."

All of us, if we are old enough to remember the period prior to 1928, recall the old-time pianist who, with his eyes glued on the screen, would accompany the events with music adapted to their mood and rhythm; and we also recall the weird and spectral feeling overtaking us when this pianist left his post for a few minutes and the film was allowed to run by itself, the darkness haunted by the monotonous rattle of the machinery. Even the silent film, then, was never mute. The visible spectacle always required, and received, an audible accompaniment which, from the very beginning, distinguished the film from simple pantomime and rather classed it—*mutatis mutandis*—with the ballet. The advent of the talkie meant not so much an "addition" as a transformation: the transformation of musical sound into articulate speech and, therefore, of quasi pantomime into an entirely new species of spectacle which differs from the ballet, and agrees with the stage play, in that its acoustic component consists of intelligible words, but differs from the stage play and agrees with the ballet in that this acoustic component is not detachable from the visual. In a film, that which we hear remains, for good or worse, inextricably fused with that which we see; the sound, articulate or not, cannot express any more than is expressed, at the same time, by visible movement; and in a good film it does not even attempt to do so. To put it briefly, the play—or, as it is very properly called, the "script"—of a moving picture is subject to what might be termed the *principle of coexpressibility.*

Empirical proof of this principle is furnished by the fact that, wherever the dialogical or monological element gains temporary prominence, there appears, with the inevitability of a natural law, the "close-up." What does the close-up achieve? In showing us, in magnification, either the face of the speaker or the face of the listeners or both in alternation, the camera transforms the human physiognomy into a huge field of action where—given the qualification of the performers—every subtle movement of the features, almost imperceptible from a natural distance, becomes an expressive event in visible space and thereby completely integrates itself with the expressive content of the spoken word; whereas, on the stage, the spoken word makes a stronger rather than a weaker impression if we are not permitted to count the hairs in Romeo's mustache.

This does not mean that the scenario is a negligible factor in the making of a moving picture. It only means that its artistic intention differs in kind from that of a stage play, and much more from that of a novel or a piece of poetry. As the success of a Gothic jamb figure depends not only upon its quality as a piece of sculpture but also, or even more so, upon its integrability with the architecture of the portal, so does the success of a movie script—not unlike that of an opera libretto—depend, not only upon its quality as a piece of literature but also, or even more so, upon its integrability with the events on the screen.

As a result—another empirical proof of the coexpressibility principle—good movie scripts are unlikely to make good reading and have seldom been published in book form; whereas, conversely, good stage plays have to be severely altered, cut, and, on the other hand, enriched by interpolations to make good movie scripts. In Shaw's *Pygmalion,* for instance, the actual process of Eliza's phonetic education and, still more important, her final triumph at the grand party, are wisely omitted; we see—or, rather, hear—some samples of her gradual linguistic improvement and finally encounter her, upon her return from the reception, victorious and splendidly arrayed but deeply hurt for want of recognition and sympathy. In the film adaptation, precisely these two scenes are not only supplied but also strongly emphasized; we witness the fascinating activities in the laboratory with its array of spinning disks and mirrors, organ pipes and dancing flames, and we participate in the ambassadorial party, with many moments of impending catastrophe and a little counterintrigue thrown in for suspense. Unquestionably these two scenes, entirely absent from the play, and indeed unachievable upon the stage, were the highlights of the film; whereas the Shavian dialogue, however severely cut, turned out to fall a little flat in certain moments. And wherever, as in so many other films, a poetic emotion, a musical outburst, or a literary conceit (even, I am grieved to say, some of the wisecracks of Groucho Marx) entirely lose contact with visible movement, they strike the sensitive spectator as, literally, out of place. It is certainly terrible when a soft-boiled he-man, after the suicide of his mistress, casts a twelve-foot glance upon her photograph and says something less-than-coexpressible to the effect that he will never forget her. But when he recites, instead, a piece of poetry as sublimely more-than-coexpressible as Romeo's monologue at the bier of Juliet, it is still worse. Reinhardt's *Midsummer Night's Dream* is probably the most unfortunate major film ever produced; and Oliver's *Henry V* owes its comparative success, apart from the all but providential adaptability of this particular play, to so many *tours de force* that it will, God willing, remain an exception rather than set a pattern. It combines "judicious pruning" with the interpolation of pageantry, nonverbal comedy and melodrama; it uses a device perhaps best designated as "oblique close-up" (Mr. Olivier's beautiful face inwardly listening to but not pronouncing the great soliloquy); and, most notably, it shifts between three levels of archaeological reality: a reconstruction of Elizabethan London, a reconstruction of the events of 1415 as laid down in Shakespeare's play, and the reconstruction of a performance of this play on Shakespeare's own stage. All this is perfectly legitimate; but, even so, the highest praise of the film will always come from those who, like the critic of *The New Yorker,* are not quite in sympathy with either the movies *au naturel* or Shakespeare *au naturel.*

As the writings of Conan Doyle potentially contain all modern mystery stories (except for the tough specimens of the Dashiell Hammett school), so do the films produced between 1900 and 1910 preestablish the subject matter and methods of the moving picture as we know it. This period produced the incunabula of the Western and the crime film (Edwin S. Porter's amazing *Great Train Robbery* of 1903) from which developed the modern gangster, adventure, and mystery pictures (the latter, if well done, is still one of the most honest and genuine forms of film entertainment, space being doubly charged with time as the beholder asks himself not only "What is going to happen?" but also "What has happened before?"). The same period saw the emergence of the fantastically imaginative film *(Méliès)* which was to lead to the expressionist and surrealist experiments (*The Cabinet of Dr. Caligari, Sang d'un Poète,* etc.), on the one hand, and to the more superficial and spectacular fairy tales à la Arabian Nights, on the other. Comedy, later to triumph in Charlie Chaplin, the still insufficiently appreciated Buster Keaton, the Marx Brothers and the pre-Hollywood creations of René Clair, reached a respectable level in Max Linder and others. In historical and melodramatic films the foundations were laid for movie iconography and movie symbolism, and in the early work of D. W. Griffith we find, not only remarkable attempts at psychological analysis *(Edgar Allan Poe)* and social criticism *(A Corner in Wheat)* but also such basic technical innovations as the long shot, the flashback and the close-up. And modest trick films and cartoons paved the way to Felix the Cat, Popeye the Sailor, and Felix's prodigious offspring, Mickey Mouse.

Within their self-imposed limitations the earlier Disney films, and certain sequences in the later ones,[1] represent, as it were, a chemically pure distillation of cinematic possibilities. They retain the most important folkloristic elements—sadism, pornography, the humor engendered by both, and moral justice—almost without dilution and often fuse these elements into a variation on the primitive and inexhaustible David-and-Goliath motif, the triumph of the seemingly weak over the seemingly strong; and their fantastic independence of the natural laws gives them the power to integrate space with time to such perfection that the spatial and temporal experi-

[1] I make this distinction because it was, in my opinion, a fall from grace when *Snow White* introduced the human figure and when *Fantasia* attempted to picturalize The World's Great Music. The very virtue of the animated cartoon is to animate, that is to say endow lifeless things with life, or living things with a different kind of life. It effects a metamorphosis, and such a metamorphosis is wonderfully present in Disney's animals, plants, thunderclouds and railroad trains. Whereas his dwarfs, glamourized princesses, hillbillies, baseball players, rouged centaurs and *amigos* from South America are not transformations but caricatures at best, and fakes or vulgarities at worst. Concerning music, however, it should be borne in mind that its cinematic use is no less predicated upon the principle of coexpressibility than is the cinematic use of the spoken word. There is music permitting or even requiring the accompaniment of visible action (such as dances, ballet music and any kind of operatic compositions) and music of which the opposite is true; and this is, again, not a question of quality (most of us rightly prefer a waltz by Johann Strauss to a symphony by Sibelius) but one of intention. In *Fantasia* the hippopotamus ballet was wonderful, and the Pastoral Symphony and "Ave Maria" sequences were deplorable, not because the cartooning in the first case was infinitely better than in the two others (*cf.* above), and certainly not because Beethoven and Schubert are too sacred for picturalization, but simply because Ponchielli's "Dance of the Hours" is coexpressible while the Pastoral Symphony and the "Ave Maria" are not. In cases like these even the best imaginable music and the best imaginable cartoon will impair rather than enhance each other's effectiveness.

Experimental proof of all this was furnished by Disney's recent *Make Mine Music* where The World's Great Music was fortunately restricted to Prokofieff. Even among the other sequences the most successful ones were those in which the human element was either absent or reduced to a minimum; Willie the Whale, the Ballad of Johnny Fedora and Alice Blue-Bonnet, and, above all, the truly magnificent Goodman Quartet.

ences of sight and hearing come to be almost interconvertible. A series of soap bubbles, successively punctured, emits a series of sounds exactly corresponding in pitch and volume to the size of the bubbles; the three uvulae of Willie the Whale—small, large and medium—vibrate in consonance with tenor, bass and baritone notes; and the very concept of stationary existence is completely abolished. No object in creation, whether it be a house, a piano, a tree or an alarm clock, lacks the faculties of organic, in fact anthropomorphic, movement, facial expression and phonetic articulation. Incidentally, even in normal, "realistic" films the inanimate object, provided that it is dynamizable, can play the role of a leading character as do the ancient railroad engines in Buster Keaton's *General* and *Niagara Falls.* How the earlier Russian films exploited the possibility of heroizing all sorts of machinery lives in everybody's memory; and it is perhaps more than an accident that the two films which will go down in history as the great comical and the great serious masterpiece of the silent period bear the names and immortalize the personalities of two big ships: Keaton's *Navigator* (1924) and Eisenstein's *Potemkin* (1925).

The evolution from the jerky beginnings to this grand climax offers the fascinating spectacle of a new artistic medium gradually becoming conscious of its legitimate, that is, exclusive, possibilities and limitations—a spectacle not unlike the development of the mosaic, which started out with transposing illusionistic genre pictures into a more durable material and culminated in the hieratic supernaturalism of Ravenna; or the development of line engraving, which started out as a cheap and handy substitute for book illumination and culminated in the purely "graphic" style of Dürer.

Just so the silent movies developed a definite style of their own, adapted to the specific conditions of the medium. A hitherto unknown language was forced upon a public not yet capable of reading it, and the more proficient the public became the more refinement could develop in the language. For a Saxon peasant of around 800 it was not easy to understand the meaning of a picture showing a man as he pours water over the head of another man, and even later many people found it difficult to grasp the significance of two ladies standing behind the throne of an emperor. For the public of around 1910 it was no less difficult to understand the meaning of the speechless action in a moving picture, and the producers employed means of clarification similar to those we find in medieval art. One of these were printed titles or letters, striking equivalents of the medieval *tituli* and scrolls (at a still earlier date there even used to be explainers who would say, *viva voce,* "Now he thinks his wife is dead but she isn't" or "I don't wish to offend the ladies in the audience but I doubt that any of them would have done that much for her child"). Another, less obtrusive method of explanation was the introduction of a fixed iconography which from the outset informed the spectator about the basic facts and characters, much as the two ladies behind the emperor, when carrying a sword and a cross respectively, were uniquely determined as Fortitude and Faith. There arose, identifiable by standardized appearance, behavior and attributes, the well-remembered types of the Vamp and the Straight Girl (perhaps the most convincing modern equivalents of the medieval personifications of the Vices and Virtues), the Family Man, and the Villain, the latter marked by a black mustache and walking stick. Nocturnal scenes were printed on blue or green film. A checkered tablecloth meant, once for all, a "poor but honest" milieu; a happy marriage, soon to be endangered by the shadows from the past, was symbolized by the young wife's pouring the breakfast coffee for her husband; the first kiss was invariably announced by the lady's gently playing with her partner's necktie and was invariably accompanied by her kicking out with her left foot. The conduct of the characters was predetermined accordingly. The poor but honest laborer who, after leaving his little house with the checkered tablecloth, came upon an abandoned baby could not but take it to his home and bring it up as best he could; the Family Man could not but yield, however temporarily, to the temptations of the Vamp. As a result these early melodramas had a highly gratifying and soothing quality in that events took shape, without the complications of individual psychology, according to a pure Aristotelian logic so badly missed in real life.

Devices like these became gradually less necessary as the public grew accustomed to interpret the action by itself and were virtually abolished by the invention of the talking film. But even now there survive—quite legitimately, I think—the remnants of a "fixed attitude and attribute" principle and, more basic, a primitive or folkloristic concept of plot construction. Even today we take it for granted that the diphtheria of a baby tends to occur when the parents are out and, having occurred, solves all their matrimonial problems. Even today we demand of a decent mystery film that the butler, though he may be anything from an agent of the British Secret Service to the real father of the daughter of the house, must not turn out to be the murderer. Even today we love to see Pasteur, Zola or Ehrlich win out against stupidity and wickedness, with their respective wives trusting and trusting all the time. Even today we much prefer a happy finale to a gloomy one and insist, at the very least, on the observance of the Aristotelian rule that the story have a beginning, a middle and an ending—a rule the abrogation of which has done so much to estrange the general public from the more elevated spheres of modern writing. Primitive symbolism, too, survives in such amusing details as the last sequence of *Casablanca* where the delightfully crooked and right-minded *préfet de police* casts an empty bottle of Vichy water into the wastepaper basket; and in such telling symbols of the supernatural as Sir Cedric Hardwicke's Death in the guise of a "gentleman in a dustcoat" *(On Borrowed Time)* or Claude Rains's Hermes Psychopompos in the striped trousers of an airline manager *(Here Comes Mister Jordan).*

The most conspicuous advances were made in directing, lighting, camera work, cutting and acting proper. But while in most of these fields the evolution proceeded continuously—though, of course, not without detours, breakdowns and archaic relapses—the development of acting suffered a sudden interruption by the invention of the talking film; so that the style of acting in the silents can already be evaluated in retrospect, as a lost art not unlike the painting technique of Jan van Eyck or, to take up our previous simile, the burin technique of Dürer. It was soon realized that acting in a silent film neither meant a pantomimic exaggeration of stage acting (as was generally and erroneously assumed by professional stage actors who more and more frequently condescended to perform in the movies), nor could dispense with stylization altogether; a man photographed while walking down a gangway in ordinary, everyday-life fashion looked like anything but a man walking down a gangway when the result appeared on the screen. If the picture was to look both natural and meaningful the acting had to be done in a manner equally different from the style of the stage and the reality of ordinary life; speech had to be made dispensable by establishing an organic relation between the acting and the technical procedure of cinephotography—much as in Dürer's prints color had been made dispensable by establishing an organic relation between the design and the technical procedure of line engraving.

This was precisely what the great actors of the silent period accomplished, and it is a significant fact that the best of them did not come from the stage, whose crystallized tradition prevented Duse's only film, *Cenere,* from being more than a priceless record of Duse. They came instead from the circus or the variety, as was the case of Chaplin, Keaton and Will Rogers; from nothing in particular, as was the case of Theda Bara, of her greater European parallel, the Danish actress Asta Nielsen, and of Garbo; or from everything under the sun, as was the case of Douglas Fairbanks. The style of these "old masters" was indeed comparable to the style of line engraving in that it was, and had to be, exaggerated in comparison with stage acting (just as the sharply incised and vigorously curved *tailles* of the burin are exaggerated in comparison with pencil strokes or brushwork), but richer, subtler and infinitely more precise. The advent of the talkies, reducing if not abolishing this difference between screen acting and stage acting, thus confronted the actors and actresses of the silent screen with a serious problem. Buster Keaton yielded to temptation and fell. Chaplin first tried to stand his ground and to remain an exquisite archaist but finally gave in, with only moderate success *(The Great Dictator).* Only the glorious Harpo has thus far successfully refused to utter a single articulate sound; and only Greta Garbo succeeded, in a measure, in transforming her style in principle. But even in her case one cannot help feeling that her first talking picture, *Anna Christie,* where she could ensconce herself, most of the time, in mute or monosyllabic sullenness, was better than her later performances; and in the second, talking version of *Anna Karenina,* the weakest moment is certainly when she delivers a big Ibsenian speech to her husband, and the strongest when she silently moves along the platform of the railroad station while her despair takes shape in the consonance of her movement (and expression) with the movement of the nocturnal space around her, filled with the real noises of the trains and the imaginary sound of the "little men with the iron hammers" that drives her, relentlessly and almost without her realizing it, under the wheels.

Small wonder that there is sometimes felt a kind of nostalgia for the silent period and that devices have been worked out to combine the virtues of sound and speech with those of silent acting, such as the "oblique close-up" already mentioned in connection with *Henry*

V; the dance behind glass doors in *Sous les Toits de Paris;* or, in the *Histoire d'un Tricheur,* Sacha Guitry's recital of the events of his youth while the events themselves are "silently" enacted on the screen. However, this nostalgic feeling is no argument against the talkies as such. Their evolution has shown that, in art, every gain entails a certain loss on the other side of the ledger; but that the gain remains a gain, provided that the basic nature of the medium is realized and respected. One can imagine that, when the cavemen of Altamira began to paint their buffaloes in natural colors instead of merely incising the contours, the more conservative cavemen foretold the end of paleolithic art. But paleolithic art went on, and so will the movies. New technical inventions always tend to dwarf the values already attained, especially in a medium that owes its very existence to technical experimentation. The earliest talkies were infinitely inferior to the then mature silents, and most of the present technicolor films are still inferior to the now mature talkies in black and white. But even if Aldous Huxley's nightmare should come true and the experiences of taste, smell and touch should be added to those of sight and hearing, even then we may say with the Apostle, as we have said when first confronted with the sound track and the technicolor film, "We are troubled on every side, yet not distressed; we are perplexed, but not in despair."

From the law of time-charged space and space-bound time, there follows the fact that the screenplay, in contrast to the theater play, *has no aesthetic existence independent of its performance, and that its characters have no aesthetic existence outside the actors.*

The playwright writes in the fond hope that his work will be an imperishable jewel in the treasure house of civilization and will be presented in hundreds of performances that are but transient variations on a "work" that is constant. The script-writer, on the other hand, writes for one producer, one director and one cast. Their work achieves the same degree of permanence as does his; and should the same or a similar scenario ever be filmed by a different director and a different cast there will result an altogether different "play."

Othello or Nora are definite, substantial figures created by the playwright. They can be played well or badly, and they can be "interpreted" in one way or another; but they most definitely exist, no matter who plays them or even whether they are played at all.

The character in a film, however, lives and dies with the actor. It is not the entity "Othello" interpreted by Robeson or the entity "Nora" interpreted by Duse; it is the entity "Greta Garbo" incarnate in a figure called Anna Christie or the entity "Robert Montgomery" incarnate in a murderer who, for all we know or care to know, may forever remain anonymous but will never cease to haunt our memories. Even when the names of the characters happen to be Henry VIII or Anna Karenina, the king who ruled England from 1509 to 1547 and the woman created by Tolstoy, they do not exist outside the being of Garbo and Laughton. They are but empty and incorporeal outlines like the shadows in Homer's Hades, assuming the character of reality only when filled with the lifeblood of an actor. Conversely, if a movie role is badly played there remains literally nothing of it, no matter how interesting the character's psychology or how elaborate the words.

What applies to the actor applies, *mutatis mutandis,* to most of the other artists, or artisans, who contribute to the making of a film: the director, the sound man, the enormously important cameraman, even the make-up man. A stage production is rehearsed until everything is ready, and then it is repeatedly performed in three consecutive hours. At each performance everybody has to be on hand and does his work; and afterward he goes home and to bed. The work of the stage actor may thus be likened to that of a musician, and that of the stage director to that of a conductor. Like these, they have a certain repertoire which they have studied and present in a number of complete but transitory performances, be it *Hamlet* today and *Ghosts* tomorrow, or *Life with Father per saecula saeculorum.* The activities of the film actor and the film director, however, are comparable, respectively, to those of the plastic artist and the architect, rather than to those of the musician and the conductor. *Stage work is continuous but transitory; film work is discontinuous but permanent.* Individual sequences are done piecemeal and out of order according to the most efficient use of sets and personnel. Each bit is done over and over again until it stands; and when the whole has been cut and composed everyone is through with it forever. Needless to say that this very procedure cannot but emphasize the curious consubstantiality that exists between the person of the movie actor and his role. Coming into existence piece by piece, regardless of the natural sequence of events, the "character" can grow into a unified whole only if the actor manages to be, not merely to play, Henry VIII or Anna Karenina throughout the entire wearisome period of shooting. I have it on the best of authorities that Laughton was really difficult to live with in the particular six or eight weeks during which he was doing—or rather being—Captain Bligh.

It might be said that a film, called into being by a co-operative effort in which all contributions have the same degree of permanence, is the nearest modern equivalent of a medieval cathedral; the role of the producer corresponding, more or less, to that of the bishop or archbishop; that of the director to that of the architect in chief; that of the scenario writers to that of the scholastic advisers establishing the iconographical program; and that of the actors, cameramen, cutters, sound men, make-up men and the divers technicians to that of those whose work provided the physical entity of the finished product, from the sculptors, glass painters, bronze casters, carpenters and skilled masons down to the quarry men and woodsmen. And if you speak to any one of these collaborators he will tell you, with perfect *bona fides,* that his is really the most important job—which is quite true to the extent that it is indispensable.

This comparison may seem sacrilegious, not only because there are, proportionally, fewer good films than there are good cathedrals, but also because the movies are commercial. However, if commercial art be defined as all art not primarily produced in order to gratify the creative urge of its maker but primarily intended to meet the requirements of a patron or a buying public, it must be said that noncommercial art is the exception rather than the rule, and a fairly recent and not always felicitous exception at that. While it is true that commercial art is always in danger of ending up as a prostitute, it is equally true that noncommercial art is always in danger of ending up as an old maid. Noncommercial art has given us Seurat's "Grande Jatte" and Shakespeare's sonnets, but also much that is esoteric to the point of incommunicability. Conversely, commercial art has given us much that is vulgar or snobbish (two aspects of the same thing) to the point of loathsomeness, but also Dürer's prints and Shakespeare's plays. For, we must not forget that Dürer's prints were partly made on commission and partly intended to be sold in the open market; and that Shakespeare's plays—in contrast to the earlier masques and intermezzi which were produced at court by aristocratic amateurs and could afford to be so incomprehensible that even those who described them in printed monographs occasionally failed to grasp their intended significance—were meant to appeal, and did appeal, not only to the select few but also to everyone who was prepared to pay a shilling for admission.

It is this requirement of communicability that makes commercial art more vital than noncommercial, and therefore potentially much more effective for better or for worse. The commercial producer can both educate and pervert the general public, and can allow the general public—or rather his idea of the general public—both to educate and to pervert himself. As is demonstrated by a number of excellent films that proved to be great box office successes, the public does not refuse to accept good products if it gets them. That it does not get them very often is caused not so much by commercialism as such as by too little discernment and, paradoxical though it may seem, too much timidity in its application. Hollywood believes that it must produce "what the public wants" while the public would take whatever Hollywood produces. If Hollywood were to decide for itself what it wants it would get away with it—even if it should decide to "depart from evil and do good." For, to revert to whence we started, in modern life the movies are what most other forms of art have ceased to be, not an adornment but a necessity.

That this should be so is understandable, not only from a sociological but also from an art-historical point of view. The processes of all the earlier representational arts conform, in a higher or lesser degree, to an idealistic conception of the world. These arts operate from top to bottom, so to speak, and not from bottom to top; they start with an idea to be projected into shapeless matter and not with the objects that constitute the physical world. The painter works on a blank wall or canvas which he organizes into a likeness of things and persons according to his idea (however much this idea may have been nourished by reality); he does not work with the things and persons themselves even if he works "from the model." The same is true of the sculptor with his shapeless mass of clay or his untooled block of stone or wood; of the writer with his sheet of paper or his dictaphone; and even of the stage designer with his empty and sorely limited section of space. It is the movies, and only the movies, that do justice to that materialistic interpretation of the universe which, whether we like it or not, pervades contemporary civilization. Excepting the very special case of the animated cartoon, the movies organize material things and persons, not a neutral medium, into a composition that receives its style, and may even become fantastic or pretervoluntarily symbolic,[2] not so much by an interpretation in the artist's mind as by the actual manipulation of physical objects and recording machinery. The medium of the movies is physical reality as such: the physical reality of eighteenth-century Versailles—no matter whether it be the original or a Hollywood facsimile indistinguishable therefrom for all aesthetic intents and purposes—or of a suburban home in Westchester; the physical reality of the Rue de Lappe in Paris or of the Gobi Desert, of Paul Ehrlich's apartment in Frankfurt or of the streets of New York in the rain; the physical reality of engines and animals, of Edward G. Robinson and Jimmy Cagney. All these objects and persons must be organized into a work of art. They can be arranged in all sorts of ways ("arrangement" comprising, of course, such things as make-up, lighting and camera work); but there is no running away from them. From this point of view it becomes evident that an attempt at subjecting the world to artistic prestylization, as in the expressionist settings of *The Cabinet of Dr. Caligari* (1919), could be no more than an exciting experiment that could exert but little influence upon the general course of events. To prestylize reality prior to tackling it amounts to dodging the problem. The problem is to manipulate and shoot unstylized reality in such a way that the result has style. This is a proposition no less legitimate and no less difficult than any proposition in the older arts.

[2] I cannot help feeling that the final sequence of the new Marx Brothers film *Night in Casablanca*—where Harpo unaccountably usurps the pilot's seat of a big airplane, causes incalculable havoc by flicking one tiny little control after another, and waxes the more insane with joy the greater the disproportion between the smallness of his effort and the magnitude of the disaster—is a magnificent and terrifying symbol of man's behavior in the atomic age. No doubt the Marx Brothers would vigorously reject this interpretation; but so would Dürer have done had anyone told him that his "Apocalypse" foreshadowed the cataclysm of the Reformation.

LIFE GOES TO THE PICTURES (1940)

By Otis Ferguson

There are the categories in art of realism and naturalism, but for the most part they have remained conveniences of designation. The truly natural and unforced, especially as applied to the ways of common life, are hardly possible in such forms of expression as music, painting, writing, because the long and uncommon discipline of these crafts has made the men in them a different breed: they are easy and at home in their job only when the job is the unnatural one of creation. Although the majority of playwrights are only second-class writers at best, and the majority of actors ham it even when they are asleep and snoring, the stage is much nearer to the actual look and push of things, if only because its people, particularly its minor people, are, after all, people.

The movies, however, are today the nearest thing ever imagined to the unaffected and unconscious process of life, as expressed in art. That takes a lot of qualification, and will be hooted at in some quarters anyway, because it is the fashion to judge movies by their worst excrescence, and I suppose much more fun that way. In theory, I imagine this distinctive quality owes most to the fact that the films combine both immediacy and an almost boundless range as to time, place, and fancy. But much of it comes directly and without forethought from their origins and audience, their rank growth as a new art. We will be at that presently.

First, there is the matter of a tradition in art as it affects its practitioners. Take writing, the most familiar of the arts today: writers are above the blind aping of tradition that becomes so ridiculous in opera singers and the vaudeville Abe and Irish. At the same time writers are marked by the occupational disease of intellectualism. If they came from the working class, it is a good bet they were odd nuts even while they were working—tolerated and even liked perhaps, but outsiders, strange with books and questioning. If they had a privileged background, they are outside the main part of the world anyway: their sympathy may be acute and wide, but has to be objective. In either event, their urge to express the world about them has had a good long soaking in the accumulation of styles that makes up the literary tradition.

We have learned, every man jack of us, only a tiny fraction of life from our personal experience. The main body of knowledge is handed down by word of mouth and, on the higher levels, by words in print (otherwise how would we know that tomatoes aren't poisonous and the world isn't flat?). And more subtly, our estimate of what is natural shifts with each new stylization of it. Milt Gross once had the last word in transcription of joosh dialack; then come people like Odets, Irwin Shaw, Jerome Weidman—and what happens? O. Henry was once the whole seamy side in neat bundles, and then comes Damon Runyon, and you can have them both. Jack London was once the strenuous life stripped to the bone, but who would follow him after Hemingway? The point which I will not labor another minute is that in all fields of presentation the world is seen through somebody else's glasses—which have been ground into a cunning instrument just as the good oculist would grind at his work: partly by inspiration, partly by relentless application, but mostly by the best use of the best tools and precepts developed in his own guarded craft.

In their forty-odd years, the movies have developed their high craftsmen, and gradually out of the craftsman's effects, an art. But forty years is nothing in art, especially such a hole-and-corner art. The movies were upon us before anyone had time to grow up and become a professor in them. They literally grew out of the people, the hundreds and thousands of people who jumped in to produce, distribute, exhibit, direct, write for, or act in a popular commodity; and the millions and millions whose demand for some kind of excitement or relaxation as available and easy as the funnies, has made the whole sky-high fantasy not only real but inevitable. The legend has it that any businessman, or even college man, can jump in, learn the ropes, and become a producer with some bold or clever stroke. The legend is that any grip on the set with ideas can substitute for an assistant cameraman someday and become Darryl Zanuck. The legend is that a director spies some handsome filling-station boy, readies him in a few pictures, and a star is born.

Legend is usually a good part hogwash, but there is justice here. For the intellectual classes, the earlier nickelodeons were houses of shame: directors, producers, exhibitors had to be recruited from the vulgar. As films gained prestige, actors, directors, and writers went over to them. If they went to Hollywood, though, there was still the feeling of cultural betrayal. It was all right to be a foreign director or cameraman, or an established name like Chaplin or Griffith. But even while someone like Edmund Wilson was awesomely mistaking an uncut travelogue for a modern epic, he was (and still is) sternly deploring the desertion of any first-rate literary hack who got the chance to hit for the Beverly Hills.

It is still true that movie people come from among just people, bringing their unconscious shabby baggage of popular life along with them. Some of them go so rapidly and so far upstage, or commercial, as to get clean out of sight. And there are very few wholly conscious of a purpose. But there is also an in-between belt of nice people who bring to the screen only their natural selves and the simple things they know. They may be technicians, or dialogue writers, or advisors, or "character" players. They may be very much in the background, and they still may be the most important aid to truth—for there was never a more relentless eye and ear for petty fraud and the easy glozing over of truth than the modern camera and sound-track.

As Lewis Jacobs reminds us in his recent history of the movies,* the films of the earliest period, hundreds upon hundreds of them, turned on incidents in the commonest of common life. But what you do not get from reading such titles as *A Plumber's Plight* is that the treatment itself is as far from life as any black-face Al Jolson is from cotton. It was only with the full flexibility of the camera and the added latitude of sound that they really had time and scope for the hundred and one details that, observed in the film's motion without checking it, take an action out of stylized presentation (however effective) and make it completely natural.

Along with the growth of naturalism there has gone an influence that is wide and unmeasurable—the old question of, Which held the mirror first, art or life? Even within our generation, some sources of our knowledge of the world have been taken over from the knowledgeable class, especially in all the more vivid departments of presentation and document in pictures. Knowledge today is so lost in a maze of simple environment that we may catch ourselves criticizing the "likelihood" of one submarine picture by a wisdom of underwa-

* *The Rise of the American Film.* New York: Harcourt, Brace, 1941.

ter techniques that could not possibly have been gained from experience. (As a matter of confessional fact, I can't today distinguish between the antiquated type of T-boat I have actually been down in, and *Submarine D-1* and *U-Boat 29.*)

Turn on yourself and ask quickly if you ever saw a tiger in the jungle. You get an image though, correct? (Any sensible tiger would probably laugh at the image you get, but that's not the point here.) Ever since the first Tarzan epics and on down through the Fox Magic Carpet of Movietone and the Armand Denis's, we have been as familiar with wild animals as Hemingway. And this goes over into character. As Alistair Cooke pointed out a couple of years ago, Churchill and Chamberlain are mere cartoon figures: the British Empire is C. Aubrey Smith. It is as familiar as tigers.

And to go even farther afield, take the common-variety American in his occupation. He is Pat O'Brien, or something like that. I remember *Here Comes the Navy,* in which O'Brien was a chief-petty-officer, for the purpose of mortifying James Cagney, seaman-second-class. He lined his company up and walked it down the dock and came front and center in a medium shot and I nearly talked out loud in the theater: "Tague (chief signalman), you sonofabitch!" (Just an old wound, gentlemen.) And then from the opposite angle, I remember being on a banana boat and watching them repair a winch, and then the second engineer knocked off and went forward, looking vaguely sardonic—and he was John Carradine to the teeth.

When I was a kid, my old man worked a starveling New England farm in a section where every other name was Lubitzcki and there was deep snow, winters, and when King Vidor made *The Wedding Night,* I liked all those hulking Polacks I had known, for the first time in my life. I worked in a bowling alley two years and my boss was a very second-rate Edward Arnold. I even did a little robbing once with a slow Dutchman and a very special-edition little Italian, and I see them occasionally even in the most faky gangster films.

This isn't a jag on autobiography, and I haven't been a fan since the days of William S. Hart, I guess. I am trying to get at a point about movies, especially as made in America. On the surface and often below it they have a magnificent realism. Their men and women, from both sides of the camera, were in so many instances a part of common life just yesterday that they haven't had time to forget it, dress it up, and bury it. Too much talk has been wasted on the tendency of the movies to type people. They do, they do. But this is the new method and here to stay, for with so many levels of life to be covered, faster and faster, they simply can't wait to develop the old-type character actor with his bag of tricks and crepe hair.

I know for a fact that Cagney can coax or shove a director until a scene from a dreamy script becomes a scene from life as Cagney remembered it. I'm sure that hundreds of lesser people—in a picture where they are well cast and let alone—dredge up out of memory, way back beyond Beverly Hills, the natural phrase and gesture which let the same life in, in spite of the director.

In such a mixture of chance, collaboration, and hurry, the real thing is often smothered by surrounding irreality, to be sure. But often —and most often—the element of clear and simple truth as it is distilled for the screen is the work of some kingpin in the organization. A director like King Vidor under a producer like Goldwyn *(The Wedding Night).* A czar-director like Alfred Hitchcock, who still has them wondering how he can openly take what is usually passed off as melodrama and get excitement out of every character along the way—his open secret, which cannot be copied, is that in spite of the requirements of speed and tension, he can stop and figure out why a person would do this if he were somebody you might meet, and if he were that real, how would he go about it? A writer-director like Rowland Brown, whether he is his own director or not, remembers so vividly his experience of childhood *as a child* that he could never make a *Wizard of Oz* or *Road to Life* (which is simply Louisa May Alcott on a collective farm, which is to say, childhood through the wrong end of a telescope). I won't forget Brown's *The Devil Is a Sissy,* but I remembered its intangibles better when I tried to set them down in review: ". . . at the time Gig's father is going to the chair, and there is that day at school and that night when nobody can sleep, Buck standing with Gig under the streetlight snapping his knuckles and nothing else to say, except in apology for his own blunderbuss of a father: 'The old man, he . . . Wull, he means all right.' This part, in the authentic schoolroom, flats and streets, was done with what struck me as straightforward and absolutely unpretentious beauty. And shrewdness too: Gig's sudden brief shift from awe and bereavement to bragging next morning was very shrewd." The stuff was there—the human relations as well as the truck-hopping, apple-swiping, and a hundred deft activities—because it was written in and allowed to come out as felt. If you throw out the moral slops of the ending, this would be the first of a perfect trilogy on low and high life in big American cities—the other two being *Public Enemy* and *The Roaring Twenties.*

In analysis, our belief in any kind of life on the screen is dependent on many things, animate or inanimate, the people seen and the people unseen who planted the line or rolled the camera or set the whole motion in tempo. A picture can thus be pure hokum and still be very true in parts, or it can be the Great Social Document of the age and never really stick for a minute. Further, I realize that this subtle combination of many forces often plays tricks on us: we think it is the actor who is fine or the director who is shrewd, when it is really that and something else too. (This should be little of our concern, but I'd like a dime for every quote I could bring in, even from established critics, praising the fine "photography" of a picture whose beauty was purely a matter of natural scenery or fine set-building.) So when you go to the vivid feeling of life to be got from a picture like *Come and Get It* (if you remember), you will find that those loggers and lumber kings were natural partly because of the magnificent documentary sequences of big-scale logging—with which they had nothing to do—and the construction of such sets as the one for the big-town saloon. All I have to do is thumb back through some old clippings to be reminded of this constant element beyond both story and character as such: "What the screen really makes out of *Ah, Wilderness* is a first-class atmosphere piece. It calls up more matters than it knows of by its sure reconstruction of the day-to-day life of the New England country in a time that is as dead but vivid in the general memory as the smell of leaves burning in piles along the gravel walks. . . . Not only the sets of stiff cluttered rooms, lawns, gas buggies, picnics, but the incidental life of the place."

Or, "*Rhodes of Africa* progresses unevenly, shirks some duties, and ends in a ponderous fussiness. The outdoor photography in Africa—the plains, hills, mines, and such mob effects as the trek north, the attack of the Matabele—is the best of the production values, being handled by a separate director, Geoffrey Barkas." (And for that matter, the work of Otto Brower and Osmond Borradaile has lightened many an African epic that otherwise falls with its own weight.)

So when we say that a film is a good picture of men working

(as we often can), we recognize the understanding and talent of many people outside the actual men at work in the story. I just wanted to get that straightened out, because there are not words enough yet for the different ways in which movies affect us. If I were to pick the Hollywood film *Black Fury* over *Kameradschaft* for "Realism" or even "Naturalism," half my readers would get black in the face. Of course Pabst's film is a monumental sketch of men working shoulder to shoulder, and way ahead of its time in a film sense. But *Black Fury* was made in another, more familiar tradition, at another time: piece by piece it is nearer to our life if only in that the life of its characters was dramatized until we actually participated in it. The film got a blast from all labor sympathizers, and in a tactical sense deserved it (if you recall, the story was a true enough story about a certain kind of union activity, but by that part-for-the-whole business of presentation seemed to stand for all union activity). However, it said more about miners and their miserable lot than anything else we've had. When those men were working, or chewing the fat, or drinking their pitiful nickels away in the bar, they were no strangers to you. Rough men and awesome, yes. But so cleverly worked into a story-pattern of cause and result, environment and hopes, that they were neither symbols nor foreigners, but people you knew and hoped the best of. You knew their work and their dinner table, their mean streets and threadbare pleasures; and everything about it was simple and just-so, through the medium of the most complex and expensive art on earth.

And then there was *Fury,* Fritz Lang's picture of a lynching, a wonderful picture through the first two-thirds. The boy was just homely and hopeless enough, saying goodbye to his girl and trying to keep his brothers out of mischief—for these were poor people, and no doubt about it. In the story he saved up enough to buy a piece of a small gas station and a cheap car, and go to fetch his girl, who had a teaching job. And all this quiet and decent life (the simple pleasures, etc.) was blown to glory in the best study of mob stupidity anyone ever saw. The audience knew who this man was, and then saw—detail after detail—the growing antagonism and mass hysteria of the small-town types who didn't know and didn't care. (Not a lot of mugging faces in close-up or fancy cutting, either.) That thing built into terrific drama, but from the ground up.

And another film, not so well known but one of John Ford's: *Prisoner of Shark Island.* I remember that above almost any "historical" film (it was the case of Dr. Mudd), if only because it got clear of period and costumes; it became to its audience a common carrier. I know nothing of Dry Tortugas, except the general climate; but I do know barrack routine and never saw it so well used to heighten illusion and tension. The bugles, rifle racks, relief of the guard, etc., were only a part of it, though. The main thing was the sweating men in that end-of-the-earth shambles, what they did and what was done to them. You got *involved* in that picture, and I believe that was brought about by such a shrewd care for the pitch and speed of every move, every detail, that there was no need for suspension of belief. Except for a few tank shots, it was one of those things that come down off the screen and pull up a chair.

It is a certain thing John Ford gets into his pictures—it is more than pure skill in the medium, for it releases the imagination of all the people working on the set. Even a hoopla Western like *Stagecoach,* admittedly made as such, packs its scenes with the same kind of likelihood; and a picture like *Submarine Patrol* is a story of the Splinter Fleet that would be accepted by veterans. In this case it isn't that Ford recaptures those gray belting north seas in winter, which job can wait for Robert Flaherty. Again, as before, it is the recreation of day-to-day relations—life in action and at mess and horsing around.

(Here we come to what the printers call Insert A, the occasion being the happy appearance of Mr. Ford's *Grapes of Wrath* before this article had got further than galley form. The film is just what such a piece was waiting for, and indeed could stand as its single illustration, for in addition to its true-as-life study of people, jalopies, Okie camps, and the roads, it had a superb job of writing, direction, and camera, and a subject worthy of the best capacities of the medium. And when that malignant clown Martin Quigley attacked the truth of the story, *Boxoffice* was able to run—in addition to other supporting documents—a remarkable juxtaposition in two columns of photographs—one of actual cars and people and Okie villages, one of stills from the picture. And on a different scale there has been that running-mate by proximity if nothing else, Milestone's version of *Of Mice and Men*—see below—another study and another proof that the truth of films can be more vivid than the truth of fiction, and still as true.)

Don't worry; this is not going to fall off into directors-I-too-have-watched-with-interest. But Lewis Milestone is another to contribute to the naturalism of the Talking Thirties by this same aptitude for letting characters talk for themselves, or making them, and covering all loose joints with details from life. *All Quiet on the Western Front* is certainly the pioneer in this period, head and shoulders. But I'd like to bring back a screwball Milestone film of 1934 that never got much play: *The Captain Hates the Sea.* Its comedy was delicious; its human content was absurdly high for such a piece of gentle spoofing; and better than anything there was that feeling about it that everybody read the script and said, This is going to be fun, and they made it so. In spite of comedy, it was just in everything, from the captain on his bridge to the fly bartender, and the only true steamer orchestra I ever saw except on a steamer. But the film is a hobby of mine, a cruise story to end cruises forever, and perhaps it is best I get off here.

Generally, you remember films by their total effect, so that if you are thinking "sea," you think of *Captains Courageous* or *Mutiny on the Bounty.* That is why directors get such a big play, as having been responsible throughout. But there are many other things to consider in this realism of life on all levels. I'll bet few remember a melodrama called *Wharf Angel,* and I wouldn't myself if it hadn't had some shots in a stokehold that were so dark, hot, and real they hurt. Of the memorable stuff in *It Happened One Night,* anyone properly conditioned to long bus-hops will have a certain nostalgia for the sequence around the Gr-yh-nd terminal and the bus itself. Anyone who has been a machinist's apprentice will remember the groundwork sequences for *Black Legion,* which wasn't an awfully well-made affair as a whole. And some will recall newspaper and magazine offices—one especially in that fast-talk piece that was ripping beyond its time, *The Front Page,* another in *Friends of Mr. Sweeney* —both hokum, of course. And so on.

As I said before, set-building for atmosphere is a responsible part of all this, but if it were the whole of it, we would have to give over to the French, who when they are good are the best in the world (take *The Lower Depths* for one, or take the René Clair carnival in *Quatorze Juillet* or the sets in *Crime and Punishment*). And for realism as such we could never put a finger on such films of the latter Soviet period as *Peasants,* where you could damn near smell the pigs and the cow-shed—in fact, nothing has ever been done so close to the elemental dirt, drudgery, and delight of farm life. No, this faster and more flexible camera eye we're considering picks up half-finished lines, personal habits, street noise, shades of daylight, and a hundred familiar things, and when done with imagination and feeling—and only then—can become as near and eloquent as the room you're in. The environment with all its familiar nuisances and pleasures, and the people in it, with all theirs. Doctor, lawyer, merchant, chief, etc.

You could stop right here and make a thesis for Hollywood as the mirror to low life, if you had to make a thesis; for its shakiest reenactments are in general those of Presidents, Morgan Partners, Supreme Court Justices, Diplomats, and such rarefied fields of the intellect as may also be spelled upper case. Colleges, for example—with the one recent exception of *Vivacious Lady,* college has had an absolute hex on producers, who have approached it with a singular mixture of trembling and football. Writing and painting, of course. (*Rembrandt* would be my exception here; *Zola* wouldn't.) And strangest of all, the ordinary run of musicians—who litter every set, every day. A danceband is still a studio blind spot: the iron rule is that everybody wears a funny hat in rehearsal or in bed; if a musician forgets and acts naturally, they have to retake the scene because that isn't the way musicians act; and a few months ago there was a producer spotting talent in New York who wouldn't listen to Bobby Hackett's cornet because, hell, he played it *down,* whereas everybody knows a cornet is played straight up in the air, balanced on the nose.

Truck drivers, linesmen, floorwalkers, train dispatchers, fighters and promoters, and the working press—the movies wade right into them. Doctors and nurses and district attorneys too. But art and thought are something special, you know, like in De Mille on the flossy. Well, let it go at that. Certainly there is everywhere in pictures a tendency to fakery and Dick Powell that has disgraced enough walks of common life to make a bookful of articles by anyone with a typewriter (and believe me it has already made several). My concern and pleasure are in movies when they are good, and rather than go nagging along with a thousand more modern instances, I will remind you of a film called *Ceiling Zero,* which I couple with *Grand Illusion* whenever I think of the best expression of men in their calling, whether at odds or together.

As what the movies recognize as a "team" I believe James Cagney and Pat O'Brien have done more than any other combination to search out and show in theater terms the obscure tie that exists between men who share the same danger, privations, and sack of Bull Durham. Often they have been cast for a simple Quirt-Flagg type of surface thing. But occasionally, working together, they have got more into it than was there to be read. And in *Ceiling Zero* they were able to let go—it was the kind of thing which was high and fascinating to audiences, dealing with the romance of flight, and which was true too, dealing with the conflict between men who only want to do the job and men who want to make money on it; with the self-destruction of one of nature's incurable wise-guys; with the life of nice people.

The picture had that quality of mutual experience and trust, mutual affection and exasperation, of a profound but tacit dedication to getting the work out, through hell and high water, that becomes the kind of bond and shared belief that is usually known only by the men sticking it out on the job. In some form or other its possibilities have been exploited in pictures, from *Beau Geste* to *Lives of a Bengal Lancer,* and it is as romantic as any straight romance. In the easy life, buckled-on routine, casual patter, and terrific high tension of this story of planes making their appointed round or crashing on it, there was something that has often been felt by men thrown together in peril or hardship, something that has always been beautiful and almost never expressed.

It was the story as much as Howard Hawks' direction; it was both as much as it was Cagney and O'Brien and all the other good people. But it was the movie-in-America even more—it was the setup to make such a thing possible and vivid, and to afford the chance to people who still remembered something of life as it appears to those who merely live it, to get in there pitching before they had become a critic or Robert Mantell, and make it live again. Like the novel, the fiction film is wide open to anyone who can use it to advantage. Unlike the novel (which please compare in its year-to-year output), and through all its silly and vicious blunders, it has taken all of actual life to be its province. And in the part of life in which the majority of people—only shadowed up to now by George Eliot and Stendhal, Millet, and Dickens and the last-gasp proletarian writers of today—are the principal characters, it has an open slate still to write on. That is the promise of the movie in America, and if there were not some token of its fulfillment, of things having been written on such a slate before this, we would not be going to movies, and talking about them.

DAVID WARK GRIFFITH (1948)

By James Agee

He achieved what no other known man has ever achieved. To watch his work is like being witness to the beginning of melody, or the first conscious use of the lever or the wheel; the emergence, coordination, and first eloquence of language; the birth of an art: and to realize that this is all the work of one man.

We will never realize how good he really was until we have the chance to see his work as often as it deserves to be seen, to examine and enjoy it in detail as exact as his achievement. But even relying, as we mainly have to, on years-old memories, a good deal becomes clear.

One crude but unquestionable indication of his greatness was his power to create permanent images. All through his work there are images which are as impossible to forget, once you have seen them, as some of the grandest and simplest passages in music or poetry.

The most beautiful single shot I have seen in any movie is the battle charge in *The Birth of a Nation.* I have heard it praised for its realism, and that is deserved; but it is also far beyond realism. It seems to me to be a perfect realization of a collective dream of what the Civil War was like, as veterans might remember it fifty years later, or as children, fifty years later, might imagine it. I have had several clear mental images of that war, from almost as early as I can remember, and I didn't have the luck to see *The Birth of a Nation* until I was in my early twenties; but when I saw that charge, it was merely the clarification, and corroboration, of one of those visions, and took its place among them immediately without seeming to be of a different kind or order. It is the perfection that I know of, of the tragic glory that is possible, or used to be possible, in war; or in war as the best in the spirit imagines or remembers it.

This is, I realize, mainly subjective; but it suggests to me the clearest and deepest aspect of Griffith's genius: he was a great primitive poet, a man capable, as only great and primitive artists can be, of intuitively perceiving and perfecting the tremendous magical images that underlie the memory and imagination of entire peoples. If he had achieved this only once, and only for me, I could not feel that he was what I believe he is; but he created many such images, and I suspect that many people besides me have recognized them, on that deepest level that art can draw on, reach, and serve. There are many others in that one film: the homecoming of the defeated hero; the ride of the Clansmen; the rapist and his victim among the dark leaves; a glimpse of a war hospital; dead young soldiers after battle; the dark, slow movement of the Union Army away from the camera, along a valley which is quartered strongly between hill-shadow and sunlight; all these and still others have a dreamlike absoluteness which, indeed, cradles and suffuses the whole film.

This was the one time in movie history that a man of great ability worked freely, in an unspoiled medium, for an unspoiled audience, on a majestic theme which involved all that he was; and brought to it, besides his abilities as an inventor and artist, absolute passion, pity, courage, and honesty. *The Birth of a Nation* is equal with Brady's photographs, Lincoln's speeches, Whitman's war poems; for all its imperfections and absurdities it is equal, in fact, to the best work that has been done in this country. And among moving pictures it is alone, not necessarily as "the greatest"—whatever that means—but as the one great epic, tragic film.

(Today, *The Birth of a Nation* is boycotted or shown piecemeal; too many more or less well-meaning people still accuse Griffith of having made it an anti-Negro movie. At best, this is nonsense, and at worst, it is vicious nonsense. Even if it were an anti-Negro movie, a work of such quality should be shown, and shown whole. But the accusation is unjust. Griffith went to almost preposterous lengths to be fair to the Negroes as he understood them, and he understood them as a good type of Southerner does. I don't entirely agree with him; nor can I be sure that the film wouldn't cause trouble and misunderstanding, especially as advertised and exacerbated by contemporary abolitionists; but Griffith's absolute desire to be fair, and understandable, is written all over the picture; so are degrees of understanding, honesty, and compassion far beyond the capacity of his accusers. So, of course, are the salient facts of the so-called Reconstruction years.)

Griffith never managed to equal *The Birth of a Nation* again, nor was he ever to strike off, in any other film, so many of those final images. Nevertheless, he found many: the strikers in *Intolerance*—the realism of those short scenes has never been surpassed, nor their shock and restiveness as an image of near-revolution; the intercutting, at the climax of that picture, between the climaxes of four parallel stories, like the swinging together of tremendous gongs; the paralyzing excitement of the melodrama near the waterfall, in *Way Down East;* Paul Revere's ride and the battle of Bunker Hill, in *America;* Danton's ride, in *Orphans of the Storm;* most subtle and remarkable of all, the early morning scene in his German film, *Isn't Life Wonderful?,* in which the ape-like Dick Sutherland pursues Carol Dempster through a grove of slender trees. All these images, and so many others of Griffith's, have a sort of crude sublimity which nobody else in movies has managed to achieve; this last one, like his images of our Civil War, seems to come out of the deep subconscious: it is an absolute and prophetic image of a nation and a people. I will always regret having missed *Abraham Lincoln,* his last film to be released: a friend has told me of its wonderful opening in stormy mid-winter night woods, the camera bearing along toward the natal cabin; and that surely must have been one of Griffith's finest images.

Even in Griffith's best work there is enough that is poor, or foolish, or merely old-fashioned, so that one has to understand, if by no means forgive, those who laugh indiscriminately at his good work and his bad. (With all that "understanding," I look forward to killing, some day, some specially happy giggler at the exquisite scene in which the veteran comes home, in *The Birth of a Nation.*) But even his poorest work was never just bad. Whatever may be wrong with it, there is in every instant, so well as I can remember, the unique purity and vitality of birth or of a creature just born and first exerting its unprecedented, incredible strength; and there are, besides, Griffith's overwhelming innocence and magnanimity of spirit; his moral and poetic earnestness; his joy in his work; and his splendid intuitiveness, directness, common sense, daring, and skill as an inventor and as an artist. Aside from his talent or genius as an inventor and artist, he was all heart; and ruinous as his excesses sometimes were in that respect, they were inseparable from his virtues, and small beside them. He was remarkably good, as a rule, in the whole middle range of feeling, but he was at his best just short of his excesses, and he tended in general to work out toward the dangerous edge. He was capable of realism that has never been beaten and he might, if he had been able to appreciate his powers as a realist, have found therein his growth and salvation. But he seems to have been a realist only by accident, hit-and-run; essentially, he was a poet. He doesn't appear ever to have realized one of the richest promises that movies hold, as the perfect medium for realism raised to the level of high poetry; nor, oddly enough, was he much of a dramatic poet. But in epic and lyrical and narrative visual poetry, I can think of nobody who has surpassed him, and of few to compare with him. And as a primitive tribal poet, combining something of the bard and the seer, he is beyond even Dovzhenko, and no others of their kind have worked in movies.

What he had above all, his ability as a craftsman and artist, would be hard enough—and quite unnecessary—to write of, if we had typical scenes before us, or within recent memory; since we have seen so little of his work in so many years, it is virtually impossible. I can remember very vividly his general spirit and manner—heroic, impetuous, tender, magniloquent, naive, beyond the endowment or daring of anybody since; just as vividly, I can remember the total impression of various major sequences. By my remembrance, his images were nearly always a little larger and wilder than life. The frame was always full, spontaneous, and lively. He knew wonderfully well how to contrast and combine different intensities throughout an immense range of emotion, movement, shadow, and light. Much of the liveliness was not intrinsic to the characters on the screen or their predicament, but was his own vitality and emotion; and much of it —notably in the amazing flickering and vivacity of his women—came of his almost maniacal realization of the importance of expressive movement.

It seems to me entirely reasonable to infer, from the extraordinary power and endurance in the memory of certain scenes in their total effect, that he was as brilliant a master of design and cutting and form as he was a composer of frames and a director of feeling and motion. But I cannot clearly remember one sequence or scene, shot by shot and rhythm by rhythm. I suspect, for instance, that analysis would show that the climactic sequence on the icy river, in *Way Down East,* is as finely constructed a piece of melodramatic storytelling as any in movies. But I can only venture to bet on this and to suggest that that sequence, like a hundred others of Griffith's, is eminently worth analysis.

My veneration for Griffith's achievements is all the deeper when I realize what handicaps he worked against, how limited a man he was. He had no remarkable power of intellect, or delicateness of soul; no subtlety; little restraint; little if any "taste," whether to help his work or harm it; Lord knows (and be thanked) no cleverness; no fundamental capacity, once he had achieved his first astonishing development, for change or growth. He wasn't particularly observant of people; nor do his movies suggest that he understood them at all deeply. He had noble powers of imagination, but little of the *intricacy* of imagination that most good poets also have. His sense of comedy was pathetically crude and numb. He had an exorbitant appetite for violence, for cruelty, and for the Siamese twin of cruelty, a kind of obsessive tenderness which at its worst was all but nauseating. Much as he invented, his work was saturated in the style, the mannerisms, and the underlying assumptions and attitudes of the nineteenth century provincial theater; and although much of that was much better than most of us realize, and any amount better than most of the styles and non-styles we accept and praise, much of it was cheap and false, and all of it, good and bad, was dying when Griffith gave it a new lease on life, and in spite of that new lease, died soon after, and took him down with it. I doubt that Griffith ever clearly knew the good from the bad in this theatricality; or, for that matter, clearly understood what was original in his work, and capable of almost unimaginably great development; and what was over-derivative, essentially non-cinematic, and dying. In any case, he did not manage to outgrow, or sufficiently to transform, enough in his style that was bad, or merely obsolescent.

If what I hear is right about the opening scene in *Abraham Lincoln,* this incapacity for radical change may have slowed him up but never killed him as an artist; in his no longer fashionable way, he remained capable, and inspired. He was merely unadaptable and unemployable, like an old, sore, ardent individualist among contemporary progressives. Hollywood and, to a great extent, movies in general, grew down from him rather than up past him; audiences, and the whole eye and feeling of the world, have suffered the same degeneration; he didn't have it in him to be amenable, even if he'd tried; and that was the end of him. Or quite possibly he was finished, as smaller men are not, as soon as he had reached the limit of his own powers of innovation, and began to realize he was only repeating himself. Certainly, anyhow, he was natural-born for the years of adventure and discovery, not for the inevitable following era of safe-playing and of fat consolidation of others' gains.

His last movie, which was never even released, was made fourteen or fifteen years ago; and for years before that, most people had thought of him as a has-been. Nobody would hire him; he had nothing to do. He lived too long, and that is one of few things that are sadder than dying too soon.

There is not a man working in movies, or a man who cares for them, who does not owe Griffith more than he owes anybody else.

UNDERGROUND FILMS (1957)

By Manny Farber

The saddest thing in current films is watching the long-neglected action directors fade away as the less talented De Sicas and Zinnemanns continue to fascinate the critics. Because they played an anti-art role in Hollywood, the true masters of the male action film—such soldier-cowboy-gangster directors as Raoul Walsh, Howard Hawks, William Wellman, William Keighley, the early, pre-*Stagecoach* John Ford, Anthony Mann—have turned out a huge amount of unprized, second-gear celluloid. Their neglect becomes more painful to behold now that the action directors are in decline, many of them having abandoned the dry, economic, life-worn movie style that made their observations of the American he-man so rewarding. Americans seem to have a special aptitude for allowing History to bury the toughest, most authentic native talents. The same tide that has swept away Otis Ferguson, Walker Evans, Val Lewton, Clarence

Williams, and J. R. Williams into near oblivion is now in the process of burying a group that kept an endless flow of interesting roughneck film passing through the theaters from the depression onward. The tragedy of these film-makers lies in their having been consigned to a Sargasso Sea of unmentioned talent by film reviewers whose sole concern is not continuous flow of quality but the momentary novelties of the particular film they are reviewing.

Howard Hawks is the key figure in the male action film because he shows a maximum speed, inner life, and view, with the least amount of flat foot. His best films, which have the swallowed-up intricacy of a good soft-shoe dance, are *Scarface, Only Angels Have Wings, His Girl Friday,* and *The Big Sleep.* Raoul Walsh's films are melancholy masterpieces of flexibility and detailing inside a lower-middle-class locale. Walsh's victories, which make use of tense, broken-field journeys and nostalgic background detail, include *They Drive by Night, White Heat,* and *Roaring Twenties.* In any Bill Wellman operation, there are at least four directors—a sentimentalist, deep thinker, hooey vaudevillian, and an expedient short-cut artist whose special love is for mulish toughs expressing themselves in drop-kicking heads and somber standing around. Wellman is at his best in stiff, vulgar, low-pulp material. In that setup, he has a low-budget ingenuity, which creates flashes of ferocious brassiness, an authentic practical-joke violence (as in the frenzied inadequacy of Ben Blue in *Roxie Hart*), and a brainless hell-raising. Anthony Mann's inhumanity to man, in which cold mortal intentness is the trademark effect, can be studied best in *The Tall Target, Winchester 73, Border Incident,* and *Railroaded.* The films of this tin-can de Sade have a Germanic rigor, caterpillar intimacy, and an original dictionary of ways in which to punish the human body. Mann has done interesting work with scissors, a cigarette lighter, and steam, but his most bizarre effect takes place in a taxidermist's shop. By intricate manipulation of athletes' bodies, Mann tries to ram the eyes of his combatants on the horns of a stuffed deer stuck on the wall.

The film directors mentioned above did their best work in the late 1940's, when it was possible to be a factory of unpretentious picture-making without frightening the front office. During the same period and later, less prolific directors also appear in the uncompromising action film. Of these, the most important is John Farrow, an urbane vaudevillean whose forte, in films like *The Big Clock* and *His*

Kind of Woman, is putting a fine motoring system beneath the veering slapstick of his eccentric characterizations. Though he has tangled with such heavyweights as Book of the Month and Hemingway, Zoltan Korda is an authentic hard-grain cheapster telling his stories through unscrubbed action, masculine characterization, and violent explorations inside a fascinating locale. Korda's best films—*Sahara, Counterattack, Cry the Beloved Country*—are strangely active films in which terrain, jobs, and people get curiously interwoven in a ravening tactility. William Keighley, in *G-Men* and *Each Dawn I Die,* is the least sentimental director of gangster careers. After the bloated philosophical safe-crackers in Huston's *Asphalt Jungle,* the smallish cops and robbers in Keighley's work seem life-size. Keighley's handling is so right in emphasis, timing, and shrewdness that there is no feeling of the director breathing, gasping, snoring over the film.

The tight-lipped creators whose films are mentioned above comprise the most interesting group to appear in American culture since the various groupings that made the 1920's an explosive era in jazz, literature, silent films. Hawks and his group are perfect examples of the anonymous artist, who is seemingly afraid of the polishing, hypocrisy, bragging, fake educating that goes on in serious art. To go at his most expedient gait, the Hawks type must take a withdrawn, almost hidden stance in the industry. Thus, his films seem to come from the most neutral, humdrum, monotonous corner of the movie lot. The fascinating thing about these veiled operators is that they are able to spring the leanest, shrewdest, sprightliest notes from material that looks like junk, and from a creative position that, on the surface, seems totally uncommitted and disinterested. With striking photography, a good ear for natural dialogue, an eye for realistic detail, a skilled inside-action approach to composition, and the most politic hand in the movie field, the action directors have done a forbidding stenography on the hard-boiled American handyman as he progresses through the years.

It is not too remarkable that the underground films, with their twelve-year-old's adventure-story plot and endless palpitating movement, have lost out in the film system. Their dismissal has been caused by the construction of solid confidence built by daily and weekly reviewers. Operating with this wall, the critic can pick and discard without the slightest worry about looking silly. His choice of best salami is a picture backed by studio build-up, agreement amongst his colleagues, a layout in *Life* mag (which makes it officially reasonable for an American award), and a list of ingredients that anyone's unsophisticated aunt in Oakland can spot as comprising a distinguished film. This prize picture, which has philosophical undertones, panfried domestic sights, risqué crevices, sporty actors and actresses, circuslike gymnastics, a bit of tragedy like the main fall at Niagara, has every reason to be successful. It has been made for that purpose. Thus, the year's winner is a perfect film made up solely of holes and evasions, covered up by all types of padding and plush. The cavity-filling varies from one prize work to another, from *High Noon* (cross-eyed artistic views of a clock, silhouettes against a vaulting sky, legend-toned walking, a big song), through *From Here to Eternity* (Sinatra's private scene-chewing, pretty trumpeting, tense shots in the dark and at twilight, necking near the water, a threatening hand with a broken bottle) to next year's winner, which will probably be a huge ball of cotton candy containing either Audrey Hepburn's cavernous grin and stiff behind or more of Zinnemann's glacéed picture-making. In terms of imaginative photography, honest acting, and insight into American life, there is no comparison between an average underground triumph *(Phenix City Story)* and the trivia that causes a critical salaam across the land. The trouble is that no one asks the critics' alliance to look straight backward at its "choices," for example, a horse-drawn truckload of liberal schmaltz called *The Best Years of Our Lives.* These ridiculously maltreated films sustain their place in the halls of fame simply because they bear the label of ART in every inch of their reelage. Praising these solemn goiters has produced a climate in which the underground picture-maker, with his modest entry and soft-shoe approach, can barely survive.

However, any day now, Americans may realize that scrambling after the obvious in art is a losing game. The sharpest work of the last thirty years is to be found by studying the most unlikely, self-destroying, uncompromising, roundabout artists. When the day comes for praising infamous men of art, some great talent will be shown in true light: people like Weldon Kees, the rangy Margie Israel, James Agee, Isaac Rosenfeld, Otis Ferguson, Val Lewton, a dozen comic-strip geniuses like the creator of "Harold Teen," and finally a half-dozen directors such as the master of the ambulance, speedboat, flying-saucer movie: Howard Hawks.

The films of the Hawks-Wellman group are *underground* for more reasons than the fact that the director hides out in subsurface reaches of his work. The hard-bitten action film finds its natural home in caves: the murky, congested theaters, looking like glorified tattoo parlors on the outside and located near bus terminals in big cities. These theaters roll action films in what, at first, seems like a nightmarish atmosphere of shabby transience, prints that seem overgrown with jungle moss, sound tracks infected with hiccups. The spectator watches two or three action films go by and leaves feeling as though he were a pirate discharged from a giant sponge.

The cutthroat atmosphere in the itch house is reproduced in the movies shown there. Hawks's *The Big Sleep* not only has a slightly gaseous, subsurface, Baghdadish background, but its gangster action is engineered with a suave, cutting efficacy. Walsh's *Roaring Twenties* is a jangling barrelhouse film, which starts with a top gun bouncing downhill, and, at the end, he is seen slowly pushing his way through a lot of Campbell's scotch broth. Wellman's favorite scene is a group of hard-visaged ball bearings standing around—for no damned reason and with no indication of how long or for what reason they have been standing. His worst pictures are made up simply of this moody wooden standing around. All that saves the films are the little flurries of bulletlike acting that give the men an inner look of credible orneriness and somewhat stupid mulishness. Mann likes to stretch his victims in crucifix poses against the wall or ground and then to peer intently at their demise with an icy surgeon's eye. Just as the harrowing machine is about to run over the wetback on a moonlit night, the camera catches him sprawled out in a harrowing image. At heart, the best action films are slicing journeys into the lower depths of American life: dregs, outcasts, lonely hard wanderers caught in a buzzsaw of niggardly, intricate, devious movement.

The projects of the underground directors are neither experimental, liberal, slick, spectacular, low-budget, epical, improving, or flagrantly commercial like Sam Katzman two-bitters. They are faceless movies, taken from a type of half-polished trash writing, that seem like a mixture of Burt L. Standish, Max Brand, and Raymond Chandler. Tight, cliché-ridden melodramas about stock musclemen. A stool pigeon gurgling with scissors in his back; a fat, nasal-voiced gang leader; escaped convicts; power-mad ranch owners with vengeful siblings; a mean gun with an Oedipus complex and migraine headaches; a crooked gambler trading guns to the redskins; exhausted GI's; an incompetent kid hoodlum hiding out in an East Side building; a sickly-elegant Italian barber in a plot to kill Lincoln; an underpaid shamus signing up to stop the blackmailing of a tough millionaire's depraved thumb-sucking daughter.

The action directors accept the role of hack so that they can involve themselves with expedience and tough-guy insight in all types of action: barnstorming, driving, bulldogging. The important thing is not so much the banal-seeming journeys to nowhere that make up the stories, but the tunneling that goes on inside the classic Western-gangster incidents and stock hoodlum-dogface-cowboy types. For instance, Wellman's lean, elliptical talents for creating brassy cheapsters and making gloved references to death, patriotism, masturbation, suggest that he uses private runways to the truth, while more famous directors take a slow, embalming surface route.

The virtues of action films expand as the pictures take on the outer appearance of junk jewelry. The underground's greatest mishaps have occurred in art-infected projects where there is unlimited cash, studio freedom, an expansive story, message, heart, and a lot of prestige to be gained. Their flattest, most sentimental works are incidentally the only ones that have attained the almond-paste-flavored eminence of the Museum of Modern Art's film library, i.e., *GI Joe, Public Enemy.* Both Hawks and Wellman, who made these overweighted mistakes, are like basketball's corner man: their best shooting is done from the deepest, worst angle. With material that is hopelessly worn out and childish *(Only Angels Have Wings),* the underground director becomes beautifully graphic and modestly human in his flexible detailing. When the material is like drab concrete, these directors become great on-the-spot inventors, using their curiously niggling, reaming style for adding background detail (Walsh); suave grace (Hawks); crawling, mechanized tension (Mann); veiled gravity (Wellman); svelte semicaricature (John Farrow); modern Gothic vehemence (Phil Karlson); and dark, modish vaudeville (Robert Aldrich).

In the films of these hard-edged directors can be found the unheralded ripple of physical experience, the tiny morbidly lifeworn detail which the visitor to a strange city finds springing out at every step. The Hawks film is as good on the mellifluous grace of the impudent American hard rock as can be found in any art work; the Mann films use American objects and terrain—guns, cliffs, boulders, an 1865 locomotive, telephone wires—with more cruel intimacy than any other film-maker; the Wellman film is the only clear shot at the mean, brassy, clawlike soul of the lone American wolf that has been taken in films. In other words, these actioneers—Mann and Hawks and Keighley and, in recent times, Aldrich and Karlson—go completely underground before proving themselves more honest and subtle than the water buffaloes of film art: George Stevens, Billy Wilder, Vittorio De Sica, Georges Clouzot. (Clouzot's most successful work, *Wages of Fear,* is a wholesale steal of the mean physicality and acrid highway inventions in such Walsh-Wellman films as *They Drive by Night.* Also, the latter film is a more flexible, adroitly ad-libbed, worked-in creation than Clouzot's eclectic moneymaker.)

Unfortunately, the action directors suffer from presentation problems. Their work is now seen repeatedly on the blurred, chopped, worn, darkened, commercial-ridden movie programs on T.V. Even in the impossible conditions of the "Late Show," where the lighting is four shades too dark and the porthole-shaped screen defeats the movie's action, the deep skill of Hawks and his tribe shows itself. Time has dated and thinned out the story excitement, but the ability to capture the exact homely-manly character of forgotten locales and misanthropic figures is still in the pictures along with pictorial compositions (Ford's *Last of the Mohicans*) that occasionally seem as lovely as anything that came out of the camera box of Billy Bitzer and Matthew Brady. The conditions in the outcast theaters—the Lyric on Times Square, the Liberty on Market Street, the Victory on Chestnut—are not as bad as TV, but bad enough. The screen image is often out of plumb, the house lights are half left on during the picture, the broken seats are only a minor annoyance in the unpredictable terrain. Yet, these action-film homes are the places to study Hawks, Wellman, Mann, as well as their near and distant cousins.

The underground directors have been saving the American male on the screen for three decades without receiving the slightest credit from critics and prize committees. The hard, exact defining of male action, completely lacking in acting fat, is a common item *only* in underground films. The cream on the top of a *Framed* or *Appointment with Danger* (directed by two first cousins of the Hawks-Walsh strain) is the eye-flicking action that shows the American body —arms, elbows, legs, mouths, the tension profile line—being used expediently, with grace and the suggestion of jolting hardness. Otherwise, the Hollywood talkie seems to have been invented to give an embarrassingly phony impression of the virile action man. The performance is always fattened either by coyness (early Robert Taylor), unction (Anthony Quinn), histrionic conceit (Gene Kelly), liberal knowingness (Brando), angelic stylishness (Mel Ferrer), oily hamming (José Ferrer), Mother's Boy passivity (Rock Hudson), or languor (Montgomery Clift). Unless the actor lands in the hands of an underground director, he causes a candy-coated effect that is misery for any spectator who likes a bit of male truth in films.

After a steady diet of undergrounders, the spectator realizes that these are the only films that show the tension of an individual intelligence posing itself against the possibilities of monotony, bathos, or sheer cliché. Though the action film is filled with heroism or its absence, the real hero is the small detail which has arisen from a stormy competition between lively color and credibility. The hardness of these films arises from the esthetic give-and-go with banality. Thus, the philosophical idea in underground films seems to be that nothing is easy in life or the making of films. Jobs are difficult, even the act of watching a humdrum bookstore scene from across the street has to be done with care and modesty to evade the type of butter-slicing glibness that rots the Zinnemann films. In the Walsh film, a gangster walks through a saloon with so much tight-roped adlibbing and muscularity that he seems to be walking backward through the situation. Hawks's achievement of moderate toughness in *Red River,* using Clift's delicate languor and Wayne's claylike acting, is remarkable. As usual, he steers Clift through a series of cornball fetishes (like the Barney Google Ozark hat and the trick handling of same) and graceful, semicollegiate business: stances and kneelings and snake-quick gunmanship. The beauty of the job is the way the cliché business is kneaded, strained against without breaking the naturalistic surface. One feels that this is the first and last hard, clamped-down, imaginative job Clift does in Hollywood—his one nonmush performance. Afterward, he goes to work for Zinnemann, Stevens, Hitchcock.

The small buried attempt to pierce the banal pulp of underground stories with fanciful grace notes is one of the important feats of the underground director. Usually, the piercing consists in renovating a cheap rusty trick that has been slumbering in the "thriller" director's handbook—pushing a "color" effect against the most resistant type of unshowy, hard-bitten direction. A mean butterball flicks a gunman's ear with a cigarette lighter. A night-frozen cowboy shudders over a swig of whisky. A gorilla gang leader makes a cannonaded exit from a barber chair. All these bits of congestion are like the lines of a hand to a good gun movie; they are the tracings of difficulty that make the films seem uniquely hard and formful. In each case, the director is taking a great chance with clichés and forcing them into a hard natural shape.

People don't notice the absence of this hard combat with low, commonplace ideas in the Zinnemann and Huston epics, wherein the action is a game in which the stars take part with confidence and glee as though nothing can stop them. They roll in parts of drug addicts, tortured sheriffs; success depending on how much sentimental bloop and artistic japery can be packed in without encountering the demands of a natural act or character. Looking back on a Sinatra film, one has the feeling of a private whirligig performance in the center of a frame rather than a picture. On the other hand, a Cagney performance under the hands of a Keighley is ingrained in a tight, malignant story. One remembers it as a sinewy, life-marred exactness that is as quietly laid down as the smaller jobs played by the Barton MacLanes and Frankie Darros.

A constant attendance at the Lyric-Pix-Victory theaters soon impresses the spectator with the coverage of locales in action films. The average gun film travels like a shamus who knows his city and likes his private knowledges. Instead of the picture-postcard sights, the underground film finds the most idiosyncratic spot of a city and then locates the niceties within the large nicety. The California Street hill in San Francisco *(Woman in Hiding)* with its old-style mansions played in perfect night photography against a deadened domestic bitching. A YMCA scene that emphasizes the wonderful fat-waisted, middle-aged physicality of people putting on tennis shoes and playing handball *(Appointment with Danger)*. The terrorizing of a dowdy middle-aged, frog-faced woman *(Born to Kill)* that starts in a decrepit hotel and ends in a bumbling, screeching, crawling murder at midnight on the shore. For his big shock effect, director Robert Wise (a sometime member of the underground) uses the angle going down to the water to create a middle-class mediocrity that outhorrors anything Graham Greene attempted in his early books on small-time gunsels.

Another fine thing about the coverage is its topographic grimness, the fact that the terrain looks worked over. From Walsh's *What Price Glory?* to Mann's *Men in War,* the terrain is special in that it is used, kicked, grappled, worried, sweated up, burrowed into, stomped on. The land is marched across in dark, threading lines at twilight, or the effect is reversed with foot soldiers in white parkas *(Fixed Bayonets)* curving along a snowed-in battleground as they watch troops moving back—in either case, the cliché effect is worked credibly inward until it creates a haunting note like the army diagonals in *Birth of a Nation.* Rooms are boxed, crossed, opened up as they are in few other films. The spectator gets to know these rooms as well as his own hand. Years after seeing the film, he remembers the way a dulled waitress sat on the edge of a hotel bed, the weird elongated adobe in which ranch hands congregate before a Chisholm Trail drive. The rooms in big-shot directors' films look curiously bulbous, as though inflated with hot air and turned toward the audience, like the high school operetta of the 1920's.

Of all these poet-builders, Wellman is the most interesting, particularly with Hopper-type scenery. It is a matter of drawing store fronts, heavy bedroom boudoirs, the heisting of a lonely service station, with light, furious strokes. Also, in mixing jolting vulgarity (Mae Clarke's face being smashed with a grapefruit) with a space composition dance in which the scene seems to be constructed before your eyes. It may be a minor achievement, but, when Wellman finishes with a service station or the wooden stairs in front of an ancient saloon, there is no reason for any movie realist to handle the subject again. The scene is kept light, textural, and as though it is being built from the outside in. There is no sentiment of the type that spreads lugubrious shadows (Kazan), builds tensions of perspective (Huston), or inflates with golden sunlight and finicky hot air (Stevens).

Easily the best part of underground films are the excavations of exciting-familiar scenery. The opening up of a scene is more concerted in these films than in other Hollywood efforts, but the most important thing is that the opening is done by roadmapped strategies that play movement against space in a cunning way, building the environment and event before your eyes. In every underground film, these vigorous ramifications within a sharply seen terrain are the big attraction, the main tent. No one does this anatomization of action and scene better than Hawks, who probably invented it—at least, the smooth version—in such 1930's gunblasts as *The Crowd Roars.* The control of Hawks's strategies is so ingenious that, when a person kneels or walks down the hallway, the movement seems to click into a predetermined slot. It is an uncanny accomplishment that carries the spectator across the very ground of a giant ranch, into rooms and out again, over to the wall to look at some faded fight pictures on a hotel wall—as though he were in the grip of a spectacular, mobile "eye." When Hawks landscapes action—the cutting between light tower and storm-caught plane in *Ceiling Zero,* the vegetalizing in *The Thing,* the shamus sweating in a greenhouse in *The Big Sleep* —the feeling is of a clever human tunneling just under the surface of terrain. It is as though the film has a life of its own that goes on beneath the story action.

However, there have been many great examples of such veining by human interactions over a wide plane. One of the special shockers, in *Each Dawn I Die,* has to do with the scissoring of a stooly during the movie shown at the penitentiary. This Keighley-Cagney effort is a wonder of excitement as it moves in great leaps from screen to the rear of a crowded auditorium: crossing contrasts of movement in three points of the hall, all of it done in a sinking gloom. One of the more ironic crisscrossings has to do with the coughings of the stuck victim played against the screen image of zooming airplanes over the Pacific.

In the great virtuoso films, there is something vaguely resembling this underground maneuvering, only it goes on above the story. Egocentric padding that builds a great bonfire of pyrotechnics over a gapingly empty film. The perfect example is a pumped-up fist fight that almost closes the three-hour *Giant* film. This ballroom shuffle between a reforming rancher and a Mexican-hating luncheonette owner is an entertaining creation in spectacular tumbling, swinging, back arching, bending. However, the endless masturbatory "building" of excitement—beautiful haymakers, room-covering falls, thunderous sounds—is more than slightly silly. Even if the room were valid, which it isn't (a studio-built chromium horror plopped too close to the edge of a lonely highway), the room goes unexplored because of the jumbled timing. The excess that is so noticeable in Stevens's brawl is absent in the least serious undergrounder, which attains most of its crisp, angular character from the modesty of a director working skillfully far within the earthworks of the story.

Underground films have almost ceased to be a part of the movie scene. The founders of the action film have gone into awkward, big-scaled productions involving pyramid-building, a passenger plane in trouble over the Pacific, and postcard Westerns with Jimmy

Stewart and his harassed Adam's apple approach to gutty acting. The last drainings of the underground film show a tendency toward moving from the plain guttural approach of *Steel Helmet* to a Germanically splashed type of film. Of these newcomers, Robert Aldrich is certainly the most exciting—a lurid, psychiatric stormer who gets an overflow of vitality and sheer love for movie-making into the film. This enthusiasm is the rarest item in a dried, decayed-lemon type of movie period. Aldrich makes viciously anti-Something movies—*Attack* stomps on Southern rascalism and the officer sect in war, *The Big Knife* impales the Zanuck-Goldwyn big shot in Hollywood. The Aldrich films are filled with exciting characterizations—by Lee Marvin, Rod Steiger, Jack Palance—of highly psyched-up, marred, and bothered men. Phil Karlson has done some surprising modern Gothic treatments of the Brinks hold-up *(Kansas City Confidential)* and the vice-ridden Southern town *(The Phenix City Story).* His movies are remarkable for their endless outlay of scary cheapness in detailing the modern underworld. Also, Karlson's work has a chilling documentary exactness and an exciting shot-scattering belligerence.

There is no longer a literate audience for the masculine picture-making that Hawks and Wellman exploited, as there was in the 1930's. In those exciting movie years, a smart audience waited around each week for the next Hawks, Preston Sturges, or Ford film—shoe-stringers that were far to the side of the expensive Hollywood film. That underground audience, with its expert voice in Otis Ferguson and its ability to choose between perceptive trash and the Thalberg pepsin-flavored sloshing with Tracy and Gable, has now oozed away. It seems ridiculous, but the Fergusonite went into fast decline during the mid-1940's when the movie market was flooded with fake underground films—plushy thrillers with neo-Chandler scripts and a romantic style that seemed to pour the gore, histrionics, decor out of a giant catsup bottle. The nadir of these films: an item called *Singapore* with Fred MacMurray and Ava Gardner.

The straw that finally breaks the back of the underground film tradition is the dilettante behavior of intellectuals on the subject of oaters. Esthetes and upper bohemians now favor horse operas almost as wildly as they like the cute, little-guy worshipings of DeSica and the pedantic, interpretive reading of Alec Guinness. This fad for Western films shows itself in the inevitable little-magazine review, which finds an affinity between the subject matter of cowboy films and the inner esthetics of Cinemah. The Hawks-Wellman tradition, which is basically a subterranean delight that looks like a cheap penny candy on the outside, hasn't a chance of reviving when intellectuals enthuse in equal amounts over Westerns by Ford, Nunnally Johnson, J. Sturges, Stevens, Delmer Daves. In Ferguson's day, the intellectual could differentiate between a stolid genre painter (Ford), a long-winded cuteness expert with a rotogravure movie scene (Johnson), a scene-painter with a notions-counter eye and a primly naïve manner with sun-hardened bruisers (John Sturges), and a *Boys' Life* nature lover who intelligently half-prettifies adolescents and backwoods primitives (Daves). Today, the audience for Westerns and gangster careers is a sickeningly frivolous one that does little more than play the garbage collector or make a night court of films. With this high-brow audience that loves banality and pomp more than the tourists at Radio City Music Hall, there is little reason to expect any stray director to try for a hidden meager-looking work that is directly against the serious art grain.

BONNIE AND CLYDE (1967)

By Pauline Kael

How do you make a good movie in this country without being jumped on? *Bonnie and Clyde* is the most excitingly American American movie since *The Manchurian Candidate.* The audience is alive to it. Our experience as we watch it has some connection with the way we reacted to movies in childhood: with how we came to love them and to feel they were ours—not an art that we learned over the years to appreciate but simply and immediately ours. When an American movie is contemporary in feeling, like this one, it makes a different kind of contact with an American audience from the kind that is made by European films, however contemporary. Yet any movie that is contemporary in feeling is likely to go further than other movies—go too far for some tastes—and *Bonnie and Clyde* divides audiences, as *The Manchurian Candidate* did, and it is being jumped on almost as hard. Though we may dismiss the attacks with "What good movie doesn't give some offense?," the fact that it is generally *only* good movies that provoke attacks by many people suggests that the innocuousness of most of our movies is accepted with such complacence that when an American movie reaches people, when it makes them react, some of them think there must be something the matter with it—perhaps a law should be passed against it. *Bonnie and Clyde* brings into the almost frighteningly public world of movies things that people have been feeling and saying and writing about. And once something is said or done on the screens of the world, once it has entered mass art, it can never again belong to a minority, never again be the private possession of an educated, or "knowing," group. But even for that group there is an excitement in hearing its own private thoughts expressed out loud and in seeing something of its own sensibility become part of our common culture.

Our best movies have always made entertainment out of the anti-heroism of American life; they bring to the surface what, in its newest forms and fashions, is always just below the surface. The romanticism in American movies lies in the cynical tough guy's independence; the sentimentality lies, traditionally, in the falsified finish when the anti-hero turns hero. In 1967, this kind of sentimentality wouldn't work with the audience, and *Bonnie and Clyde* substitutes sexual fulfillment for a change of heart. (This doesn't quite work, either; audiences sophisticated enough to enjoy a movie like this one are too sophisticated for the dramatic uplift of the triumph over impotence.)

Structurally, *Bonnie and Clyde* is a story of love on the run, like the old Clark Gable–Claudette Colbert *It Happened One Night* but turned inside out; the walls of Jericho are psychological this time, but they fall anyway. If the story of Bonnie Parker and Clyde Barrow seemed almost from the start, and even to them while they were living it, to be the material of legend, it's because robbers who are loyal to each other—like the James brothers—are a grade up from garden-variety robbers, and if they're male and female partners in crime and young and attractive they're a rare breed. The Barrow gang had both family loyalty and sex appeal working for their legend. David Newman and Robert Benton, who wrote the script for *Bonnie and Clyde,* were able to use the knowledge that, like many of our other famous outlaws and gangsters, the real Bonnie and Clyde seemed to others to be acting out forbidden roles and to relish their roles. In contrast with secret criminals—the furtive embezzlers and other crooks who lead seemingly honest lives—the known outlaws capture the public imagination, because they take chances, and because, often, they enjoy dramatizing their lives. They know that newspaper readers want all the details they can get about the criminals who do the terrible things they themselves don't dare to do, and also want the satisfaction of reading about the punishment after feasting on the crimes. Outlaws play to this public; they show off their big guns and fancy clothes and their defiance of the law. Bonnie and Clyde established the images for their own legend in the photographs they posed for: the gunman and the gun moll. The naïve, touching doggerel ballad that Bonnie Parker wrote and had published in newspapers is about the roles they play for other people contrasted with the coming end for them. It concludes:

> Someday they'll go down together;
> They'll bury them side by side;
> To few it'll be grief—
> To the law a relief—
> But it's death for Bonnie and Clyde.

That they did capture the public imagination is evidenced by the many movies based on their lives. In the late forties, there were *They Live by Night,* with Farley Granger and Cathy O'Donnell, and *Gun Crazy,* with John Dall and Peggy Cummins. (Alfred Hitchcock, in the same period, cast these two Clyde Barrows, Dall and Granger, as Loeb and Leopold, in *Rope.*) And there was a cheap—in every sense—1958 exploitation film, *The Bonnie Parker Story,* starring Dorothy Provine. But the most important earlier version was Fritz Lang's *You Only Live Once,* starring Sylvia Sidney as "Joan" and Henry Fonda as "Eddie," which was made in 1937; this version, which was one of the best American films of the thirties, as *Bonnie and Clyde* is of the sixties, expressed certain feelings of its time, as this film expresses certain feelings of ours. (*They Live by Night,* produced by John Houseman under the aegis of Dore Schary, and directed by Nicholas

Ray, was a very serious and socially significant tragic melodrama, but its attitudes were already dated thirties attitudes: the lovers were very young and pure and frightened and underprivileged; the hardened criminals were sordid; the settings were committedly grim. It made no impact on the postwar audience, though it was a great success in England, where our moldy socially significant movies could pass for courageous.)

Just how contemporary in feeling *Bonnie and Clyde* is may be indicated by contrasting it with *You Only Live Once,* which, though almost totally false to the historical facts, was *told* straight. It is a peculiarity of our times—perhaps it's one of the few specifically modern characteristics—that we don't take our stories straight any more. This isn't necessarily bad. *Bonnie and Clyde* is the first film demonstration that the put-on can be used for the purposes of art. *The Manchurian Candidate almost* succeeded in that, but what was implicitly wild and far-out in the material was nevertheless presented on screen as a straight thriller. *Bonnie and Clyde* keeps the audience in a kind of eager, nervous imbalance—holds our attention by throwing our disbelief back in our faces. To be put on is to be put on the spot, put on the stage, made the stooge in a comedy act. People in the audience at *Bonnie and Clyde* are laughing, demonstrating that they're not stooges—that they appreciate the joke—when they catch the first bullet right in the face. The movie keeps them off balance to the end. During the first part of the picture, a woman in my row was gleefully assuring her companions, "It's a comedy. It's a comedy." After a while, she didn't say anything. Instead of the movie spoof, which tells the audience that it doesn't need to feel or care, that it's all just in fun, that "we were only kidding," *Bonnie and Clyde* disrupts us with "And you thought we were only kidding."

This is the way the story was told in 1937. Eddie (Clyde) is a three-time loser who wants to work for a living, but nobody will give him a chance. Once you get on the wrong side of the law, "they" won't let you get back. Eddie knows it's hopeless—once a loser, always a loser. But his girl, Joan (Bonnie)—the only person who believes in him—thinks that an innocent man has nothing to fear. She marries him, and learns better. Arrested again and sentenced to death for a crime he didn't commit, Eddie asks her to smuggle a gun to him in prison, and she protests, "If I get you a gun, you'll kill somebody." He stares at her sullenly and asks, "What do you think they're going to do to me?" He becomes a murderer while escaping from prison; "society" has made him what it thought he was all along. *You Only Live Once* was an indictment of "society," of the forces of order that will not give Eddie the outcast a chance. "We have a right to live," Joan says as they set out across the country. During the time they are on the run, they become notorious outlaws; they are blamed for a series of crimes they didn't commit. (They do commit holdups, but only to get gas or groceries or medicine.) While the press pictures them as desperadoes robbing and killing and living high on the proceeds of crime, she is having a baby in a shack in a hobo jungle, and Eddie brings her a bouquet of wild flowers. Caught in a police trap, they die in each other's arms; they have been denied the right to live.

Because *You Only Live Once* was so well done, and because the audience in the thirties shared this view of the indifference and cruelty of "society," there were no protests against the sympathetic way the outlaws were pictured—and, indeed, there was no reason for any. In 1958, in *I Want to Live!* (a very popular, though not very good, movie), Barbara Graham, a drug-addict prostitute who had been executed for her share in the bludgeoning to death of an elderly woman, was presented as gallant, wronged, morally superior to everybody else in the movie, in order to strengthen the argument against capital punishment, and the director, Robert Wise, and his associates weren't accused of glorifying criminals, because the "criminals," as in *You Only Live Once,* weren't criminals but innocent victims. Why the protests, why are so many people upset (and not just the people who enjoy indignation), about *Bonnie and Clyde,* in which the criminals *are* criminals—Clyde an ignorant, sly near psychopath who thinks his crimes are accomplishments, and Bonnie a bored, restless waitress-slut who robs for excitement? And why so many accusations of historical inaccuracy, particularly against a work that is far more accurate historically than most and in which historical accuracy hardly matters anyway? There is always an issue of historical accuracy involved in any dramatic or literary work set in the past; indeed, it's fun to read about Richard III vs. Shakespeare's Richard III. The issue is always with us, and will always be with us as long as artists find stimulus in historical figures and want to present their versions of them. But why didn't movie critics attack, for example, *A Man for All Seasons*—which involves material of much more historical importance—for being historically inaccurate? Why attack *Bonnie and Clyde* more than the other movies based on the same pair, or more than the movie treatments of Jesse James or Billy the Kid or Dillinger or Capone or any of our other fictionalized outlaws? I would suggest that when a movie so clearly conceived as a new version of a legend is attacked as historically inaccurate, it's because it shakes people a little. I know this is based on some pretty sneaky psychological suppositions, but I don't see how else to account for the use only against a *good* movie of arguments that could be used against almost all movies. When I asked a nineteen-year-old boy who was raging against the movie as "a cliché-ridden fraud" if he got so worked up about other movies, he informed me that that was an argument *ad hominem*. And it is indeed. To ask why people react so angrily to the best movies and have so little negative reaction to poor ones is to imply that they are so unused to the experience of art in movies that they fight it.

Audiences at *Bonnie and Clyde* are not given a simple, secure basis for identification; they are made to feel but are not told *how* to feel. *Bonnie and Clyde* is not a serious melodrama involving us in the plight of the innocent but a movie that assumes—as William Wellman did in 1931 when he made *The Public Enemy,* with James Cagney as a smart, cocky, mean little crook—that we don't need to pretend we're interested only in the falsely accused, as if real criminals had no connection with us. There wouldn't be the popular excitement there is about outlaws if we didn't all suspect that—in some cases, at least—gangsters must take pleasure in the profits and glory of a life of crime. Outlaws wouldn't become legendary figures if we didn't suspect that there's more to crime than the social workers' case studies may show. And though what we've always been told will happen to them—that they'll come to a bad end—does seem to happen, some part of us wants to believe in the tiny possibility that they can get away with it. Is that really so terrible? Yet when it comes to movies people get nervous about acknowledging that there must be some fun in crime (though the gleam in Cagney's eye told its own story). *Bonnie and Clyde* shows the fun but uses it, too, making comedy out of the banality and conventionality of that fun. What looks ludicrous in this movie isn't *merely* ludicrous, and after we have laughed at ignorance and helplessness and emptiness and stupidity and idiotic deviltry, the laughs keep sticking in our throats, because what's funny isn't only funny.

In 1937, the movie-makers knew that the audience wanted to believe in the innocence of Joan and Eddie, because these two were lovers, and innocent lovers hunted down like animals made a tragic love story. In 1967, the movie-makers know that the audience wants to believe—maybe even prefers to believe—that Bonnie and Clyde were guilty of crimes, all right, but that they were innocent in general; that is, naïve and ignorant *compared with us.* The distancing of the sixties version shows the gangsters in an already legendary period, and part of what makes a legend for Americans is viewing anything that happened in the past as much simpler than what we are involved in now. We tend to find the past funny and the recent past campy-funny. The getaway cars of the early thirties are made to seem hilarious. (Imagine anyone getting away from a bank holdup in a tin lizzie like that!) In *You Only Live Once,* the outlaws existed in the same present as the audience, and there was (and still is, I'm sure) nothing funny about them; in *Bonnie and Clyde* that audience is in the movie, transformed into the poor people, the Depression people, of legend—with faces and poses out of Dorothea Lange and Walker Evans and *Let Us Now Praise Famous Men.* In 1937, the audience felt sympathy for the fugitives because they weren't allowed to lead normal lives; in 1967, the "normality" of the Barrow gang and their individual aspirations toward respectability are the craziest things about them—not just because they're killers but because thirties "normality" is in itself funny to us. The writers and the director of *Bonnie and Clyde* play upon our attitudes toward the American past by making the hats and guns and holdups look as dated as two-reel comedy; emphasizing the absurdity with banjo music, they make the period seem even farther away than it is. The Depression reminiscences are not used for purposes of social consciousness; hard times are not the reason for the Barrows' crimes, just the excuse. "We" didn't make Clyde a killer; the movie deliberately avoids easy sympathy by picking up Clyde when he is already a cheap crook. But Clyde is not the urban sharpster of *The Public Enemy;* he is the hick as bank robber—a countrified gangster, a hillbilly killer who doesn't mean any harm. People so simple that they are alienated from the results of their actions—like the primitives who don't connect babies with copulation—provide a kind of archetypal comedy for us. It may seem like a minor point that Bonnie and Clyde are presented as not mean and sadistic, as having killed only when cornered; but in terms of legend, and particularly movie legend, it's a major one. The "classic" gangster films showed gang members betraying each other and viciously murdering the renegade who left to join another gang; the gang-leader hero no sooner got to the top than he was betrayed by someone he had trusted or someone he had double-crossed. In contrast, the Barrow gang represent family-style crime. And Newman and Benton have been acute in emphasizing this—not making them victims of society (they are never that, despite Penn's cloudy efforts along these lines) but making them absurdly "just-folks" ordinary. When Bonnie tells Clyde to pull off the road—"I want to talk to you"—they are in a getaway car, leaving the scene of a robbery, with the police right behind them, but they are absorbed in family bickering: the traditional all-American use of the family automobile. In a sense, it is the absence of sadism—it is the violence without sadism—that throws the audience off balance at *Bonnie and Clyde*. The brutality that comes out of this innocence is far more shocking than the calculated brutalities of mean killers.

Playfully posing with their guns, the real Bonnie and Clyde mocked the "Bloody Barrows" of the Hearst press. One photograph shows slim, pretty Bonnie, smiling and impeccably dressed, pointing a huge gun at Clyde's chest as he, a dimpled dude with a cigar, smiles back. The famous picture of Bonnie in the same clothes but looking ugly squinting into the sun, with a foot on the car, a gun on her hip, and a cigar in her mouth, is obviously a joke—her caricature of herself as a gun moll. Probably, since they never meant to kill, they thought the "Bloody Barrows" were a joke—a creation of the lying newspapers.

There's something new working for the Bonnie-and-Clyde legend now: our nostalgia for the thirties—the unpredictable, contrary affection of the prosperous for poverty, or at least for the artifacts, the tokens, of poverty, for Pop culture seen in the dreariest rural settings, where it truly seems to belong. Did people in the cities listen to the Eddie Cantor show? No doubt they did, but the sound of his voice, like the sound of Ed Sullivan now, evokes a primordial, pre-urban existence—the childhood of the race. Our comic-melancholic affection for thirties Pop has become sixties Pop, and those who made *Bonnie and Clyde* are smart enough to use it that way. Being knowing is not an artist's highest gift, but it can make a hell of a lot of difference in a movie. In the American experience, the miseries of the Depression are funny in the way that the Army is funny to draftees—a shared catastrophe, a leveling, forming part of our common background. Those too young to remember the Depression have heard about it from their parents. (When I was at college, we used to top each other's stories about how our families had survived: the fathers who had committed suicide so that their wives and children could live off the insurance; the mothers trying to make a game out of the meals of potatoes cooked on an open fire.) Though the American derision of the past has many offensive aspects, it has some good ones, too, because it's a way of making fun not only of our forebears but of ourselves and our pretensions. The toughness about what we've come out of and what we've been through—the honesty to see ourselves as the Yahoo children of yokels—is a good part of American popular art. There is a kind of American poetry in a stickup gang seen chasing across the bedraggled backdrop of the Depression (as true in its way as Nabokov's vision of Humbert Humbert and Lolita in the cross-country world of motels)—as if crime were the only activity in a country stupefied by poverty. But Arthur Penn doesn't quite have the toughness of mind to know it; it's not what he means by poetry. His squatters'-jungle scene is too "eloquent," like a poster making an appeal, and the Parker-family-reunion sequence is poetic in the gauzy mode. He makes the sequence a fancy lyric interlude, like a number in a musical (*Funny Face,* to be exact); it's too "imaginative"—a literal dust bowl, as thoroughly becalmed as Sleeping Beauty's garden. The movie becomes dreamy-soft where it should be hard (and hard-edged).

If there is such a thing as an American tragedy, it must be funny. O'Neill undoubtedly felt this when he had James Tyrone get up to turn off the lights in *Long Day's Journey Into Night.* We are bumpkins, haunted by the bottle of ketchup on the dining table at San Simeon. We garble our foreign words and phrases and hope that at least we've used them right. Our heroes pick up the wrong fork, and the basic figure of fun in the American theatre and American movies is the man who puts on airs. Children of peddlers and hod carriers don't feel at home in tragedy; we are used to failure. But, because of the quality of American life at the present time, perhaps there can be no real comedy—nothing more than stupidity and "spoof"—without true horror in it. Bonnie and Clyde and their partners in crime are comically bad bank robbers, and the backdrop of poverty makes their holdups seem pathetically tacky, yet they rob banks and kill people; Clyde and his good-natured brother are so shallow they never think much about anything, yet they suffer and die.

If this way of holding more than one attitude toward life is already familiar to us—if we recognize the make-believe robbers whose toy guns produce real blood, and the Keystone cops who shoot them dead, from Truffaut's *Shoot the Piano Player* and Godard's gangster pictures, *Breathless* and *Band of Outsiders*—it's because the young French directors discovered the poetry of crime in American life (from our movies) and showed the Americans how to put it on the screen in a new, "existential" way. Melodramas and gangster movies and comedies were always more our speed than "prestigious," "distinguished" pictures; the French directors who grew up on American pictures found poetry in our fast action, laconic speech, plain gestures. And because they understood that you don't express your love of life by denying the comedy or the horror of it, they brought out the poetry in our tawdry subjects. Now Arthur Penn, working with a script heavily influenced—one might almost say inspired—by Truffaut's *Shoot the Piano Player,* unfortunately imitates Truffaut's artistry instead of going back to its tough American sources. The French may tenderize their American material, but we shouldn't. That turns into another way of making "prestigious," "distinguished" pictures.

Probably part of the discomfort that people feel about *Bonnie and Clyde* grows out of its compromises and its failures. I wish the script hadn't provided the upbeat of the hero's sexual success as a kind of sop to the audience. I think what makes us not believe in it is that it isn't consistent with the intelligence of the rest of the writing—that it isn't on the same level, because it's too manipulatively clever, too much of a gimmick. (The scene that shows the gnomish gang member called C.W. sleeping in the same room with Bonnie and Clyde suggests other possibilities, perhaps discarded, as does C.W.'s reference to Bonnie's liking his tattoo.) Compromises are not new to the Bonnie-and-Clyde story; *You Only Live Once* had a tacked-on coda featuring a heavenly choir and William Gargan as a dead priest, patronizing Eddie even in the afterlife, welcoming him to Heaven with "You're free, Eddie!" The kind of people who make a movie like *You Only Live Once* are not the kind who write endings like that, and, by the same sort of internal evidence, I'd guess that Newman and Benton, whose Bonnie seems to owe so much to Catherine in *Jules and Jim,* had more interesting ideas originally about Bonnie's and Clyde's (and maybe C.W.'s) sex lives.

But people also feel uncomfortable about the violence, and here I think they're wrong. That is to say, they *should* feel uncomfortable, but this isn't an argument *against* the movie. Only a few years ago, a good director would have suggested the violence obliquely, with reaction shots (like the famous one in *The Golden Coach,* when we see a whole bullfight reflected in Anna Magnani's face), and death might have been symbolized by a light going out, or stylized, with blood and wounds kept to a minimum. In many ways, this method is more effective; we feel the violence more because so much is left to our imaginations. But the whole point of *Bonnie and Clyde* is to rub our noses in it, to make us pay our dues for laughing. The dirty reality of death—not suggestions but blood and holes—is necessary. Though I generally respect a director's skill and intelligence in inverse ratio to the violence he shows on the screen, and though I questioned even the Annie Sullivan–Helen Keller fight scenes in Arthur Penn's *The Miracle Worker,* I think that this time Penn is right. (I think he was also right when he showed violence in his first film, *The Left Handed Gun,* in 1958.) Suddenly, in the last few years, our view of the world has gone beyond "good taste." Tasteful suggestions of violence would at this point be a more grotesque form of comedy than *Bonnie and Clyde* attempts. *Bonnie and Clyde* needs violence; violence is its meaning. When, during a comically botched-up getaway, a man is shot in the face, the image is obviously based on one of the most famous sequences in Eisenstein's *Potemkin,* and the startled face is used the same way it was in *Potemkin*—to convey in an instant how someone who just happens to be in the wrong place at the wrong time, the irrelevant "innocent" bystander, can get it full in the face. And at that instant the meaning of Clyde Barrow's character changes; he's still a clown, but *we've* become the butt of the joke.

It is a kind of violence that says something to us; it is something that movies must be free to use. And it is just because artists must be free to use violence—a legal right that is beginning to come under attack—that we must also defend the legal rights of those film-makers who use violence to sell tickets, for it is not the province of the law to decide that one man is an artist and another man a no-talent. The no-talent has as much right to produce works as the artist has, and not only because he has a surprising way of shifting from one category to the other but also because men have an inalienable right to be untalented, and the law should not discriminate against lousy "artists." I am not saying that the violence in *Bonnie and Clyde* is legally acceptable because the film is a work of art; I think that

Bonnie and Clyde, though flawed, is a work of art, but I think that the violence in *The Dirty Dozen,* which isn't a work of art, and whose violence offends me *personally,* should also be legally defensible, however morally questionable. Too many people—including some movie reviewers—want the law to take over the job of movie criticism; perhaps what they really want is for their own criticisms to have the force of law. Such people see *Bonnie and Clyde* as a danger to public morality; they think an audience goes to a play or a movie and takes the actions in it as examples for imitation. They look at the world and blame the movies. But if women who are angry with their husbands take it out on the kids, I don't think we can blame *Medea* for it; if, as has been said, we are a nation of mother-lovers, I don't think we can place the blame on *Oedipus Rex.* Part of the power of art lies in showing us what we are *not* capable of. We see that killers are not a different breed but are *us* without the insight or understanding or self-control that works of art strengthen. The tragedy of *Macbeth* is in the fall from nobility to horror; the comic tragedy of *Bonnie and Clyde* is that although you can't fall from the bottom you can reach the same horror. The movies may set styles in dress- or love-making, they may advertise cars or beverages, but art is not examples for imitation—that is not what a work of art does for us—though that is what guardians of morality *think* art is and what they want it to be and why they think a good movie is one that sets "healthy," "cheerful" examples of behavior, like a giant all-purpose commercial for the American way of life. But people don't "buy" what they see in a movie quite so simply; Louis B. Mayer did not turn us into a nation of Andy Hardys, and if, in a film, we see a frightened man wantonly take the life of another, it does not encourage us to do the same, any more than seeing an ivory hunter shoot an elephant makes us want to shoot one. It may, on the contrary, so sensitize us that we get a pang in the gut if we accidentally step on a moth.

Will we, as some people have suggested, be lured into imitating the violent crimes of Clyde and Bonnie because Warren Beatty and Faye Dunaway are "glamorous"? Do they, as some people have charged, confer glamour on violence? It's difficult to see how, since the characters they play are horrified by it and ultimately destroyed by it. Nobody in the movie gets pleasure from violence. Is the charge based on the notion that simply by their presence in the movie Warren Beatty and Faye Dunaway make crime attractive? If movie stars can't play criminals without our all wanting to be criminals, then maybe the only safe roles for them to play are movie stars—which, in this assumption, everybody wants to be anyway. After all, if they played factory workers, the economy might be dislocated by everybody's trying to become a factory worker. (Would having criminals played by dwarfs or fatties discourage crime? It seems rather doubtful.) The accusation that the beauty of movie stars makes the antisocial acts of their characters dangerously attractive is the kind of contrived argument we get from people who are bothered by something and are clutching at straws. Actors and actresses are *usually* more beautiful than ordinary people. And why not? Garbo's beauty notwithstanding, her Anna Christie did not turn us into whores, her Mata Hari did not turn us into spies, her Anna Karenina did not make us suicides. We did not want her to be ordinary looking. Why should we be deprived of the pleasure of beauty? Garbo could be all women in love because, being more beautiful than life, she could more beautifully express emotions. It is a supreme asset for actors and actresses to be beautiful; it gives them greater range and greater possibilities for expressiveness. The handsomer they are, the more roles they can play; Olivier can be anything, but who would want to see Ralph Richardson, great as he is, play Antony? Actors and actresses who are beautiful start with an enormous advantage, because we love to look at them. The joke in the glamour charge is that Faye Dunaway has the magazine-illustration look of countless uninterestingly pretty girls, and Warren Beatty has the kind of high-school good looks that are generally lost fast. It's the roles that make *them* seem glamorous. Good roles do that for actors.

There is a story told against Beatty in a recent *Esquire*—how during the shooting of *Lilith* he "delayed a scene for three days demanding the line 'I've read *Crime and Punishment* and *The Brothers Karamazov*' be changed to 'I've read *Crime and Punishment* and *half* of *The Brothers Karamazov*.'" Considerations of professional conduct aside, what is odd is why his adversaries waited three days to give in, because, of course, he was right. That's what the character he played *should* say; the other way, the line has no point at all. But this kind of intuition isn't enough to make an actor, and in a number of roles Beatty, probably because he doesn't have the technique to make the most of his lines in the least possible time, has depended too much on intuitive non-acting—holding the screen far too long as he acted out self-preoccupied characters in a lifelike, boringly self-conscious way. He has a gift for slyness, though, as he showed in *The Roman Spring of Mrs. Stone,* and in most of his films he could hold the screen—maybe because there seemed to be something going on in his mind, some kind of calculation. There was something smart about him—something shrewdly private in those squeezed-up little non-actor's eyes—that didn't fit the clean-cut juvenile roles. Beatty was the producer of *Bonnie and Clyde,* responsible for keeping the company on schedule, and he has been quoted as saying, "There's not a scene that we have done that we couldn't do better by taking another day." This is the hell of the expensive way of making movies, but it probably helps to explain why Beatty is more intense than he has been before and why he has picked up his pace. His business sense may have improved his timing. The role of Clyde Barrow seems to have released something in him. As Clyde, Beatty is good with his eyes and mouth and his hat, but his body is still inexpressive; he doesn't have a trained actor's use of his body, and, watching him move, one is never for a minute convinced he's impotent. It is, however, a tribute to his performance that one singles this failure out. His slow timing works perfectly in the sequence in which he offers the dispossessed farmer his gun; there may not be another actor who would have dared to prolong the scene that way, and the prolongation until the final "We rob banks" gives the sequence its comic force. I have suggested elsewhere that one of the reasons that rules are impossible in the arts is that in movies (and in the other arts, too) the new "genius"—the genuine as well as the fraudulent or the dubious—is often the man who has enough audacity, or is simpleminded enough, to do what others had the good taste not to do. Actors before Brando did not mumble and scratch and show their sweat; dramatists before Tennessee Williams did not make explicit a particular substratum of American erotic fantasy; movie directors before Orson Welles did not dramatize the techniques of film-making; directors before Richard Lester did not lay out the whole movie as cleverly as the opening credits; actresses before Marilyn Monroe did not make an asset of their ineptitude by turning faltering misreadings into an appealing style. Each, in a large way, did something that people had always enjoyed and were often embarrassed or ashamed about enjoying. Their "bad taste" shaped a new accepted taste. Beatty's non-actor's "bad" timing may be this kind of "genius"; we seem to be watching him *think out* his next move.

It's difficult to know how Bonnie should have been played,

because the character isn't worked out. Here the script seems weak. She is made too warmly sympathetic—and sympathetic in a style that antedates the style of the movie. Being frustrated and moody, she's not funny enough—neither ordinary, which, in the circumstances, would be comic, nor perverse, which might be rather funny, too. Her attitude toward her mother is too loving. There could be something funny about her wanting to run home to her mama, but, as it has been done, her heading home, running off through the fields, is unconvincing—incompletely motivated. And because the element of the ridiculous that makes the others so individual has been left out of her character she doesn't seem to belong to the period as the others do. Faye Dunaway has a sixties look anyway—not just because her eyes are made up in a sixties way and her hair is wrong but because her personal style and her acting are sixties. (This may help to make her popular; she can seem prettier to those who don't recognize prettiness except in the latest styles.) Furthermore, in some difficult-to-define way, Faye Dunaway as Bonnie doesn't keep her distance—that is to say, an *actor's* distance—either from the role or from the audience. She doesn't hold a characterization; she's in and out of emotions all the time, and though she often hits effective ones, the emotions seem *hers,* not the character's. She has some talent, but she comes on too strong; she makes one conscious that she's a willing worker, but she doesn't seem to know what she's doing—rather like Bonnie in her attempts to overcome Clyde's sexual difficulties.

Although many daily movie reviewers judge a movie in isolation, as if the people who made it had no previous history, more serious critics now commonly attempt to judge a movie as an expressive vehicle of the director, and a working out of his personal themes. Auden has written, "Our judgment of an established author is never simply an aesthetic judgment. In addition to any literary merit it may have, a new book by him has a historic interest for us as the act of a person in whom we have long been interested. He is not only a poet . . . he is also a character in our biography." For a while, people went to the newest Bergman and the newest Fellini that way; these movies were greeted like the latest novels of a favorite author. But Arthur Penn is not a writer-director like Bergman or Fellini, both of whom began as writers, and who (even though Fellini employs several collaborators) compose their spiritual autobiographies step by step on film. Penn is far more dependent on the talents of others, and his primary material—what he starts with—does not come out of his own experience. If the popular audience is generally uninterested in the director (unless he is heavily publicized, like DeMille or Hitchcock), the audience that is interested in the art of movies has begun, with many of the critics, to think of movies as a directors' medium to the point where they tend to ignore the contribution of the writers —and the directors may be almost obscenely content to omit mention of the writers. The history of the movies is being rewritten to disregard facts in favor of celebrating the director as the sole "creative" force. One can read Josef von Sternberg's autobiography and the text of the latest books on his movies without ever finding the name of Jules Furthman, the writer who worked on nine of his most famous movies (including *Morocco* and *Shanghai Express*). Yet the appearance of Furthman's name in the credits of such Howard Hawks films as *Only Angels Have Wings, To Have and Have Not, The Big Sleep,* and *Rio Bravo* suggests the reason for the similar qualities of good-bad-girl glamour in the roles played by Dietrich and Bacall and in other von Sternberg and Hawks heroines, and also in the Jean Harlow and Constance Bennett roles in the movies he wrote for *them.* Furthman, who has written about half of the most entertaining movies to come out of Hollywood (Ben Hecht wrote most of the other half), isn't even listed in new encyclopedias of the film. David Newman and Robert Benton may be good enough to join this category of unmentionable men who do what the directors are glorified for. The Hollywood writer is becoming a ghostwriter. The writers who succeed in the struggle to protect their identity and their material by becoming writer-directors or writer-producers soon become too rich and powerful to bother doing their own writing. And they rarely have the visual sense or the training to make good movie directors.

Anyone who goes to big American movies like *Grand Prix* and *The Sand Pebbles* recognizes that movies with scripts like those don't have a chance to be anything more than exercises in technology, and that this is what is meant by the decadence of American movies. In the past, directors used to say that they were no better than their material. (Sometimes they said it when they weren't even up to their material.) A good director can attempt to camouflage poor writing with craftsmanship and style, but ultimately no amount of director's skill can conceal a writer's failure; a poor script, even well directed, results in a stupid movie—as, unfortunately, does a good script poorly directed. Despite the new notion that the direction is everything, Penn can't redeem bad material, nor, as one may surmise from his *Mickey One,* does he necessarily know when it's bad. It is not fair to judge Penn by a film like *The Chase,* because he evidently did not have artistic control over the production, but what happens when he does have control and is working with a poor, pretentious mess of a script is painfully apparent in *Mickey One*—an art film in the worst sense of that term. Though one cannot say of *Bonnie and Clyde* to what degree it shows the work of Newman and Benton and to what degree they merely enabled Penn to "express himself," there are ways of making guesses. As we hear the lines, we can detect the intentions even when the intentions are not quite carried out. Penn is a little clumsy and rather too fancy; he's too much interested in being cinematically creative and artistic to know when to trust the script. *Bonnie and Clyde* could be better if it were simpler. Nevertheless, Penn is a remarkable director when he has something to work with. His most interesting previous work was in his first film, *The Left Handed Gun* (and a few bits of *The Miracle Worker,* a good movie version of the William Gibson play, which he had also directed on the stage and on television). *The Left Handed Gun,* with Paul Newman as an ignorant Billy the Kid in the sex-starved, male-dominated Old West, has the same kind of violent, legendary, nostalgic material as *Bonnie and Clyde;* its script, a rather startling one, was adapted by Leslie Stevens from a Gore Vidal television play. In interviews, Penn makes high, dull sounds—more like a politician than a movie director. But he has a gift for violence, and, despite all the violence in movies, a gift for it is rare. (Eisenstein had it, and Dovzhenko, and Buñuel, but not many others.) There are few memorable violent moments in American movies, but there is one in Penn's first film: Billy's shotgun blasts a man right out of one of his boots; the man falls in the street, but his boot remains upright; a little girl's giggle at the boot is interrupted by her mother's slapping her. The mother's slap—the seal of the awareness of horror—says that even children must learn that some things that look funny are not only funny. That slap, saying that only idiots would laugh at pain and death, that a child must develop sensibility, is the same slap that *Bonnie and Clyde* delivers to the woman saying "It's a comedy." In *The Left Handed Gun,* the slap is itself funny, and yet we suck in our breath; we do not dare to laugh.

Some of the best American movies show the seams of cuts and the confusions of compromises and still hold together, because there is enough energy and spirit to carry the audience over each of the weak episodes to the next good one. The solid intelligence of the writing and Penn's aura of sensitivity help *Bonnie and Clyde* triumph over many poorly directed scenes: Bonnie posing for the photograph with the Texas Ranger, or—the worst sequence—the Ranger getting information out of Blanche Barrow in the hospital. The attempt to make the Texas Ranger an old-time villain doesn't work. He's in the tradition of the mustachioed heavy who foreclosed mortgages and pursued heroines in turn-of-the-century plays, and this one-dimensional villainy belongs, glaringly, to spoof. In some cases, I think, the writing and the conception of the scenes are better (potentially, that is) than the way the scenes have been directed and acted. If Gene Hackman's Buck Barrow is a beautifully controlled performance, the best in the film, several of the other players—though they are very good—needed a tighter rein. They act too much. But it is in other ways that Penn's limitations show—in his excessive reliance on meaning-laden closeups, for one. And it's no wonder he wasn't able to bring out the character of Bonnie in scenes like the one showing her appreciation of the fingernails on the figurine, for in other scenes his own sense of beauty appears to be only a few rungs farther up that same cultural ladder.

The showpiece sequence, Bonnie's visit to her mother (which is a bit reminiscent of Humphrey Bogart's confrontation with his mother, Marjorie Main, in the movie version of *Dead End*), aims for an effect of alienation, but that effect is confused by all the other things attempted in the sequence: the poetic echoes of childhood (which also echo the child sliding down the hill in *Jules and Jim*) and a general attempt to create a frieze from our national past—a poetry of poverty. Penn isn't quite up to it, though he is at least good enough to communicate what he is trying to do, and it is an attempt that one can respect. In 1939, John Ford attempted a similar poetic evocation of the legendary American past in *Young Mr. Lincoln;* this kind of evocation, by getting at how we *feel* about the past, moves us far more than attempts at historical re-creation. When Ford's Western evocations fail, they become languorous; when they succeed, they are the West of our dreams, and his Lincoln, the man so humane and so smart that he can outwit the unjust and save the innocent, is the Lincoln of our dreams, as the Depression of *Bonnie and Clyde* is the

Depression of our dreams—the nation in a kind of trance, as in a dim memory. In this sense, the effect of blur is justified, is "right." Our memories *have* become hazy; this is what the Depression has faded into. But we are too conscious of the technical means used to achieve this blur, of the *attempt* at poetry. We are aware that the filtered effects already include our responses, and it's too easy; the lines are good enough so that the stylization wouldn't have been necessary if the scene had been played right. A simple frozen frame might have been more appropriate.

The editing of this movie is, however, the best editing in an American movie in a long time, and one may assume that Penn deserves credit for it along with the editor, Dede Allen. It's particularly inventive in the robberies and in the comedy sequence of Blanche running through the police barricades with her kitchen spatula in her hand. (There is, however, one bad bit of editing: the end of the hospital scene, when Blanche's voice makes an emotional shift without a corresponding change in her facial position.) The quick panic of Bonnie and Clyde looking at each other's face for the last time is a stunning example of the art of editing.

The end of the picture, the rag-doll dance of death as the gun blasts keep the bodies of Bonnie and Clyde in motion, is brilliant. It is a horror that seems to go on for eternity, and yet it doesn't last a second beyond what it should. The audience leaving the theatre is the quietest audience imaginable.

Still, that woman near me was saying "It's a comedy" for a little too long, and although this could have been, and probably was, a demonstration of plain old-fashioned insensitivity, it suggests that those who have attuned themselves to the "total" comedy of the last few years may not know when to stop laughing. Movie audiences have been getting a steady diet of "black" comedy since 1964 and *Dr. Strangelove, Or: How I Learned to Stop Worrying and Love the Bomb.* Spoof and satire have been entertaining audiences since the two-reelers; because it is so easy to do on film things that are difficult or impossible in nature, movies are ideally suited to exaggerations of heroic prowess and to the kind of lighthearted nonsense we used to get when even the newsreels couldn't resist the kidding finish of the speeded-up athletic competition or the diver flying up from the water. The targets have usually been social and political fads and abuses, together with the heroes and the clichés of the just preceding period of film-making. *Dr. Strangelove* opened a new movie era. It ridiculed *everything* and *everybody* it showed, but concealed its own liberal pieties, thus protecting itself from ridicule. A professor who had told me that *The Manchurian Candidate* was "irresponsible," adding, "I didn't like it—I can suspend disbelief only so far," was overwhelmed by *Dr. Strangelove:* "I've never been so involved. I had to keep reminding myself it was only a movie." *Dr. Strangelove* was clearly intended as a cautionary movie; it meant to jolt us awake to the dangers of the bomb by showing us the insanity of the course we were pursuing. But artists' warnings about war and the dangers of total annihilation never tell us how we are supposed to regain control, and *Dr. Strangelove,* chortling over madness, did not indicate any possibilities for sanity. It was experienced not as satire but as a confirmation of fears. Total laughter carried the day. A new generation enjoyed seeing the world as insane; they *literally* learned to stop worrying and love the bomb. Conceptually, we had already been living with the bomb; now the mass audience of the movies—which is the youth of America—grasped the idea that the threat of extinction can be used to devaluate everything, to turn it all into a joke. And the members of this audience do love the bomb; they love feeling that the worst has happened and the irrational are the sane, because there is the bomb as the proof that the rational are insane. They love the bomb because it intensifies their feelings of hopelessness and powerlessness and innocence. It's only three years since Lewis Mumford was widely acclaimed for saying about *Dr. Strangelove* that "unless the spectator was purged by laughter he would be paralyzed by the unendurable anxiety this policy, once it were honestly appraised, would produce." Far from being purged, the spectators are paralyzed, but they're still laughing. And how odd it is now to read, *"Dr. Strangelove* would be a silly, ineffective picture if its purpose were to ridicule the characters of our military and political leaders by showing them as clownish monsters—stupid, psychotic, obsessed." From *Dr. Strangelove* it's a quick leap to *MacBird* and to a belief in exactly what it was said we weren't mean to find in *Dr. Strangelove.* It is not war that has been laughed to scorn but the possibility of sane action.

Once something enters mass culture, it travels fast. In the spoofs of the last few years, everything is gross, ridiculous, insane; to make sense would be to risk being square. A brutal new melodrama is called *Point Blank* and it is. So are most of the new movies. This is the context in which *Bonnie and Clyde,* an entertaining movie that has some feeling in it, upsets people—people who didn't get upset even by *Mondo Cane.* Maybe it's because *Bonnie and Clyde,* by making us care about the robber lovers, has put the sting back into death.

FILM AS HIGH ART

In this section I've grouped some representative pieces by critics who have demanded of movies the same degree of complexity and subtlety they would demand of any other art form. They have consistently evaluated movies by the highest standards, deriving their ideals from fiction, drama, painting and the greatest films of the past. (See John Simon's "A Critical Credo" in Section III for a full statement of this position.) Since critics interested only in high art see very few films they like, or at least very few that come up to the level at which critic and film face one another on terms of equality, their writing walks a tightrope from piece to piece, with unbounded respect for movies on one side and virtually unbounded contempt for them on the other. When these critics fall, I needn't tell you on which side they most frequently land. At its best, highbrow writing on movies is marked by a passionate love for quality and an equally passionate detestation of shoddiness of any sort; by precision of thought and ingenuity of attack; by high-spirited wit and, occasionally, aphoristic brilliance. At its worst, it is marked by sourness, repetitiveness, lack of proportion; and it is haunted by the cynical suspicion on the part of certain readers that the critic has chosen movies as the art form guaranteed to display most frequently the superiority of his personal taste. For instance, when a critic has to quote Rilke (in German, of course) as a way of dismissing a pathetic Hollywood comedy about the trials of marriage, obviously something is wrong. At the least, it suggests that the critic should be writing about Rilke and not about Hollywood comedies.

The highbrows are at their best in close readings of the movie art they love, and I've chosen four such examples here.

Harry Alan Potamkin, who died tragically young (at thirty-three in 1933), was born in Philadelphia, moved to Paris in the twenties, and settled in New York in 1929 for the remainder of his life. For a while he was easily the most powerful writer among the many young intellectuals who got excited about movies in the twenties and wrote about them for the arts reviews and little magazines of the period. This piece, written in 1929, before a heavy infusion of Marxism thickened Potamkin's prose disastrously,* reflects the enthusiasm of a time when it first seemed possible that movies could equal the greatest aesthetic and spiritual experiences of the past. In Dreyer's masterpiece, *The Passion of Jeanne d'Arc,* the incessant close-ups and rhythmic editing created feelings approaching religious ecstasy in Potamkin and in many viewers since.

The literary critic William Troy wrote movie reviews for *The Nation* from 1933 to 1935. In this piece on Fritz Lang's *M,* which Troy compares favorably to Eugene O'Neill's *Mourning Becomes Electra* (a bold and accurate judgment), Troy proposes that the cinema, with its more flexible symbolic and poetic resources, is better suited than naturalistic drama for the revival, in modern terms, of the spirit of classical tragedy. Stanley Kauffmann, film critic of *The New Republic* almost continuously since 1959, has acknowledged Troy's reviews as a model for his own work. Kauffmann is a liberal critic who has been especially impressive in his tough-minded resistance to liberal pieties, particularly in the American cinema. However, in order to emphasize the informal connection with Troy, I've chosen this grave and beautiful piece on *La Notte,* in which Kauffmann asserts that cinema is best able to sustain the spirit of tragedy by going *beyond* classical plot logic. For Kauffmann, Antonioni's film is that rarity, an avant-garde work that connects with the audience emotionally.

Dwight Macdonald wrote occasional pieces on movies in the thirties and forties when his principal interests as a journalist were

*Others may not agree. Some of Potamkin's most ambitious later essays—on Eisenstein, Pudovkin, Pabst, and other subjects—can be found in *Hound & Horn: Essays on Cinema,* Arno Press, 1972.

political (including the politics of culture); by the time he came to write a regular film column for *Esquire* in 1960 (the column lasted until 1966), Macdonald was this country's acknowledged master of polemical writing—both the roughhouse and gentler varieties. Here, in fine good humor, he chastises some of the too-serious serious critics of the early sixties who demanded of Fellini's *8 1/2* a profundity that wasn't intended. For Macdonald, *8 1/2* is essentially a social comedy (he evokes Lubitsch), an exhilarating play of surfaces: Like *Citizen Kane,* the film was complicated but not obscure, an "easy" great film which did not require translation "from the language of art into the language of philosophy."

Ingmar Bergman is one artist who occasionally requires a great deal of interpretation; but before interpretation comes elucidation. John Simon, his notorious belligerency here out of sight, has written a fine, straightforward appreciation of *The Passion of Anna,* an evocation of the film in all its richness of detail. This is one of those rare cases in which a critic's personality seems to vanish, apparently consumed by the greater sensibility of the artist. This sort of disappearing act—a form of homage—is of course an illusion created by humility and sheer hard work.—*Ed.*

THE PASSION OF JEANNE D'ARC (1929)*

By Harry Alan Potamkin

We are always waiting in the cinema for the eventual film which will be the vindication of the major cinema devices. We are always waiting for the film down to essentials and yet conveying a profound human experience. For the craft of the movie, like the craft of any other art, is performance—of camera, of film, of player, of screen. (Mr. Alexander Bakshy has stated these four as the different cinema performances on movements, a fundamental statement.) But as an art conclusive the cinema must find its source in experience and its final meaning in experience. Where is the motion picture—we are always asking—profound in its exploitation of performance, and profound in its transmission of experience? This query is the key to the importance of plot in the movie not as detailed or episodic narrative but as subject-matter. The consideration of plot as narrative has been the cause and result of the movie's literalness (particularly in America) and the inability to include in the formation of the moving picture the inferences of the theme, much more important than the narrative. This inability has prevented a film so dramatically effective as Feyder's recent *Thérèse Raquin* (adapted from Zola's novel) from being a film of permanent importance.

In brief, we are always waiting for a film reduced but with passionate human content. The purity of passionate apprehension. A film mindful of the plot as the subject-matter of life. A film using the legitimate emphasis of the camera (or other kino instruments) and realizing an experience of form and content completely fused and fluid. We are always waiting for the expression of a perspicacious knowledge of the medium, and of the matter it is to convert into and by means of itself. The American film has realized in its literalness a pleasant but shallow ease of sequence. The German has stressed, in the main, the device as virtuosity rather than as an incorporate, revealing utility. The Swedish film, like the notable *Atonement of Gosta Berling,* is a rigorous life-exposition, but it has not fully grasped the principle of the conversion of the subject matter. The French

*The film, completed in 1928, took one year to reach America.

movie on the whole is too banal or too pretty or too frivolous (without being lively) to merit our interest. Yet the film which in this instance satisfies our anticipation is a French film. Its achievement may be explained by the fact that its director is a Dane, Carl Th. Dreyer. The film is *The Passion of Jeanne d'Arc*.

This profound and truly passionate motion picture concerns itself with the last day of Jeanne, the day of excruciating torment. The scenario is the combined work of the director and Joseph Delteil, the dadaist who wrote the prize-winning book on The Maid. It is, I hope, no libel of M. Delteil to suspect that the disciplining will of the director (a prime essential in the cinema industry today) kept the narrative within the strenuous limits of reverence. Reverence is a portion of the intensity of this film, an intensity to which everything submits—the decor by Jean Victor-Hugo, the photography of Maté, with its superb statement of personalities by the skin-textures and moles. In total accord with this intense and intensive exploitation of the subject-matter (remember there is really no plot here, only the last moment—the queries, the betrayal, the final conflagration), is the use of the succession of individual cinephotos. These are not close-ups (there is no "closing up" in the bland movie way), not stills (for the angles and curves are lovely and illuminating), but the bold concentration of individual faces and figures in the active, critical, voracious eye of the camera. This would suggest a static series of pictures, not Mr. Bakshy's "dynamic sequence," rather the mere physical basis of filming than the esthetic aspiration of the cinema. But it attests to Carl Dreyer's genius that the sequence is eminently fluid, dramatic, rhythmic. The succession has a definite time-order, a definite plastic arrangement in the time-order of exquisite curves (the performers exploited by the camera) and bodily angles, a definite utilization of the screen as the receptive instrument (advocated long ago by Mr. Bakshy, but very seldom realized), and a gradual almost unsuspected rise to the final mob explosion. There are diagonal curves of the moving performers, vertical inclines, a forehead above the lower frame boldly duplicating the moderated masses of the background.

There is no extraneous detail in the film. Not once does a detail fail to directly relate and contribute to the subject-matter. At one point, Jeanne sees the grave-digger pull up a skull. Unnecessary? Obvious? There is a swift succession, almost staccato in its brevity, to a field of flowers. The previous detail becomes inevitable, poignant. In fact, the entire film has that virtue, that at any moment the detail on the screen validates what preceded it. This is rhythm, this is art. The beautiful flight of birds, as Jeanne is perishing, the mother suckling her child—the former might be a sentimentalism, the latter a surrealistic simplicism; but by the severe control of the director, they become terrible convictions of the world that would let one who loved free flight perish bound, and one who herself would such life burn at the stake. Creation against desolation!

The torment of the young peasant girl, "called Jeannette at home," convinced in her childishness and mysticism of her divine mission, becomes the emotional experience of the spectator. Her fears, persistent under the insistent examination, become heavy with the burden of the torment, become luminous with the momentary glamor and memory stirred by the queries. The heavy tear imparts to the spectator the sense of the days and months of anguish the girl has endured in her steadfastness to her inspiration. The luminous tear elucidates the girl's origins, her free fields, her home, and the momentum of the inspiration that has urged her into this betrayal. The tears of Falconetti, the portrayer of Jeanne, are not the tears of a Clara Bow, insipid, irritating, fraudulent. Her eyes enamored of God borrow no stage-pantomime, but with the grained skin and parched lips, the clipped hair, and chained walk, reveal the entire enterprise of God and land within the girl's body. Falconetti faithfully submits to the intensity of the unit, enters into it, and expresses it while she expresses Jeanne. She is the conception. She is the film. An identical loyalty is manifested by each of the accurately chosen, thoroughly participating cast. No specious prettiness, but hardiness, man in his physical variousness, man in his spiritual diversity serving the same master—Interest. The Interest of State, the Interest of God. Jeanne, serving God, alone of all has served herself, her systemic soul-and-body. She as the servant of herself becomes the everlasting, the others are left to weep upon the torment they have connived. The State alone (Warwick) remains unperturbed, save to halt the conflagration of Jeanne which threatens to burn down the power of England in Rouen. As no prologue was needed, no epilogue is asked for and no commentary from the distance of several centuries. How superior to Shaw's Joan! The inference all embodied in the unit-structure, not tagging along like loose threads, nor stressed like a moral to a fable. One fault alone disturbs the perfection of this grand film, a fault easily eliminated: there are too many captions, well written though they are. Fewer captions jotted in the staccato brevity of many of the images that pass almost before one sees them—these would have better suited the film's attitude, and not served to weaken (even if in the minutest degree, as the captions do at present) the demanding simplicity and rigorousness of this beautiful work.

The Passion of Jeanne d'Arc is an historical film, but not a costume film; an historical film that is contemporaneous in its universal references. *The Passion of Jeanne d'Arc* is a religious film, but not a sanctimonious film. Life, it urges, is transcendent. It is a transcendent film.

M (1933)*

By William Troy

M, the German-language film, is based on the crimes and the final apprehension by the police of the famous child murderer of Düsseldorf. Certainly no subject could be more inherently horrible, more dangerously open to a facile sensationalism of treatment. Yet such are the tact and the genius with which Fritz Lang has handled it that the result is something at once more significant than either the horror story, pure and simple, represented by *Caligari* and the *Rue Morgue,* or the so-called psychological "document" of the type which Germany has sent us so often in the past. The result is, in fact, a film which answers to most of the demands of classical tragedy. In the first place Lang has concentrated his interest not on the circumstances but on the social and human consequences of the crimes. We are shown a whole city thrown into panic by what is for every class the least pardonable of all acts of violence. The police have

*The film, completed in 1931, took two years to reach America.

failed in their efforts to find the criminal; the underworld of crooks, thieves, and beggars, in order to guarantee their own security, organize themselves in a man hunt. At the end it is the latter and not the police who ferret out the guilty one in the dark recesses of a factory storeroom. All this, of course, provides a formal suspense more sustained than would any playing on the usual modes of physical horror. It also provides a certain nervous relief. The horror, as is proper and necessary in the films, is conveyed by implication rather than representation. It is implied through a very few miraculously appropriate symbols—a child's toy balloon caught in a telegraph wire, a child's ball rolling to a stop from the scene of the crime. Blood-lust is identified with the strain of Grieg which the criminal whistles whenever the passion is upon him. The whole pattern—lust, the victim, and the circumstances—is symbolized in the frame of glittering knives in which the criminal, staring in a shop window, sees the image of his latest victim reflected. Because these symbols are one and all visual or aural, peculiar to the talking screen, they serve to make *M* of the very highest technical interest. But they are not enough to explain why it may also be considered a great tragedy. For the crystallization of these symbols in an emotion absolutely realized in the spectator and effecting in him a genuine Aristotelian catharsis, the flawless acting of Peter Lorre is perhaps finally responsible. In his rendering of the paralysis of frustrated lust in the scene on the café terrace, for example, he gives us an intuition of the conflict of will and desire such as we are accustomed to only in the great classic dramas when they are played by great tragic actors. And in the last scene, when he stands at bay before the assembled underworld seated in judgment, his wide-eyed, inarticulate defense is made the equivalent of those long passages of rhetoric at the close of Greek or Elizabethan plays in which the hero himself is forced to admit his helplessness before the forces which have undone him. The modern psychopath, through Peter Lorre's acting, attains to the dignity of the tragic hero. It does not matter that the forces are no longer on the outside. They are perhaps the more ruthless for being inside him. The *moirae* may be given different names by the doctors, the judges, and the audience, but they have lost none of their ancient inevitability.

The last thing that may be said about *M,* therefore, is that it confirms our belief in the continued vitality of the tragic emotion. Few other attempts to substitute for the old gods, fates, or destiny a modern fatalism of psychological mechanisms have been so successful. The difficulty has seemed at times (as in O'Neill's *Electra*) that the latter are too subjective ever to take the place of the former. But it may only have been some failure or insufficiency of the artistic process at work. It may be that Fritz Lang and Peter Lorre are better artists in their fields than most of those who have sought to revive tragedy in our time. Or it may be—and *M* gives strength to the supposition—that the cinema is able to supply a language for modern tragic experience that is at once fresher, more various, and more poetic than the flat statement of naturalistic drama. Our speech, we are often enough told, has suffered in the marketplace. Our language symbols are abraded and our rhythms dissolved. But through the distinct symbols and closer pantomimic acting possible on the screen the whole world of tragic reality may once again be reopened to us.

LA NOTTE (1962)

By Stanley Kauffmann

Michelangelo Antonioni's *La Notte* is so perfectly congruent with our concerns, so piercingly honest, that it is close to a personal experience. Such an acutely subjective reaction is not always the purpose of art, but it is his purpose and he has achieved it.

The story is spare. In Milan live Giovanni and Lidia, a novelist and his wife, childless, in their thirties, married some years, affectionate with each other but no longer in love. The film covers about eighteen hours in their lives: a visit to a dying friend in a hospital; a publication-day party for Giovanni's new book (which he fears may be his last); a long lonely walk by Lidia through the city; their visit to a night club where they see an erotic balancing act; an all-night party at a millionaire's villa where each of them meets someone who —temporarily, at least—attracts him. At dawn they cross the huge lawn together, the tired dance band still playing. Behind some trees they sit. She reads to him a tender love letter, addressed to her. He asks her who wrote it. "You did," she replies. Stung with anguish for his lost love, he seizes her. At first she denies him, saying she doesn't love him any more. He persists and she gradually acquiesces. The film ends with the couple making love on the grass. Whether they will be able to remake their love is undecided.

The film has no plot. It is a series of events given their dynamics by the depth of character of the two people passing through them: a man and a woman, once in love, who still live with and like each other but who have floated apart out of fingertip's reach. Seen through their eyes, vibrated through their nervous systems, the incidents in the film—sometimes unremarkable in themselves—take on the proportions of a pilgrimage. This is because their relationship is not sexual *ennui* or a stage in marital intrigue; it is the result of their being perceptive people in a world inimical to confidence, therefore inimical to lasting love. With no sense of strain whatever, this pair step forward as protagonists of the age's love tragedy: the lack of a whole, oriented self to give in love.

I must make it clear that this is not just one more European film about "the moral collapse of our time"—the label that every lurid French or Italian film carries to justify its luridness. *La Notte* is certainly concerned with the theme of Yeats' *Second Coming;* the best *do* lack all conviction, while the worst *are* full of passionate intensity. (See the millionaire host.) The film exists in an ambience that is post-Hitler, post-Stalin, post-Bomb, in a society caught between the far-reaching but iron-lined avenues of Marxism and, on the other hand, a creeping corpulence fed extensively by military preparations to deter Marxism.

But Antonioni is no glib, self-scratching Jeremiah. He is not merely past outmoded hope, he is past despair. He looks at this new environment as his home and, having decided not to die, lives. His characters are in their habitat and know it; they face the task of imagining a viable future. As for their marriage, we see them discovering the geography of the island on which they are cast, recognizing that other lovers are at best excursions that will only take them to other islands, that in the fact of mutual compassion there is justification for compassion, that they can stay together because they are somewhat consecrated by knowledge of each other's weaknesses and by the time they have passed together. The film finishes without rosiness but with the cleanliness of scouring candor, a sense that the worst is known.

"I know what to write," says Giovanni, "but I don't know how to write it." Like every artist in history, he sees more than he is capable of expressing, but, unlike them, he has no relevant framework within which to strive. He no longer knows how to speak or the point in speaking. "A writer is an anachronism," he says, "doing something that can't be done yet by machines." The horrible moment for him comes when his industrialist-host offers to take him out of his anachronism with a job as corporation historian and publicity director; an offer made with all the lubricity of the materialist ego that knows how to reinforce itself with the quasi-idealistic. The horror of the offer is that Giovanni realizes its aptness. The job would at least fill a gap in him, even though he knows it would be one long, plump suicide. But the real purification by this horror comes near the end when he tells Lidia of the offer and she says, "Why not?" When she who knows him and has admired him can say that, it is rock bottom for him. Her bland acceptance is the shock that may reawaken him and connect him with a revised world.

As for Lidia, the death of their friend Tommaso is the end of her last link with selfless love. Tommaso, who was never physically her lover, worshiped her, and almost convinced her (she says) that she was intelligent. Giovanni spoke to her only of himself "and I loved it"; but now all that is left of Giovanni for her is an ego that doubts itself. The loss of Tommaso's love—the only one without ego—is like losing parents a second time. She is reconciled to loneliness, even to her husband's quest for illusions of refreshment in other women, both because she is no longer jealous and because she wishes him well. But at the end, if she is not convinced that he is again capable of his former love, she at least knows that he realizes this and is ashamed of it, instead of accepting it; and in that shame is a possible seed.

Marcello Mastroianni, as Giovanni, gives a performance of utter comprehension and delicacy that *begins* by being true and then goes on to harrow us. Jeanne Moreau, who plays Lidia, has seemed to me until now a film actress in the least complimentary sense, a woman whose performances were for the most part albums of varyingly interesting photographs. Under Antonioni's hand, what was semblance has become vitalized. "The director," he says, "must know how to demand," and he has demanded well of her. She moves through this film like a sad suite of airs. Her face, elegiac and passionate, seems to brood over this film, even when she is absent.

Monica Vitti, brunette in this film, has a less complex role as the millionaire's daughter, but gives it waywardness without coyness and sex with sensibility. Bernhard Wicki (the director of *The Bridge*) endows his brief appearance as Tommaso with the clarity of the dying and the pride of a man who has faced his limitations—all this so sharply that the later news of his death makes us feel a loss.

As for Antonioni himself: I have now seen *La Notte* three times and I speak carefully when I say that I think he is making a new art form. In this film, even more strikingly than in *L'Avventura,* he is forging a new language apposite to a changed world. For a society theistically based and teleologically organized, the concepts of drama that derived substantially from Aristotle have sufficed for centuries. The film was born to that inheritance and, out of it, still produces fine works (although with a perceptibly increasing tinge of nostalgia). Antonioni has seen the dwindling force of this inheritance and is finding means to supplement it. He is achieving what many contemporary artists in his and other fields are seeking and not often with his success: renewal of his art rather than repetition.

Jackson Pollock, Hans Hofmann, and their kin are exponents of dissatisfaction rather than recreation. The anti-novelists, in their frustration with the limits of the conventional novel, ask readers to share their professional problems rather than to be affected as readers. Brecht jostled the traditional drama healthily, but his theater is didactic, aimed toward a different godhead—a temporal one that now seems sterile to many. The so-called Theater of the Absurd faces reality rigorously and poetically, but a theater of images and no characters is limited to disembodied effects—and each author seems to have one reiterated effect. Who needs to see another play by Beckett or Ionesco or Pinter? In films, too, the avant-garde—Cocteau and many others—have tried to find new methods; but they, too, have to concentrated on the attempt that they have neglected to communicate much content. A more conventional artist, Ingmar Bergman feels present spiritual hungers as keenly as anyone, but his films so far, for all their superb qualities, exemplify Mulligan's line to Dedalus: "You have the cursed jesuit strain in you, only it's injected the wrong way."

Antonioni, however, seems to be making the miracle: finding a way to speak to us about ourselves today without crankily throwing away all that went before and without being bound by it. He is reshaping the idea of the content of film drama, discarding ancient and less ancient concepts, redirecting traditional audience expectations toward immersion in character rather than conflict of character. He is reshaping time itself in his films, taking it out of its customary synoptic form, wringing intensity out of its distention, daring to ask us to "live through" experiences with less distillation, deriving his drama from the very texture of such experiences and their juxtaposition, rather than from formal clash and climax and resolution. Fundamentally, he gives us characters whose drama consists in facing life minute after minute rather than in moving through organized plots with articulated obstacles; who have no well-marked cosmos to use as a tennis player uses a court; who live and die without the implication of a divine eye that sees their virtues (whether men do or not) and cherishes them.

John Grierson once said that when a director dies, he becomes a photographer; but Antonioni gets emotional utility—in a film about *people*—out of surfaces and compositions. He uses photography for enrichment, not for salon gasps: for example, the scene where Lidia goes for a ride in the rain with a man and the downpour seems to put the car in danger of dissolution.

The sequence that best represents Antonioni's style is the one in which Lidia slips away from the publisher's party and wanders through the streets. Conditioned as we are, we *expect* something; we think she is off to meet a lover, or to kill herself, or to get involved in an accident. But nothing happens; and everything happens. She strolls past a bus conductor eating a sandwich and is fascinated by his existence and his appetite in the same universe with her; she passes two men laughing uproariously at a joke and she smiles, too, although she has not heard it, anxious to join them, to be one of the human race; she encounters a crying child and kneels briefly and unsuccessfully to comfort it; she tears a flake of rust off a corroding wall; she sees two young men punching each other ferociously, watches horrified, then screams for them to stop. (The victor thinks she must be attracted to him and starts to pursue her, and so Antonioni touches another old tribal nerve.) Then in the suburbs she watches some boys shooting off rockets. She finds she is in a neighborhood that she and Giovanni used to visit years before. She telephones him and he drives out to pick her up.

By drama-school definition, it is not a cumulative dramatic sequence. It is a miniature recapitulation, deftly done, of the possibilities of life: a child and an old woman, a man eating and a man punching, sunlight on a fountain and a greasy lewd stallkeeper. Antonioni holds it all together with something like the surface tension of liquids and, by not commenting, comments. It is essentially as drastic a revolution as abstract expressionist painting or Beckett's litanylike dialogue, but Antonioni has not estranged us in order to speak to us about loneliness; he has not sacrificed the link of recognition to make new images; he has not had to use absurdity to convey the absurd.

Of every directorial technique he is an easy master. I specify only two. His use of sound: the low-pitched conversation in the hospital is interrupted by the passage of a helicopter like a pause in music so that the hushed key will not become tedious. His symbolism (which is unobtrusive): the mushroom cloud of smoke that envelops the boy who fires the rocket, and the fact that Giovanni meets Lidia after her walk in front of a long-abandoned church.

For me, Antonioni has made in *La Notte* and in *L'Avventura* the most subtly truthful theatrical works about the relation of the sexes since Joyce's *Exiles*. But he has done more. In *La Notte* he has used a vitiated marriage as a metaphor of the crisis of faith in our age, the faith within which profoundest love and pettiest whim have always been contained. He has used his camera as a hound of non-heaven ranging through the streets of Milan to find the beauty in necessity, the assurance in knowing that one can live without assurances. This film leaves us less deceived; thus with the truth in us less encumbered.

8 1/2: FELLINI'S OBVIOUS MASTERPIECE (1964)

By Dwight Macdonald

I can't say that Fellini has been one of my favorite directors. *The White Sheik* I thought crude compared to Antonioni's comparable tragicomedy about a similar milieu, *The Lady Without the Camellias.* For all its poetic realism, *La Strada* left a sentimental aftertaste, mostly because of the performance of Fellini's wife, Giulietta Masina, which was praised for just the quality that put me off: her miming, which recalled all too faithfully the original creators of the style—Langdon, Keaton and Chaplin. My favorite up to now has been *Cabiria* (1957), a Dickensian mixture of realism, pathos and comedy; Mrs. Fellini also played the lead, this time with more restraint. The much-admired *I Vittelloni* (1953) I've seen only on a tiny 16-millimeter screen; it looked good, but my eye isn't practiced enough to know how it would look full-size.* The also admired *La Dolce Vita* I thought sensationalized, inflated and cinematically conventional, despite some brilliant episodes which (like the unbrilliant ones) made their point before they were half over. And Fellini's episode in *Boccaccio 70* was even worse than De Sica's: a stertorous laboring of a theme—censors are secretly prurient—that was probably considered hackneyed by Menander. But now Fellini has made a movie that I can't see any way not to recognize as a masterpiece.

This portrait of the artist as a middle-aged man is the most brilliant, varied and entertaining movie I've seen since *Citizen Kane.* I saw it twice in as many weeks, and the second time I discovered many points that had escaped me in the first viewing,

*I have seen it full-size since this was written and it *didn't* look good. I think it one of those historically important films like Visconti's *La Terra Trema,* Godard's *Breathless* and (possibly) Resnais' *Hiroshima, Mon Amour* which haven't worn well because their innovations have become commonplace—too successful, in a sense—while there isn't enough else in them to engage our interest today. The antidramatic naturalism which fifteen years ago was exciting in *I Vitelloni* has become so familiar that the film now looks pedestrian, faded.

so headlong is its tempo, so fertile its invention. What I had found exciting the first time still seemed so, nor was I conscious of any *longueurs,* with two exceptions: the night visit to the tower (Guido's talk with Rosella merely verbalized what had already been shown to our eyes) and the scene in the car between Guido and Claudia (her "How big will my part be" would have been enough to make the point). A great deal is packed into every scene, like *Kane:* of well-observed detail; of visual pleasure; of fine acting in minor roles (Guido Alberti's The Producer, Edra's La Saraghina, Madeleine Lebeau's Actress). And finally, like *Kane,* it deals with large topics like art, society, sex, money, aging, pretense and hypocrisy—all that Trollope wrote about in *The Way We Live Now*—just the opposite of these cautious little (though not short) art films that lingeringly explore some tiny area of impingement between three undefined characters or, if the director feels in an epic mood, four.

The action, or Argument, is as simple as its development is complex. Guido (played by Marcello Mastroianni with style, humor and delicacy) is a famous director who has retreated to an Italian seaside health resort to avoid a breakdown and to finish the script of a spectacular of stupefying banality about the flight to another planet of the survivors of a nuclear war. The script is long overdue: a huge Canaveral-type launching tower has been erected on the beach—it cost a real $140,000 in the real film, we are told by the Joseph E. Levine handout which is also real, relatively—cast, producer, technicians, everybody is waiting around while costs tick along like a taxi meter as Guido tries to break through his Creative Block, and meanwhile to placate and if possible evade their persistent demands. His mistress arrives (a full-bodied, empty-headed soubrette right out of a Franz Lehár operatta—really wonderful performance by Sandra Milo) and is presently followed by his wife (Anouk Aimée manages to look astringent and attractive simultaneously), necessitating another series of evasions and placations that are all the more difficult because his relation to each is unsatisfactory since he is still, in middle age, trying to square the sexual circle: to possess without being possessed, to take without giving. His personal and professional lives are thus speeding toward catastrophe on parallel tracks. It happens. Mistress and wife finally clash in a scene of irretrievable social horror. The movie comes to smash at a huge publicity party the producer gives to force Guido's hand. Badgered by questions he can't answer, since the script is still hardly begun, Guido crawls under a buffet table and shoots himself. He springs back to life at once and begins to solve all his problems, emotional as well as cinematic, in a happy ending that has been widely deplored.

There are three kinds of reality in *8 1/2,* and the film proceeds with constant shifting of gears between them. (Like *Marienbad,* but a secular version of that hieratic mystery: quick, humorous, jazzy, direct—you always know what gear you're in.) There is Guido's real present, as outlined above. There are his memories of his boyhood and of his dead parents. And there are his Walter Mitty daydreams of a harmonious realm of *luxe, calme, et volupté* in which all his problems are magically solved: the artist's world of creative fantasy. Its symbol is a beautiful young girl in white who keeps materializing and fading away throughout the film, and seems to be a kind of Muse. After his wife and his mistress have disastrously collided, Guido leans back in his café chair, closes his eyes (behind dark glasses), and revises the scene so that the wife compliments the mistress on her dress, and the two are presently waltzing together; since this works so well, Guido's editing goes all the way, and we have the lovely, and witty, harem fantasy, which poeticizes Freudian ideas about the libido even as it parodies them.

Everything flows in this protean movie, constantly shifting between reality, memory, and fantasy. Free association is its structural principle. A description of just what happens in two sequences may give some idea; I make no claim for detailed accuracy for these notes taken in the dark; they are merely what one viewer saw, or thought he saw. The first comes early in the film; the second covers the last half hour or so.

(1) A bedroom in a shabby hotel. Guido asks Carla, his mistress, to make up like a whore and go out into the corridor and come into the room as if to an unknown client. Carla: "Oh, good—we've never tried *that* before!" But she keeps spoiling the mood by chattering about her husband. (She's always trying to get Guido to give him a job: "He's serious, not pushy at all, that's his tragedy," she says in an earlier scene. "He knows more about Roman history than anybody. You'd like him.") Also by remarking, as Guido makes her up:

"just like one of your actresses"; and, as she goes out, wrapped in a sheet, "I don't think I'd like that kind of life, I'm a homebody, really." (Cf. Proust's Charlus trying to get the hard-working youth he's hired to whip him in the male brothel to admit he's really a brutal criminal—the young man is shocked, he's the only support of an invalid mother, he insists, to Charlus's disgust.) She spoils it completely when she comes in, flourishing a bottle of mineral water—"The landlady gave it to me for my stomach." It's a hopeless anticlimax when she flings wide the sheet. . . . Guido sleeps while Carla reads a comic book; both sleep. . . . A black-robed woman, seen from behind, appears; Guido wakes; she gestures to him to follow. . . . He is in a great weedy cemetery bounded by two long lines of high crumbling walls in which are niches and tombs. He talks with his dead father and mother (the woman in black). His father complains, in a reasonable tone and with precise gestures, as one explains why a new flat won't do, that his tomb is uncomfortably cramped; Guido listens sympathetically. . . . The producer and his assistant appear and complain to his parents that Guido is lazy and irresponsible; the parents agree he has always been a problem. . . . Guido helps his father back into his grave, tenderly, a dutiful son. He kisses his mother goodbye, she suddenly embraces him passionately and kisses him on the mouth, turning into a younger woman (his wife, as we find later).

(2) Interior of a movie theatre, empty except for Guido, who is isolated with his contemptuous collaborator; lower down we see his wife with her sister and friends, and the producer with his entourage. Guido must at last choose the cast, from screen tests; no more stalling, the producer warns, I can make it tough for you if you force me to. Wife's party murmur approval, everybody glares at Guido. The critic-collaborator, sitting just behind him, begins again to tell him how stupid his ideas are. Guido listens courteously, as always, then (beginning of shortest fantasy-sequence) raises one finger. Two assistants take the critic by the arms, lead him into the aisle, put a black hood over his face, a rope around his neck, and hang him. Back to reality: shot of Guido with his collaborator, undamaged, still sitting behind him. Producer calls for projectionist to begin; screen is lit by a blazing rectangle of light that is switched off at once. Beginning of longest fantasy, which lasts to the end, with dreams inside dreams inside dreams; from now on, despite some misleading illusions of reality, we are inside

Guido's head. The screen tests are not for parts in the science-fiction movie Guido is supposed to be making, but for roles in his own story, i.e., in the movie we have been watching: wife, mistress, La Saraghina, etc. The producer sees nothing strange, since he's now in Guido's head too, and keeps demanding that a choice be made. But Guido says they're all bad. Only the originals will do, after all, since no matter how talented the massive actress who imitates La Saraghina, she isn't the real thing.

A man whispers to Guido, as he sits dejectedy watching the tests, that Claudia, whom he knew years ago as a young actress, wants to see him about a part. Guido follows him eagerly, is excited to find that Claudia (played by Claudia Cardinale) looks exactly like the Muse (also played by Cardinale) he has already encountered several times in mysterious and frustrating circumstances. He takes her for a night drive in his sports car to talk it over. The first thing she says is, "How big will my part be?" . . . Cut to a provincial town square, old houses facing each other, a baroque gateway closing one end, the whole giving the effect of an oblong room open to the sky: camera peers through the only window that is lit and we see Claudia the Muse, all in white, against white walls, setting a white table with fruit and wine—a lovely, poetic glimpse. (Gianni di Venanzo's photography alone would make *8 1/2* worth seeing.) Guido and the other Claudia drive into the square, but now all the windows are dark —his Muse has fled before her earthly (and earthy) twin. Stopping the car, Guido tries to explain his troubles to Claudia. "It's because you don't know how to make love," she replies, with a smile implying she could teach him. No, you're wrong, he insists, a woman cannot change a man. "Then you brought me here, you cheated me, and there's no part for me?" "Yes, there's no part for you," he replies wearily, "and there's no movie." Suddenly they are blinded by the headlights of three cars that roar into the square, bearing the producer and his aides. The producer tells Guido he has decided to get things started with a big press conference and party at the launching tower tomorrow morning. They all get into the cars and drive off. . . .

The journalists and cast and guests are gathered at the tower on the beach; it is cold and windy. (Someone says, "You kept us waiting so long—look, it's almost winter.") Waiters behind long tables with elaborate foods and drinks. Guido arrives, tries to escape, is seized by the arms and dragged to the speakers' table, past a lineup of reporters shouting questions in various languages. Everybody surges up to the table—more questions, pleas, insults—skirts and tablecloths billow in the wind, which is getting stronger—bedlam, babel, a Mad Hatter's press conference. Guido refuses to say anything since he has not even cast the movie yet. Producer, venomous aside: "I'll break you, I'll see that you never make another picture, you're ruining me." Guido dives under the table, crawls along on hands and knees, people reach down to grab him, he pulls out a pistol, puts it to his temple, a loud report. . . .

Guido alone on the beach except for some workmen on the towers. "Take it down," he shouts up at them, "all of it." Collaborator-critic appears, Guido explains he's decided not to make the picture. "You're absolutely right," says the critic, "I respect you." They get into Guido's car, the critic drones on congratulating Guido on having the courage not to make a mediocre film "that will leave a mark on the sands of time like the deformed footprint of a cripple." As Guido starts to drive away, the magician from an earlier scene—an old friend who seems to have occult powers—appears in front of the car in his top hat and tails, his face made up dead white with red lips and darkened eyes like a clown, smiling his professional smile (manic yet gentle) and pointing with his wand. Guido looks out of the car and sees his father and mother, who wave to him, then Claudia the Muse, smiling and beckoning, then the others from his past and present, all dressed in white. (The critic is still explaining why it's impossible to create in this age—he cannot see these people.) Guido gets out of the car, takes up his director's bullhorn and begins to arrange everybody; he has decided to make an entirely different movie, about himself—his memories, his women, his creative problems—in short, the movie we have just seen. Like Prospero in another drama with a most implausible happy ending, he summons them all: parents, wife, mistress, producer, technicians, actors, the Muse Claudia, even himself as a boy who leads a gay little parade of musical clowns. And they all come, walking up from the sea, pouring down from the steps of the launching tower, linking hands with Guido and his wife in a long line that dances along a seawall to the tinny blare of the circus band. The last shot is of the ten-year-old Guido, dressed in his seminarian's uniform (now white instead of black), strutting along proudly in front of his band.

Most of the critics have objected to this finale as bogus, escapist, sentimental, a specious "solution" that is incongruous with what has gone before, a happy ending arbitrarily tacked on, etc. In a generally favorable review in *Sight and Sound,* for instance, Eric Rhode writes in solemn disapproval: "Both Guido and Fellini show themselves incapable of making a distinction between the truths of the mind and those of behavior. The self-reflective spirit can swiftly turn narcissistic, and although Guido may confront his inner world, he fails to confront his social obligations." Or, as a psychiatrist objected to me: "He has failed to integrate reality and fantasy." This is all true—no confronting of social obligations, no integration of the real and the unreal, and plenty of escapism. I didn't for a minute believe that Guido had changed: the reconciliation with his wife—he asks her if their marriage can't be "saved" and she replies, "I can try if you will help me"—was unintegrated fantasy, as was the affectionate kiss he gives his mistress. On the plane of real behavior, his wife will continue to be censorious, his mistress will continue to be vulgar, and he will continue to betray both of them and will still greedily try to get love without giving love. The most that has happened in the "real" world is that Guido has achieved some insight—"I am what I am and not what I want to be"—which may or may not influence his future behavior; probably not. But he has triumphed in the "unreal" world of fantasy, which for him is the real one, since it is there he creates. In the sphere of the imagination, he *has* faced up to his problems and resolved them, for there he has made a work of art that hangs together and is consistent with itself. (I could never understand why "art for art's sake" is usually sneered at—for what better sake?) All through *8 1/2* Guido (and Fellini) are escaping from one kind of reality, but only in order to rush boldly and recklessly into another kind, the artist's kind. In this sense, the finale is consistent with what has gone before—and, in fact, its logical conclusion.

John Francis Lane wrote in a recent issue of *Sight and Sound:* "I'm afraid that however fond we may be of the director of *I Vitelloni* we are not really deeply concerned about his intellectual and sexual fetishes. Fellini has been too honest, too courageous, too sincere. He has made a film director's notebook, and I am not surprised that directors everywhere (even those who usually hate Fellini's films) love this picture." I think the implication of self-indulgent narcissism in the first sentence is wrong. Granted that, as Fellini was the first to insist ("more than a confession . . . my testament"), Guido is himself and *8 1/2* is his own Life and Hard Times, I think the miracle is how tough-minded his autobiography is, how he has been able to see himself at a distance, neither self-sparing nor self-flagellating, a wonderful Latin moderation throughout, realistic and ironic. Guido's hat, for instance, clerical black but worn at a lady-killing slant and with a worldly twist, is a perfect symbol of Fellini's own ambivalent feelings about the Church. Or there is the clowning he often uses to preserve his humanity in the movie jungle, such as kneeling between the marble lions at the foot of the hotel's grand stairway, salaaming and ululating gibberish salutations to the producer making his stately descent. Nothing duller than someone else's fetishes and neuroses, agreed, but I think in *8 1/2* Fellini has found the objective forms in which to communicate his subjective explorations.

A major theme of the film is aging, which obviously worries Fellini. He expresses it not in Bergmanesque symbols or narcissistic musings, but in episodes that arise naturally out of the drama: the elderly patients lining up for the curative waters; the senile cardinal; Guido's friend, the aging diplomat (who looks very much like him, with a decade or two added) who is divorcing his wife to marry one of his daughter's school friends and whom we see, doggedly jaunty, doing the twist with his nymphet fiancée, sweat pouring from a face set in an agonized grin; the aging actress who desperately cries out to Guido as he tries to escape politely: "I am a very passionate woman—you'll see!"; the magician reading the dowager's thoughts: "You would like to live another hundred years." One of the most sympathetic traits of Guido is the patience, gentleness, humor—the good manners of an old and tolerant culture—with which he responds to the reproaches of everybody around him, reproaches all the more irritating because they are justified. He is less patient, however, when the nerve of old age is touched. He encourages an old stagehand with acting ambitions to do a soft-shoe dance and croak out a song, then dismisses him brutally. *Memento mori.* So with the half dozen dignified old men his assistant has rounded up for extra parts: "How old are you?" he asks each. "Seventy-one," "sixty-three," "eighty-four," etc. "You're not old enough," he says, turning away contemptuously. The theme is stated most fully in a scene in the corridor outside the production office (where everybody has been working in a Kafkaesque-bureaucratic frenzy at three in the morning) when Guido is waylaid by his elderly assistant director,

Conocchia, who begins by weeping into his handkerchief ("You don't trust me, you won't let me help you, you tell me nothing, I was once your friend"), and works himself up into a rage: "I've been in movies thirty years—we used to do things you'd never dare!" Guido, who has been listening with his usual ironical patience, like a man waiting for a thunderstorm to pass, suddenly explodes: "Get out, leave me alone, you . . . old man!" (Two young men from the production office poke their heads out: *"Vecchio? Vecchio?"*) But Conocchia has the last word. "You're not the man you used to be!" he shouts as Guido walks away.

I hazard that *8 1/2* is Fellini's masterpiece precisely because it is about the two subjects he knows the most about: himself and the making of movies. He doesn't have to labor his points, he can move freely, quickly, with the ease of a man walking about his own home. And so much can be suggested in so little footage! That tall, aristocratic blonde, for instance, Guido glimpses several times in the hotel. She fascinates him because she looks like the heroine of an international spy thriller; he never meets her (the closest he comes is to put her into his dream harem), but he does overhear her end of a long-distance telephone conversation, which sounds like a bad movie script but which vastly intrigues him. Several kinds of parody are intertwined in this tiny episode: of movie clichés, of Guido's romantic eroticism, and—a feedback—of a man whose job it is to fabricate these glamorous stereotypes, himself falling for them. Successful parody is possible only when the parodist feels "at home with" (significant phrase) his subject. This familiarity also means that Fellini is able to keep *8 1/2* right down to earth, so that what might have been one more labored exercise in fantasy—like De Sica's *Miracle in Milan,* for instance—is spontaneous, lifelike and often very funny. I think Fellini has become the greatest master of social comedy since Lubitsch.

8 1/2 takes us further inside the peculiar world of movie-making than any other film I know. I once asked the Argentine director, Torre Nilsson, why important movie directors seem to lose their creative powers so much more often—and completely—than major artists in other fields. (I was thinking of Welles and Hitchcock.) He replied: "In movies, once you make a success, you become public property; you are overwhelmed with fame, money, women, admirers, promoters, and you can never get away from it. A painter or writer or composer creates by himself, but directors have to have hundreds of other people around all the time. So they burn themselves out early." When I saw *8 1/2,* I saw what he meant. Guido is distracted in the literal sense: "to divide [the mind, attention, etc.] between objects." They're all here: the highbrow journalist who asks about his philosophy, and also the lowbrow one—"Couldn't you tell me something about your love life?"; the producer who bullies him about the production schedule and the accountants who nag him about costs; the property man who begs Guido to take on as extras his giggling teen-age "nieces"; the playboy who wants him to sit up all night drinking; the man who waylays him in the lobby, waving a script: "It shows the necessity of universal disarmament; only a man of your courage and integrity could do it"; the press agents and tourists and mistresses, including his own. All there, and each wants a slice of him.

The reviews of *8 1/2* in the newspapers and in magazines like *Newsweek* and *The New Yorker* have been enthusiastic. The public likes it, too. But the "little-magazine" critics have been cool and wary, as though they felt they were being conned. Their objections, remarkably uniform, suggest to me that the trouble with serious film criticism today is that it is too serious.

> All these sequences are so magnificently filmed that the breath is hardly left to voice a query as to what they mean. Gianni di Venanzo's black-and-white photography and Piero Gherardi's sets and costumes provide such visual magic that it seems pointless to make philosophical reservations on the film's content. Yet the sheer beauty of Fellini's film . . . is deceiving us. (John Francis Lane in *Sight and Sound.*)

He goes on to complain of "pretentiousness of subject matter" and "artistic inflation." It's true, beauty and art are deceivers ever. The pea is never under the shell Fellini has given us every reason to believe contains it. In James and Conrad this is called ambiguity.

> The trouble seems to come from another quarter—moral and intellectual content. Fellini's last three films seem to me to rank in merit according to the amount of "meaning" in each. *La Dolce Vita* fairly reeked of "meaning," with its Christ symbols, parallels to Dante, moral indictment of a contemporary life style, and what not. [This is not ironical—D.M.] The *Boccaccio '70* episode had its little fabulated moral. But *8 1/2* has little or no intellectual content. The difference shows in the very titles. *La Dolce Vita* evokes a moral tradition of some kind. *The Temptation of Dr. Antonio* (with

its echo of "The Temptation of St. Anthony") prepares us for religious allegory. But *8 1/2* drives us right back into Fellini's biography. . . . The artist's promise of a moral or intellectual "point" bribes us (me) to take part in his (my) illicit fantasies. Without an intellectual superstructure, his personal fantasy fails to engage other persons. (Norman N. Holland in *Hudson Review.*)

It would be needlessly cruel to comment on these stiff-jointed lucubrations, though I can't help wondering what the quotes around meaning mean. Does he "mean" it? In addition to his other burdens, Mr. Holland groans under a massive load of primitive Freudianism. Maybe this explains why he dares to express openly a puritan nervousness when confronted by useless beauty that his colleagues express more discreetly.

Since *La Dolce Vita,* Fellini's films have been following a trend that certainly culminates in *8 1/2*. [Briefest trend in cultural history since the only Fellini film between *Vita* and *8 1/2* was the half-hour episode in *Boccaccio 70*—D.M.] It is the triumph of style over content. At the end of *8 1/2* we are excited not because Fellini has told us something significant about the artistic process, but because he has found such a visually exciting metaphor for his idea that it does not matter if this idea is not quite first-rate. . . . Nothing very significant is said about illusion and reality, dream and art. (Gary Carey in *The Seventh Art.*)

True that when it comes to making significant statements about illusion and reality and other high topics, Fellini is "not quite first-rate" compared to, say, Dr. Erwin Panofsky, of the (Princeton) Institute of Advanced Studies, whose 1934 essay, "Style and Medium in the Moving Pictures," is a classic. But I doubt that Dr. Panofsky, a modest and sensible man, would claim he could have made *8 1/2,* any more than Fellini, also sensible if not modest, would aspire to a professorship of, say, Cinematic Philosophy. Mr. Carey ends his review on the usual sub-puritan note: "*8 1/2* is really a visual experience, its only profundity resting there." And what better resting place?

Fellini's latest "autobiographical" oddity. . . . The nicest possible thing one could say is that he had had the guts to try and shove this particular form of lachrymose sexuality into the environs of art. . . . Of course, the result is horrendously pretentious. . . . She [Anouk Aimée as the wife] is where Fellini's vulgarity positively beckons us into attention and in so doing ruins a fantasy. He just can't deal with the grown-up issues she incarnates. But as a cinematic outlet for the imagination—the sort of stuff a director like Fellini *can* cope with . . . the film is extraordinary. . . . *8 1/2* looks marvelous and doesn't matter much of a damn. (John Coleman in the London *New Statesman.*)

No comment.

The tone is never sure, but falters between irony and self-pity, between shamefaced poeticism and tongue-tied self-mockery. . . . The second failure . . . [is] ignorance. . . . *8 1/2* piles problem upon problem, which is permissible; but sheds no light, which is not. . . . Fellini, apparently afraid of becoming a self-repeater with diminishing returns as so many famous Italian directors have become, tries for something new: symbolism, metaphysics, solid intellectual content. . . . What made Fellini's early films great . . . was their almost total avoidance of intellectualizing. (John Simon in *The New Leader.*)

The first sentence seems to me about as obtuse or perverse or both as you could get in eighteen words: I detected no self-pity, but on the contrary was impressed by the objectivity with which Fellini presented himself and his most personal worries; the poeticism was real poetry, and it was far from shamefaced, in fact it was blatant, exuberant; and any critic who could apply the adjective "tongue-tied" to Fellini, always fluent to the point of garrulity, must have an ax to grind. Mr. Simon's was a polemical one: his review is unique in finding nothing to praise in *8 1/2.* The closest he comes is: "Despite two or three good scenes [not specified] it is a disheartening fiasco." (It pains me to write thus, or should anyway, since I respect Mr. Simon's critical acumen so much that I wrote an introduction to his recent collection of essays, *Acid Test.*) Why "ignorance" is a fault in an artist I don't see, nor why he has to solve any problems except those of constructing a work of art, which are difficult enough. Shakespeare was a bit of an ignoramus—"little Latin and less Greek" —nor do we expect *King Lear* to "shed light" on geriatrics. I agree that Fellini is no thinker, and that he is at his worst when he intellectualizes. I also agree that "all the principal characters . . . are sublimely dichotomous," that "the dialogue bulges with antinomies," and that Fellini isn't in the same league as "the great masters of ambiguity—Pirandello, Brecht, Valéry, Eliot." Compared to that Yankee lineup, he's a busher. But all this is beside the point since, at least as I read *8 1/2,* Fellini is *not* trying for "symbolism, metaphysics [or] solid intellectual content."

This brings me to the crux of my quarrel with the all-too-serious critics (an exception was Jack Hirschman's jazzy paean in *Film Quarterly*) and indeed to what I see as the crux of the film itself. Because it is technically sophisticated, and because it deals with major areas of experience, these critics look for philosophical depths in a movie which is superficial—I think deliberately—in every way except as a work of art. They call Fellini a phony for not delivering the goods, but I don't see his signature on their bill of lading. On the contrary, some of the best comedy in his film is provided by intellectuals: the affected young beauty who has written a treatise on "The Solitude of Modern Man in the Contemporary Theater"; the highbrow British reporter who pesters Guido with questions like, "Is it that you cannot communicate? Or is that merely a mask?" And above all the collaborator who has been assigned to help Guido complete his script —an eye-glassed, beaknosed superintellectual whose lean face is fixed in lines of alert, sour suspicion. This personage—listed in the cast credits as The Writer, and played with waspish authority by Jean Rougeul—is endlessly articulate about the script; it's narcissistic ("just another film about your childhood"), romantic, pretentious, tasteless, and mindless: "Your main problem is the film lacks ideas, it has no philosophical base. It's merely a series of senseless episodes. . . . It has none of the merits of the avant-garde film and all the drawbacks." How can a director make more explicit his rationale? Life imitated art, as elsewhere in this strange film* and the actual highbrow critics reacted to *8 1/2* much as The Writer did to Guido's script. Several people I've talked to—and I must admit there is as much conversational as printed opposition to *8 1/2*—have suggested that The Writer is merely a ploy by Fellini to disarm his critics by making all their points in advance; they might have added the American woman who at the end shouts, "He's lost. He hasn't anything to say." Maybe. But he was a good prophet. For the "serious" critics have by now become habituated to profound, difficult

*"Fellini found himself embarked, with costly sets built and stars under contract, on a kind of explanatory sequel to *La Dolce Vita,*" reports *The New Statesman.* When he found this didn't work, he did what Guido did—switched to a film about himself, that is, about a famous director who finds himself blocked on a film. Reality came as close to overwhelming Fellini as it did Guido. According to *Sight and Sound:* "Two weeks before *8 1/2* opened in Rome he still hadn't made up his mind how to end it."

films that must be "interpreted" from the language of art (what's on the screen) into the language of philosophy (what what's on the screen "really means"). It began with Bergman (whom I've always thought strongest at his shallowest) and reached a comic climax in the recent efforts of Franco-American *auteur* critics to read *The Birds* as a morality play about Modern Civilization, and a pathetic one in the efforts of almost everybody to make sense out of that triumph of non- and indeed anti-sense, *Last Year at Marienbad*—everybody except its creators, who said they themselves disagreed on what it "meant."

The off-putting quality of *8 1/2* for all but the less intellectualized critics (and the public) is that it is nothing but a pleasurable work of art which might have been directed by Mozart—and there were no doubt pundits in his day who deplored the frivolous way he played around with Masonic symbolism in *The Magic Flute.* It is a worldly film, all on the surface: humorous, rhetorical, sensuous, lyrical, witty, satiric, full of sharply realistic detail and also of fantastic scenes like the great one in the steam bath. The essence of *8 1/2* is here: the visual panache of the movie-makers making their way down the stairs, swathed in sheets like Roman senators and wreathed in smoky steam like the damned going down to hell, terrific but also just a touch burlesque on Biblical spectaculars—the loudspeaker, "Guido, Guido. His Eminence will see you now"—the burlesque becoming strident as Guido's colleagues push around him, warning, "Don't hold anything back from His Eminence," while they ask him to put in a word for them, and then turning to satire, as Guido stands before the aged Cardinal (also wrapped in a sheet, bony neck and chest bare, mist swirling about him like God's mantle) and complains, "I'm not happy, Your Eminence." "Why should you be, my son?" the Cardinal replies with unexpected vigor. "That's not your job in life. . . . *Nulla salvatio extra ecclesiam.* . . . That which is not of God is of the Devil." The scene closes with an exterior shot of a small cellar window that swings slowly shut as if excluding the sinner *(extra ecclesiam)* from the heaven within. There is plenty of symbolism here, indeed every shot is a metaphor, but they are all as obvious as the closing window. This is perhaps the difficulty; nothing for the interpretative tooth to mumble, no Antonionian *angst,* no Bergmanesque Godhead, no Truffaut-style existential Absurd to perplex us. Like Baroque art, of which it is a belated golden ray, *8 1/2* is complicated but not obscure. It is more Handel than Beethoven—

objective and classical in spirit as against the romantic subjectivism we are accustomed to. It's all there, right on the surface, like a Veronese or a Tiepolo.

One could drop still another name, the greatest of all. Is there not something Shakespearean in this range of human experience expressed in every mode from high lyric to low comic, from the most formal rhetoric to the most personal impressionism? And don't the critics remind one of those all-too-serious students who try to discover "Shakespeare's philosophy" and always fail because Shakespeare hadn't any; his "ideas" were all *ad hoc;* their function was to solve dramatic rather than philosophical problems. As Jack Hirschman writes: "Fellini has . . . come free of that awful psycho-philosophical air which pervades *La Dolce Vita.* . . . In *8 1/2* people are on earth not because they are destined to be trapped by cultural despair, but because they are destined to play out the roles of their individual realities."

Finally, in *8 1/2* Fellini steals from everybody, just like Shakespeare. "Theft" on this scale becomes synthesis: *8 1/2* is an epitome of the history of cinema. His thefts are creative because they are really borrowings, which are returned with the fingerprints of the thief all over them. The childhood episodes are Bergmanesque chiaroscuro, as is the great scene on the beach when La Saraghina dances for the schoolboys, which echoes, right down to the brutal beat of the music, an even greater beach scene, that between the soldiers and the clown's wife at the beginning of *Naked Night:* but this is a Latin Bergman, sensuous and dramatic and in no way profound. When Guido and his wife quarrel in the hotel bedroom, the bleak failure to make contact (and the austere photography) recall Antonioni, but *this* alienated couple don't suffer in silence, they yell at each other. The early scene in the rest-cure garden is full of heroic close-ups à la Eisenstein, but they are used (like "The Ride of the Valkyries" thundered out by the hotel band) for satiric counterpoint to the aging, prosaic faces of the invalids. The general structure—a montage of tenses, a mosaic of time blocks—recalls *Intolerance, Kane,* and *Marienbad,* but in Fellini's hands it becomes light, fluid, evanescent. And delightfully obvious.

THE PASSION OF ANNA (1970)

By John Simon

Ingmar Bergman's *A Passion* (released here as *The Passion of Anna*) records the interplay of four people on the small Swedish island where Bergman lives, the microcosm into which he likes to fit his far-ranging universal visions. The main character is Andreas Winkelman, a man who has relegated his feelings as far inside, and other people as far outside and away from him, as possible. He has, we learn at one point, been in prison: he had passed bad checks, been drunk, and violently resisted arrest. We also gather that his wife, a sculptress, left him. From the vast number of books in his house, we deduce that he is some kind of littérateur. We do not even know how these few data interrelate, if indeed they do. Yet this sketchy Andreas is the perfect carrier for the psychic disease he suffers from, and its articulate mouthpiece.

Certain island neighbors begin to impinge on his life. Anna Fromm comes to use his telephone when hers is out of order, makes a highly emotional plea to someone called Elis with reference to her dead husband and child, is rebuffed in some money matter, and departs distraught. In the handbag she leaves behind, Andreas discovers a farewell letter from her late husband, also called Andreas. The letter points out that though the couple love each other, they cannot help inflicting reciprocal psychic and physical torture, and must separate. When Winkelman goes to return the letter, Anna is asleep, but her dearest friends, Eva and Elis Vergérus, invite him in; he politely refuses.

He does, however, come to dinner one day. Here he learns that Elis is a famous architect who has been commissioned to build a cultural center in Milan, though he is totally cynical about the project, culture, and life in general. His wife, Eva, appears to be a charming, easy-going young woman, placidly dependent on her husband, yet Andreas has previously come upon her dozing in her car in broad daylight, because of a fierce insomnia she suffers from at night. But the big surprise of the evening is the somewhat mousy Anna's vehement tirade against cynicism, disbelief, and lies. As she holds up her memories of a happy, truth-telling marriage that sustain her through life, Andreas remembers the letter from his namesake. That night, having been invited to sleep over, he is awakened by the screams of Anna, who has had some dreadful nightmare.

Next morning, Elis takes Andreas to the handsome old mill he has turned into a studio; tells him about the car accident in which Anna, who drove, escaped with injuries, while her husband and child were killed; and shows him a huge, carefully filed collection of photographs. These, taken by himself as well as clipped from all over, show human beings and faces in every kind of situation, but particularly in emotional crises. It emerges that the dead Andreas was a potential genius, and that, though they loved each other, he and Anna fought constantly. Although Andreas promises to pose for Elis, he is upset by the architect's cynical bitterness, especially by the casual revelation that Elis's wife had been the dead Andreas's mistress, "quite above board."

Andreas goes on a binge, howls his name across the winter landscape, collapses, and is eventually dragged home by Johan Andersson, a lowly firewood-peddler, to whom he has been kind on occasion. Eva, bored and restless during one of Elis's absences on business, comes to Andreas and has a brief fling with him, all the while protesting her love for her husband, whom she cannot meaningfully reach. Andreas goes to Elis's studio to be photographed; Elis extracts a confession of his crime and imprisonment, but agrees to underwrite a bank loan for him, even engages him to write up his architectural notes, thus obligating and subjugating Andreas all the more. We learn from Eva, in an effusion of sympathy, that Andreas and Anna have become lovers, and the rest of the film concerns their unsuccessful affair. By slow stages of attrition, they reach the point where each comes close to killing the other and must, finally, part.

Now *A Passion* does have a central weakness: a good deal of it has to be taken on faith, on somebody's word; we do not even find out such basic things as the source of Andreas's income. But it is a weakness that reinforces two of the main themes. First, that things are not as people say they are—because all speakers lie, deceive themselves, or are simply ignorant—and still we sometimes have to believe them, for there is nothing else to go on. Second, that people so utterly lose the sense of their identity that their professions, like everything else about them, become irrelevant, interchangeable. The fact that Andreas's house has no electric light and can nevertheless harbor a functioning TV set and other electrical appliances is a genuine inconsistency, but a slight one.

What enchants in *A Passion* is the evocative power of the photography, although this is only Bergman's second color film. Sven Nykvist, the cinematographer, has caught in the outdoor shots a thin, almost constipated color: the austerely wintry woods and blur of a distant sea, the anemic skies with a beclouded sun that looks like a reflector beam rendered impotent by fog—these have a way of emerging as faintly tinted lithographs, beautiful but chilling. Yet it is indoors that Bergman and Nykvist work their greatest wonders. In every indoor sequence a certain color or color combination significantly predominates, without the obtrusiveness of such experiments in recent films by Fellini, Antonioni, and others.

Thus in a moment of contentment, like the dinner party, everything is an opulent bronze color, a bronze that happily subsumes the flush of animated faces and the gold of candlelight. When Eva comes to visit Andreas, they play a favorite dance record from his student days, "Always Romantic"—it is almost the only time there is music on the soundtrack—and, for a while, the whole film goes red. This is introduced by a quick shot of a light streaming through a red pane on the front door: Bergman admits that he is about to use a filmic device, but one that faithfully records the red light of nascent passion turned on in the mind. It is not a harsh, declamatory red, like that of the pool scene in *Fellini Satyricon;* it is rather the coral glow of healthy cheeks or remembered sunsets, appetizing rather than strident.

Even more impressive are the seemingly natural color tonalities that are nevertheless emotionally slanted. The morning after Andreas's and Eva's dalliance, things take on a lividly viridescent cast—the hues, as it were, of faint nausea, shame, regret. Again, during Winkelman's and Anna's last car ride in a downpour, everything around them is in the silver-gray, gunmetal domain: the colors of metallic, cutting truth. And what makes the grayness even chillier is that it follows a sequence with a burning stable, all flaming red. Throughout the film, color schemes not only express moods but also contrast pointedly with the colors of what has been or is to come.

Sometimes, however, it is the combination of several colors

that is brilliantly provocative. So, in Elis's studio, the architect tempts Andreas with a liquor cabinet suddenly flung open. From among the very white walls there gleams out a dazzling array of variously colored liquor bottles, a veritable hoard of the Nibelungs or some other devilish treasure. Elis himself, in black and white quasi-clerical garb, surrounded by flame-red cardboard boxes, looks like a priest of hell.

The most eloquent device is the use of color and movement together. Thus the dinner party is all static closeups of burnished, warm gold, casting its grace over the solo arias each quartet member delivers in high style. But just as Anna finishes her paean to truth and love, Bergman cuts to a shot we have already seen: the dead Andreas's tortured farewell letter, with the camera moving in extreme closeup across the typescript. The letter is on grayish paper, particularly sobering after the golden glow, and the intense magnification gives the typed characters pathetically frazzled edges. The inexorable lateral movement of the camera, in strong contrast to its previous indulgent lingering over a face, is especially suggestive. This was the movement of the typewriter cylinder as the first Andreas wrote the words that were vainly trying to free him from his impossible relationship with Anna; and it is also the movement of the perusing eyes of the second Andreas, who, despite this dark knowledge, will be drawn into an equally gray affair with the woman. A lateral seesaw movement, then, that unites the two Andreases.

Or take the scene where Andreas and Eva begin their brief affair. Coming after an incarnadine sequence, it is all grays and blacks. Paradoxical but right: there is nothing "Always Romantic" about this fling, a mere humdrum, furtively snatched anodyne. And so, in front of a twilight-gray window, two faces in black silhouette play out an amazing ballet of teasing little comings together and drawings apart: the two dark, wavy lines of the profiles dance a *pas de deux* whose fluctuations are equally beautiful as human lovemaking and as sheer animated abstraction. Finally, the profiles merge in a long kiss and sink out of the image, leaving behind only a window frame dividing the film frame into unequal gray parts. Through the upper, larger one we dimly perceive a red barn: something like an abstract expressionist painting by Rothko or Gottlieb. And during all these pleasant preliminaries to sex with Andreas, Eva is telling him of her frustrated love for her husband, Elis.

Sound is no less important than sight in *A Passion*—whether it is dialogue, poetic, piercing, cogent; or simply sound: church bells, hammering, heavy breathing, the crisply impersonal clink of dishes during a loveless breakfast or, in an ugly, humiliating outdoor fight that follows, the crying of wind and crash of waves from afar. Bergman manipulates natural sounds as if they were notes in music: when desultory sheep bells become the very voice of melancholy isolation; or when a drunken Andreas bellows out his name into the silent recesses of winter, hoping for some answering voice to confirm his identity, and the obbligato of rusty and guttural foghorns offers only a mixture of mockery and indifference. And when Andreas eagerly fumbles with the papers he finds in Anna's bag, the unfurling of that letter with its message of physical and psychic violence is magnified in volume from a mere crinkling to a premonitory, doomful clatter.

These sounds sometimes echo one another. At the climax of Anna's horrible Easter dream (which in its themes, images, tone and shift to black-and-white photography alludes to the dreams of the heroine of *Shame,* and may very well be an outtake from that preceding and related film), Anna comes upon the mangled body of her dead son. We see her scream repeatedly, but the only sound we hear is the ticking of a clock. It is time that is the true enemy, the traducer who delivers us to death; the sound of the clock (which accompanied some previous scenes with cheerfully hypocritical innocence) churns away like a sick heartbeat about to explode. And this is an Easter dream; so much for resurrection.

What does get resurrected is that ticking. At the very end of the film, when Anna may have intended to drive both of them into death, she nevertheless answers Andreas's last question with words that are full of genuine love and humility. Then she drives off, perhaps forever. Now Andreas is left alone on the soggy, muddy road, and we see him in a long shot pacing hither and yon. But this is no ordinary pacing: one direction is that of Anna and staying together, the other is that of continued loneliness and exile from experience. As he keeps reversing his way, the camera slowly comes closer, as if to discover some resolution in his face. At the same time, the image, already grainy, begins to decompose even further, and, once again, we hear that ominous ticking of the clock. When the camera closes in on Andreas, overexposure makes him only just visible: he collapses in the mud, unable to choose either direction. Over the ticking comes the narrator's voice: "This time his name was Andreas

Winkelman," and the film ends in a whiteout. Yes, and the last time his name was Andreas Fromm. But that, surely, is not the only parallel intended. Another time his name will be yours, mine, Everyman's.

What is the philosophic content of *A Passion?* The insufficiency of life, the central hollowness beneath the sporadically rich surface. Note how brilliantly Bergman turns his spare chamber quartet into a prodigally orchestrated symphony. Andreas the brooder is complemented by Elis the inquirer (his last name, Vergérus, is that of the doctor in *The Magician,* another ruthless dissector in search of an ultimate truth), but an Elis who has to admit that his photographs provide no answer to the riddle of life. Anna, the self-deluding seeker for truth through love, is complemented by Eva, the unfulfilled wife who resorts to little affairs, dabbling and mendacious. And from here the film extends farther, upward and downward.

Upward there is the Vietnam war, which briefly but harrowingly appears on a television set. Downward there is the devastation in the animal kingdom wreaked by a maniac loose on the island, who goes about slashing sheep to death, hanging puppies, and setting horses on fire. People suspect the humble recluse Johan, Andreas's friend, and with vicious, blind cruelty drive the wood-peddler to death. Yet the crimes, for Johan was innocent, continue. Now there is a scene in which all these themes coalesce. Andreas and Eva are watching the Saigon chief of police gleefully executing away when a dull thud outside draws them from their TV set. A bird—it must have been frightened, Andreas says—accidentally collided in the dark with a wall of the house, and is now in agony. Andreas has to kill it with a stone, much like the stones with which the islanders hounded Johan to death.

But the simple Johan became suspect after a lost law case drove him into seclusion, just as Andreas withdrew after his unhappy bout with the law. The bird has to be killed; yet how horrible is its blood on Andreas's hands! It died because of darkness, aloneness, fright; in a similar lonely state of panic Andreas became an outlaw. So loneliness makes us suspicious and suspect; all of us are hangmen and victims, both of others and ourselves. And the death of the bird coincides exactly with the Vietnam executions on TV.

Bergman's overall mastery is accurately reflected in his mastery of detail. Two examples out of many: when Eva and Andreas have become lovers, there is a closeup of her face, horizontal across the screen, framed from below by Andreas's shoulder and beard, and from above by his bent arm around her. But this enfolding is not circular: what encloses and partly cuts off Eva's face is a lozenge, a diamond shape. Even the protection of intimacy we offer one another is not rounded and soft; it is diamond-hard and cold. And, again, when Andreas and Anna are having that terrible last fight in the rain-battered car, a toy bear suspended from the rear-view mirror jiggles between their faces grotesquely and piteously, duplicating the motions of Andreas's dachshund, which the maniac had hanged from a tree. The fine thing here is that no obvious symbol, no one-for-one comparison forces itself upon us. Rather, there are suggestions of several things: that the maniac, though Johan has died miserably, is still on the loose; that there are objective correlatives for our anguish in the world around us, inanimate things that fill up with our anger and hurt; and that what twists and trembles between Andreas and Anna, love turned to hate, is as deadly as any killer's madness.

As usual, the acting of Bergman's "repertory company" is magisterial. Liv Ullmann's Anna is a characterization of inexhaustible variety, ranging from healthy peasant to self-deluding rationalizer, from avenging angel to cracked porcelain figurine, which the touch of truth will shatter. When she tells Andreas about her marriage and the fatal accident, in a series of closeups in which the camera angle varies ever so slightly yet brilliantly, and the color of her eyes is picked up by the blue-green fabric of her armchair, she exudes an elemental womanliness and humanity that contrast profoundly and pitifully with the untruths she is uttering. Bibi Andersson's Eva is like Blake's "Songs of Innocence and Experience" recited simultaneously: this is someone playing an existential game, but you never know (any more than she does) whether the game is knowing or naïve, whether she is kicking the ball or whether she is herself the ball that is being kicked. Take the marvelous little scene when, after the night of lovemaking with Andreas, Eva gets into her car and is about to drive off but jumps out and—with a strange, out-of-context intensity—kisses the bemused Andreas seeing her off. Then she leaps back into the car and really drives away. That kiss, though; what was it? An attempt to turn fleshliness, retroactively, into sisterliness? The farewell to a passion that cannot continue, but wants to die with a crescendo? Or just a spontaneous outburst of tenderness from a woman whose impulses are squelched by her husband? There is something so rich in the lapidariness of Miss Andersson's performance that all three meanings inhere in the single gesture.

Then there is Erland Josephson's architect, cynical, smug, full of quiet bravado, yet subtly revealing fissures in his façade. When his wife and Andreas share a moment of tenderness at his studio while he is turning off a radio playing Bach, and then comes back in warningly humming the melody (the only other, almost subliminal, appearance of music on the sound track), the ominous expression on Elis's face subsumes pain, vindictiveness, and the visible effort to cover up the rift in its composure. Josephson conveys this welter of conflicting impulses in the record time of, I estimate, three seconds. As for Max von Sydow's Andreas, I am exhausted from the labor of ferreting out new superlatives, which every successive performance by this actor requires. His great talent lies in perfectly fusing strength and weakness, as if they had been run through a blender, so that what comes out is so much of a piece that you do not know whether a given movement or inflection is an upsurge of power or a paroxysm of impotence. He can look noble and beautiful when he is saying something abject or terrible; he can do something contemptible and make it appear the essence of manliness. He is, in short, a master of ambiguity.

And speaking of ambiguity, *A Passion* contains a curious, much debated device. At four points the action of the film stops, and one of the four principals (each gets his turn) is given the chance to discuss, as an actor or private person, the character he or she is portraying. What the problems of enacting the role are, what the portrayer thinks the mainsprings of the character to be, what the character might develop into after the end of the film. One justification for the device is that it comes at moments of almost unbearable tension, and provides relief—to be sure, not comic relief, but relief through Brechtian distancing. It also affords a more expressly analytical view of the character, in accordance with Brechtian precepts, and a chance to evaluate him in the additional context of the actor's opinions. Finally, the device permits us to see how different these actors are in real life, how far beyond their quotidian selves their artistry has taken them.

The film has been exploitatively renamed in America by United Artists *The Passion of Anna,* with supposed suggestions of a woman in heat. But it must clearly be *a* passion: Anna's, Eva's, Elis's, Andreas's—anybody's. All these passions intersect, merge for a moment, feed on and destroy one another. Together, they spell a passion of suffering, like Christ's, only here the collective Calvary of all mankind.

CRITICAL METHOD

What eventually became the preface to Robert Warshow's posthumous collection of essays, *The Immediate Experience,* was first written by him in 1954 as an application for a Guggenheim Fellowship. In this essay, Warshow, with characteristic clarity and modesty, explains his dissatisfaction with two earlier serious types of film criticism, both of which, he says, "have tended to slight the fundamental *fact* of movies, a fact at once aesthetic and sociological but also something more." Warshow proposes simple candor and an act of self-integration ("I have not brought Henry James to the movies or the movies to Henry James, but I hope I have shown that the man who goes to the movies is the same man who reads James") as the only solution for intellectuals faced with a medium that is both popular culture and art. "A man watches a movie, and a critic must acknowledge that he is that man." This may seem self-evident *now* (film criticism having grown increasingly personal, even confessional), but when Warshow wrote these words intellectuals frequently twisted themselves into knots trying to find some suitable framework for discussing movies—anything but admit how much they enjoyed the fantasies on screen or how far their own fantasies were implicated. Warshow's essays helped do away with a lot of the old condescension and hypocrisy.

John Simon's "A Critical Credo" proposes unlimited (and largely unrealized) possibilities for film and a traditional function of upholding standards and improving taste for film criticism. His insistence on the evil of bad movies is both a stirring testimonial to the power of art and a useful justification for extreme critical violence; certainly *evil* must be met with stern measures. Simon remains one of those critics who have concerned themselves strictly with aesthetic evaluation, never with the "something more" in movies that has fascinated Warshow and so many others.

Most critics, I believe, have oscillated between a platonic view (such as Simon's) of ideal artistic solutions against which all specific attempts must be ruthlessly measured, and the more pragmatic approach of judging each film by how well it fulfills the expectations of its *type,* even when these expectations are rather modest (Is movie X a *good* low-budget horror film?). Critics relying exclusively on the first attitude are endlessly attacking films for failing to do what they never set out to do; critics relying exclusively on the second can easily fall into a slack, complacent acceptance of modest ambitions, never challenging the "given."

The debate in the sixties between Andrew Sarris and Pauline Kael over the value of Sarris's formulation of the *auteur* theory may be familiar to some readers, but I saw no reason to omit it on that account: It remains the closest thing we have had to a *Kulturkampf* (there were numerous allies on both sides) in the history of American film criticism and the basic issues haven't diminished in importance. In addition, keeping these statements in print is the only way of preventing further misrepresentation. For instance, Sarris did not assert that directors were responsible for everything creative in movies or that all directors were *auteurs* or that all films by directors who *were auteurs* should be considered of equal interest or value. (Nor does Sarris function as an *auteurist* in everything he writes. To indicate the diversity of his interests, I've included here his review of *State of Siege,* in which the multiple images of critic as public figure, as citizen, as aesthete, as skeptical post-Orwell liberal, as civil libertarian, etc., all come into brilliant focus in a single article.) On the other side of the argument, Kael has never been *against* directors assuming creative control of moviemaking; if you read her with any care at all, you can see she is arguing for a different definition of *auteur*—the director who writes his own scripts as well as directs, rather than the director (as Sarris would have it) who works within the studio system and imposes his personality on the material given to him.

The reader will notice that I have omitted Sarris's first (1962) "tentative" formulation of the theory—the article that Kael attacks. I did so for two reasons: a) she herself summarizes the piece at great length; and b) Sarris answers some of her criticisms in a later (1968) and richer exposition of his ideas, the essay, included here, that served as the introduction to his best-known work, *The American Cinema. The American Cinema,* often called "the *auteurist* bible," is an attempt to rewrite American film history in terms of the careers of individual directors, starting with the greatest and working down to those of lesser interest. Sarris looked for thematic consistency as well as quality, evaluating a director's work as a coherent or incoherent whole, as personal expression or impersonal craftsmanship—in any case, as a totality. For obvious reasons, then, *auteur* criticism is of greater value in judging new films by directors with a body of work behind them than new films by young directors who have no established themes or styles to evaluate. Indeed, it was partly the fear that *auteur* critics would respond inadequately to what is *new* in film art that drove Kael to such extremes of anger.

If one judges by ultimate influence (leaving aside the question of who is right), it appears that Sarris won the battle. The reorganization of film studies at universities, the flood of books on directors, the revival of many obscure American films in directors' retrospectives (obviously not the *only* way films are revived), the attitudes of young critics and scholars (some of whom have used *auteur* criticism as a mere convenience), the greater emphasis on directorial personality in the work of older critics, the portraits of Sarris's *auteurs* in the popular public television series, "The Men Who Made the Movies"—all of this attests to the progress of the *auteur* theory in the world outside film magazines.

Which is not to say that *auteurism* has passed through a single season without explicit challenge. One of the most important challenges was Richard Corliss's book *Talking Pictures* (1974), from which I have reprinted the introduction. Corliss's work, avowedly "a response to and expansion of Sarris's *The*

American Cinema," also traces thematic patterns and consistencies, but in the work of screenwriters, rather than directors. Corliss's principal quarrel with the *auteur* theory is that it largely relinquished its original intention of analyzing visual style as the key to directorial temperament, settling instead into analysis of thematic structure. Since the *theme* of a movie, says Corliss, is the writer's province, not the director's, the writer who imposes his ideas on a variety of directors should be valued as a central creative force in film history. The *auteur* turns out to be an author after all.

In effect, Corliss is calling for a more detailed and scholarly version of the old film-is-a-collaborative-art attitude. Ideally, film criticism would consist of a painstaking, detective-like routine, in which the creative contributions of directors, writers, cinematographers, set-designers, actors, and producers all would be included as variables in any given judgment.—*Ed.*

PREFACE TO THE IMMEDIATE EXPERIENCE* (1954)

By Robert Warshow

The movies—and American movies in particular—stand at the center of that unresolved problem of "popular culture" which has come to be a kind of nagging embarrassment to criticism, intruding itself on all our efforts to understand the special qualities of our culture and to define our own relation to it. That this relation should require definition at all is the heart of the problem. We are all "self-made men" culturally, establishing ourselves in terms of the particular choices we make from among the confusing multitude of stimuli that present themselves to us. Something more than the pleasures of personal cultivation is at stake when one chooses to respond to Proust rather than Mickey Spillane, to Laurence Olivier in *Oedipus Rex* rather than Sterling Hayden in *The Asphalt Jungle.* And when one has made the "right" choice, Mickey Spillane and Sterling Hayden do not disappear; perhaps no one gets quite out of sight of them. There is great need, I think, for a criticism of "popular culture" which can acknowledge its pervasive and disturbing power without ceasing to be aware of the superior claims of the higher arts, and yet without a bad conscience. Such a criticism finds its best opportunity in the movies, which are the most highly developed and most engrossing of the popular arts, and which seem to have an almost unlimited power to absorb and transform the discordant elements of our fragmented culture.

Serious film criticism has tended to fall into two general types. The first is that criticism which seeks to validate the film's claim to a position of "equality" among the older arts, emphasizing in one way or another the formal qualities of the medium and the self-consciousness of the film artist. Such criticism is likely to base itself on some fairly clear concept of the "cinematic" and to use this as

*This Preface originally formed the Statement of Project submitted with the application for a Guggenheim Fellowship, October 1954. Several paragraphs at the end, relevant only to the application, have been deleted.

a standard of judgment. Depending on the critic's predilections, he may think of the "cinematic" as residing primarily in visual patterns (a view which leads toward abstract films) or as residing primarily in the medium's power of "truthful" representation (a view which leads toward documentary films). In either case, it is typical of this criticism to place great stress on matters of technique, to minimize the importance of film actors in favor of directors (who are regarded as the artists of the medium), and, very often, to deplore the introduction of sound, and especially of dialogue, as having impaired the purity of the medium. In this category of criticism are such well-known works as Rudolf Arnheim's *Film als Kunst* (1931) and Sergei Eisenstein's *The Film Sense* (1942) and *Film Form* (1949).

More recently there has developed a second type of criticism which either minimizes the aesthetic problem or ignores it altogether, treating the films (along with other forms of popular culture) as indexes to mass psychology or, sometimes, the "folk spirit." Criticism of this sort ranges from the discovery of direct correspondences between the movies and life (e.g., the prevalence of themes of violence in American movies either reflects or encourages violence in American life) to the complex and "deep" interpretations of psychoanalysis (e.g., the relegation of women to a minor role in Western movies, and the supposedly "phallic" character of the Western hero's gun, indicate a latent homosexuality in the movie audience). Ideas of film aesthetics need not be excluded, but they are subordinate to the primary aim of sociological analysis. Thus, the sociological critic who is alive to the aesthetics of the movies will not make the mistake of assuming that the effect of a film can be conveyed by recounting its plot, or that the repetition of a theme is necessarily a measure of its importance, but he will still be concerned with those elements which he believes to be affecting or expressing "the audience" rather than with what he himself responds to. Sometimes, indeed, the sociological critic may try to resolve this difficulty—if he feels it as a difficulty—by a kind of forced identification with "the audience"; sociology and aesthetics then become one, "mass psychology" is likely to become "myth," and aesthetic value is likely to be identified with "mythic" intensity. The detached (if not necessarily objective) tone of social science is more typical, however, and if there are value judgments, they usually refer not to the films in themselves but to the social facts which the films are believed to reflect. Excellent examples of this type of criticism are Siegfried

Kracauer's *From Caligari to Hitler* (1947), a study of German films during the period of the Weimar Republic, and Nathan Leites and Martha Wolfenstein's *Movies: A Psychological Study* (1950). David Riesman has also made use of the films in his more general studies of American life.

No student of the films can fail to acknowledge his debt to the brilliant work that has been done in these two broad fields of criticism; out of that work has emerged the general outline within which all future discussion must find its place. I think it may be said nevertheless that both these approaches, in their separate ways, have tended to slight the fundamental *fact* of the movies, a fact at once aesthetic and sociological but also something more. This is the actual, immediate experience of seeing and responding to the movies as most of us see them and respond to them. A critic may extend his frame of reference as far as it will bear extension, but it seems to me almost self-evident that he should start with the simple acknowledgment of his own relation to the object he criticizes; at the center of all truly successful criticism there is always a man reading a book, a man looking at a picture, a man watching a movie. Critics of the films, caught in the conflict between "high culture" and "popular culture," have too often sought to evade this confrontation.

The sociological critic is likely to be the more guilty, holding the experience of the movies entirely at arm's length. Indeed, it might be said that he pretends not to go to the movies at all; he merely investigates a social or psychological "phenomenon"—something, that is, which involves others. Even when he does try to acknowledge his own part in the experience, it is only by treating himself as one of the "others," just as a psychiatrist may observe the symptoms of neurosis in himself but by the very act of observation achieves a kind of momentary exemption. The aesthetic critic, on the other hand, may be perfectly willing to acknowledge his relation to the object—but only after he has transformed the object. For what he seeks in the films is almost always something that he can recognize as "legitimate" to the world of art—which is to say, analogous to the effects of other art forms on their highest levels. He goes to the movies, he would have us believe, as one goes to concerts or the ballet. No doubt his claim is often a truthful one; there is art in the movies, and there is an "art" cinema. Many of the products of the "art" cinema well deserve all the praise they have received. And yet, I think, one cannot long frequent the "art" cinema or read much of the criticism which upholds it without a sense of incompleteness and even of irrelevance. Really the movies are not quite that "legitimate" —they are still the bastard child of art, and if in the end they must be made legitimate, it will be a changed household of art that receives them. (Something of the sort has happened with the novel, I think.) The process cannot be rushed, and the critic whose chief concern is to advance the film's claim to legitimacy is evading the issue. The sociological critic says to us, in effect: It is not *I* who goes to see the movies; it is the audience. The aesthetic critic says: It is not the *movies* I go to see; it is art.

To state what seems to me the proper course for film criticism is not so easy as to express my sense of the shortcomings of the older approaches. I can do best, I think, by writing in personal terms.

I have gone to the movies constantly, and at times almost compulsively, for most of my life. I should be embarrassed to attempt an estimate of how many movies I have seen and how many hours they have consumed. At the same time, I have had enough serious interest in the products of the "higher" arts to be very sharply aware that the impulse which leads me to a Humphrey Bogart movie has little in common with the impulse which leads me to the novels of Henry James or the poetry of T. S. Eliot. That there is a connection between the two impulses I do not doubt, but the connection is not adequately summed up in the statement that the Bogart movie and the Eliot poem are both forms of art. To define that connection seems to me one of the tasks of film criticism, and the definition must be first of all a personal one. A man watches a movie, and the critic must acknowledge that he is that man.

I also know very well that I do not go to the movies in order to discover what impulses are moving "the audience," though I am willing to make such discoveries when they happen to present themselves to me. Here again, it is I who go to the movies (perhaps I should say: alas!) not the sociologist in me, if there is a sociologist in me. And it must be that I go to the movies for the same reason that the "others" go: because I am attracted to Humphrey Bogart or Shelley Winters or Greta Garbo; because I require the absorbing immediacy of the screen; because in some way I take all that nonsense seriously. For I must make one more confession: I have seen a great many very bad movies, and I know when a movie is bad, but I have rarely been bored at the movies; and when I have been bored, it has usually been at a "good" movie.

I have been writing about the movies, off and on, since 1947, and in the past few years it seems to me I have been able to recognize in my work a point of view—perhaps I mean only a vocabulary—that begins to be adequate to the complexities of the subject, doing some justice to the claims both of art and of "popular culture," and remaining also, I hope, in touch with the basic relation of spectator and object. I have felt my work to be most successful when it has seemed to display the movies as an important element in my own cultural life, an element with its own qualities and interesting in its own terms, and neither esoteric nor alien. The movies are part of my culture, and it seems to me that their special power has something to do with their being a kind of "pure" culture, a little like fishing or drinking or playing baseball—a cultural fact, that is, which has not yet fallen altogether under the discipline of art. I have not brought Henry James to the movies or the movies to Henry James, but I hope I have shown that the man who goes to the movies is the same as the man who reads James. In the long run, I hope that my work may even make some contribution to the "legitimization" of the movies; but I do not think one can make such a contribution by pretending that "legitimization" has already taken place.

I propose now to produce a book of essays on the movies, dealing with various key aspects of the subject, which will adequately express this point of view. While I believe that I have by now developed a kind of "theory" of the movies, and would expect this theory to emerge from my book, it will be in no sense a theoretical work. There are many theories of the movies—who would not wish to be the Aristotle of a new art form? My own ambition, in the present work, is only to produce a body of criticism dealing with specific films and types of films, with certain actors, certain themes, and with two or three of the general problems which may point towards a theory. If it is successful, the book should bring its readers pleasure and illumination in connection with one of the leading elements in modern culture, and perhaps go some way towards resolving the curious tension that surrounds the problem of "popular culture." At the best, I hope the volume may possibly be a contribution to literature . . .

CIRCLES AND SQUARES: JOYS AND SARRIS (1963)

By Pauline Kael

. . . the first premise of the *auteur* theory is the technical competence of a director as a criterion of value . . . The second premise of the *auteur* theory is the distinguishable personality of the director as a criterion of value . . . The third and ultimate premise of the *auteur* theory is concerned with interior meaning, the ultimate glory of the cinema as an art. Interior meaning is extrapolated from the tension between a director's personality and his material . . .

Sometimes a great deal of corn must be husked to yield a few kernels of internal meaning. I recently saw *Every Night at Eight,* one of the many maddeningly routine films Raoul Walsh has directed in his long career. This 1935 effort featured George Raft, Alice Faye, Frances Langford and Patsy Kelly in one of those familiar plots about radio shows of the period. The film keeps moving along in the pleasantly unpretentious manner one would expect of Walsh until one incongruously intense scene with George Raft thrashing about in his sleep, revealing his inner fears in mumbling dream talk. The girl he loves comes into the room in the midst of his unconscious avowals of feeling, and listens sympathetically. This unusual scene was later amplified in *High Sierra* with Humphrey Bogart and Ida Lupino. The point is that one of the screen's most virile directors employed an essentially feminine narrative device to dramatize the emotional vulnerability of his heroes. If I had not been aware of Walsh in *Every Night at Eight,* the crucial link to *High Sierra* would have passed unnoticed. Such are the joys of the auteur theory.

—*Andrew Sarris, "Notes on the* Auteur *Theory in 1962,"* Film Culture, *Winter 1962–1963.*

Perhaps a little more corn should be husked; perhaps, for example, we can husk away the word "internal" (is "internal meaning" any different from "meaning"?). We might ask why the link is "crucial"? Is it because the device was "incongruously intense" in *Every Night at Eight* and so demonstrated a try for something *deeper* on Walsh's part? But if his merit is his "pleasantly unpretentious manner" (which is to say, I suppose, that, recognizing the limitations of the script, he wasn't trying to do much) then the incongruous device was probably a misconceived attempt that disturbed the manner—like a bad playwright interrupting a comedy scene because he cannot resist the opportunity to tug at your heartstrings. We might also ask why this narrative device is "essentially feminine": is it more feminine than masculine to be asleep, or to talk in one's sleep, or to reveal feelings? Or, possibly, does Sarris regard the device as feminine because the listening woman becomes a sympathetic figure and emotional understanding is, in this "virile" context, assumed to be essentially feminine? Perhaps only if one accepts the narrow notions of virility so common in our action films can this sequence be seen as "essentially feminine," and it is amusing that a critic can both support these clichés of the male world and be so happy when they are violated.

This is how we might quibble with a different *kind* of critic but we would never get anywhere with Sarris if we tried to examine what he is saying sentence by sentence.

So let us ask, what is the meaning of the passage? Sarris has noticed that in *High Sierra* (not a very good movie) Raoul Walsh repeated an uninteresting and obvious device that he had earlier used in a worse movie. And for some inexplicable reason, Sarris concludes that he would not have had this joy of discovery without the *auteur* theory.

But in every art form, critics traditionally notice and point out the way the artists borrow from themselves (as well as from others) and how the same devices, techniques, and themes reappear in their work. This is obvious in listening to music, seeing plays, reading novels, watching actors; we take it for granted that this is how we perceive the development or the decline of an artist (and it may be necessary to point out to *auteur* critics that repetition without development is decline). When you see Hitchcock's *Saboteur* there is no doubt that he drew heavily and clumsily from *The 39 Steps,* and when you see *North by Northwest* you can see that he is once again toying with the ingredients of *The 39 Steps*—and apparently having a good time with them. Would Sarris not notice the repetition in the Walsh films without the *auteur* theory? Or shall we take the more cynical view that without some commitment to Walsh as an *auteur,* he probably wouldn't be spending his time looking at these movies?

If we may be permitted a literary analogy, we can visualize Sarris researching in the archives of the *Saturday Evening Post,* tracing the development of Clarence Budington Kelland, who, by the application of something like the *auteur* theory, would emerge as a much more important writer than Dostoyevsky; for in Kelland's case Sarris's three circles, the three premises of the *auteur* theory, have been consistently congruent. Kelland is technically competent (even "pleasantly unpretentious"), no writer has a more "distinguishable personality," and if "interior meaning" is what can be extrapolated from, say, *Hatari!* or *Advise and Consent* or *What Ever Happened to Baby Jane?* then surely Kelland's stories with their attempts to force a bit of character and humor into the familiar plot outlines are loaded with it. Poor misguided Dostoyevsky, too full of what he has to say to bother with "technical competence," tackling important themes in each work (surely the worst crime in the *auteur* book) and with his almost incredible unity of personality and material leaving you nothing to extrapolate from, he'll never make it. If the editors of *Movie* ranked authors the way they do directors, Dostoyevsky would probably be in that almost untouchable category of the "ambitious."

It should be pointed out that Sarris's defense of the *auteur* theory is based not only on aesthetics but on a rather odd pragmatic statement: "Thus to argue against the *auteur* theory in America is to assume that we have anyone of Bazin's sensibility and dedication to provide an alternative, and we simply don't." Which I take to mean that the *auteur* theory is necessary in the absence of a critic who wouldn't need it. This is a new approach to aesthetics, and I hope Sarris's humility does not camouflage his double-edged argument. If his aesthetics is based on expediency, then it may be expedient to point out that it takes extraordinary intelligence and discrimination and taste to *use* any theory in the arts, and that without those qualities, a theory becomes a rigid formula (which is indeed what is happening among *auteur* critics). The greatness of critics like Bazin in France and Agee in America may have something to do with their using their full range of intelligence and intuition, rather than relying on formulas. Criticism is an art, not a science, and a critic who follows rules will fail in one of his most important functions: perceiving what is original and important in *new* work and helping others to see.

THE OUTER CIRCLE

. . . the first premise of the *auteur* theory is the technical competence of a director as a criterion of value.

This seems less the premise of a theory than a commonplace of judgment, as Sarris himself indicates when he paraphrases it as, "A great director has to be at least a good director." But this commonplace, though it *sounds* reasonable and basic, is a shaky premise: sometimes the greatest artists in a medium bypass or violate the simple technical competence that is so necessary for hacks. For example, it is doubtful if Antonioni could handle a routine directorial assignment of the type at which John Sturges is so proficient *(Escape from Fort Bravo* or *Bad Day at Black Rock),* but surely Antonioni's *L'Avventura* is the work of a great director. And the greatness of a director like Cocteau has nothing to do with mere technical competence: his greatness is in being able to achieve his own personal expression and style. And just as there were writers like Melville or Dreiser who triumphed over various kinds of technical incompetence, and who were, as artists, incomparably greater than the facile technicians of their day, a new great film director may appear whose very greatness is in his struggling toward grandeur or in massive accumulation of detail. An artist who is not a good technician can indeed create new standards, because standards of technical competence are based on comparisons with work already done.

Just as new work in other arts is often attacked because it violates the accepted standards and thus seems crude and ugly and incoherent, great new directors are very likely to be condemned precisely on the grounds that they're not even good directors, that they don't know their "business." Which, in some cases, is true, but does it matter when that "business" has little to do with what they want to express in films? It may even be a hindrance, leading them to banal slickness, instead of discovery of their own methods. For some, at least, Cocteau may be right: "The only technique worth having is the technique you invent for yourself." The director must be judged on the basis of what he produces—his films—and if he can make great films without knowing the standard methods, without the usual craftsmanship of the "good director," then that is the way he works. I would amend Sarris's premise to, "In works of a lesser rank, technical competence can help to redeem the weaknesses of the material." In fact it seems to be precisely this category that the *auteur* critics are most interested in—the routine material that a good craftsman can make into a fast and enjoyable movie. What, however, makes the *auteur* critics so incomprehensible, is not their *preference* for works of this category (in this they merely follow the lead of children who also prefer simple action films and westerns and horror films to works that make demands on their understanding) but their truly astonishing inability to exercise taste and judgment *within* their area of preference. Moviegoing kids are, I think, much more reliable guides to this kind of movie than the *auteur* critics: every kid I've talked to knows that Henry Hathaway's *North to Alaska* was a surprisingly funny, entertaining movie and *Hatari!* (classified as a "masterpiece" by half the *Cahiers* Conseil des Dix, Peter Bogdanovich, and others) was a terrible bore.

THE MIDDLE CIRCLE

. . . the second premise of the *auteur* theory is the distinguishable personality of the director as a criterion of value.

Up to this point there has really been no theory, and now, when Sarris begins to work on his foundation, the entire edifice of civilized standards of taste collapses while he's tacking down his floorboards. Traditionally, in any art, the personalities of all those involved in a production have been a factor in judgment, but that the *distinguishability* of personality should in itself be a criterion of value completely confuses *normal* judgment. The smell of a skunk is more distinguishable than the perfume of a rose; does that make it better? Hitchcock's personality is certainly more distinguishable in *Dial M for Murder, Rear Window, Vertigo,* than Carol Reed's in *The Stars Look Down, Odd Man Out, The Fallen Idol, The Third Man, An Outcast of the Islands,* if for no other reason than because Hitchcock repeats while Reed tackles new subject matter. But how does this distinguishable personality function as a criterion for judging the works? We recognize the hands of Carné and Prévert in *Le Jour se Lève,* but that is not what makes it a beautiful film; we can just as easily recognize their hands in *Quai des Brumes*—which is not such a good film. We can recognize that *Le Plaisir* and *The Earrings of Madame de . . .* are both the work of Ophuls, but *Le Plaisir* is not a great film, and *Madame de . . .* is.

Often the works in which we are most aware of the personality of the director are his worst films—when he falls back on the devices he has already done to death. When a famous director makes a good movie, we look at the movie, we don't think about the director's personality; when he makes a stinker we notice his familiar touches because there's not much else to watch. When Preminger makes an expert, entertaining whodunit like *Laura,* we don't look for his personality (it has become part of the texture of the film); when he makes an atrocity like *Whirlpool,* there's plenty of time to look for his "personality"—if that's your idea of a good time.

It could even be argued, I think, that Hitchcock's uniformity, his mastery of tricks, and his cleverness at getting audiences to respond according to his calculations—the feedback he wants and gets from them—reveal not so much a personal style as a personal theory of audience psychology, that his methods and approach are not those of an artist but a prestidigitator. The *auteur* critics respond just as Hitchcock expects the gullible to respond. This is not so surprising—often the works *auteur* critics call masterpieces are ones that seem to reveal the contempt of the director for the audience.

It's hard to believe that Sarris seriously attempts to apply "the distinguishable personality of the director as a criterion of value" because when this premise becomes troublesome, he just tries to brazen his way out of difficulties. For example, now that John Huston's work has gone flat* Sarris casually dismisses him with: "Huston is virtually a forgotten man with a few actors' classics behind him . . ." If *The Maltese Falcon,* perhaps the most high-style thriller ever made in America, a film Huston both wrote and directed, is not a director's film, what is? And if the distinguishable personality of the director is a criterion of value, then how can Sarris dismiss the Huston who comes through so unmistakably in *The Treasure of Sierra Madre, The African Queen,* or *Beat the Devil,* or even in a

*And, by the way, the turning point came, I think, not with *Moby Dick,* as Sarris indicates, but much earlier, with *Moulin Rouge.* This may not be so apparent to *auteur* critics concerned primarily with style and individual touches, because what was shocking about *Moulin Rouge* was that the content was sentimental mush. But critics who accept even the worst of Minnelli probably wouldn't have been bothered by the fact that *Moulin Rouge* was soft in the center, it had so many fancy touches at the edges.

muddled Huston film like *Key Largo?* If these are actors' movies, then what on earth is a director's movie?

Isn't the *auteur* theory a hindrance to clear judgment of Huston's movies and of his career? Disregarding the theory, we see some fine film achievements and we perceive a remarkably distinctive directorial talent; we also see intervals of weak, half-hearted assignments like *Across the Pacific* and *In This Our Life.* Then, after *Moulin Rouge,* except for the blessing of *Beat the Devil,* we see a career that splutters out in ambitious failures like *Moby Dick* and confused projects like *The Roots of Heaven* and *The Misfits,* and strictly commercial projects like *Heaven Knows, Mr. Allison.* And this kind of career seems more characteristic of film history, especially in the United States, than the ripening development and final mastery envisaged by the *auteur* theory—a theory that makes it almost de rigeur to regard Hitchcock's American films as superior to his early English films. Is Huston's career so different, say, from Fritz Lang's? How is it that Huston's early good—almost great—work must be rejected along with his mediocre recent work, but Fritz Lang, being sanctified as an *auteur,* has his bad recent work praised along with his good? Employing more usual norms, if you respect the Fritz Lang who made *M* and *You Only Live Once,* if you enjoy the excesses of style and the magnificent absurdities of a film like *Metropolis,* then it is only good sense to reject the ugly stupidity of *Journey to the Lost City.* It is an insult to an artist to praise his bad work along with his good; it indicates that you are incapable of judging either.

A few years ago, a friend who reviewed Jean Renoir's University of California production of his play *Carola,* hailed it as "a work of genius." When I asked my friend how he could so describe this very unfortunate play, he said, "Why, of course, it's a work of genius. Renoir's a genius, so anything he does is a work of genius." This could almost be a capsule version of the *auteur* theory (just substitute *Hatari!* for *Carola*) and in this reductio ad absurdum, viewing a work is superfluous, as the judgment is a priori. It's like buying clothes by the label: this is Dior, so it's good. (This is not so far from the way the *auteur* critics work, either.)

Sarris doesn't even play his own game with any decent attention to the rules: it is as absurd to praise Lang's recent bad work as to dismiss Huston's early good work; surely it would be more consistent if he also tried to make a case for Huston's bad pictures? That would be more consistent than devising a category called "actors' classics" to explain his good pictures away. If *The Maltese Falcon* and *The Treasure of Sierra Madre* are actors' classics, then what makes Hawks's *To Have and Have Not* and *The Big Sleep* (which were obviously tailored to the personalities of Bogart and Bacall) the work of an *auteur?*

Sarris believes that what makes an *auteur* is "an élan of the soul." (This critical language is barbarous. Where else should élan come from? It's like saying "a digestion of the stomach." A film critic need not be a theoretician, but it is necessary that he know how to use words. This might, indeed, be a first premise for a theory.) Those who have this élan presumably have it forever and their films reveal the "organic unity" of the directors' careers; and those who don't have it—well, they can only make "actors' classics." It's ironic that a critic trying to establish simple "objective" rules as a guide for critics who he thinks aren't gifted enough to use taste and intelligence ends up—where, actually, he began—with a theory based on mystical insight. This might really make demands on the *auteur* critics if they did not simply take the easy way out by arbitrary decisions of who's got "it" and who hasn't. Their decisions are not merely not based on their theory; their decisions are *beyond* criticism. It's like a woman's telling us that she feels a certain dress *does* something for her: her feeling has about as much to do with critical judgment as the *auteur* critics' feeling that Minnelli *has* "it," but Huston never had "it."

Even if a girl had plenty of "it," she wasn't expected to keep it forever. But this "élan" is not supposed to be affected by the vicissitudes of fortune, the industrial conditions of moviemaking, the turmoil of a country, or the health of a director. Indeed, Sarris says, "If directors and other artists cannot be wrenched from their historical environments, aesthetics is reduced to a subordinate branch of ethnography." May I suggest that if, in order to judge movies, the *auteur* critics must wrench the directors from their historical environments (which is, to put it mildly, impossible) so that they can concentrate on the detection of that "élan," they are reducing aesthetics to a form of idiocy. Élan as the permanent attribute Sarris posits can only be explained in terms of a cult of personality. May I suggest that a more meaningful description of élan is what a man feels when he is working at the height of his powers—and what we respond to in works of art with the excited cry of "This time, he's really done it" or "This shows what he could do when he got the chance" or "He's found his style" or "I never realized he had it in him to do anything so good," a response to his joy in creativity.

Sarris experiences "joy" when he recognizes a pathetic little link between two Raoul Walsh pictures (he never does explain whether the discovery makes him think the pictures are any better) but he wants to see artists in a pristine state—their essences, perhaps?—separated from all the life that has formed them and to which they try to give expression.

THE INNER CIRCLE

The third and ultimate premise of the *auteur* theory is concerned with interior meaning, the ultimate glory of the cinema as an art. Interior meaning is extrapolated from the tension between a director's personality and his material.

This is a remarkable formulation: it is the opposite of what we have always taken for granted in the arts, that the artist expresses himself in the unity of form and content. What Sarris believes to be "the ultimate glory of the cinema as an art" is what has generally been considered the frustrations of a man working against the given material. Fantastic as this formulation is, it does something that the first two premises didn't do: it clarifies the interests of the *auteur* critics. If we have been puzzled because the *auteur* critics seemed so deeply involved, even dedicated, in becoming connoisseurs of trash, now we can see by this theoretical formulation that trash is indeed their chosen province of film.

Their ideal *auteur* is the man who signs a long-term contract, directs any script that's handed to him, and expresses himself by shoving bits of style up the crevasses of the plots. If his "style" is in conflict with the story line or subject matter, so much the better—more chance for tension. Now we can see why there has been so much use of the term "personality" in this aesthetics (the term which seems so inadequate when discussing the art of Griffith or Renoir or Murnau or Dreyer)—a routine, commercial movie can sure use a little "personality."

Now that we have reached the inner circle (the bull's eye turns out to be an empty socket) we can see why the shoddiest films are often praised the most. Subject matter is irrelevant (so long as it isn't treated sensitively—which is bad) and will quickly be disposed of by *auteur* critics who know that the smart director isn't responsible for that anyway; they'll get on to the important subject—his *mise-en-scène.* The director who fights to do something he cares about is a square. Now we can at least begin to understand why there was such contempt toward Huston for what was, in its way, a rather extraordinary effort—the *Moby Dick* that failed; why *Movie* considers Roger Corman a better director than Fred Zinnemann and ranks Joseph Losey next to God, why Bogdanovich, Mekas, and Sarris give their highest critical ratings to *What Ever Happened to Baby Jane?* (mighty big crevasses there). If Carol Reed had made only movies like *The Man Between*—in which he obviously worked to try to make something out of a ragbag of worn-out bits of material—he might be considered "brilliant" too. (But this is doubtful: although even the worst Reed is superior to Aldrich's *Baby Jane,* Reed would probably be detected, and rejected, as a man interested in substance rather than sensationalism.)

I am angry, but am I unjust? Here's Sarris:

> A Cukor who works with all sorts of projects has a more developed abstract style than a Bergman who is free to develop his own scripts. Not that Bergman lacks personality, but his work has declined with the depletion of his ideas largely because his technique never equaled his sensibility. Joseph L. Mankiewicz and Billy Wilder are other examples of writer-directors without adequate technical mastery. By contrast, Douglas Sirk and Otto Preminger have moved up the scale because their miscellaneous projects reveal a stylistic consistency.

How neat it all is—Bergman's "work has declined with the depletion of his ideas largely because his technique never equaled his sensibility." But what on earth does that mean? How did Sarris perceive Bergman's sensibility except through his technique? Is Sarris saying what he seems to be saying, that if Bergman had developed more "technique," his work wouldn't be dependent on his ideas? I'm afraid this *is* what he means, and that when he refers to Cukor's "more developed abstract style" he means by "abstract" something unrelated to ideas, a technique not dependent on the content of the films. This is curiously reminiscent of a view common enough in the business world, that it's better not to get too involved, too personally interested in business problems, or they take over your life; and besides, you don't function as well when you've lost your objectivity. But this is the *opposite* of how an artist works. His technique, his *style,* is determined by his range of involvements, and his preference for certain themes. Cukor's style is no more *abstract*(!) than Bergman's: Cukor has a range of subject matter that he can handle and when he gets a good script within his range (like *The Philadelphia Story* or *Pat and Mike*) he does a good job; but he is at an immense *artistic* disadvantage, compared with Bergman, because he is dependent on the ideas of so many (and often bad) scriptwriters and on material which is often alien to his talents. It's amusing (and/or depressing) to see the way *auteur* critics tend to downgrade writer-directors—who are in the *best* position to use the film medium for personal expression.

Sarris does some pretty fast shuffling with Huston and Bergman; why doesn't he just come out and admit that writer-directors are disqualified by his third premise? They can't arrive at that "interior meaning, the ultimate glory of the cinema" because a writer-director has no tension between his personality and his material, so there's nothing for the *auteur* critic to extrapolate from.

What is all this nonsense about extrapolating "interior" meaning from the tension between a director's personality and his material? A competent commercial director generally does the best he can with what he's got to work with. Where is the "tension"? And if you can locate some, what kind of meaning could you draw out of it except that the director's having a bad time with lousy material or material he doesn't like? Or maybe he's trying to speed up the damned production so he can do something else that he has some *hopes* for? Are these critics honestly (and futilely) looking for "interior meanings" or is this just some form of intellectual diddling that helps to sustain their pride while they're viewing silly movies? Where is the tension in Howard Hawks's films? When he has good material, he's capable of better than good direction, as he demonstrates in films like *Twentieth Century, Bringing Up Baby, His Girl Friday;* and in *To Have and Have Not* and *The Big Sleep* he demonstrates that with help from the actors, he can jazz up ridiculous scripts. But what "interior meaning" can be extrapolated from an enjoyable, harmless, piece of kitsch like *Only Angels Have Wings;* what can the *auteur* critics see in it beyond the sex and glamor and fantasies of the highschools boys' universe—exactly what the mass audience liked it for? And when Hawks's material and/or cast is dull and when his heart isn't in the production—when by the *auteur* theory he should show his "personality," the result is something soggy like *The Big Sky*.

George Cukor's modest statement, "Give me a good script and I'll be a hundred times better as a director"* provides some notion of how a director may experience the problem of the given material. What can Cukor do with a script like *The Chapman Report* but try to kid it, to dress it up a bit, to show off the talents of Jane Fonda and Claire Bloom and Glynis Johns, and to give the total production a little flair and craftsmanship. At best, he can make an entertaining bad movie. A director with something like magical gifts *can* make a silk purse out of a sow's ear. But if he has it in him to do more in life than make silk purses, the triumph is minor—even if the purse is lined with gold. Only by the use of the *auteur* theory does this little victory become "ultimate glory." For some unexplained reason those traveling in *auteur* circles believe that making that purse out of a sow's ear is an infinitely greater accomplishment than making a solid carrying case out of a good piece of leather (as, for example, a Zinnemann does with *From Here to Eternity* or *The Nun's Story*).

I suppose we should be happy for Sirk and Preminger, elevated up the glory "scale," but I suspect that the "stylistic consistency" of, say, Preminger, could be a matter of his *limitations*, and that the only way you could tell he made some of his movies was that he used the same players so often (Linda Darnell, Jeanne Crain, Gene Tierney, Dana Andrews, et al., gave his movies the Preminger look). But the argument is ludicrous anyway, because if Preminger shows stylistic consistency with subject matter as varied as *Carmen Jones, Anatomy of a Murder,* and *Advise and Consent,* then by any rational standards he should be attacked rather than elevated. I don't think these films are stylistically consistent, nor do I think Preminger is a

*In another sense, it is perhaps immodest. I would say, give Cukor a clever script with light, witty dialogue, and he will know what to do with it. But I wouldn't expect more than glossy entertainment. (It seems almost too obvious to mention it, but can Sarris really discern the "distinguishable personality" of George Cukor and his "abstract" style in films like *Bhowani Junction, Les Girls, The Actress, A Life of Her Own, The Model and the Marriage Broker, Edward, My Son, A Woman's Face, Romeo and Juliet, A Double Life?* I wish I could put him to the test. I can only *suspect* that many *auteur* critics would have a hard time seeing those telltale traces of the beloved in their works.)

great director—for the very simple reason that his films are consistently superficial and facile. (*Advise and Consent,* an *auteur* "masterpiece"—Ian Cameron, Paul Mayersberg, and Mark Shivas of *Movie* and Jean Douchet of *Cashiers du Cinéma* rate it first on their ten best lists of 1962 and Sarris gives it his top rating—seems not so much Preminger-directed as other-directed. That is to say, it seems calculated to provide what as many different groups as possible want to see: there's something for the liberals, something for the conservatives, something for the homosexuals, something for the family.) An editorial in *Movie* states: "In order to enjoy Preminger's films the spectator must apply an unprejudiced intelligence; he is constantly required to examine the quality not only of the characters' decisions but also of his own reactions," and "He presupposes an intelligence active enough to allow the spectator to make connections, comparisons and judgments." May I suggest that this spectator would have better things to do than the editors of *Movie* who put out Preminger issues? They may have, of course, the joys of discovering links between *Centennial Summer, Forever Amber, That Lady in Ermine,* and *The Thirteenth Letter,* but I refuse to believe in these ever-so-intellectual protestations. The *auteur* critics aren't a very *convincing* group.

I assume that Sarris's theory is not based on his premises (the necessary causal relationships are absent), but rather that the premises were devised in a clumsy attempt to prop up the "theory." (It's a good thing he stopped at three: a few more circles and we'd really be in hell, which might turn out to be the last refinement of film tastes—Abbott and Costello comedies, perhaps?) These critics work embarrassingly hard trying to give some semblance of intellectual respectability to a preoccupation with mindless, repetitious commercial products—the kind of action movies that the restless, rootless men who wander on Forty-second Street and in the Tenderloin of all our big cities have always preferred just because they could respond to them without thought. These movies soak up your time. I would suggest that they don't serve a very different function for Sarris or Bogdanovich or the young men of *Movie*—even though they devise elaborate theories to justify soaking up their time. An educated man must have to work pretty hard to set his intellectual horizons at the level of *I Was a Male War Bride* (which, incidentally, wasn't even a good *commercial* movie).

"Interior meaning" seems to be what those in the know know.

It's a mystique—and a mistake. The *auteur* critics never tell us by what divining rods they have discovered the élan of a Minnelli or a Nicholas Ray or a Leo McCarey. They're not critics; they're inside dopesters. There must be another circle that Sarris forgot to get to —the one where the secrets are kept.

OUTSIDE THE CIRCLES, OR WHAT IS A FILM CRITIC?

I suspect that there's some primitive form of Platonism in the underbrush of Sarris's aesthetics.* He says, for example, that "Bazin's greatness as a critic . . . rested in his disinterested conception of the cinema as a universal entity." I don't know what a "universal entity" is, but I rather imagine Bazin's stature as a critic has less to do with "universals" than with intelligence, knowledge, experience, sensitivity, perceptions, fervor, imagination, dedication, lucidity—the traditional qualities associated with great critics. The role of the critic is to help people see what is in the work, what is in it that shouldn't be, what is not in it that could be. He is a good critic if he helps people understand more about the work than they could see for themselves; he is a great critic, if by his understanding and feeling for the work, by his passion, he can excite people so that they want to experience more of the art that is there, waiting to be seized. He is not necessarily a bad critic if he makes errors in judgment. (Infallible taste is inconceivable; what could it be measured against?) He is a bad critic if he does not awaken the curiosity, enlarge the interests and understanding of his audience. The art of the critic is to transmit his knowledge of and enthusiasm for art to others.

I do not understand what goes on in the mind of a critic who thinks a *theory* is what his confrères need because they are not "great" critics. Any honest man can perform the critical function to the limits of his tastes and powers. I daresay that Bogdanovich and V. F. Perkins and Rudi Franchi and Mark Shivas and all the rest of the new breed of specialists know more about movies than some people and could serve at least a modest critical function if they could remember that art is an expression of human experience. If they are men of feeling and intelligence, isn't it time for them to be

*This might help to explain such quaint statements as: Bazin "was, if anything, generous to a fault, seeking in every film some vestige of the cinematic art"—as if cinema were not simply the movies that have been made and are being made, but some preëxistent entity. If Bazin thought in these terms, does Sarris go along with him?

a little ashamed of their "detailed criticism" of movies like *River of No Return?*

I believe that we respond most and best to work in any art form (and to other experience as well) if we are pluralistic, flexible, relative in our judgments, if we are eclectic. But this does not mean a scrambling and confusion of systems. Eclecticism is not the same as lack of scruple; eclecticism is the selection of the best standards and principles from various systems of ideas. It requires more care, more orderliness to be a pluralist than to apply a single theory. Sarris, who thinks he is applying a single theory, is too undisciplined to recognize the conflicting implications of his arguments. If he means to take a Platonic position, then is it not necessary for him to tell us what his ideals of movies are and how various examples of film live up to or fail to meet his ideals? And if there is an ideal to be achieved, an objective standard, then what does élan have to do with it? (The ideal could be achieved by plodding hard work or by inspiration or any other way; the method of achieving the ideal would be as irrelevant as the "personality" of the creator.) As Sarris uses them, vitalism and Platonism and pragmatism do not support his *auteur* theory; they undermine it.

Those, like Sarris, who ask for objective standards seem to want a theory of criticism which makes the critic unnecessary. And he *is* expendable if categories replace experience; a critic with a single theory is like a gardener who uses a lawn mower on everything that grows. Their desire for a theory that will solve all the riddles of creativity is in itself perhaps an indication of their narrowness and confusion; they're like those puzzled, lost people who inevitably approach one after a lecture and ask, "But what is your basis for judging a movie?" When one answers that new films are judged in terms of how they extend our experience and give us pleasure, and that our ways of judging how they do this are drawn not only from older films but from other works of art, and theories of art, that new films are generally related to what is going on in the other arts, that as wide a background as possible in literature, painting, music, philosophy, political thought, etc., helps, that it is the wealth and variety of what he has to bring to new works that makes the critic's reaction to them valuable, the questioners are always unsatisfied. They wanted a simple answer, a formula; if they approached a chef they would probably ask for the one magic recipe that could be followed in all cooking.

And it is very difficult to explain to such people that criticism is exciting just because there is no formula to apply, just because you must use everything you are and everything you know that is relevant, and that film criticism is particularly exciting just because of the multiplicity of elements in film art.

This range of experience, and dependence on experience, is pitifully absent from the work of the *auteur* critics; they seem to view the movies, not merely in isolation from the other arts, but in isolation even from their own experience. Those who become film specialists early in life are often fixated on the period of film during which they first began going to movies, so it's not too surprising that the *Movie* group—just out of college and some still in—are so devoted to the films of the forties and fifties. But if they don't widen their interests to include earlier work, how can they evaluate films in anything like their historical continuity, how can they perceive what is distinctive in films of the forties? And if they don't have interests outside films, how can they evaluate what goes on in films? Film aesthetics as a distinct, specialized field is a bad joke: the *Movie* group is like an intellectual club for the intellectually handicapped. And when is Sarris going to discover that aesthetics is indeed a branch of ethnography; what does he think it is—a sphere of its own, separate from the study of man in his environment?

SOME SPECULATIONS ON THE APPEAL OF THE *AUTEUR* THEORY

If relatively sound, reasonably reliable judgments were all that we wanted from film criticism, then *Sight and Sound* might be considered a great magazine. It isn't, it's something far less—a good, dull, informative, well-written, safe magazine, the best film magazine in English, but it doesn't satisfy desires for an excitement of the senses. Its critics don't often outrage us, neither do they open much up for us; its intellectual range is too narrow, its approach too professional. (If we recall an article or review, it's almost impossible to remember which Peter or which Derek wrote it.) Standards of quality are not enough, and *Sight and Sound* tends to dampen enthusiasm. *Movie,* by contrast, seems spirited: one feels that these writers do, at least, love movies, that they're not condescending. But they too, perhaps even more so, are indistinguishable read-alikes, united by fanaticism in a ludicrous cause; and for a group that discounts content and story, that believes the director is the *auteur* of what gives the film value, they show an inexplicable fondness—almost an obsession—for detailing plot and quoting dialogue. With all the zeal of youth serving an ideal, they carefully reduce movies to trivia.

It is not merely that the *auteur* theory distorts experience (all theory does that, and helps us to see more sharply for having done so) but that it is an aesthetics which is fundamentally anti-art. And this, I think, is the most serious charge that can possibly be brought against an aesthetics. The *auteur* theory, which probably helped to liberate the energies of the French critics, plays a very different role in England and with the *Film Culture* and New York *Film Bulletin* *auteur* critics in the United States—an anti-intellectual, anti-art role.

The French *auteur* critics, rejecting the socially conscious, problem pictures so dear to the older generation of American critics, became connoisseurs of values in American pictures that Americans took for granted, and if they were educated Americans, often held in contempt. The French adored the American gangsters, and the vitality, the strength, of our action pictures—all those films in which a couple of tough men slug it out for a girl, after going through hell together in oil fields, or building a railroad, or blazing a trail. In one sense, the French were perfectly right—these were often much more skillfully made and far more interesting visually than the movies with a message which Americans were so proud of, considered so *adult.* Vulgar melodrama with a fast pace can be much more exciting—and more honest, too—than feeble, pretentious attempts at drama—which usually meant just putting "ideas" into melodrama, anyway. Where the French went off was in finding elaborate intellectual and psychological meanings in these simple action films. (No doubt we make some comparable mistakes in interpreting French films.)

Like most swings of the critical pendulum, the theory was a *corrective,* and it helped to remind us of the energies and crude strength and good humor that Europeans enjoyed in our movies. The French saw something in our movies that their own movies lacked; they admired it, and to some degree, they have taken it over and used it in their own way (triumphantly in *Breathless* and *Shoot the Piano Player,* not very successfully in their semi-American thrillers). Our movies were a product of American industry, and in a sense, it was America itself that they loved in our movies—our last frontiers, our robber-barons, our naiveté, our violence, our efficiency and speed and technology, our bizarre combination of sentimentality and inhuman mechanization.

But for us, the situation is different. It is good for us to be reminded that our mass culture is not altogether poisonous in its effect on other countries, but what is appealingly exotic—"American"—for them is often intolerable for us. The freeways of cities like Los Angeles may seem mad and marvelous to a foreign visitor; to us they are the nightmares we spend our days in. The industrial products of Hollywood that we grew up on are not enough to satisfy our interests as adults. We want a great deal more from our movies than we get from the gangster carnage and the John Ford westerns that Europeans adore. I enjoy some movies by George Cukor and Howard Hawks but I wouldn't be much interested in the medium if that were all that movies could be. We see many elements in foreign films that *our* movies lack. We also see that our films have lost the beauty and innocence and individuality of the silent period, and the sparkle and wit of the thirties. There was no special reason for the French critics, preoccupied with *their* needs, to become sensitive to *ours.* And it was not surprising that, in France, where film directors work in circumstances more comparable to those of a dramatist or a composer, critics would become fixated on American directors, not understanding how confused and inextricable are the roles of the front office, the producers, writers, editors, and all the rest of them —even the marketing research consultants who may pretest the drawing powers of the story and stars—in Hollywood. For the French, the name of a director *was* a guide on what American films to see; if a director was associated with a certain type of film that they liked, or if a director's work showed the speed and efficiency that they enjoyed. I assume that anyone interested in movies uses the director's name as some sort of guide, both positive and negative, even though we recognize that at times he is little more than a stage manager. For example, in the forties, my friends and I would keep an eye out for the Robert Siodmak films and avoid Irving Rapper films (except when they starred Bette Davis whom we wanted to see even in bad movies); I avoid Mervyn LeRoy films (though I went to see *Home Before Dark* for Jean Simmons's performance); I wish I could avoid Peter Glenville's pictures but he uses actors I want to see. It's obvious that a director like Don Siegel or Phil Karlson does a better job with what he's got to work with than Peter Glenville, but that doesn't mean there's any pressing need to go see every tawdry little gangster picture Siegel or Karlson directs; and perhaps if they tackled more difficult subjects they wouldn't do a better job than Glenville. There is no rule or theory involved in any of this, just simple discrimination; we judge the man from his films and learn to predict a little about his next films, we don't judge the films from the man.

But what has happened to the judgment of the English and New York critics who have taken over the *auteur* theory and used it to erect a film aesthetics based on those commercial movies that answered a need for the French, but which are not merely ludicrously inadequate to our needs, but are the results of a system of production that places a hammerlock on American directors? And how can they, with straight faces, probe for deep meanings in these products? Even the kids they're made for know enough not to take them seriously. How can these critics, sensible enough to deflate our overblown message movies, reject the total content of a work as unimportant and concentrate on signs of a director's "personality" and "interior meaning"? It's understandable that they're trying to find movie art in the loopholes of commercial production—it's a harmless hobby and we all play it now and then. What's incomprehensible is that they *prefer* their loopholes to unified film expression. If they weren't so determined to exalt products over works that attempt to express human experience, wouldn't they have figured out that the *mise-en-scène* which they seek out in these products, the director's personal style which comes through despite the material, is only a mere suggestion, a hint of what an artist can do when he's in control of the material, when the whole film becomes expressive? Isn't it obvious that *mise-en-scène* and subject material—form and content—can be judged separately only in bad movies or trivial ones? It must be black comedy for directors to read this new criticism and discover that films in which they felt trapped and disgusted are now said to be their masterpieces. It's an aesthetics for 1984: failure is success.

I am too far from the English scene to guess at motives, and far away also from New York, but perhaps close enough to guess that the Americans (consciously or unconsciously) are making a kind of social comment: like the pop artists, the New Realists with their comic strips and Campbell's soup can paintings, they are saying, "See what America is, this junk is the fact of our lives. Art and avant-gardism are phony; what isn't any good, is good. Only squares believe in art. The artifacts of industrial civilization are the supreme truth, the supreme joke." This is a period when men who consider themselves creative scoff at art and tradition. It is perhaps no accident that in the same issue of *Film Culture* with Sarris's *auteur* theory there is a lavishly illustrated spread on "The Perfect Filmic

Appositeness of Maria Montez"—a fairly close movie equivalent for that outsized can of Campbell's soup. The editor, Jonas Mekas, has his kind of social comment. This is his approach to editing a film magazine: "As long as the 'lucidly minded' critics will stay out, with all their 'form,' 'content,' 'art,' 'structure,' 'clarity,' 'importance'—everything will be all right, just keep them out. For the new soul is still a bud, still going through its most dangerous, most sensitive stage." Doesn't exactly make one feel welcome, does it? I'm sure I don't know what the problem is: are there so many "lucidly minded" critics in this country (like Andrew Sarris?) that they must be fought off? And aren't these little "buds" that have to be protected from critical judgments the same little film makers who are so convinced of their importance that they can scarcely conceive of a five-minute film which doesn't end with what they, no doubt, regard as the ultimate social comment: the mushroom cloud rising? Those "buds" often behave more like tough nuts.

Sarris with his love of commercial trash and Mekas who writes of the "cul-de-sac of Western culture" which is "stifling the spiritual life of man" seem to have irreconcilable points of view. Sarris with his joys in Raoul Walsh seems a long way from Mekas, the spokesman for the "independent film makers" (who couldn't worm their way into Sarris's outer circle). Mekas makes statements like "The new artist, by directing his ear inward, is beginning to catch bits of man's true vision." (Dear Lon Chaney Mekas, please get your ear out of your eye. Mekas has at least one thing in common with good directors: he likes to dramatize.) But to love trash and to feel that you are stifled by it are perhaps very close positions. Does the man who paints the can of Campbell's soup love it or hate it? I think the answer is both: that he is obsessed by it as a fact of our lives and a symbol of America. When Mekas announces, "I don't want any part of the Big Art Game" he comes even closer to Sarris. And doesn't the *auteur* theory fit nicely into the pages of an "independent film makers" journal when you consider that the work of those film makers might compare very unfavorably with good films, but can look fairly interesting when compared with commercial products? It can even look original to those who don't know much film history. The "independent film makers," Lord knows, are already convinced about their importance as the creative figures—the *auteurs;* a theory which suggested the importance of writing to film art might seriously damage their egos. They go even farther than the *auteur* critics' notion that the script is merely something to transcend: they often act as if anyone who's concerned with scripts is a square who doesn't dig film. (It's obvious, of course, that this aesthetic based on images and a contempt for words is a function of economics and technology, and that as soon as a cheap, lightweight 16mm camera with good synchronous sound gets on the market, the independent film makers will develop a different aesthetic.)

The *auteur* theory, silly as it is, can nevertheless be a dangerous theory—not only because it constricts the experience of the critics who employ it, but because it offers nothing but commercial goals to the young artists who may be trying to do something in film. *Movie* with its celebration of Samuel Fuller's "brutality" and the Mackie Mekas who "knows that everything he has learned from his society about life and death is false" give readers more of a charge than they get from the limp pages of *Sight and Sound* and this Journal.* This is not intended to be a snide remark about *Sight and Sound* and *Film Quarterly:* if they are not more sensational, it is because they are attempting to be responsible, to hoard the treasures of our usable past. But they will be wiped off the cinema landscape, if they can't meet the blasts of anti-art with some fire of their own.

The union of Mekas and Sarris may be merely a marriage of convenience; but if it is strong enough to withstand Sarris's "Hello and Goodbye to the New American Cinema" (in the *Village Voice,* September 20, 1962), perhaps the explanation lies in the many shared attitudes of the Mekas group and the *auteur* critics. Neither group, for example, is interested in a balanced view of a film; Mekas says he doesn't believe in "negative criticism" and the *auteur* critics (just like our grammar-school teachers) conceive of a review as "an appreciation." The directors they reject are so far beyond the pale that their films are not even considered worth discussion. (Sarris who distributes zero ratings impartially to films as varied as *Yojimbo, The Manchurian Candidate,* and *Billy Budd* could hardly be expected to take time off from his devotional exercises with Raoul Walsh to explain why these films are worthless.) Sarris, too, can resort to the language of the hipster—"What is it the old jazz man says of his art? If you gotta ask what it is, it ain't? Well, the cinema is like that." This is right at home in *Film Culture,* although Sarris (to his everlasting credit) doesn't employ the accusatory, paranoid style of Mekas:

*I.e., *Film Quarterly.—Ed.*

"You criticize our work from a purist, formalistic and classicist point of view. But we say to you: What's the use of cinema if man's soul goes rotten?" The "you" is, I suppose, the same you who figures in so much (bad) contemporary prophetic, righteous poetry and prose, the "you" who is responsible for the Bomb and who, by some fantastically self-indulgent thought processes, is turned into the enemy, the *critic.* Mekas, the childlike, innocent, pure Mekas, is not about to be caught by "the tightening web of lies"; he refuses "to continue the Big Lie of Culture." I'm sure that, in this scheme, any attempt at clear thinking immediately places us in the enemy camp, turns us into the bomb-guilty "you," and I am forced to conclude that Mekas is not altogether wrong—that if we believe in the necessity (not to mention the beauty) of clear thinking, we are indeed his enemy. I don't know how it's possible for anyone to criticize his work from a "purist, formalistic and classicist point of view"—the method would be too far from the object; but can't we ask Mekas: is man's soul going to be in better shape because your work is protected from criticism? How much nonsense dare these men permit themselves? When Sarris tells us, "If the *auteur* critics of the Fifties had not scored so many coups of clairvoyance, the *auteur* theory would not be worth discussing in the Sixties," does he mean any more than that he has taken over the fiats of the *auteur* critics in the fifties and goes on applying them in the sixties? Does he seriously regard his own Minnelli-worship as some sort of objective verification of the critics who praised Minnelli in the fifties? If that's his concept of critical method, he might just as well join forces with other writers in *Film Culture.* In addition to Mekas ("Poets are surrounding America, flanking it from all sides,") there is, for example, Ron Rice: "And the beautiful part about it all is that you can, my dear critics, scream protest to the skies, you're too late. The Musicians, Painters, Writers, Poets and Film-Makers all fly in the same sky, and know Exactly where It's "AT." Rice knows where he's at about as much as Stan Brakhage who says, "So the money vendors have begun it again. To the catacombs then . . ." In the pages of *Film Culture* they escape from the money changers in Jerusalem by going to the catacombs in Rome. "Forget ideology," Brakhage tells us, "for film unborn as it is has no language and speaks like an aborigine." We're all familiar with Brakhage's passion for obstetrics, but does being a primitive man mean being a foetus? I don't understand that unborn aborigine talk, but I'm prepared to believe that grunt by grunt, or squeal by squeal, it will be as meaningful as most of *Film Culture.* I am also prepared to believe that for Jonas Mekas, culture is a "Big Lie." And Sarris, looking for another culture under those seats coated with chewing gum, coming up now and then to announce a "discovery" like Joanne Dru, has he found his spiritual home down there?

Isn't the anti-art attitude of the *auteur* critics, both in England and here, implicit also in their peculiar emphasis on virility? (Walsh is, for Sarris, "one of the screen's most virile directors." In *Movie* we discover: "When one talks about the heroes of *Red River,* or *Rio Bravo,* or *Hatari!* one is talking about Hawks himself . . . Finally everything that can be said in presenting Hawks boils down to one simple statement: here is a man.") I don't think critics would use terms like "virile" or "masculine" to describe artists like Dreyer or Renoir; there is something too *limited* about describing them this way (just as when we describe a woman as sensitive and feminine, we are indicating her *special* nature). We might describe Kipling as a virile writer but who would think of calling Shakespeare a virile writer? But for the *auteur* critics calling a director virile is the highest praise because, I suggest, it is some kind of assurance that he is not trying to express himself in an art form, but treats movie-making as a professional job. (*Movie:* Hawks "makes the very best adventure films because he is at one with his heroes . . . Only Raoul Walsh is as deeply an adventurer as Hawks . . . Hawks' heroes are all professionals doing jobs—scientists, sheriffs, cattlemen, big game hunters: real professionals who know their capabilities . . . They know exactly what they can do with the available resources, expecting of others only what they know can be given.") The *auteur* critics are so enthralled with their narcissistic male fantasies (*Movie:* "Because Hawks' films and their heroes are so genuinely mature, they don't need to announce the fact for all to hear") that they seem unable to relinquish their schoolboy notions of human experience. (If there are any female practitioners of *auteur* criticism, I have not yet discovered them.) Can we conclude that, in England and the United States, the *auteur* theory is an attempt by adult males to justify staying inside the small range of experience of their boyhood and adolescence—that period when masculinity looked so great and important but art was something talked about by poseurs and phonies and sensitive-feminine types? And is it also their way of making a comment on our civilization by the suggestion that trash is the true film art? I ask; I do not know.

A CRITICAL CREDO (1967)

By John Simon

The most important thing to remember about film criticism is that it is not fundamentally different from any other kind of criticism. But because criticism itself remains such a largely misunderstood and therefore feared and hated concept, it may be well to posit one's general critical credo before proceeding to film criticism proper. Now if there is anything the public avoids more than criticism, it is discussions and theories of criticism; yet these, consumed in moderation, could serve as useful energizers of both criticism and the audience, leading, I hesitate to say to better art, but at least to better conditions for art, which is not so very different a thing.

Matthew Arnold called poetry the criticism of life; it is not impossible to invert the formula and call criticism the poetry of life. For if I understand Arnold correctly, he means that poetry, by setting before man an ideal existence with thought and feeling performing to the utmost of their capacities, urges him to recognize the insufficiencies of the routine he calls living and directs him toward the heights. If this is so, then true criticism, which renders explicit the achievements and shortcomings of art—man's noblest aspiration—is in fact a kind of poetry, a poetry of hate for what is ugly or false, and of love for what is beautiful and true. I realize that it has become unfashionable in life—let alone in criticism—to use terms like "ugly" and "beautiful," but I accept the charge of being unfashionable with satisfaction and even, I confess, with pride.

The most common attacks on criticism (and especially on movie criticism, which, being as yet young and feeble, can least defend itself) are either that it is unconstructive or that it is unnecessary. Unnecessary, apparently, because the public can think for itself: if a book, a painting, a film is good, it will be accepted; if it is bad, it will fail. What need, then, for critics? The most obvious answer is that the world of art is full of works whose true worth or worthlessness took far too long to be comprehended, and that even if time does sit in just and inexorable judgment, its courts are apt to be as cruelly procrastinatory as those described by Dickens and Kafka. To the extent that criticism can accelerate the verdict of the ages, it can speed up the coming of pleasure and enlightenment, and, no less important, spare us the waste of what as mortals we have the least of—time.

Without criticism there would be no dialogue, and it is staggering to contemplate what would have been the history—if any—of government, education, philosophy, psychiatry, and any other important discipline of learning or aspect of life without dialectics, without the chance of both sides being heard and hearing each other. Without criticism, the artist receives no serious answer; we must, on solid empirical evidence, consider failure or success with the mass of one's contemporaries as nothing more than a snort from the crowd, to be interpreted however one pleases. It is not important that the critical answer be that of an infallible oracle—what oracle ever was that?—it matters merely that a critical answer be the best of which a sensitive, experienced, eloquent, and honest mind and sensibility are capable. Thereby a purposeful issue is joined: the keen yet bloodless struggle for human fulfillment, which it was once permissible to call the pursuit of truth and beauty.

But what of "destructive" criticism, which is far and wide alleged to be bad? The terms "constructive" and "destructive," as applied to criticism, have no meaning whatever. There is only good and bad criticism. What indeed might "constructive" mean in reference to a critique? From the author in question, "Like me, don't knock me!" which is an absurd request. From the pedagogue, "Show him or her where and how the thing could be improved!" But any genuine artist would resent the critic's offering to remake his work; only school compositions can so be treated by teachers, and it may be that even they should not. I cannot write someone else's book, play, or scenario for him; I can only point out where and why he lost me—and that, I suppose, would already be called "destructive" criticism. To the casual layman, "constructive" criticism would be, "Go easy on him, he is doing his best." But this is the worst fallacy of all: it assumes that art does not really matter. If a surgeon's patients die on him, one after the other, does one excuse him by saying he did his best? Can a statesman's, a military commander's, an educator's errors be excused so cheaply? No; because those things *matter*. Whereas art, it would seem, does not.

But to the critic to whom art is important, sacred, and, ultimately, coextensive with life itself, to produce bad art and to condone it—and thereby give rise to further bad art and finally drive out the good—are the two most heinously dangerous sins imaginable. And the most destructive. Still the temperate person will say, "All right, forget about 'destructive' and 'constructive'—but couldn't you just be more moderate in your dislikes?" Different evils need different modes of attack: from Swiftian *saeva indignatio* to subtle puncturing, from "more in sorrow than in anger" to *reductio ad absurdum,* one chooses whichever method is most suitable; or, if one is less versatile, whichever method one is best suited to. The critic's words are his tools, or weapons, and he would be foolish and incompetent if he did not use them to the utmost of his, and their, ability. If the critic is mistaken or too harsh, time eventually proves him wrong—much more quickly than it would a bad artist, because here it can rely on the enthusiastic help of the critic's colleagues. The genuine artist cannot be destroyed by words: It is not the *Quarterly,* "savage and tartarly," but consumption that killed John Keats. And the man who slings mud pies at the Venus de Milo hits only himself.

Good criticism and bad criticism, then; but what constitutes good criticism? Perhaps it is easiest to begin by defining the commonest kind of bad criticism, which is not criticism at all but reviewing. Reviewing is something that newspaper editors have invented: it stems from the notion that the critic is someone who must see with the eyes of the Average Man or Typical Reader (whoever that is) and predict for his fellows what their reaction will be. To this end, the newspapers carefully screen their reviewers to be representative common men, say, former obituary writers or mail-room clerks, anything but trained specialists. To accept such a reviewer as critic and guide is like expecting school children to teach one another, or patients in a hospital ward to undertake one another's cure. A critic excites the public's curiosity, wonder, suspicion, rage, and enthusiasm; a reviewer elicits mostly one of two reactions: "Good! That's another one I don't have to see!" or "Great! I like it already." Both reactions stifle thought instead of encouraging the audience and, with luck, even the artist to grow.

Now the good critic is, first and foremost, a teacher. One problem, among many, with our education is that it ends. After a certain number of years, always too few, the last textbook is shut, the door closes on the last classroom, and we are free—free not only to desist from all further learning, but also to forget what we have learned so far. How many of us can pass up such a golden opportunity? This is where the critic comes in. With cogency, suasion, passion, charm he induces us to think, to widen our horizons, to open yet another book, to reconsider a snap judgment, to see something from a loftier vantage point, in historic perspective, and using more and truer touchstones. Good criticism of any kind—of movies, ballet, architecture, or whatever—makes us think, feel, respond; if we then agree or disagree is less important than the fact that our faculties have been engaged and stretched. Good criticism informs, interprets, and raises the ultimate questions, the unanswerable ones that everyone must try to answer none the less. This is teaching of the highest order.

Secondly, the true critic is an artist. "Criticism is a good thing, but poetry is a better," wrote Richard Le Gallienne. As a poet, he had every reason to preconize poetry; as a bad one, every reason to patronize criticism. But even the most enthusiastic practitioner of criticism, if he is not Oscar Wilde, would refrain from placing it above poetry; it would, however, be wrong to deny that a good piece of criticism must be as well written and shaped as, *mutatis mutandis,* a poem, a story, or a personal essay. It is, therefore, in its own way a work of art. As that remarkable but still underrated German playwright, poet, and novelist Frank Wedekind put it, "Without doubt, the systematic execution of a critique written with a sense of responsibility is a more difficult, worthy, and, even for art, more valuable task than the writing of mediocre plays." And he went on, "Critic and author are . . . different stages of development of the same calling. The two are collaborators on the same project." The critic, as that enlightened poet Pierre Reverdy saw him, *"fait, avec plus de liberté, l'office du meilleur ami."* But the artist will accept the friendship of the critic only if he recognizes in him a fellow-artist. Why should friendship become misalliance? In his occasionally *outré* but generally highly perceptive essay "The Critic as Artist," Wilde observed, "the critic is he who exhibits to us a work of art in a form different from that of the work itself, and the employment of a new material is a critical as well as a creative element." Wilde called criticism "a creation within a creation" and so the purest form of creativity, and indeed the piece of criticism that cannot be read by a civilized and concerned person without knowledge of the work or artist discussed is not a true critique. And that which can be so read is more than a review; it is a work of the contemplative imagination, a work of art. So we can read Longinus or Lessing, Sainte-Beuve or Hazlitt, without more than a general awareness of the writers that were their points of departure. And in reading a drama review of Shaw or Beerbohm it is scarcely necessary to have seen the production in question to savor the matter and the manner of the review as literature. Of which one of our film critics is this true? How many people now writing about movies are worth reading even when the particular film is still fresh in our memories, and our desire to discuss it still sovereign?

Thirdly, the critic is or should be a thinker. In an age when philosophy has removed itself into theology or science or even, of all places, literary criticism, it becomes incumbent on the critic to turn philosopher. To quote Wilde's essay once more, "the highest Criticism . . . is the record of one's own soul." In other words, the critic must have a world view, which, however one may wish to disguise it, is a moral position. Nothing is more suspect in criticism nowadays than a moral position, and yet there can be no criticism without one. The moment something appears to us better or worse than something else, we are being moralists—for aesthetics is the morality of art, just as morality is the aesthetics of living. But if criticism cannot do without morality, it can easily remain unaware of its underlying morality, and the penalty for such unawareness is inferior criticism. What form this morality will take is comparatively unimportant; it may be—and I myself would wish it to be—neither an established system nor the systematization of a yet unestablished one. It should be, as nearly as I can describe it, a relevance to human life, an elegance of spirit, a generosity and adventuresomeness of outlook, and above all, a concept or intimation of what the ideal solution to an artistic problem would be, and the dogged insistence on measuring every performance against the envisioned model. It should never judge something, as is commonly done, on how well it fulfills its own aims, for by that standard, if it sets out to be only junk, junk will have to be found excellent. Essential too is an awareness of reconciled opposites: of the joy inherent in tragedy and of the pathos no true comedy can be without.

But I am not trying to develop a whole critical philosophy here. I am merely pleading for, or insisting on, the necessity of a realized philosophy translated into artistic expression as the irreducible minimum of the true critic's equipment. And it will be useful to bear always in mind the statement of the great sixteenth-century Spanish Jesuit Baltasar Gracián: "Not only in words, but also in works is lying practiced, and the latter form of lying is much the more dangerous."

With these general remarks out of the way, we may pass to considerations pertaining specifically to film criticism. The problem here is acute: Whereas the other arts seem to be blessed with more or less the critics they deserve—with modern music, painting, and sculpture receiving, as their just deserts, the most inept kind of criticism—film, which may well be the salient and vital art form of our day is getting hardly less incompetent criticism as a gratuitous insult. The main trouble is that most intellectuals, even if willing to concede that film is an art, would not consider criticizing it an art or even a serious occupation, perhaps because there are not enough serious film critics, or indeed serious films, around to get a meaningful dialogue started. A case in point is Kenneth Tynan, whose drama criticism was, whatever particulars one might cavil with, manifestly serious (and let me make clear, once and for all, that by serious I do not mean long-faced), but whose film criticism, however much one may enjoy it, is patently frivolous. The fundamental problem, I suppose, is that film is being taken, ultimately, as an "entertainment" as opposed to a work of art, as if art and entertainment were mutually exclusive or, at least, separate entities, as form and content or meaning and style were once thought to be. While no one today would dare to think of form and content as separate or, except for purposes of classroom demonstration, separable, it still seems the most natural thing to erect a fence between the few films that "have something to say" and the many that are "merely amusements," and, apparently, come up with roughly equal endorsement for films in both groups, albeit by a double standard involving different scales.

Now I submit that the first responsibility of the film critic is to recognize that there is, to be sure, a superficial difference between comedy and tragedy, and a profound one between good and bad, but that to view and review *all* films as anything but an art is at best trivial and at worst stupid—always bearing in mind that I am talking of the serious critic. Suppose that I were speaking here as a literary critic, seriously and literarily (as opposed to banteringly or sociologically), and discussed the works of Herman Wouk or Leon Uris or

James Michener. I should justly be considered, *ipso facto,* critically, if not indeed mentally, incompetent. But if, as a film critic, I were to present a rapturous tribute to the films of a Blake Edwards or Otto Preminger, or if I were to disgorge high-sounding effusions about the work of Godard or Chabrol (and, who knows, perhaps even that of Stan Brakhage or Jack Smith), I would be listened to with earnestness and deference, as if I were not dealing with men who are, in one case, hacks and charlatans, in the other, pretentious flounderers—and this despite the fact that one or the other of them may have stumbled on something useful, may have a certain facility, and may have even, *mirabile dictu,* turned out a passable film.

The point is that the critic—as distinguished from the historian, the sociologist, the collector, the faddist—has no business considering entertainment as an end in itself, any more than he may consider art, in film or elsewhere, as something dreary and unentertaining. This does not mean, of course, that the critic should refuse to review a so-called entertainment film: we do not as yet have enough films that are art, or even aspiring to that condition, yet serious criticism must go on. To adapt a saying of Clemenceau's, the reviewing of films, such as they may be, is much too serious a matter to be left in the hands of mere reviewers. And it is crucial to remember that there is no genuine entertainment without artistry, just as there can be no art that is unabsorbing, i.e., boring. There is, however this proviso: Artistry is not quite on the same level as art.*

A distinguished Polish film-maker and teacher remarked to me not long ago that we talk so much about film as art, yet there have been in the whole history of the cinema thus far no more than, at best, two works of indubitable art. I think that the number is higher, though not very much higher; I must also, in principle, agree. Hardly anyone writing about film today would maintain, for example, that D. W. Griffith was not an artist; yet, to me, he is the epitome of the nonartist, no matter how much he may have contributed to the *technique* of the film. I would say that Griffith is to the art of cinema what Achilles Tatius was to the art of the novel. Or that Griffith did for film what Sackville and Norton, the authors of *Gorboduc,* did for

*Allowances must, I suppose, be made for such a category as "failed art." *Paradise Regained,* or most of Blake's prophetic books, for example, are art in intention, and do not make the compromises of pseudoart. But works which intelligent readers (except, perhaps, contemporaries struck by their timeliness) will read only under duress might as well be considered failed or nonart.

the English drama. And this, clearly, not because a film like *Birth of a Nation* is morally objectionable, but because it is artistically and intellectually insufficient.

This might begin to sound like support for all those potentially qualified film critics who prefer to abstain because of the grim prospect of bringing superior equipment to bear on nothing or next to nothing. It might be suggested here that Aristotle was able to write extraordinarily fine dramatic criticism at a time when there were only a half dozen dramatists worth considering. But the position of the film critic today is truly anomalous: It is to be confronted with an art that, even though it has done remarkably well in the short span of six decades, has not had anywhere near enough time to develop fully; and to confront it with a critical discipline that, even if only in related fields, has acquired a vast tradition and imposing expertise and sophistication. The main thing the critic can do while waiting for the day when it will be possible to limit oneself to writing serious criticism about serious films for serious publications is, with every means at his command, to help bring about that day.

The age is eminently ripe for film to become a true art. For this is only possible when something newer and more profitable exists to syphon off the most irresponsible, inartistic, greedy elements from an older art. "It is unimaginable," wrote Friedrich Dürrenmatt, "what would have to be played on the stage nowadays if film had not been invented and the screenwriters were turning out stage plays." This statement can now be revised: It is inconceivable what trash would be put on film these days if television had not been invented, and the TV writers were functioning as scenarists. As it is, far too many of them are.

The next responsibility of the critic is to recognize the difficulties inherent in the form of film. There are simple and complex arts. Fiction, for example, is a simple art, based on the word. So too is painting, based—until recently, anyway—on the image. Conversely, ballet, opera, film are complex arts. Although this is not a value judgment, implying that complex arts are superior to simple ones, or vice versa, writing good criticism of a complex art presents a multiplicity of problems. Now, to make things a little easier for the critic, one aspect of a complex art usually far surpasses the others in importance. Ballet is perfectly possible without costumes and sets, and even music has been dropped in some recent experiments. Opera could do without words, using nonsense syllables, which most librettos quite successfully approximate already. Modern composers, like Stravinsky, have t nded to use the voice purely as an instrument; and even the best texts are likely to be of little avail: What the elaborate orchestration does not swallow, the singer's diction cert inly will.

But film is the o complex art in which two main components are equally important: text and cinematography, that is, word and image. The youthful critic, contemptuous of words and proud, like the young film-maker, of "thinking in film"—which means, I suppose, perceiving the whole work as images—should beware: Words are no less important than pictures. But the old-school critic should also be wary: Pictures are no less important than words. A film that is all image and poor words is like a beautiful woman who, the moment she opens her mouth, offends us. We cannot love her. But neither can we love a brilliantly eloquent woman who is ugly as sin. In any case, the relation between image and word is much more intimate than some people realize: Even in silent or near-silent films the mind tends to translate seen actions into words—so that the word, excluded, creeps in by the back door.

Now because film is such a complex—perhaps, indeed, a total—art, the ideal film critic would have to be conversant with cinematography, literature, acting techniques, painting and sculpture (form and composition), music, dance (film musicals), and in view of the generally poor subtitles, as many foreign languages as possible. Can one encompass all this? I dare say that when T. S. Eliot gave as *the* requirement for a critic that he be "very intelligent," he was not thinking of the film critic. Otherwise, I suspect, he would have had to say "very, very intelligent." But ironically, as we shall see, it is precisely some of the least intelligent people who wander into film criticism.

We have now reached the point where it is appropriate to indicate some of the things a film critic should not be. Film criticism, like film-making, is a field that attracts the anti-intellectual—whether he be an intellectual turned sour, or a bona fide anti-intellectual of long standing. Now, whereas film-making does not require a rational basis, film criticism does. Yet it is all too readily conceived of as some kind of game, if not, indeed, a con-game, or even a form of public defiance—something withal that enjoys enough of a vogue to make it look like work. Thus, for example, the people who evolved and practice the *auteur* theory were playing a faddist in-game, which does not begin to hold up under rational scrutiny, yet they were able to corner a large part of the critical market. (I use the unsavory metaphor advisedly.) But film criticism, again like film, has particular appeal for an even worse crowd, the lunatic fringe, because it offers a perfect substitute world. The fact that film, of all arts, comes closest to looking both like life and like dreams, both like palpable reality and like wish-fulfillments made manifest, makes it the preferred medium for escape: it has neither the arrant artifices and inescapable limitations of the theatre, nor the crippling self-censorship and disintoxicating commercials of television to cope with. Thus it invites us on a voyage where all is *luxe, calme et volupté,* or, if we would rather, *luxe, frénésie et volupté,* and the seekers of artificial paradises flock right in. Consider the so-called Underground Cinema with its party fun and games that become films, and its film screenings that turn into fun and game parties in an uninterrupted daisy chain, nonworld without end. And, in due time, the lunatic fringe evolves its own critics, even while it gradually wears down the resistance of those reviewers initially opposed to it.

And even when it is not the fanatical movie buff who turns critic, the temptation is great for the critic to become a movie buff, which is the exact opposite of being a critic. Because the history of film is short and because film comes at one automatically, the way a book, for instance, does not, the critic may be seduced into trying to see as nearly every film as possible. Only, though the history of film may indeed be short, it is also extremely wide: the output is tremendous. What self-respecting literary critic would try to keep up with every novel, or even every slightly better novel, that comes along, to say nothing of all the other literary genres? That way lies madness. So, if our man is not already a madman when he becomes a film critic, he stands an excellent chance of ending up as one.

Yet, heaven knows, the film critic needs every bit of lucidity and resourcefulness to do justice to a job in which mountains of difficulty insist on mistaking him for Mohammed. It is part of the critic's responsibility to be unremittingly aware of the almost insuperable problems that face him the moment he wishes to be more than the reviewer of a specific film that happens to come his way, or, given that situation, to write something that will have widespread and lasting value.

A book can be read slowly and reread. The painting usually, though nowadays not always, stands still; it is also available in reproduction. Music places score, text (if there is one), and recordings into one's hands. Even the ballet critic has the advantage of viewing and reviewing certain ballets over and over again, and thus knowing at least some of the staples of the repertoire practically by heart. In film, even where a printed script is obtainable, the critic depends on a few notes—often, because they have to be scribbled in haste and darkness, illegible—and on his evanescent memory of a fleeting experience.

And even if a cinemathèque is at the critic's disposal—but how many of us are so privileged?—he still cannot take the film home with him and ponder it at leisure. True, some film lending libraries are beginning to be heard of, but they are as yet only little more than a tantalizing promise, a drop in the bucket, and the problems surrounding lending libraries being what they are, it is doubtful that this bucket will ever quench anyone's thirst. To be sure, new inventions may come along, but I am not trying to practice Utopian criticism here. In any case, the critic will eventually need to have his own film library, just as today's literary critic and scholar has his own essential books. But even that is not the end of our problems. However much access the critic may have to films, his readers will most likely not have it. In this way it becomes, in the large number of cases, hard or impossible for the reader to verify the critic's contentions. But, worst of all, there is no way of accurately *quoting* film: Still photographs can barely do justice to stationary objects of art; dialogue conveys only a fragment of what happens in a film. Verbal evocation also has a hard time of it: If you use technical terminology to explain shots and camera movements, you may very well lose your reader, and will certainly end up boring him; if you use impressionistic, imaged prose, unless you are very skillful indeed, you may wander far afield. Thus a genuine understanding, let alone a dialogue, between critic and reader is almost impossible.

As if all this were not enough, the film critic is also up against a space problem, though, unlike greater powers with such problems, he is not asking for the moon, merely for enough space in a paper or magazine to develop his ideas and impressions. But the space accorded him is usually quite insufficient, precisely because film, as we said before, has so many components. Consequently it is the rarest thing to find a review that can begin to do justice to the manifold achievements and lacks of the film it deals with.

And there is apt to be yet a further obstacle. Because film represents such a large financial investment for the producers, the honestly outspoken critic, if he is working for an influential publication, becomes a threat to Hollywood. As a result, many are the tales of critics losing their jobs, or not even getting them, because of pressure—direct or indirect, actual or merely anticipated—from the big film companies.

If one contemplates the obstacles I have just enumerated, one might well consider undertaking to write film criticism an act of singular, if not suicidal, desperation. And yet, more than ever, good film criticism is needed. For, even though film production is more massive, far-flung, and ambitious than ever, the average quality has not substantially progressed since the time when Pablo Neruda's solitary gentleman took his newly seduced girl out for an evening,

> *y la lleva a los miserables cinematógrafos*
> *donde los héroes son potros y príncipes apasionados . . .*

(and he takes her to the wretched movies/where the heroes are horses or passionate princes), and, I might add, there is usually not that much difference between the two. The first and last responsibility of the film critic, then, is—prepare yourselves for a thundering truism—to raise the standard of motion pictures.

Unfortunately this is not nearly so self-evident as it might be to one segment of the population: the movie reviewers. To be sure, they will all tell you that they are in love with excellence; meanwhile, however, they are perfectly happy in their sordid concubinage with the second-rate. How depressingly they will latch on to this scene or that brief moment, gush over some very funny bit performer or a few clever little directorial touches. Now I am myself pathetically grateful for the slightest bit of genuine quality or inventiveness, in whichever corner of a movie I can track it down, but that does not mean that I am willing to forgo my appetite for the best in the work as a whole, or that I will bend over backward to justify that whole by one or two tolerable parts. It is not enough to love the good, it is also necessary to hate the bad; indeed, I submit that he who does not hate the bad cannot truly love the good. *Qui bene amat, bene castigat:* there is no rodless way of bringing up the movie industry, a big, fat, and extraordinarily corrupt baby. Of course, one is not infallible, but one must believe that one is: Nothing is less interesting to a reader than lack of conviction, unless it be lack of wit or poetry.

Yes, those two are the chief gifts the gods can bestow on a film critic: a poetic style to evoke the lovelinesses, the subtleties, the excitement of film; and a coruscating wit, whose edge is sharp enough—I draw the image from C. B. De Mille's *The Crusades*—to cut a falling feather in two. If you have those two qualities, you do not need anything else—except, needless to say, a point of view; but it is unlikely that a critic who is a poet and a wit would lack a point of view.

If you are a true film critic (or, for that matter, a true critic of any art form), there are three questions that are bound to haunt you wherever you go. They are, in fact, the same question manifesting itself in three guises, rather like Robert Graves's Triple Goddess. Its most commonplace form is, "Have you liked *anything* lately?" If this question embarrasses you, because, indeed, you haven't liked anything lately, you might just as well turn in your critic's hat immediately. If this question does not embarrass you, because you've liked quite a few things recently, you might also just as well turn in your hat. If, however, you are a real critic, you simply stare brazenly at the questioner and say, "There were a good many films I would have liked to like." Or, "It is press agents who are in the business of liking films."

Now for the second form of the haunting question, usually uttered with a patronizing sneer, "Do you *like* movies?" The obvious answer to this would be, "Yes, more than you; otherwise I would not accept so many substitutes." But politeness may be preferable, in which case it is good to have to hand a memorized list of favorite films; it does not matter how old they are, the mere quantity and rapid-fire comeback will silence the interrogator. My own favorite dozen, my all-time greats, in no particular order, is as follows: Ingmar Bergman's *The Naked Night* and *Smiles of a Summer Night,* Federico Fellini's *The White Sheik* and *I Vitelloni,* Antonioni's *L'Avventura,* Kurosawa's *The Seven Samurai,* Orson Welles's *Citizen Kane,* Jean Renoir's *The Rules of the Game,* René Clément's *Forbidden Games,* Marcel Carné's *The Children of Paradise,* Andrzej Wajda's *Kanal,* and one film of Chaplin's, which, I confess, refuses to remain the same one but varies according to which of three—*The Gold Rush, City Lights,* or *Modern Times*—I have seen last.

But sometimes the question arises in its third, most formidably pseudolearned avatar. "Why do you insist on judging the film according to some hypothetical notion of what ought to be there, rather than on what is actually there?" The answer to that may be simple: "Because there is nothing there." Yet, in some cases, that may be putting it too strongly: Something may be there, albeit scarcely worth serious discussion. Of course, sometimes it is these very somethings that give rise to the most heated discussions and impassioned partisanship—in which case, one may have to take a stand. But whatever you do, never abandon that image of perfection at the back of your head, on which the film, superimposed, must fit like identical triangles; unless, that is, the film is better than your image of perfection, in which case drop the image.

And however bad the general state of film criticism may be, there have been and always will be critics from whom our hypostatized ideal critic might learn something. To speak only of American criticism, with which I am most familiar, I should like an ideal critic to acquire the passionate scrupulousness, the constantly self-searching enthusiasm of James Agee, the modesty and social awareness of Robert Warshow, the background information and scrappiness of Pauline Kael, the gentlemanly dignity of Stanley Kauffmann, and the idiosyncratic raciness of Dwight Macdonald. If all these virtues cannot be used simultaneously, let him practice them by turns, applying each where it is most called for, as a painter does his colors. And by all means let him have some virtues no other critic has, virtues that none of us has even dreamt of. The very worst thing such an ideal critic might do is to be wrong. And even that is not fatal, if we believe Henry de Montherlant: "Je suis convaincu que les oeuvres qui durent ne durent que par des malentendus, par toute la littérature dont la posterité les entoure, littérature où les intentions véritables des auteurs finissent par être noyées du tout et perdues de vue." But, for all that, it is preferable to aim, to the utmost of one's emotional sensitivity and intellectual power, at being right.

TOWARD A THEORY OF FILM HISTORY—INTRODUCTION TO THE AMERICAN CINEMA (1968)

By Andrew Sarris

I. THE FOREST AND THE TREES

The cinema by any definition is still very young, but it is already old enough to claim not only its own history but its own archaeology as well. The earliest artifacts have been traced back to the 1880's and 1890's in the United States, France, or England, depending on the nationality of the archaeologist. Conflicting proofs and patents of invention have been submitted for Thomas A. Edison, William Kennedy, Laurie Dickson, William Friese-Greene, Louis Aimé Augustin Le Prince, Louis and Auguste Lumière, and many other shadowy figures out of the nineteenth-century camera obscura of art, science, and capitalism.

To the extent that the cinema is a creature of the scientific spirit, it has inherited expectations of infinite development and improvement. It is as if this machine art were designed to transcend the vagaries of human inspiration. A Shakespeare may appear once in a millennium, but the express train of twentieth-century history cannot wait a century or even a decade for the world to be remade from the moonbeams of a movie projector. Too much was expected of the medium, and too little was demanded of its scholars. The extravagant rhetoric of disillusionment obscured the incredibly perfunctory attention given to thousands upon thousands of movies. Therefore the first task of a theory of film history is to establish the existence of these thousands of movies as a meaningful condition of the medium.

Even though most movies are only marginally concerned with the art of the cinema, the notion of quality is difficult to grasp apart from the context of quantity. Comprehension becomes a function of comprehensiveness. As more movies are seen, more cross-references are assembled. Fractional responsibilities are more precisely defined; personal signatures are more clearly discerned.

It follows that comprehensive film scholarship from primary sources depends for its motivation upon a pleasurable response to the very act of moviegoing. Conversely, the compleat film historian must be recruited from the ranks of the authentic moviegoers rather than the slummers from the other arts. Not that an uncritical enthusiasm for movies is desirable in our chronicler. Film history devoid of value judgments would degenerate into a hobby like bridge or stamp collecting, respectable in its esoteric way, but not too revelatory. Or, as has been more the fashion, the collectivity of movies could be clustered around an idea, usually a sociological idea befitting the mindlessness of a mass medium.

The trouble up to now has been not seeing the trees for the forest. But why should anyone look at thousands of trees if the forest itself be deemed aesthetically objectionable? Of course, the forest to which I refer is called Hollywood, a pejorative catchword for vulgar illusionism. Hollywood is a foresty word rather than a treesy word. It connotes conformity rather than diversity, repetition rather than variation. The condescending forest critic confirms his preconceptions by identifying those elements that Hollywood movies have in common. Thus he also justifies his random sampling of Hollywood's output. If you've seen one, you've seen 'em all. And if you've seen a few, you certainly don't need to see them all. Hence the incessant carping on Hollywood "clichés:" Boy Meets Girl. The Happy Ending. The Noble Sacrifice. The Sanctity of Marriage. The Gangster Gets His Just Deserts. The Cowboy Outdraws the Villain. Girl and Boy Feel a Song Coming On. Presumably if you've laughed at one such convention, you've laughed at them all.

There is no denying that Hollywood movies emerge through a maze of conventions. Pressures from the studio, the censor, and the public have left their mark on film history. There is no artistic justification for the handcuffing of Burgess Meredith's George after he has mercifully shot the Lennie of Lon Chaney, Jr., in *Of Mice and Men.* Nor for the arrest of Gale Sondergaard at the end of *The Letter.* Nor for the mysterious going-away tears shed by Carole Lombard's Amy in *They Knew What They Wanted.* The citations of censor-dictated punishments of crime and sin could take up volumes and volumes. Hollywood movies have been hobbled also by front-office interference and a Scribean script policy that decreed the simplest, singlest, and most vulgar motivations for characters.

But the forest critic is not concerned with particulars. It is the system that he despises. It is the system that he blames for betraying the cinema. This curious feeling of betrayal dominates most forest histories to the point of paranoia. Somewhere on the western shores of the United States, a group of men have gathered to rob the cinema of its birthright. If the forest critic be politically oriented, he will describe these coastal conspirators as capitalists. If aesthetically oriented, he will describe them as philistines. Either way, an entity called the cinema has been betrayed by another entity called Hollywood. It is hard to find a parallel to this stern attitude in any of the other arts. A bad novel is not reviewed as if the author and publisher had betrayed literature. A bad painting is not castigated for disgracing the medium that produced Poussin and Delacroix. Perhaps the closest parallel can be found in certain critical attitudes toward the type of play performed on Broadway, London's West End, and the Parisian boulevards. The factor shared by theatre and cinema in this regard is the possession of buildings in which the public gathers to watch plays or films as the particular edifice complex dictates. The forest critic cannot help wondering what would happen if these buildings were consecrated to what he considers to be genuine art. What he seeks is the union of crowd spectacle with coterie taste. His generally liberal leanings convince him that the masses can indeed be saved from their own vulgarities.

The forest critic is not entirely lacking in historical proofs of betrayal. An unimpeachable witness such as George Stevens has testified: "When the movie industry was young, the film-maker was its core and the man who handled the business details his partner . . . When he finally looked around, he found his partner's name on the door. Thus the film-maker became the employee, and the man who had the time to attend to the business details became the head of the studio." The so-called system can be blamed for the blighted careers of D. W. Griffith, Josef von Sternberg, Orson Welles, Erich von Stroheim, and Buster Keaton, and for the creative frustrations of innumerable other directors. The problem with these examples is that in most instances the forest critics repudiated the afflicted directors long before the industry curtailed their careers. Forest critics have never championed individuality for its own sake. A Griffith has been denounced for not keeping up with the times. A Sternberg has been condemned for his preoccupation with eroticism. A Welles has been flayed for his flamboyant egotism. The principle of the forest has been upheld at the expense of the topmost trees, and this is indeed the supreme irony of forest criticism. Far from welcoming diversity, the forest critic seeks a new uniformity. He would have Hollywood march off en masse like Birnam Wood to whatever Dunsinane the forest critic desires. Instead of one version of *The Grapes of Wrath,* there would be three hundred. Instead of one biography of Émile Zola, there would be a thousand critiques of anti-Semitism throughout the ages. Every movie would deal Realistically with a Problem in Adult Terms, or employ the Materials of the Medium in a Creative Manner. Thus the goals of forest criticism are ultimately impersonal. If John Ford decides to make a thirties adventure movie like *Seven Women* in the sixties, he is hopelessly out of step with cinemah. Similarly Charles Chaplin's *Countess from Hong Kong,* Orson Welles's *Falstaff,* and Howard Hawks's *El Dorado* are not synchronized with the express train of history. The medium marches on at its own pace. It is impervious to the melancholy twilight periods of its greatest artists.

The forest critic has had recourse to other snobberies over the years, and brief rebuttals to the battle cries of foreign "art" films, documentary, and the avant-garde might be in order at this point. In fact, the same careless arguments are heard today. The same rebuttals obviously apply.

THE FOREIGN FILM IS BETTER: The first serious cults of the foreign film sprang up in the twenties around the German and Russian cinemas, notable respectively for expressive camera mobility and revolutionary theories of montage. The giants of this era were Murnau, Lang, and Pabst in Germany, and Eisenstein, Pudovkin, and Dovjenko in Russia. The French cinema of Renoir, Vigo, Becker, Cocteau, Pagnol, Duvivier, Carné, Feyder, and Autant-Lara attracted some cultists in the thirties and early forties. The Italian neorealism of Rossellini, Visconti, and De Sica dominated the late forties and early fifties. The current line of the xenophiles among American critics is less localized. Hollywood's alleged betters may be found in Sweden (Ingmar Bergman), Denmark (Carl Dreyer), Japan (Mizoguchi, Kurosawa, Ozu), India (Satyajit Ray), Poland (Has, Polanski, Skolimowski, Wajda), not to mention the familiar hunting grounds of France, Italy, and England. Film for film, Hollywood can hold its own with the rest of the world. If there have been more individualized works from abroad, there have also been fewer competent ones. If

Hollywood yields a bit at the very summit, it completely dominates the middle ranges, particularly in the realm of "good-bad" movies and genres. Invidious comparisons are inevitable to some extent because of the arithmetic of distribution. Since a lower percentage of foreign films are available in America, indiscriminate viewing of Hollywood movies leads to an unscientific sampling of merit. Language barriers and the sheer exoticism of the unknown contribute to critical distortions. By the same token, American movies are often overrated abroad.

DOCUMENTARY FILMS ARE MORE REALISTIC THAN FICTIONAL MOVIES, HENCE MORALLY AND AESTHETICALLY SUPERIOR: One might just as well say that books of nonfiction are more truthful than novels. A great deal of semantic confusion is caused here by the duality of the cinema as a recording medium like the printing press, phonography, radio, lithography, and television, and as an art form.

AVANT-GARDE FILMS POINT THE WAY FOR COMMERCIAL MOVIES: It is difficult to think of any technical or stylistic innovations contributed by the avant-garde. Avant-garde critics and film-makers have had to be dragged screaming into the eras of sound, color, and wide-screen. Avant-garde impulses seem to be channeled toward the shattering of content taboos, political, religious, and sexual. Luis Buñuel and René Clair have come out of the avant-garde, and some think that Cocteau never left it, but few avant-garde mannerisms stand for long the withering gaze of the camera.

Though the forest critic may still point to foreign "art" films, the documentary, and the avant-garde, he knows full well that the masses he wants to save are enthralled more by ordinary movies than by lofty cinema. He himself is fascinated by the vulgar spectacles he deplores in his scholarly treatises, and in his fascination is the secret of his yearning. If the stupidities on the screen can stir even his own refined sensibilities, what ecstasies would he not experience if the dream mechanism were controlled by tastes comparable to his own? Greta Garbo edited by the *Partisan Review,* and all that. The forest critic cannot admit even to himself that he is beguiled by the same vulgarity his mother enjoys in the Bronx. He conceals his shame with such cultural defense mechanisms as pop, camp, and trivia, but he continues to sneak into movie houses like a man of substance visiting a painted woman. If he understood all the consequences involved, he would not want movies liberated from their vulgar mission. He appreciates the fact that always and everywhere there were temples of temptation dedicated to the kind of furtive pleasure that was mercifully free from the stink of culture. Nonetheless his intellectual guilt compels him to deny serious purpose and individual artistry to the mass spectacles he has been educated to despise.

The forest critic makes the mistake of crediting the power of the medium for making a "bad" movie seem entertaining. He overlooks the collectivity of creation in which "good" and "bad" can co-exist. Greta Garbo is genuinely "good" in *Camille* and Robert Taylor is genuinely "bad." George Cukor's direction of Garbo is extraordinary, but his direction of Laura Hope Crews is much too broad. In that same year (1937) Ernst Lubitsch obtained a restrained performance from Miss Crews in *Angel.* Thus our notions of "good" and "bad" are cast adrift in a sea of relativity. The collectivity that makes the cinema the least personal of all the arts also redeems most movies from complete worthlessness. But collectivity is not necessarily impersonality. Collectivity may just as easily be a collection of distinctive individualities. Ideally the strongest personality should be the director, and it is when the director dominates the film that the cinema comes closest to reflecting the personality of a single artist. A film history could reasonably limit itself to a history of film directors. It would certainly be a good start toward a comprehensive film history, but it would hardly explain everything to be found in thousands of movies. Nor is there any theory that would explain everything for all time. The performances of Humphrey Bogart, for example, seem more meaningful today than they did in their own time. By contrast, the image of Greer Garson has faded badly.

Film history is both films *in* history and the history of films. The forest critic tends to emphasize the first approach at the expense of the second. He treats the movies of the thirties as responses to the Great Depression. By this criterion, few movies met their responsibilities to the oppressed and the underprivileged. For every *I Was a Fugitive from a Chain Gang* and *Our Daily Bread,* there were a score of "Thou Swell" romances in which money was no object. Yet the escapism of the thirties was as much a reflection of the Great Depression as any topical film on unemployment. The most interesting films of the forties were completely unrelated to the War and the Peace that followed. Throughout the sound era, the forest critic has been singling out the timely films and letting the timeless ones fall by the wayside. Unfortunately, nothing dates faster than timeliness. Hence the need for perpetual revaluation.

II. THE AUTEUR THEORY

I first employed the term "auteur theory" in an article entitled "Notes on the Auteur Theory in 1962" (*Film Culture* No. 27, Winter 1962–63). The article was written in what I thought was a modest, tentative, experimental manner. It was certainly not intended as the last word on the subject. Indeed, it invited debate in a dialectical spirit of pooled scholarship, though without much hope of attracting attention in a publication with a readership of less than ten thousand. I had been writing articles in *Film Culture* for seven years without fueling any fires of controversy, but on this occasion a spark was ignited in far-off San Francisco by a lady critic with a lively sense of outrage. As often happens, the attack on the theory received more publicity than the theory itself. Unfortunately, the American attacks on the auteur theory only confirmed the backward provincialism of American film criticism. Not that the auteur theory is beyond criticism. Far from it. What is beyond criticism is the historical curiosity required to discuss any critical theory on film. A character in Bernardo Bertolucci's *Before the Revolution* observes that you can argue only with those with whom you are in fundamental agreement. "Let us polemicize," a Polish critic once wrote me. The affectionate aggressiveness of this attitude demands a modicum of mutual respect and a tradition of scholarly community sadly lacking in American film criticism.

First of all, the auteur theory, at least as I understand it and now intend to reaffirm it, claims neither the gift of prophecy nor the option of extracinematic perception. Directors, writers, actors (even critics) do not always run true to form, and the critic can never assume that a bad director will always make a bad film. No, not always, but almost always, and that is the point. What is a bad director but a director who has made many bad films? Hence, the auteur theory is a theory of film history rather than film prophecy. Of the directors listed in this book's* Pantheon, Flaherty, Griffith, Keaton, Lubitsch, Murnau, and Ophuls are dead. Lang, Renoir, and Sternberg are involuntarily inactive, Chaplin, Ford, and Welles involuntarily inter-

*I.e., in Sarris's *The American Cinema.—Ed.*

mittent. Only Hawks and Hitchcock of this group still enjoy reasonable commercial viability as they pass into their seventies, but it is difficult to imagine that their ultimate critical standing will be at stake in the next few seasons. Auteur criticism has been accused of sentimentality toward old directors. In Hollywood, particularly, you're only as good as your last picture, and no one in that power-oriented micropolis wants to waste time on has-beens. Since auteur criticism is based on an awareness of the past, it finds the work of old directors rich in associations. Not the work of all old directors, however. William Wellman, Henry King, and Frank Lloyd are not without their defenders, but the sum totals of their careers reveal more debits than credits. The ranking of directors is based on total rather than occasional achievement.

But why rank directors at all? Why all the categories and lists and assorted drudgeries? One reason is to establish a system of priorities for the film student. Another is the absence of the most elementary academic tradition in cinema. The drudgeries in the other, older, arts are performed by professional drudges. Film scholarship remains largely an amateur undertaking. In America especially, a film historian must double as a drudge. The rankings, categories, and lists establish first of all the existence of my subject and then my attitude toward it. "Taste," Paul Valéry remarked, "is made of a thousand distastes." François Truffaut's *Politique des auteurs,* first promulgated in the *Cahiers du Cinéma* No. 31 of January 1954, can be credited (or blamed) for the polemical stance of the term "auteur."

Politique des auteurs referred originally to the policy at *Cahiers* to be for some directors and against others. For Truffaut, the best film of Delannoy was less interesting than the worst film of Renoir. This was an extreme example of the *politique* in action. It served as a shock statement for the criticism of cruelty. The term "auteur" is more perplexing, as I should be the first to recognize after all the controversies the term has caused me. Strictly speaking, "auteur" means "author," and should be so translated when the reference is to literary personalities. When Truffaut writes of Gide or Giraudoux, and refers to them incidentally as "auteurs," there is no special point being made, and "author" is both an adequate and accurate translation. It is another matter entirely when Truffaut describes Hitchcock and Hawks as "auteurs." "Author" is neither adequate nor accurate as a translation into English mainly because of the inherent literary bias of the Anglo-American cultural Establishment. In terms of this bias, Ingmar Bergman did not become an author until his screenplays were published in cold print. The notion that a non-literary director can be the author of his films is difficult to grasp in America. Since most American film critics are either literary or journalistic types with no aspirations or even fantasies of becoming film directors, the so-called auteur theory has had rough sledding indeed. Truffaut's greatest heresy, however, was not in his ennobling direction as a form of creation, but in his ascribing authorship to Hollywood directors hitherto tagged with the deadly epithets of commercialism. This was Truffaut's major contribution to the anti-Establishment ferment in England and America.

However, Truffaut cannot be considered a systematic historian of the American cinema. Nor a comrade in arms for Anglo-American auteurists and New Critics. Truffaut, Godard, Chabrol, Rohmer, Rivette, and other *Cahiers* critics may have stimulated the Anglo-American New Criticism into being, but they did not long sustain its heresies. Of course, even *Cahiers* criticism was never so monolithic as its more vulgar American antagonists supposed. Nor were (or are) all French critics and periodicals camped under the *Cahiers* standard. Nor does the *nouvelle vague* constitute a continuing advertisement for auteur criticism. The critics of each country must fight their own battles within their own cultures, and no self-respecting American film historian should ever accept Paris as the final authority on the American cinema.

If Truffaut's *Politique des auteurs* signaled a break with anything, it was with a certain segment of the French cinema that was dominated (in Truffaut's view) by a handful of scriptwriters. The target was the well-upholstered, well-acted, carefully motivated "Tradition of Quality" represented by Claude Autant-Lara, Marcel Carné, René Clair, René Clément, Henri Clouzot, André Cayatte, Jean Delannoy, Marcel Pagliero, and a host of even lesser figures. This "Old Guard" was responsible for films like *Devil in the Flesh, The Red and the Black, Forbidden Games, Gervaise, Wages of Fear, Diabolique, Justice Is Done,* and *Symphonie Pastorale,* in short, what American reviewers considered the class of French film-making into the late fifties. Against these alleged creatures of fashion, Truffaut counterposed Jean Renoir, Max Ophuls, Robert Bresson, Jacques Becker, Jean Cocteau, and Jacques Tati as authentic auteurs. Truffaut was involved in nothing less than changing the course of the French cinema. His bitterest quarrels were with film-makers, whereas the bitterest quarrels of the New Critics in England and America were with other critics. Truffaut's critical antagonists in Paris were generally not guilty of condescending to the American cinema. The editors of *Positif* may have preferred Huston to Hitchcock, and the MacMahonists may have preferred Losey to Hawks, but no faction had to apologize for its serious analyses of American movies. Even the French Marxists denounced the more capitalistic output from Hollywood in intellectually respectful terms. Long before the giddy rationalizations of pop, camp, and trivia, French critics were capable of discussing such lowbrow genres as Westerns and *policiers* with a straight face. The fact that many French critics had small English and less American actually aided them in discerning the visual components of a director's style.

Nevertheless a certain perversity in Truffaut's position still haunts the auteur theory and the New Criticism. Truffaut used American movies as a club against certain snobbish tendencies in the French cinema. This suggests the classic highbrow gambit of elevating lowbrow art at the expense of middle-brow art. Auteur critics are particularly vulnerable to the charge of preferring trash to art because they seek out movies in the limbo of cultural disrepute. An anti-auteur critic can score points simply by citing the titles of alleged auteur masterpieces. Without having seen the films, is anyone likely to believe that *Kiss Me Deadly* is more profound than *Marty,* that *Seven Men from Now* is more artistically expressive than *Moby Dick,* that *Baby Face Nelson* is more emotionally effective than *The Bridge on the River Kwai,* that *Bitter Victory* is more psychologically incisive than *The Defiant Ones,* that *Rio Bravo* is more morally committed than *The Nun's Story,* that *Gun Crazy* will outlive *The Heiress* or that *Psycho* will be admired long after *A Man for All Seasons* has been forgotten? Again, these propositions cannot be seriously debated. One kind of critic refuses to cope with a world in which a movie called *Baby Face Nelson* could possibly be superior to *The Bridge on the River Kwai.* The other kind of critic refuses to believe that a movie called *Baby Face Nelson* could possibly be less interesting than *The Bridge on the River Kwai.* One of the fundamental correlations in auteur criticism is that between neglected directors and neglected genres. To resurrect Ford and Hawks, it is necessary also to resurrect the Western. To take Minnelli seriously, it is necessary to take musicals seriously. However, auteur criticism is quite distinct from genre criticism. Genre criticism of the Western, for example, presupposes an ideal form for the genre. Directors may deviate from this form, but only at their own peril. The late Robert Warshow's celebrated essay on the Western described how a variety of directors failed to achieve Warshow's idealized archetype of the genre. By contrast, auteur criticism of the Western treats the genre as one more condition of creation.

Ultimately, the auteur theory is not so much a theory as an attitude, a table of values that converts film history into directorial autobiography. The auteur critic is obsessed with the wholeness of art and the artist. He looks at a film as a whole, a director as a whole. The parts, however entertaining individually, must cohere meaningfully. This meaningful coherence is more likely when the director dominates the proceedings with skill and purpose. How often has this directorial domination been permitted in Hollywood? By the most exalted European standards, not nearly enough. Studio domination in the thirties and forties was the rule rather than the exception, and few directors had the right of final cut. Educated Americans were brought up on the jaundiced Hollywood chronicles of F. Scott Fitzgerald, Nathanael West, John Dos Passos, Ring Lardner, and John O'Hara. The vulgar but vital producer-entrepreneur was the sun king in these sagas, and sensitive literary types were left out in the shade. In retrospect, however, the studio system victimized the screenwriter more than the director. It was not merely a question of too many scribes spoiling the script, although most studios deliberately assigned more than one writer to a film to eliminate personal idiosyncrasies, whereas the director almost invariably received sole credit for direction regardless of the studio influences behind the scenes. This symbol of authority was not entirely lacking in substance even in Hollywood, or perhaps especially in Hollywood where the intangibles of prestige loom large. There were (and are) weak and strong directors as there were weak and strong kings, but film history, like royal history, concerns those who merely reign as well as those who actually rule. Indeed, the strength of a John Ford is a function of the weakness of a Robert Z. Leonard just as the strength of a Louis XIV is a function of the weakness of a Louis XVI. The strong director imposes his own personality on a film; the weak director allows the personalities of others to run rampant. But a movie is a movie, and if by chance Robert Z. Leonard should reign over a respectable production like *Pride and Prejudice,* its merits are found elsewhere than in the director's personality, let us say in Jane Austen, Aldous Huxley, Laurence Olivier, Greer Garson, and a certain tradition of gentility at Metro-Goldwyn-Mayer. Obviously, the auteur theory cannot possibly cover every vagrant charm of the cinema. Nonetheless, the listing of films by directors remains the most reliable index of quality available to us short of the microscopic evaluation of every film ever made.

Even the vaunted vulgarity of the movie moguls worked in favor of the director at the expense of the writer. A producer was more likely to tamper with a story line than with a visual style. Producers, like most people, understood plots in literary rather than cinematic terms. The so-called "big" pictures were particularly vulnerable to front-office interference, and that is why the relatively conventional genres offer such a high percentage of sleepers. The culturally ambitious producer usually disdained genre films, and the fancy dude writers from the East were seldom wasted on such enterprises. The auteur theory values the personality of a director precisely because of the barriers to its expression. It is as if a few brave spirits had managed to overcome the gravitational pull of the mass of movies. The fascination of Hollywood movies lies in their performance under pressure. Actually, no artist is ever completely free, and art does not necessarily thrive as it becomes less constrained. Freedom is desirable for its own sake, but it is hardly an aesthetic prescription.

However, the auteur critic does not look to the cinema for completely original artistic experiences. The cinema is both a window and a mirror. The window looks out on the real world both directly (documentation) and vicariously (adaptation). The mirror reflects what the director (or other dominant artist) feels about the spectacle. Modern cinema tends to fog up the window in order to brighten the reflection. It would seem that a theory that honored the personality of a director would endorse a cinema in which a director's personality was unquestionably supreme. Paradoxically, however, the personalities of modern directors are often more obscure than those of classical directors who were encumbered with all sorts of narrative and dramatic machinery. The classical cinema was more functional than the modern cinema. It knew its audience and their expectations, but it often provided something extra. This something extra is the concern of the auteur theory.

The auteur theory derives its rationale from the fact that the cinema could not be a completely personal art under even the best of conditions. The purity of personal expression is a myth of the textbooks. The camera is so efficient a manufacturer of "poetic" images that even a well-trained chimpanzee can pass as a "film poet." For all its viciousness and vulgarity, the Hollywood system imposed a useful discipline on its directors. The limited talents of a Gregory La Cava could be focused on an exquisite department-store-window whimsy involving Claudette Colbert and a family of mannequins. The genre expectations of *She Married Her Boss* took care of the rest of the movie, but in those few moments in the department-store window, the La Cava touch was immortalized as a figure of style.

Nonetheless the auteur theory should not be defended too strenuously in terms of the predilections of this or that auteur critic. Unfortunately, some critics have embraced the auteur theory as a shortcut to film scholarship. With a "you-see-it-or-you-don't" attitude toward the reader, the particularly lazy auteur critic can save himself the drudgery of communication and explanation. Indeed, at their worst, auteur critiques are less meaningful than the straightforward plot reviews that pass for criticism in America. Without the necessary research and analysis, the auteur theory can degenerate into the kind of snobbish racket that is associated with the merchandizing of paintings. The burden of proof remains with the critic, auteur-oriented or otherwise, and no instant recipes of aesthetic wisdom will suffice. Welles is not superior to Zinnemann "of course," but only after an intensive analysis of all their respective films. Where the auteur critic parts company with the anti-auteur critic is in treating every Welles film as well as every Zinnemann film as part of a career whole. The auteur critic thus risks the resentment of the reader by constantly judging the present in terms of the past. The auteur critic must overcome this resentment by relating the past to the present in the most meaningful way possible. Fortunately, readers are becoming more rather than less knowledgeable about the past with each passing year.

Ian Cameron's article "Films, Directors and Critics" in *Movie* of September 1962 raises an interesting objection to the auteur theory: "The assumption which underlies all the writing in *Movie* is that the director is the author of a film, the person who gives it any distinctive quality. There are quite large exceptions, with which I shall deal later. On the whole we accept the cinema of directors, although without going to the farthest-out extremes of the *la politique des auteurs* which makes it difficult to think of a bad director making a good film and almost impossible to think of a good director making a bad one."

Cameron was writing particularly of the policy at *Cahiers du Cinéma* in which the films of favored directors were invariably assigned to the specialists in those directors. The result was that no favored director was ever panned. Ironically, Cameron and his colleagues found themselves in the same bind in *Movie* when David Lean's *Lawrence of Arabia* came up for consideration. Since none of the *Movie* critics liked Lean or the film enough to search for meanings in the mise-en-scène, *Lawrence* was left in the lurch without any review at all. Cameron defended the exclusion on the grounds that the best review of any film will be written by the critic who best understands the film, usually because he is the most sympathetic to it. Cameron, like the editors of *Cahiers,* thus upheld the criticism of enthusiasm as a criterion for his publication. Why does this sound so heretical in the United States? Simply because most movie reviewers fancy themselves as magistrates of merit and paid taste consultants for the public. The "best" movie reviewer is the "toughest" movie reviewer, and a reputation is made and measured by the percentage of movies the reviewer pans. The more movies panned, the more honest the reviewer. Everyone knows how assiduously the movie companies seek to corrupt the press. Hence, what better proof of critical integrity than a bad notice? Besides, the journalistic beat of the movie reviewer takes in all movies, not just the ones he likes. The highbrow critic can pick and choose; the lowbrow reviewer must sit and suffer. Walter Kerr has defined the difference between reviewing and criticism as the difference between assuming that your reader has not seen the work in question and assuming that he has. Reviewing is thus a consumer report for the uninitiated; criticism a conversation with one's equals. It is the economic structure of the cinema that gives the reviewer more power than the critic, but whereas in the other arts the critic makes up in academic prestige what he lacks in the market power of the reviewer, the film scholar has until very recently lacked both power and prestige. That is why film scholars can be slandered as "cultists" by philistinish movie reviewers.

However, the more fastidious film publications neglect their obligations to the medium by restricting their critiques to the films and directors they like. The film scholar should see as much as possible and write about as much as possible. To avoid passing judgment on a film because of lack of sympathy is an act of intellectual arrogance. Nothing should be beneath criticism or contempt. I take a transcendental view of the role of a critic. He must aspire to totality even though he knows that he will never attain it. This transcendental view disposes of the either/or tone of many opponents of the auteur theory. This tone suggests that the critic must make an irrevocable choice between a cinema of directors and a cinema of actors, or between a cinema of directors and a cinema of genres, or between a cinema of directors and a cinema of social themes, and so on. The transcendental view of the auteur theory considers itself the first step rather than the last stop in a total history of the cinema. Eventually we must talk of everything if there is enough time and space and printer's ink. The auteur theory is merely a system of tentative priorities, a pattern theory in constant flux. The auteur critic must take the long view of cinema as if every film would survive in some vault forever. Auteur criticism implies a faith in film history as a continuing cultural activity. The last thing an auteur critic desires is to keep a reader from seeing a movie. Debate is encouraged, but the auteur critic is committed to the aesthetic values he has derived from the artists who have inspired him. The auteur critic seeks to communicate the excitement he has felt to his readers, but he does not substitute his own sensibility for that of the artist under analysis. The ideal auteur critic should sacrifice his own personality to some extent for the sake of illuminating the personality of the director. In practice, however, no critic can entirely escape the responsibility of his own values. Elucidation must yield at some point to evaluation. All that is meaningful is not necessarily successful. John Ford's sentimentality in *The Informer* is consistent with the personality he expresses throughout his career, but the film suffers from the sentimentality just the same. Alfred Hitchcock's *Marnie* makes a meaningful statement about sexual relationships, but the script and acting leave much to be desired. *Red Line—7000* is no less personal a project for Howard Hawks than *El Dorado,* but there is all the difference in the world between the self-parody of *Red Line* and the self-expression of *El Dorado.* Orson Welles manifests his vision of the world with more lucidity and grace in *The Magnificent Ambersons* than in *Macbeth,* and Sternberg is more poetic, if less personal, in *Morocco* than in *Anatahan.* Even the greatest directors have their ups and downs. No one has ever suggested the contrary. At a certain level of achievement, however, even the failures of a director can be fascinating. Actually, a careful analysis of a director's career often turns up neglected masterpieces that replace the "official" masterpieces. Ford, for example, is seldom cited for *Steamboat 'Round the Bend* and *The Searchers,* but these films look more interesting today than *The Informer* and *The Grapes of Wrath.*

The best directors generally make the best films, but the directors must be discovered through their films. "That was a good movie," the critic observes. "Who directed it?" When the same answer is given over and over again, a pattern of performance emerges. The critic can talk about meaning and style in the work of a director. But how does a critic determine whether a movie is good or bad? This is a more difficult question. At first, there was only the vaguest idea of what a movie should be like to qualify as a work of art. Then as more and more movies were made, it was possible to impose relative standards. D. W. Griffith was the first great film-maker simply because his films were so much more accomplished than anyone else's.

After Griffith, film criticism became richer in associations. If Aristotle had been alive to write a *Poetics* on film, he would have begun with D. W. Griffith's *Birth of a Nation* as the first definition of a feature film as a work of bits and pieces unified by a central idea. Griffith is thus one of the definitions of cinema. Subsequent definitions include Murnau, Lang, Lubitsch, Flaherty, Eisenstein, Dreyer, Hitchcock, Renoir, Ford, *et al.* In every instance, the film preceded the film-maker in the critic's consciousness. The films have continued to accumulate more than fifty years after *Birth of a Nation.* The bits and pieces have multiplied beyond measure. The auteur theory is one of several methods employed to unify these bits and pieces into central ideas.

To look at a film as the expression of a director's vision is not to credit the director with total creativity. All directors, and not just in Hollywood, are imprisoned by the conditions of their craft and their culture. The reason foreign directors are almost invariably given more credit for creativity is that the local critic is never aware of all the influences operating in a foreign environment. The late Robert Warshow treated Carl Dreyer as a solitary artist and Leo McCarey as a social agent, but we know now that there were cultural influences in Denmark operating on Dreyer. *Day of Wrath* is superior by any standard to *My Son John,* but Dreyer is not that much freer an artist than McCarey. Dreyer's chains are merely less visible from our vantage point across the Atlantic.

The art of the cinema is the art of an attitude, the style of a gesture. It is not so much *what* as *how.* The *what* is some aspect of reality rendered mechanically by the camera. The *how* is what the French critics designate somewhat mystically as mise-en scène. Auteur criticism is a reaction against sociological criticism that enthroned the *what* against the *how.* However, it would be equally fallacious to enthrone the *how* against the *what.* The whole point of a meaningful style is that it unifies the *what* and the *how* into a personal statement. Even the pacing of a movie can be emotionally expressive when it is understood as a figure of style. Of course, the best directors are usually fortunate enough to exercise control over their films so that there need be no glaring disparity between *what* and *how.* It is only on the intermediate and lower levels of filmmaking that we find talent wasted on inappropriate projects.

Not all directors are auteurs. Indeed, most directors are virtually anonymous. Nor are all auteurs necessarily directors. There is much more of Paddy Chayefsky than of Arthur Hiller in *The Americanization of Emily,* which is another way of saying that *Emily* is written but not really directed. Players, particularly comic players, are their own auteurs to varying degrees. It can be argued that Leo McCarey directed the funniest picture of the Marx Brothers in *Duck Soup,* but he can hardly be credited with molding their anarchic personalities. The trouble with the Marx Brothers, in comparison with Chaplin, Keaton, and Lloyd in the silent era, was that they never controlled their own films either as directors or producers. W. C. Fields did his most memorable turns as unrelated bits of vaudeville in the muck of third-rate scenarios. We remember fragments more than we remember films. Even Garbo was of only fragmentary interest in Robert Z. Leonard's *Susan Lennox—Her Fall and Rise.* Would Garbo's image be as lustrous today without her performances in *Camille* (George Cukor), *Ninotchka* (Ernst Lubitsch), and *Queen Christina* (Rouben Mamoulian)? Good sequences in bad movies can be cited *ad infinitum, ad gloriam.* How about good performances by bad actors? Or good novels by bad novelists? Good and bad seem to become less frivolous matters with acting and writing than with direction.

Most cultivated people know what they like and what is art in acting and writing, but direction is a relatively mysterious, not to say mystical, concept of creation. Indeed, it is not creation at all, but rather a very strenuous form of contemplation. The director is both the least necessary and most important component of film-making. He is the most modern and most decadent of all artists in his relative passivity toward everything that passes before him. He would not be worth bothering with if he were not capable now and then of a sublimity of expression almost miraculously extracted from his money-oriented environment.

STATE OF SIEGE (1973)

By Andrew Sarris

PART I

If *State of Siege* had happened to arrive in America under ordinary circumstances as a commercial enterprise seeking a payoff and a playoff in a capitalistic country, a political analysis of the material would have seemed supplementary if not indeed superfluous. A movie is a movie is a movie and all that. Unfortunately, *State of Siege* has been rather conveniently converted into a cause célèbre under the auspices of the allegedly American Film Institute. The issues have become George Stevens, Jr., and Freedom of Expression rather than the images, sounds, and alleged "facts" of *State of Siege.* Ever since George Stevens, Jr., disinvited *State of Siege* from the opening series of screenings at the AFI Theatre at the Kennedy Center, we have had alarums and excursions and pronouncements and perorations. Indeed, people were busy signing petitions and striking moral poses in support of freedom of expression even before they had seen the movie. As Nichols and May once reminded us in their classic skit on the quiz-show scandals, moral issues are ever so much more fun than real issues. And especially when the culprit is such an easy, harmless, safe target as the infinitely vulnerable American Film Institute. For the record, however, my own position on the moral issue of freedom of expression has never varied by a hair's-breadth over the years. I am flatly opposed to all censorship, be it applied to *State of Siege* or *Deep Throat* or *Birth of a Nation* or *Triumph of the Will* or every last racist flicker of the old cowboy-injun flicks. My commitment to cinema and all other forms of artistic expression is unconditional.

As it happened, I had submitted my resignation from the Board of Directors of the American Film Institute a few days before the controversy over the Costa-Gavras movie erupted. As only one out of 37 members of the board, I hardly intended to overdramatize my departure. I have too often criticized others for grandstand plays not to feel uncomfortable over one of my own. Also, I have always been very careful to make a distinction between reasons and excuses. My basic reason for resigning? I had too many other obligations. That's all, folks. I did not resign because George Stevens, Jr., had the temerity to ignore my political predilections by inviting Richard the Third to the John Ford dinner. I did not resign because *State of Siege* was disinvited, and I did not resign because George Stevens, Jr., had refused to resign or even relent.

My role at the AFI was always too marginal for any administrative megalomania to take hold. I enjoyed my association with Roger Stevens and George Stevens, Jr., and all the other members of the board and the staff. I must confess also that sitting on the board with such star eminences as Gregory Peck and Charlton Heston always gave me a Through-the-Looking-Glass feeling of being a villainous character actor in a movie about Greg or Chuck as an idealistic executive looking right through my darkly circled night-school CPA eyes into my evil corporation-raiding soul, and thus foiling all my nefarious plans. I mean that I was suddenly on the wrong side of the movie screen, and my muse beckoned me back into the creative and critical sanctuary of that darkness in which I had always been destined to function in my proper role.

Nonetheless, I still stand behind the American Film Institute and its objectives, particularly in the crucial area of archival preservation. I believe also that the Institute should assume more responsibility in the encouragement of film scholarship, a domain that has been shrinking in the AFI budget ever since the ouster of Jim Kitses, Estelle

Changas, and Paul Schrader from Greystone. After all, it is a community of film scholars we can thank for the continuing interest in John Ford's career through the sixties and the seventies, and not the assembled Hollywood and Washington stuffed shirts at the Ford dinner. But I shall have more to say about that Ford dinner after I have disposed of all the questions connected with *State of Siege.*

I have talked with both parties to the dispute: George Stevens, Jr., and Roger Stevens for the AFI, and Costa-Gavras for the film. I have now seen the movie, and checked the reviews of Vincent Canby, Judith Crist, Kathleen Carroll, and Archer Winsten. I have also benefited from some instant research on the subject. But it is very hard to know where to begin, and so I will just sort of spill all over from Rome and Paris to Montevideo, from New York to Washington, from *The Battle of Algiers* to *Z,* from fact to fiction all the way to dialectical distortion and the poisonous poetics of partisanship.

First, I can understand why George Stevens, Jr., was upset when he saw the movie and thought of it being screened a few yards from a bust of John F. Kennedy. As a Kennedyite and Washingtonian (and McGovernite too, let us remember), Stevens remembers too many flag-draped coffins, and too many widows' weeds and grieving children to accept the murder of an American on the screen as a parable of Marxist justice. Even an American like Daniel A. Mitrione, for whom few tears were shed around the world at the time of his death. An ethnic police chief from Richmond, Indiana, on a dubious mission for the A.I.D. first in the Dominican Republic, then Brazil, then finally and fatally in Uruguay, is hardly the stuff of which memorable martyrs are made.

Costa-Gavras and Franco Solinas have concentrated on Mitrione as the focal point of all American foreign policy, and indeed of all social evil in the world. However, the film is fictionalized to the extent of using assumed names. Hence, Mitrione is called Philip Michael Santore, but the American flag and the Alliance for Progress, and every aspect of American involvement with Latin America is tied up with Mitrione in a Montevideo cellar. Of course, *State of Siege* was shot not in Montevideo or in any part of Uruguay, but in nearby less chilly Chile. One senses the steep topography of Chile in the early shots of police roadblocks snarling traffic. For the Marxist sensibility, all of South America and indeed all the world is governed by the same laws of oppression, exploitation, and expropriation. The well-publicized statement of Franco Solinas, screenwriter of *State of Siege,* is clear enough:

"We haven't sought to make a suspense film. We wanted to ask the public a question—not in the classic sense, will he die? But is he or is he not responsible? Guilt not in the traditional sense—he has killed, he has robbed—but much greater. A responsibility of a political nature. Our point of view is not romantic. We are not giving a discourse on morality. We do not seek to establish whether Santore is good or bad. Santore interests us because he represents a system which is bad for the majority of men."

In his telegram to the members of the Board of Directors of the American Film Institute, George Stevens, Jr., declared: "Sometime ago we announced plans to premiere *State of Siege* in the AFI Theatre at the Kennedy Center. Though I had not, at that time, seen the film, I made the decision based on my respect for the filmmaking abilities of its creators. I have now seen the film and discovered it deals with a theme which makes it an inappropriate choice for the showing that has been planned for it as part of our opening at the Kennedy Center.

"*State of Siege* deals, according to published statements by the authors, with an event which actually happened in 1970, the political assassination of an American A.I.D. official, Daniel Mitrione, at the hands of guerrillas in Uruguay. Our decision to provide this film with its U.S. premiere in the opening days of the new motion picture theater in the Kennedy Center was a serious mistake, particularly in the wake of recent events which saw the assassination of the American Ambassador and the chargé d'affaires in the Sudan by Arab terrorists.

"Moreover, it appears to me that this film rationalizes an act of political assassination; and I think it undesirable to initiate programing at the John F. Kennedy Center with such a film. I hope any disappointment Costa-Gavras might feel over this will be balanced by the knowledge that his film and the statement he makes within it will be available to the American public in theaters throughout the country of which the film is highly critical."

Stevens later told me he had first been alerted to a possible problem with *State of Siege* when he was having dinner with Max Palevsky, the film's financial backer. Palevsky reportedly remarked that he was surprised to see *State of Siege* go into Kennedy Center. Stevens then made his request to see the film. I first learned of the cancellation when a reporter from the Washington *Post* called to ask my reaction, first to the cancellation, and then to the fact that Stevens had substituted for *State of Siege* one of my alleged "faves," Jacques Rivette's *L'Amour Fou,* as if I had engineered the whole thing to pay off Jacques Rivette. For just an instant, I felt a twinge of Nixonian nastiness toward the *Post,* but it passed, and I pleaded ignorance of the whole dispute.

When I attended the press conference given by Don Rugoff to explain his own position and that of the film's director and screenwriter, there were several interesting plays on words, first as to whether Stevens really meant "rationalization" or "justification." Costa-Gavras and Solinas insisted on making a distinction between the former, which they considered a valid approach to the subject and the latter, invalid. Don Rugoff then made the distinction between assassination and "reluctant" execution, and I popped up to ask what the difference was as far as Mitrione was concerned, and I felt waves of hostility surging over me from all over the auditorium. Mitrione was a non-person that morning, even though an unreasonable replica is now serving as mayor of nearby Philadelphia, and another may be in City Hall come 1974.

My curiosity over the film now thoroughly whetted, I went to see *State of Siege* at the Beekman at its first public performance in New York. At first, I felt the kind of documentary diffuseness I associated more with *The Battle of Algiers* than with *Z.* I was thoroughly familiar with both Costa-Gavras and Solinas, having seen all their work with other writers and directors, and thus spotted the tensions between them. Costa-Gavras flashy, intuitive, fatalistic, almost tragic; Solinas solid, theoretical, dialectical, almost lucid. With Costa-Gavras there was the swirling public occasion with the sardonic Greek Marxist chorus, on this occasion O. E. Hasse as the raisonneur. With Solinas there was the documentary authentication of fictional detail, the torture gadgets shipped in diplomatic pouches from Disneyland training ground in Texas. Step by step, Solinas will instruct us in all the picturesque details of an American conspiracy to enslave the world. It is the same story everywhere, one of the guerrilla interrogators declares: Algeria, Cuba, Vietnam.

Of the reviewers thus far, only Vincent Canby has expressed any reservations about the factual background of the narrative. One would never know from this picture that Uruguay was in a state of civil disorder largely because of the malaise induced by a rampaging inflation, the same kind of inflation which brought Hitler to power in Germany. However, Costa-Gavras and Solinas cannot be faulted for neglecting the bread-and-butter issues of economics. Nothing would be more effective in keeping audiences away from the theater. American complicity in South American torture is a much more effective ploy for the box office, and there is undeniably American complicity in our support and recognition of regimes which torture their citizens, but I really wonder if Algeria, Cuba, and North Vietnam are exempt from the distressingly long list of countries whose dictatorial regimes practice some form of repressive torture. Where does the guilt begin and where does it end, and do Costa-Gavras and Solinas really mean to imply that repressive torture is exclusively the mechanism of capitalistic countries? Why is Mitrione any more the logical product of capitalism than Stalin is the logical product of Marxism?

When I spoke with Costa-Gavras and Solinas, they countered my objection that there was a tendency nowadays to attack the evils of one country's regime against another country's landscape. Thus, I argued, the film versions of the Solzhenitsyn novels were shot in Norway *(One Day in the Life of Ivan Denisovich)* and Denmark *(The Ninth Circle), Z* was shot in Algeria, *The Confession* in France, and now *State of Siege* in Chile. But, they responded, the purpose of ideological cinema is not necessarily to convert the enemy, but to enrich the consciousness of one's supporters. Why shouldn't the left have its own entertainments?

I can't find much to quarrel with in this unusually modest statement of intention. I could even agree with Costa-Gavras and Solinas that all cinema is ideological either by commitment or default. In this sense, *The Godfather* may well be Nixonian by default as *Sound of Music* is Eisenhowerian by evangelical zeal. Why then should I quibble over the discrepancies and distortions in *State of Siege* when there is so much in the film that does attest accurately to the state of the world in our time? I suppose it is because I don't like it when a film tries to outsmart me by juggling its categories between fact and fiction. And also, I feel that Costa-Gavras and Solinas have chosen to exploit libertarian ideas in which they do not really believe. Hence, there is in *State of Siege* a recurring reference to the supposedly sacred Constitution, to the principles of democracy and judicial restraint and parliamentary pluralism, and to the rights of nations to govern their own affairs without outside interference. However, the Tupamaros were a small group of middle-class intellectuals who rejected democratic methods of persuasion. They hardly served as examples of capitalistic exploitation, being closer to our own Weathermen than to Fanon's *Wretched of the Earth.* But from the moment they first appear on the screen, they are romanticized in a way that can only be called Hollywoodian. They seem to travel perpetually in pairs, virile young man with pretty but idealistic young girl. No overt macho here. The Theodorakis percussive rhythms accompanying the capers of the Tupamaros are sympathetically pulse-stirring. There are flashes of comedy relief and humor. It's all such a lark to "expropriate" cars by luring dumb drivers with pretty decoys, and then brandishing guns all over the place. It *is* funny to wrap a middle-aged American in a rug so that his bald pate is sticking out. I could hear the audience giggling. It wasn't quite as exciting as blowing up French men, women, and children in *The Battle of Algiers.* That was really an orgasmic thrill. Perhaps Costa-Gavras and Solinas are not quite ready to rationalize the "reluctant" execution of the Jewish athletes in Munich, but Mitrione, alias Santore, alias Yves Montand as dialectical antagonist for the hooded inquisitors of the left, will do for the moment.

Yves Montand's casting is the movie's biggest coup. Montand gives Santore more gravity, dignity, lucidity, and moral stature than any mere police chief from Richmond, Indiana, would ever dream of demanding from central casting. And it is this inspired casting which gives the movie the tiniest semblance of the objectivity and ambiguity granted to it by those reviewers who have chosen to swallow it whole. Otherwise, every frame of the film is loaded with one-sided propaganda. Indeed, the frames themselves are often gilded with obtrusively oversized officer's hats left over from *Catch-22.* Renato Salvatori, who is especially adept at playing the fascist buffoon for Costa-Gavras, acts more with his ridiculous hat than with his sympathetically primitive face. The fascists are often distorted through the mercilessly derisive lenses of grotesque caricature; the Tupamaros are almost invariably seen in modestly heroic middle shots.

What then of the double layer of the film? It serves merely to imply a causal relationship between every manifestation of the American system and Mitrione. But is it Mitrione as an American, or is it Mitrione as a policeman in any society in the world that is at issue here? Let us say that we comfortable Manhattanites prefer not to know what our Mitriones are doing in the back rooms of station houses throughout the city, the country, and even the world. The order which we seek and which perhaps we now even crave cannot be purchased cheaply. But how much terror would it take in our own immediate neighborhood for us to call Mitrione back from his grave to save us?

Costa-Gavras and Solinas can mince all the words they want. If they do not rationalize or justify assassination by the Tupamaros, they certainly romanticize and sentimentalize it. For example, we see the atrocities of the repressive regime in all its graphic (almost pornographic) detail, but Costa-Gavras never shows us the Tupamaros actually killing Yves Montand. Why not? We saw Montand clobbered again and again in *Z* when he was the good guy being assassinated by the bad guys. Why not now when he is the sympathetically bad guy being "reluctantly" executed by the good guys? Were Costa-Gavras and Solinas afraid that their "rationalization" of leftist terror would leave a bad taste in the viewer's mouth if the viewer were treated to the spectacle of a breathing human flame being snuffed out in the name of a principle?

In *Z*, if you remember, a postscript told us of subsequent developments in Greek politics, all depressingly bad and reactionary. Strangely, there was no postscript to the activities of the Tupamaros. The American fascists go on as before under the watchful Eye of the People, but of the Tupamaros what? Normally, a movie ends when it chooses to end, and the critic has no business pushing it forward in time. Unfortunately, no one thus far seemed interested in checking out what ever happened to the other two officials kidnapped along with Mitrione, namely, American agronomist Dr. Claude L. Fly and Brazilian consul Gomides. On the bus in which the various guerrillas meet in turn to vote on the execution of Santore, the leader is asked about the fate of the other two captives, and the leader answers that they are innocent and will be released in a few days unharmed. The audience is left with the impression that this is precisely what happened. Both men *were* released, but only after a million-dollar ransom was paid for the Brazilian, and only after Claude L. Fly suffered a heart attack during his eight-month captivity. Eight months, not three days. Meanwhile, this same group of Tupamaros had kidnapped the British ambassador to Uruguay, and later another group kidnapped a French woman journalist. A million-dollar ransom was asked for Fly also, but his family couldn't raise the money, and they severely criticized both the Nixon administration and the Uruguayan government for not negotiating with the Tupamaros. The Tupamaros later kidnapped the attorney general from Montevideo, released him after two weeks, and then kidnapped one U. Pereira Reverbel, President Pacheco's confidant and director of the state-owned telephone company for the second time in three years, while he was sitting in a dentist's chair. He pulled a gun but was beaten unconscious and taken out of the building bundled in a blanket.

The British ambassador, describing his ordeal upon arriving in England, said that the kidnappers looked like Ku Klux Klansmen in their masks and that they were about university age. He termed conditions of his imprisonment "abominable," but added that the kidnappers gave him books to read. In that respect, Claude L. Fly wrote a 600-page diary which the Tupamaros delivered with him when he was released. I have not been able to determine whether or not Fly died a short time later as a result of his ordeal, but it was a chance comment of Roger Stevens's that led me along this line of inquiry. There is at once a comic opera aspect and a note of prophetic horror in the full story of the Tupamaros. *State of Siege* does not begin to tell this story in all its historical, sociological, and psychological complexity. But if Costa-Gavras and Solinas had not come along with their provocative movie, I would never have bestirred myself to brush away all the cobwebs from the Mitrione affair. They have thus made me rethink much of my politics and poetics.

What upsets me most in *State of Siege* is not the anti-Americanism, and certainly not the anti-capitalism, but rather the dramatized deliberation of a group of idealists as they prepare to kill an ideological enemy in cold blood. If I believe in anything as a matter of unyielding personal principle, I believe in the total abolition of capital punishment everywhere in the world, and especially in the United States. I don't believe premeditated political murder can ever be sanctified by a poll of the murderers, and, consequently, I cannot participate vicariously in the murder of Mitrione when we have seen already that even Eichmann's execution failed so dismally as psychological retribution that there seems to be an unconscious fear in Israel of another Nazi war criminal doddering into the dock with traumatic irrelevance to the horror of history.

I am willing to believe Stevens rejected *State of Siege* more for its imagery than for its ideology. Still, Stevens was ethically wrong in first inviting and then disinviting a film, the makers of which never sought the honor of an AFI screening in the first place. The feelings of an honored filmmaker should be considered of more import than the feelings of official Washington. Even on the most tactical level, Stevens would have lost nothing by having allowed official Washington to be outraged a bit. So far New York doesn't seem to be outraged at all. Our national self-hatred seems so insatiable that the ideological disapproval of America shared by Costa-Gavras and Solinas seems mild by comparison. There is at least a part of me wondering why Costa-Gavras and Solinas don't go home to take pot-shots at Pompidou and the Pope. It is that same part of me that warms to Jane Fonda, but gets turned off by Vanessa Redgrave. Social criticism should begin at home, and if America has had a bad habit of exporting its presumed virtue abroad, Europeans have an equally bad habit of thinking they can diagnose all America's ills with a quick course in Berlitz and a very short interview with Allen Ginsberg. The strange thing is that *State of Siege* is a great deal more fun as a movie-movie than I seem willing to give it credit for, and both Costa-Gavras and Solinas are a great deal more sympathetic than I seem willing to concede. Perhaps it is the critical and audience reaction that has turned me off from this very skillfully wrought spectacle. So go see it without fail while I prepare to plunge more deeply into its curious paradoxes in Part II, now that I have discussed some of its surface aspects.

PART II

All Greeks are exiles at heart. When they are not in flight from their impoverished geography, they are in retreat from their glorious history. They are officially the most beloved of all minorities, and emotionally the most beleaguered. After all, the rocky, arid, unproductive soil of Greece is hardly the ideal terrain for a national pedestal. Being of Greek descent myself, I believe I have as much right as any non-Greek to have a theory about Greeks.

All my life I have heard condescendingly kind words about Greeks and Greece from non-Greeks. These kind words seemed always to have been designed to make me feel like an unfortunate orphan who had lost his illustrious ancestors a very long time ago. It was therefore in character for the so-called civilized world to repay its debt to Greece by looting the country of almost all its art treasures. There is consequently more of the glory of Ancient Hellas in New York, London, Paris, Berlin, and other museum metropolises than there is in the barren wastes of Greece itself. In this respect, we might say that Lord Elgin loved Greece with the dreadful efficiency of Genghis Khan.

But then who could expect Hellenophiles around the world to entrust modern Greeks with the heritage of Ancient Greece? Even Byron was supposed to have become disillusioned with the brawling Balkan tribe he found foraging on the sites of his romantic visions. He journeyed in quest of nineteenth-century Pericleans, and all he found was a procession of pushcart vendors, who can be found nowadays on any streetcorner in New York beginning the very tedious task of amassing great fortunes.

However, I do not profess to be a professional Greek even in this supposed year of the ethnics. I have very rarely socialized with my ancestral compatriots unless their cultural interests happened to coincide with mine at any given moment. And although I have visited London and Paris fairly regularly since 1961, I never managed to make it to Greece until 1968, and even then and in the following year I never bothered to venture beyond Athens with its open-air cinemas at the walls of which young Costa-Gavras used to leap up and down to get a free view of the screen. The respective birthplaces of my father and mother are not too far from where Costa-Gavras was born, but I have little desire to visit these ancestral locales. Somehow I don't want to repeat Byron's mistake by forcing a pathetic patina of rot and ruin and poverty to fulfill the heroic fantasies my father left behind as his only legacy. Besides, my roots and memories are in Brooklyn and Queens and Manhattan, and not in the Peloponnesian ports from which Greek kings once sailed to reclaim Helen from the Trojans. Still, there were moments in 1968 and 1969 when I sat in the syntagma in Athens with the ghostly feeling that I had been sitting there always in spiritual harmony with my true people, and that some part of me would never leave again.

Perhaps it is true that you can't go home again, but it may also be true that you can never entirely escape the ghosts from the grave. Modern Greece has been politically and often bloodily divided ever since King Otto assumed the throne in 1830. The Monarchists and the Republicans have struggled for power ever since. Nowadays they call each other Fascists and Communists. Even the language has reflected this division with the Cretan dialect of Venizelos and Kazantzakis contending with the Constantinian Katharevousa in which

I was instructed by a succession of very genteel Greek-American teachers.

From everything I have read of the early life of Costa-Gavras in Greece, I know instinctively that his mother and my mother would never get along. I have had many affectionate arguments over Papadopoulos with my mother, but in the crunch I don't think I could turn her over to revolutionary or even reformist authorities for political rectification. Nor would I be particularly overjoyed to see my bourgeois relatives in Athens butchered or even badgered in an "objectively" justified revolution. I don't argue their case or their cause, but there is enough of them in me, and of me in them, to keep me effectively apathetic about the political situation. If the alternative to Papadopoulos and the coarse colonels were some ideal democratic Eden which combined economic justice with political and intellectual freedom, and which excluded the influence and domination of Big Powers, East or West, I would have no problem making the sentimental choice Costa-Gavras has suggested in his last three movies. But I find it naïve to think that any small country (except possibly Switzerland) can find happiness and prosperity in the Big Power-Multinational Corporation maelstrom of today's power politics. Hence, Greece, Czechoslovakia, Uruguay—each in its own way is a pathetic anachronism, a clucking victim of those Big Power Predators: the Eagle and the Bear.

But what of the tortures and arbitrary imprisonments Costa-Gavras complains about in his movies? Of course, I'm opposed to torture and arbitrary imprisonment. Who isn't? But is it more important to condemn a wicked system in which torture and arbitrary imprisonment are possible, or to single out wicked men at random in a melodramatic fashion? If indeed the late Daniel Mitrione practiced torture in Central and South America, and I notice now that that fact is in some dispute, would not a concern with habeas corpus and due process be relevant to the situation? But such a concern applies only if we are talking about politics rather than poetics. When we shift to poetics, the problem is of a different order. Then we must ask if the melodrama surrounding Mitrione is a valid pretext for indoctrinating the audience with a Marxist view of American economic imperialism in South America and the Third World. Most reviewers seem to think it is. Look at the ITT scandals and the Watergate follies, they say. Look at Daniel Ellsberg and Ray Dirks in the dock and on the carpet for exposing chicanery in high places while the worst culprits get off scot-free. Certainly, the most morbid Marxist would be hard put to think up a plot as sordid as Watergate or the Equity Funding Corporation with a computer actually programmed for fraud.

We are ready to believe the worst about anyone and anything. Thus, Costa-Gavras and Solinas do not have to prove their case against Mitrione alias Santore. They merely have to shout: *"J'accuse!"* and the mob will do the rest. For some reviewers, the daily headlines fill in the blank spaces of *State of Siege*. Judith Crist, for example, considers the machinations of ITT in Chile as full confirmation of what Costa-Gavras and Solinas impute to Mitrione in Uruguay, Brazil, and the Dominican Republic. Now, no one can accuse Judith Crist, Archer Winsten, and Kathleen Carroll of being systematic Marxists or anti-Americans. None of these critics has ever been unduly enchanted with Jean-Luc Godard's brand of Marxist-Leninist cinema in recent years. It isn't really a movie, they complain of just everything Godard has done in the past five years, and even before. Godard seems boring and self-indulgent whereas Costa-Gavras seems exciting and entertaining. But if anything, Godard's politics are more radical than Costa-Gavras's. Having recently interviewed Godard and Jean-Pierre Gorin at the Algonquin, I retain an image of two field-jacketed fugitives from Mao's Ninth Army walking across the media-hardened indifference of the dining room. By contrast, Costa-Gavras and Solinas at the relatively palatial Pierre evoke the elegant middle-class leftism of the brightest salons in Paris and Rome. And yet in the esoteric reaches of world structuralism, Godard is still regarded as a stylistic force, and Costa-Gavras merely as a manipulative entertainer with a weakness for sacrificing form to effect. It is this perverseness in the structuralist scene in Paris against which Mary McCarthy was reacting when she declared in a recent symposium in the *Partisan Review* that she did indeed enjoy *Z*, as if the topmost towers of *Tel Quel*, *Cinéthique*, and the newly structured *Cahiers du Cinéma* would topple in shock from such vulgar impudence. My own reading of Costa-Gavras from his films has always been that he was nothing if not passionately pragmatic.

But when I finally did meet him, I found that my previous insights were only partially confirmed. In a sense, we both belong to a multinational firm of film sensibilities and we are both limited in our power, our choices and options, he as a filmmaker and I as a film critic. On the gut issues, he is probably closer to radical anarchism, and I to liberal skepticism, and this is perhaps the widest chasm possible between two sensibilities in the modern world. I state my bias openly so that my instinctive resistance to his movies may be taken by the reader as a personal idiosyncrasy. I have read elsewhere that Costa-Gavras's father fought on the EAM or losing side of the Greek Civil War, which in its way was as traumatic a struggle between left and right as the Spanish Civil War. One could not expect a direct victim of the Truman Doctrine to grow up with a warm feeling for American Manifest Destiny anywhere in the world. But have the movie-movies of Costa-Gavras radicalized the world any more than has the anticinema of Godard? Or do they serve, as Luis Buñuel suggested to Carlos Fuentes of all subversive movies, merely as a means of expressing a margin of dissent from established authority?

It is significant that violence and/or torture figure very centrally in all three Costa-Gavras political films. Costa-Gavras told me that he had imported a tragic vision of life into the French cinema from both his Greek background and from the American movies he always admired. Orson Welles once remarked that tragedy in the English-speaking world since Shakespeare had become inseparable from melodrama. By contrast, French tragedy since Racine is locked in the mind, the will, and the language. Thus, as Shaw once noted, whereas English-speaking intellectuals tend to disguise their feelings as ideas, French intellectuals tend to disguise their ideas as feelings, the difference precisely between Shakespeare and Racine.

Curiously, the most feeling I ever sensed in a Costa-Gavras came through in his very first movie, a nonpolitical exercise entitled *The Sleeping Car Murders,* particularly in the relationship between the wisely world-weary detective played by Yves Montand and his surrogate son played by Jacques Perrin. There was an odd sweetness and intensity to this relationship, which, in retrospect, takes on an autobiographical coloration. I am beginning to understand Costa-Gavras's feeling for tragedy as I have always understood his image of himself as an exile. It is a feeling that is evidenced in the looks people give one another in flashbacks as if they already know that things are going to end very badly. With a natively somber artist like Costa-Gavras, life does not really begin until someone has died. But tragic feelings and tragic looks do not constitute a tragic vision. There is more of a tragic vision in Mizoguchi and in Ophuls and even in Sergio Leone than there is in Costa-Gavras. And least of all is there a tragic vision in *State of Siege.* Why not? Simply because Costa-Gavras and Solinas do not display the slightest interest in Daniel Mitrione as a human being. Time and again, the recurring images of memory and celebration threaten to break through into personal reverie, but they always stop safely on the other side of congealed politics. What was it really like for a police chief from Richmond, Indiana, to await death in a Montevideo cellar? For that matter, what was it really like to be a police chief in Richmond, Indiana? Costa-Gavras doesn't really care. He has convinced himself somehow that life is a collective experience within certain prescribed ideological limits, and the Enemy is invariably vulgar, corrupt, perverted, and, when Yves Montand plays the lead, pathetically deceived. But tragic feelings divorced from individual, idiosyncratic personal destiny result only in sentimental politics.

Hence, *State of Siege* reminds me of nothing so much as those old Warners historical allegories like *The Life of Emile Zola* and *Juarez* with a touch of *Watch on the Rhine.* The assassinated pacifist leader in *Z* was a combination Zola, Dreyfus, and Juarez, and the "reluctant" execution of Maximilian in *Juarez* bears more than a passing resemblance to the "reluctant" execution of Mitrione in *State of Siege.* It remained for Lillian Hellman's *Watch on the Rhine* to dramatize how some murders were less evil than others, and how the end sometimes justified the means, especially when Mother Russia was being menaced by fascist Finland. But then why shouldn't the left have its own John Wayne-type genre entertainment? I prefer to see left and right as arbitrary points on a circle of human illusions rotating endlessly around lonely, alienated exiles from Eden in search of a meaning to life before the darkness of death. My poetics are therefore even less in tune with *State of Siege* than are my politics. However, it is possible that Costa-Gavras may have decided that to let his tragic feelings come through all the way in his political films would make him tactically guilty of the Sin of Despair. Art and Revolution. Choose One. I choose Art.

INTRODUCTION: NOTES ON A SCREENWRITER'S THEORY, 1973—INTRODUCTION TO TALKING PICTURES (1973)

By Richard Corliss

1. *THESIS: THE DIRECTOR AS* AUTEUR

I was driving by Otto Preminger's house last night—or is it "a house by Otto Preminger"?

—Burt Kennedy, 1971

It's a full decade now since Andrew Sarris published, in *Film Culture* magazine, his two-part Americanization of the *politique des auteurs.* At the time it could be taken as a thoughtful and provocative challenge to that near-monopoly in serious English-language film criticism, the Social Dialectic. Refreshingly, Sarris examined films as the creations of artists rather than of social forces—whether capitalist, communist, or fascist—and, in doing so, he helped liberate the scrupulous study of American film from the numbing strictures of solemnity. We could finally admit without shame that the best Hollywood movies succeeded not only as delightful entertainments but as art works rivaling those from the culture capitals of Europe.

Sarris wasn't the first American to argue that "the director is the author of a film." Hollywood itself had accepted this policy in the silent days, when directors received billing just below their stars; *The Rise of the American Film* and *The Liveliest Art* devote long chapters to the careers of Hollywood *metteurs-en-scène;* even Bosley Crowther, back in 1940, seconded William Wyler's assertion that "the final responsibility for a picture's quality rests solely and completely upon the shoulders of the man who directed it." But it was Sarris's call to arms that started the auteur revolution. First the specialized journals, then the mass-market magazines, then *The New York Times, Cue,* and *TV Guide* began crediting directors not only with authorship but with ownership: "Arthur Hiller's *Love Story.*" By the time the trend had reached Hollywood, it had become something of a joke. Thus *Play It Again, Sam*—starring Woody Allen, screenplay by Woody Allen, from a play by Woody Allen—is heralded in the screen credits as "A Herbert Ross Film."

Sarris's version of the *politique* was extraordinarily helpful in calling attention to neglected American directors in a fistful of infra dig genres, but it may have done more harm than good in citing the director as the sole author of his film. What could have begun a systematic expansion of American film history—by calling attention to anonymous screenwriters, cinematographers, art directors, and, yes, even actors—bogged down in an endless coronation of the director as benevolent despot, in his enshrinement as solitary artist, with his collaborating craftsmen functioning merely as paint, canvas, bowl of fruit, and patron.

By establishing the director as the Creator of a Work of Art, the auteurists were falling into the same critical traps that had snared the no-less-well-meaning Social Realism crowd some thirty years earlier. The notion persists that a work of art is the product of one man working alone to carve a personal vision out of the marble of his sensibility. Ideally, perhaps, but not invariably—and, in Hollywood, not even generally. Yet this notion, very romantic and very American, is the basis upon which most recent film histories stand. It is so basic that it is taken for granted: in the standard book-length studies of Sternberg and Stevens, Hitchcock and Hawks, the critics' auteur bias is a given that needn't be proven.

A number of critical labels have to be spindled and mutilated before we can begin to appreciate the collaborative complexity of American cinema more fully. ART VS. ENTERTAINMENT: a rather precious distinction by now, since any supremely entertaining movie should reveal deeper (or at least broader) levels upon further viewings, and since any work of art cannot help but entertain, if only in the viewer's delight in discovering it. SOLITARY ART VS. CORPORATE ART: The fact that Chartres, or *Charade,* was the work of a number of individuals contributing their unique talents to a corporate enterprise doesn't necessarily make either work less "artistic" than, say, Van Gogh's "Wildflowers" or Snow's *Wavelength.* It just makes it more difficult for the critic to assign sole authorship, which is more a critical convenience than a value judgment—or should be, anyway.

THE CREATIVE ARTIST VS. THE INTERPRETIVE ARTIST: Both Stanley Donen and Michael Snow are, shall we say, artists; but Snow is a creative artist and Donen an interpretive artist. Snow is almost literally a film *maker,* collaborating with his film strips and his Movieola in an intimate, incestuous way that has very little to do with the way Donen collaborates with his scriptwriter, actors, and technicians. The traditional view was that the solitary, creative artist produced Art, while the corporate, interpretive craftsman produced Entertainment. It would seem that the auteur theory, which one might have assumed would demolish this old canard, is actually reinforcing it. If Donen is worthy of sustained critical study (and I believe he is), so are, say, Arthur Freed, Gene Kelly, Betty Comden and Adolph Green, Richard Avedon, George Abbott, Cary Grant, Peter Stone, Christopher Challis, and all the other talented men and women whose careers intersected Donen's at mutually felicitous points.

Cinema is not the only medium in which authorship is bestowed upon the director (or, for that matter, the art director—as witness John Simon's recent critical study, *Ingmar Bergman Directs,* which the title page describes, in a type size equal to Mr. Simon's credit, as "a creation of Halcyon Enterprises"!). Determining authorship in the theater can be a complicated business. Is Harold Pinter the "author" of *Old Times?* Most assuredly. And yet the difference between the London and New York productions of the play amounted to more than a subtle shift in tone, or even in effect; it was a difference in *meaning.* As played by Colin Blakely (London), the Deeley character was the audience's very vulnerable identity figure; as played by Robert Shaw (New York), he was a self-deceiving boor. As played by Vivien Merchant (London), the Anna character was menacing, predatory; as played by Rosemary Harris (New York), she was helpful, sympathetic. Same author, same director, same pauses—but different casts and, almost, two different plays.

It's probably fair to consider Tom O'Horgan the prime mover (whether as creator or defiler) of his later theatrical extravaganzas, because he shapes, packages, controls his productions as completely as, say, Ken Russell controls *his* films. In a less mannerist vein, the Broadway career of Elia Kazan—whose collaborations with Tennessee Williams, Arthur Miller, and S. N. Behrman, among others, were both intense and enduring—could be profitably studied for Kazan's personal approach to themes and styles. But could he exercise "directorial authority" as powerfully on Broadway as in Hollywood? In one case at least, *yes:* at his insistence, Williams wrote an entirely new third act for *Cat on a Hot Tin Roof.* To be sure (and to be lamented), one can*not* study Kazan's theater work, because his productions died on closing night, while his playwrights' scripts live on in book form. One reason for directorial supremacy in the cinema may be that, there, the reverse is true: screenplays are rarely published (and barely consulted even then), while the films made from them are available at the flick of a TV channel selector.

William Wyler was absolutely right to hold the director responsible for "a picture's quality"—just as a conductor is responsible for the composer's symphony, or a contractor for the architect's plans. But he must also be responsible *to* something: the screenplay. With it, he can do one of three things: ruin it, shoot it, or improve it. Realizing a screenplay is the director's job; transcending it is his glory. Despite the Writers Guild's immemorial gripes, directing is a fine art, not a lead-pipe cinch (as too many screenwriters have proved when they tried to direct a picture).

Andrew Sarris has said that the directors he prefers are those with an unconscious—who, presumably, speak from the soul, and not from the scenario. I think that this statement also suggests why Sarris prefers a director's cinema to a writer's. One restraint on the poetic tendencies of a screenwriter-oriented critic, as opposed to those of an auteurist, is that the screenwriter *makes* words and situations occur, while the director *allows* actions to occur. Thus, the process of creating a screenplay is more formal, less mystical than the image, which is created by the director, photographer, designer, and actors. This inexactness of the visual process gives the auteurist an opportunity to infer reams and realms of metaphysical nuance. Typewriter keys seem to spring to the paper with grandiose generalizations: "a world of . . . ," "the cinema of . . ." And since the director allowed these filmic epiphanies to take place, who's to say he didn't *make* them happen?

This is the notion of the artist as inspired dervish—literally "inspired." The Muse breathes the spirit into a director, and he exhales this inspiration, filling the sound stage with a magic that affects cast and crew and results in a privileged moment. To the great directors, making their greatest films, this fantasy may apply.

One gets the feeling that John Ford creatively controlled every moment of *The Searchers,* from first opening door to last closing door. But the greatness of even so controlled a film as *Psycho* is partly due to Anthony Perkins' performance, which at least extended, and probably transcended, Hitchcock's understanding of Norman Bates's character.

The director *is* right in the middle of things. At the very least, he's on the sound stage while the cinematographer is lighting the set that the art director has designed and, later, while the actors are speaking the lines that the screenwriter wrote. At best, he steers all these factors (story, actors, camera) in the right *direction,* to the extent that many films are indeed dominated by his personality—though not, perhaps, in the way the auteurists mean. The phrase "directorial personality" may make more sense if it's taken quite literally. Anyone who's seen Stanley Donen or Sam Peckinpah or Howard Hawks or Radley Metzger in action knows that the effective director is usually a man with a strong, persuasive personality. He has to combine the talents of salesman (to get a job in the first place), tough guy (to make the technicians respond to his commands), and best friend (to coax a good performance out of a volatile actress). Whether he directs with a riding crop (Stroheim), an icy stare (Sternberg), or some lightweight banter (Cukor), his personality is often crucial to the success of a film. The importance of a director's personal—or even visual—style is not a question here, only the assumption that he creates a style out of thin air instead of adapting it to the equally important styles of the story and performers.

Indeed, if auteur criticism had lived up to its early claim to be truly concerned with visual style, there would be no need for any systematic slighting of the screenwriter. Given a certain text, or pretext, the director could be said to weave the writer's design into a personal, visual subtext through the use of camera placement and movement, lighting, cutting, direction of actors, etc. Such a *politique* would go far toward elucidating the work of superior *metteurs-en-scène* on the order of Cukor, Donen, Michael Curtiz, Mitchell Leisen, and Don Siegel. But visual style is not the auteurist's major interest. Auteur criticism is essentially theme criticism; and themes—as expressed through plot, characterization, and dialogue—belong primarily to the writer.

2. *ANTITHESIS: THE SCREENWRITER AS* AUTEUR

In my opinion, the writer should have the first and last word in filmmaking, the only better alternative being the writer-director, but with the stress on the first word.

—Orson Welles, 1950

The cry *"cherchez l'auteur"* can lead unwary film scholars astray when the auteur happens to be the author—or rather, when the script is the basis of a film's success. As often as not, when a fine film is signed by a middle-rung director, the film's distinctive qualities can be traced to the screenwriter. There's no need to rescue Mitchell Leisen, Garson Kanin, Sam Wood, and William D. Russell from the underworld of neglected directors simply because each was fortunate enough to direct a comedy written, in his best period, by Norman Krasna (*Hands Across the Table, Bachelor Mother, The Devil and Miss Jones,* and *Dear Ruth,* respectively). The direction of these films *is* usually adroit and sensitive, and the presence of charming comediennes enhances them even further; but the delightfully dominant personality behind the screen is undoubtedly Krasna's.

Krasna's "mistaken-identity" theme, which he milked for more than thirty years, is as unmistakable as an Eric Rohmer plot—but he's hardly the only Hollywood screenwriter with thematic or tonal obsessions. Ben Hecht's penny-ante cynicism, Preston Sturges's apple-pie-in-the-face Americana, Frank Tashlin's breast fixation, Peter Stone's schizophrenia, George Axelrod's impotent Svengalis, Howard Koch's *liebestod* letters, Borden Chase's wagon trains of Western Civilization, Abraham Polonsky's economic determinism, Billy Wilder's creative con men, Samson Raphaelson's aristocratic *bourgeoisie,* Garson Kanin and Ruth Gordon's eccentric marriages, Dudley Nichols's instant redemption, Joseph L. Mankiewicz's endless articulation, Dalton Trumbo's gilt-edged propaganda, Robert Riskin's demogogic populism, Sidney Buchman's democratic republicanism, Jules Furthman's noble adventurers, Charles Lederer's sassy misanthropy, Ring Lardner, Jr.'s brassy misogyny, Terry Southern's practical joking, Erich Segal's ivy-covered sentimentality, Jules Feiffer's cartoon morality plays, David Newman and Robert Benton's likable losers . . . look at the films of these screenwriters half as closely as an auteurist would examine the work of Otto Preminger or Robert Mulligan, and chances are you'll find yourself staring at some dominant theme or style or plot or mood—some strong personal trait of film authorship. After all, film is (as Andrew Sarris has observed) essentially a dramatic medium; and the screenwriters are the medium's dramatists.

It's clear that some method of classification and evaluation is necessary, both to identify and to assess the contribution of that overpaid but unsung *genus* known as the screenwriter. But that is a game that conceals even more pitfalls than does the Sarris Hit Parade of Directors. Once the auteur scholar accepts the myth of the omnipotent director—that nonexistent Hawks or Stevens who writes, produces, photographs, acts in, and edits every film he makes—his game is won. Indeed, even the stanchest adherent of the *politique des collaborateurs* can be fairly sure that the director of record is the man who hollered "Action!" and "Cut!"—though his importance in controlling what went on between those two commands may be disputed. But the size of a screenwriter's contribution to any given film is often more difficult to ascertain.

A writer may be given screen credit for work he didn't do (as with Sidney Buchman on *Holiday*), or be denied credit for work he did do (as with Sidney Buchman on *The Awful Truth*). The latter case is far more common than the former. Garson Kanin co-wrote *The More the Merrier,* but his name didn't appear on-screen because he had already been inducted into the wartime Army. Ben Hecht toiled for seven days rewriting the first nine reels of *Gone With the Wind,* but David O. Selznick wanted Sidney Howard's name to appear alone on the screenplay. Michael Wilson wrote the screenplay for *Friendly Persuasion* and co-scripted *The Bridge on the River Kwai* and *Lawrence of Arabia,* but the Hollywood blacklist kept his name off all three films, and the writing Oscar for *Kwai* was awarded to Pierre Boulle, who had nothing at all to do with the film adapted from his novel.

The American Screen Writers Guild has a ridiculous rule that disallows screenplay credit to any director who has not contributed at least fifty percent of the dialogue—ridiculous if only because it permits auteur critics to infer that their favorite directors consistently contributed, say, forty-nine percent. (When the Guild discovered that *Bad Company,* a script by the writing team of Benton and Newman, was going to be directed by Benton, it routinely scheduled an arbitration hearing to determine whether director Benton was stealing a credit on poor writer Newman's script!) In Europe, the auteurists tell us, things are more enlightened: there, the director receives screenplay credit whether he wrote anything or not. Certainly Bergman, Fellini, Antonioni, Chabrol, Truffaut (all writers before they were directors) work either as sole authors or as collaborators—and not just as editors—on their screenplays. But reliable sources indicate that *Tout Va Bien,* the new "Godard" film, was written solely by Jean-Pierre Gorin; and Luis Buñuel has admitted in print that he contributed not one word of dialogue to Jean-Claude Carrière's script for *Le Charme Discret de la Bourgeoisie,* although Bruñuel is listed ahead of Carrière as an author of the screenplay. Joseph Losey, who never takes screenplay credit, says he works as closely with the screenwriter as he does with the cinematographer, editor, and actors—should he share official credit with these collaborators as well? Losey needn't worry: auteur critics would have him share credit with *nobody.*

In the Golden Age of Hollywood, things were a bit different. A director would be given a script and instructed to start shooting Monday; so much for shaping a personal vision through creative rewriting. But what about the screenwriter who specializes in adaptations? Who's the auteur then? It's true that, in the case of a Donald Ogden Stewart, the problem is more subtle. Few screenwriters can boast a more impressive list of credits than Stewart's. As with George Cukor, the director for whom he produced his finest scripts, Stewart's "filmography is his most eloquent defense." Both Stewart and Cukor, however, had the good luck to be assigned adaptations of some of the wittiest and most actable theater pieces of their time—*Holiday, The Women* (for which Stewart received no screen credit), *The Philadelphia Story,* and *Edward, My Son*—and Stewart's transferrals of these works from stage to screen adhered closely to both the spirit and the letter of the originals.

Stewart's achievement should not be dismissed; many screenwriters failed at the delicate craft he mastered. But, as with directors, one can distinguish several layers of screenwriting authorship: the indifferent work of a mediocre writer, whether it's an original script or an adaptation (which we may call procrustean); the gem-polishing of a gifted adapter like Stewart (protean); and the creation of a superior original script, like Herman J. Mankiewicz's *Citizen Kane* or Abraham Polonsky's *Body and Soul* (promethean). When faced with the career of a Stewart, the critic who has discarded the convenience of the auteur theory must compare Stewart's adaptations with the source works, in hopes of detecting such changes as plot compression or expansion, bowdlerization, addition or deletion of dialogue, and differences in theme and tone. At worst, this research will exhaust and discourage the critic; at best, it will convince him that the creation of a Hollywood movie involves a complex weave of talents, properties, and personalities.

When a screenwriter, like Preston Sturges or George Axelrod, has a distinctive authorial tone, his contributions to films with multiple script credits can usually be discerned. But the hallmark of many fine screenwriters is versatility, not consistency. Subject matter dictates style. Given the Cheshire Cat nature of these writers, how are we to know which part of the *Casablanca* script is the work of the sophisticated but self-effacing Howard Koch, and which part was written by Julius and Philip Epstein? Well, recent archaeological studies have indicated that the Epsteins began to rework the plot of an unproduced play, *Everybody Comes to Rick's* (which has, in sketch form, most of the film's characters, including a Negro named Sam who is told to "Play it, Sam," and plays "As Time Goes By"), but then were called to the War; and that Koch developed these contributions into the final, full-blooded screenplay.

We don't have many of these memoirs, though—screenwriters being a notoriously underinterviewed breed (ever read one with Herman Mankiewicz?)—and since most Hollywood egos are approximately the size of the Graf Zeppelin, the accounts of screenwriters may be taken with the same pillar of salt we keep handy for directors' interviews and actors' autobiographies. Nevertheless, a screenwriter's work should and can be judged by analyzing his entire career, as is done with a director. If a writer has been associated with a number of favorite films, if he has received sole writing credit on some of these films, and if we can decipher a common style in films with different directors and actors, an authorial personality begins to appear. The high polish and understated irony of Koch's other work—from his script for the Mercury Theatre *War of the Worlds,* through his ten-year tenure at Warners, to his late-forties scripts for *Letter from an Unknown Woman* and *No Sad Songs for Me*—and his fulfillment of our three conditions, give credence to this account of the writing of *Casablanca.*

In fact, most of the best Hollywood screenwriters were sole authors of a substantial number of scripts.

The paucity of critical and historical literature makes all screenwriters "Subjects for Further Research." The cavalier group headings on the following lists are meant only to emphasize the tentative nature of the classification. As more films are seen from the writers' point of view, names will be shuffled from one list to another. Ultimately, each of them, and many more, should have an artistic identity clear enough to make such capricious classification unnecessary. Until that enlightened time comes to pass, we must make do with an Acropolis of Screenwriters something like this one—which considers only the writers who are evaluated in this book.*

Parthenon. Borden Chase, Betty Comden and Adolph Green, Ben Hecht, Nunnally Johnson, Garson Kanin (and Ruth Gordon), Howard Koch, Frank S. Nugent, Samson Raphaelson, Preston Sturges, Billy Wilder.

Erechtheion. George Axelrod, Sidney Buchman, Jules Feiffer, Norman Krasna, Ernest Lehman, Herman J. Mankiewicz, David Newman and Robert Benton, Abraham Polonsky, Casey Robinson, Peter Stone.

Propylaea. Charles Brackett, Delmer Daves, Jules Furthman, Buck Henry, Ring Lardner, Jr., Charles Lederer, Joseph L. Mankiewicz, Robert Riskin, Morrie Ryskind, Frank Tashlin.

Outside the Walls. Edwin Justus Mayer, Dudley Nichols, Erich Segal, Terry Southern, Dalton Trumbo.

All of these screenwriters—even those infidels muttering curses outside our Acropolis walls—deserve monographs or books devoted to their Hollywood careers. If the critical winds reverse themselves, and if publishers' generosity to unsalable film books continues, dawn may yet break over a bookshelf stocked with such titles as *The Cinema of Samson Raphaelson* and *The Collected Letters of Howard Koch.*

In the main, the screenwriters who appear in this book are those who, by adapting their conspicuous talents to the Byzantine demands of the trade, developed the most successful screenwriting techniques. Success usually begat power, and power begat authority. By authority is meant the right to complete your own script without being forced to surrender it to the next fellow on the assembly line,

*I.e., in Corliss's *Talking Pictures.—Ed.*

the right to consult with any actor or director who wants changes, and the right to fight for your film through the taffy pull of front-office politics, pressure groups, and publicists. If directors have been pre-eminent in Hollywood since long before the arrival of the auteur theory, it is probably because, among all of Tinseltown's employees, they were the ones with the most power.

3. *SYNTHESIS: THE MULTIPLE* AUTEUR

There was the era of the actor, when a film was its star, and we had Mary Pickford, Douglas Fairbanks, Greta Garbo. Then we had the era of the director, and the films of King Vidor, Sternberg, Feyder and Clair. A new era is beginning: that of the author. After all, it's the author who makes a film.

—Jean Renoir, 1939

Despite their own kvetching about functional impotence in the moviemaking process, and despite the criminal negligence of a new breed of critics, screenwriters have done so much in making a film entertaining, moving, even ennobling. But such has been the factory nature of the Hollywood movie that writers can still do *only* so much. A screenwriter is, as often as not, the middleman between the author of the original property and the director—and the man who gets his hands on the flypaper last is the one whose fingerprints will show up first. The writers' movement in the thirties and forties, inextricably bound up with inter-Guild hostilities and jealousies as it was, drew its limited power by sucking as much blood as possible from the *metteur-en-scène* as the Directors Guild would allow. The effect of the auteur theory was to steal back whatever authority (and authorship) the writers had usurped: at best, it was proposed, the writer writes a script but the director makes the film. The two crafts were seen as riding on opposite sides of a seesaw, with the weight of contemporary critical opinion deciding which group was to be left stranded in the air.

Perhaps a synthesis of these presumably antithetical functions is in order. The films that receive the highest praise in this book are those whose writers and directors—in creative association with the actors and technicians—worked together toward a collaborative vision. You could call *Citizen Kane* either the culmination of Herman Mankiewicz's dreams or the beginning of Orson Welles' nightmares, but it would be silly to ignore either man's contribution. Who is the auteur of *Ninotchka:* Ernst Lubitsch, or the Charles Brackett–Billy Wilder–Walter Reisch team, or Greta Garbo? Obviously, all of them. I've tried in this book to make a case for the screenwriter without libeling either the director or the actor. Once the contribution of all these crafts—individually and collectively—have been accepted and examined, studies of other vital film collaborators could begin and be meshed into a giant matrix of coordinate talents. One ultimate result of this process of synthesis should be to open the critical shutter a few more stops upon that strange and glorious hybrid: the artistic-entertaining, solitary-corporate, creative-interpretive talking picture.

GENRES

Writing about film genres is a notoriously hazardous task. Just defining a genre is difficult enough. How many films are necessary to make up an authentic genre? How does one distinguish a genre from a cycle or a trend? How does one evaluate a given genre film—by its adherence to some ideal type in the critic's head, by its willingness to work variations on the type, or by its eagerness to deny the conventions of the type altogether? If originality matters to a critic more than anything else, then isn't he saying that a genre film cannot be truly first-rate, that every great film, by definition, is *sui generis*—a genre of its own kind? Despite all these confusions (and there are many more), genre criticism continues to exert a fascination for critics and sociologists, and for obvious reasons. When certain settings, narrative conventions, and moral/social conflicts are repeated (with variations) through decades, they must be telling us something essential about the capabilities of the medium and the nature of the audience. The latter possibility has always been particularly intriguing. Presumably, if the audience wasn't powerfully drawn to what a given genre was saying about America, the audience would stop going and the genre would die out (which has happened in many cases). Most critics feel that it is only in genre films that the audience yields up its soul, not in film classics or in the occasional huge hit whose popularity becomes a mystery once the preoccupations of the season have passed.

When genre criticism is bad, it's really insufferably bad—presumptuous, overgeneralized, less valuable than a good accurate review of a single film. More than any other kind of criticism, it requires intellectual *tact.* In his famous piece on silent comedy, James Agee confined himself to the evocation of a language—a language no longer spoken but still comprehensible to those who might hear it. This long piece never proposes a theory of comedy; it consists almost entirely of precise descriptions of appearance, movement, gesture, and rhythm, and some of these notations are as decisive and fiercely concentrated as great poetry. Silent comedy appealed to Agee's love of physical heroism; since it was a form of *vanished* heroism, he felt free to let out his full Southern eloquence, by turns celebratory and elegiac.

Of course Agee is brutally unfair to talking comedy (he doesn't even mention the screwball comedies of the thirties, one of the richest of all American film genres), thereby illustrating an abiding problem of genre criticism: Once a critic has set up his ideals, he finds it hard to be generous to films that differ from the type. A similar problem arises in Robert Warshow's essay on the Western; Warshow appears to be dismissing some of the most important and interesting Westerns because they don't fit the pattern he has established. Still, this is one of the most satisfying pieces of film criticism ever written in this country. In his introduction to Warshow's *The Immediate Experience,* Lionel Trilling praised Warshow's noble clarity of phrase, and compared this essay to the work of Hazlitt and Orwell. The moral universe of the classic Western, as Warshow describes it, is even more beautiful and haunting to us now than it was twenty years ago: The values Warshow celebrates have disappeared from Westerns, indeed from all movies, and nearly everyone feels the loss. Reading this essay should silence forever those educated simpletons who say that movies are worthless because they don't tell the truth. Warshow loved truth as much as anyone, but he also saw the moral and aesthetic necessity for myth. If he had lived into the sixties and seventies (he died in 1955, only thirty-seven years old), one imagines he would have become increasingly depressed by a culture that systematically undermined all its myths, debunking everything and everybody, with the unhappy result of leaving us all up in the air believing in nothing.

In her piece on the science fiction films of the fifties and early sixties, Susan Sontag sidesteps the problem of the ideal type by setting up a number of alternate models equal in value. She is determined to understand what the genre is saying, rather than to evaluate its success as art. As a result, for some readers this piece may seem more like sociological speculation than criticism, but I still find it irresistible for its deadpan (and often very funny) descriptions of large-scale disaster as an aesthetic and "sensuous" experience, and for its sober elaboration of what that experience reveals of the viewer's psychology.

For both Sontag and Paul Schrader (in his piece on *film noir*), the movies are a good place to study the dark side of postwar popular culture. Schrader's piece may be only a series of "notes" (as he calls them), but it suggests the mixture of stylistic, historical, and sociological speculation that any successful example of genre criticism must contain. Since Schrader subsequently wrote the screenplays for such films as *Taxi Driver* and *Obsession,* the article is also intriguing for what it suggests of his preoccupations and ambitions.—*Ed.*

COMEDY'S GREATEST ERA (1949)

By James Agee

In the language of screen comedians four of the main grades of laugh are the titter, the yowl, the bellylaugh and the boffo. The titter is just a titter. The yowl is a runaway titter. Anyone who has ever had the pleasure knows all about a bellylaugh. The boffo is the laugh that kills. An ideally good gag, perfectly constructed and played, would bring the victim up this ladder of laughs by cruelly controlled degrees to the top rung, and would then proceed to wobble, shake, wave and brandish the ladder until he groaned for mercy. Then, after the shortest possible time out for recuperation, he would feel the first wicked tickling of the comedian's whip once more and start up a new ladder.

The reader can get a fair enough idea of the current state of screen comedy by asking himself how long it has been since he has had that treatment. The best of comedies these days hand out plenty of titters and once in a while it is possible to achieve a yowl without overstraining. Even those who have never seen anything better must occasionally have the feeling, as they watch the current run or, rather, trickle of screen comedy, that they are having to make a little cause for laughter go an awfully long way. And anyone who has watched screen comedy over the past ten or fifteen years is bound to realize that it has quietly but steadily deteriorated. As for those happy atavists who remember silent comedy in its heyday and the bellylaughs and boffos that went with it, they have something close to an absolute standard by which to measure the deterioration.

When a modern comedian gets hit on the head, for example, the most he is apt to do is look sleepy. When a silent comedian got hit on the head he seldom let it go so flatly. He realized a broad license, and a ruthless discipline within that license. It was his business to be as funny as possible physically, without the help or hindrance of words. So he gave us a figure of speech, or rather of vision, for loss of consciousness. In other words he gave us a poem, a kind of poem, moreover, that everybody understands. The least he might do was to straighten up stiff as a plank and fall over backward with such skill that his whole length seemed to slap the floor at the same instant. Or he might make a cadenza of it—look vague, smile like an angel, roll up his eyes, lace his fingers, thrust his hands palms downward as far as they would go, hunch his shoulders, rise on tiptoe, prance ecstatically in narrowing circles until, with tallow knees, he sank down the vortex of his dizziness to the floor, and there signified nirvana by kicking his heels twice, like a swimming frog.

Startled by a cop, this same comedian might grab his hatbrim with both hands and yank it down over his ears, jump high in the air, come to earth in a split violent enough to telescope his spine, spring thence into a coattail-flattening sprint and dwindle at rocket speed to the size of a gnat along the grand, forlorn perspective of some lazy back boulevard.

Those are fine clichés from the language of silent comedy in its infancy. The man who could handle them properly combined several of the more difficult accomplishments of the acrobat, the dancer, the clown and the mime. Some very gifted comedians, unforgettably Ben Turpin, had an immense vocabulary of these clichés and were in part so lovable because they were deep conservative classicists and never tried to break away from them. The still more gifted men, of course, simplified and invented, finding out new and much deeper uses for the idiom. They learned to show emotion through it, and comic psychology, more eloquently than most language has ever managed to, and they discovered beauties of comic motion which are hopelessly beyond reach of words.

It is hard to find a theater these days where a comedy is playing; in the days of the silents it was equally hard to find a theater which was not showing one. The laughs today are pitifully few, far between, shallow, quiet and short. They almost never build, as they used to, into something combining the jabbering frequency of a machine gun with the delirious momentum of a roller coaster. Saddest of all, there are few comedians now below middle age and there are none who seem to learn much from picture to picture, or to try anything new.

To put it unkindly, the only thing wrong with screen comedy today is that it takes place on a screen which talks. Because it talks, the only comedians who ever mastered the screen cannot work, for they cannot combine their comic style with talk. Because there is a screen, talking comedians are trapped into a continual exhibition of their inadequacy as screen comedians on a surface as big as the side of a barn.

At the moment, as for many years past, the chances to see silent comedy are rare. There is a smattering of it on television—too often treated as something quaintly archaic, to be laughed at, not with. Some two hundred comedies—long and short—can be rented for home projection. And a lucky minority has access to the comedies in the collection of New York's Museum of Modern Art, which is still incomplete but which is probably the best in the world. In the near future, however, something of this lost art will return to regular theaters. A thick straw in the wind is the big business now being done by a series of revivals of W. C. Fields's memorable movies, a kind of comedy more akin to the old silent variety than anything which is being made today. Mack Sennett now is preparing a sort of pot-pourri variety show called *Down Memory Lane* made up out of his old movies, featuring people like Fields and Bing Crosby when they were movie beginners, but including also interludes from silents. Harold Lloyd has re-released *Movie Crazy,* a talkie, and plans to revive four of his best silent comedies *(Grandma's Boy, Safety Last, Speedy* and *The Freshman).* Buster Keaton hopes to remake at feature length, with a minimum of dialogue, two of the funniest short comedies ever made, one about a porous homemade boat and one about a prefabricated house.

Awaiting these happy events we will discuss here what has gone wrong with screen comedy and what, if anything, can be done about it. But mainly we will try to suggest what it was like in its glory in the years from 1912 to 1930, as practiced by the employees of Mack Sennett, the father of American screen comedy, and by the four most eminent masters: Charlie Chaplin, Harold Lloyd, the late Harry Langdon and Buster Keaton.

Mack Sennett made two kinds of comedy: parody laced with slapstick, and plain slapstick. The parodies were the unceremonious burial of a century of hamming, including the new hamming in serious movies, and nobody who has missed Ben Turpin in *A Small Town Idol,* or kidding Erich von Stroheim in *Three Foolish Weeks* or as *The Shriek of Araby,* can imagine how rough parody can get and still remain subtle and roaringly funny. The plain slapstick, at its best, was even better: a profusion of hearty young women in disconcerting bathing suits, frisking around with a gaggle of insanely incompetent policemen and of equally certifiable male civilians sporting museum-piece mustaches. All these people zipped and caromed about the pristine world of the screen as jazzily as a convention of water bugs. Words can hardly suggest how energetically they collided and bounced apart, meeting in full gallop around the corner of a house; how hard and how often they fell on their backsides; or with what fantastically adroit clumsiness they got themselves fouled up in folding ladders, garden hoses, tethered animals and each other's headlong crosspurposes. The gestures were ferociously emphatic; not a line or motion of the body was wasted or inarticulate. The reader may remember how splendidly upright wandlike old Ben Turpin could stand for a Renunciation Scene, with his lampshade mustache twittering and his sparrowy chest stuck out and his head flung back like Paderewski assaulting a climax and the long babyish black hair trying to look lionlike, while his Adam's apple, an orange in a Christmas stocking, pumped with noble emotion. Or huge Mack Swain, who looked like a hairy mushroom, rolling his eyes in a manner patented by French Romantics and gasping in some dubious ecstasy. Or Louise Fazenda, the perennial farmer's daughter and the perfect low-comedy housemaid, primping her spit curl; and how her hair tightened a good-looking face into the incarnation of rampant gullibility. Or snouty James Finlayson, gleefully foreclosing a mortgage, with his look of eternally tasting a spoiled pickle. Or Chester Conklin, a myopic and inebriated little walrus stumbling around in outsize pants. Or Fatty Arbuckle, with his cold eye and his loose, serene smile, his silky manipulation of his bulk and his satanic marksmanship with pies (he was ambidextrous and could simultaneously blind two people in opposite directions).

The intimate tastes and secret hopes of these poor ineligible dunces were ruthlessly exposed whenever a hot stove, an electric fan or a bulldog took a dislike to their outer garments: agonizingly elaborate drawers, worked up on some lonely evening out of some God-forsaken lace curtain; or men's underpants with big round black spots on them. The Sennett sets—delirious wallpaper, megalomaniacally scrolled iron beds, Grand Rapids *in extremis*—outdid even the underwear. It was their business, after all, to kid the squalid braggadocio which infested the domestic interiors of the period, and that was almost beyond parody. These comedies told their stories to the unaided eye, and by every means possible they screamed to it. That is one reason for the India-ink silhouettes of the cops, and for convicts and prison bars and their shadows in hard sunlight, and for barefooted husbands, in tigerish pajamas, reacting like dervishes to stepped-on tacks.

The early silent comedians never strove for or consciously thought of anything which could be called artistic "form," but they achieved it. For Sennett's rival, Hal Roach, Leo McCarey once devoted almost the whole of a Laurel and Hardy two-reeler to pie-throwing. The first pies were thrown thoughtfully, almost philosophically. Then innocent bystanders began to get caught into the vortex. At full pitch it was Armageddon. But everything was calculated so nicely that until late in the picture, when havoc took over, every pie made its special kind of point and piled on its special kind of laugh.

Sennett's comedies were just a shade faster and fizzier than life. According to legend (and according to Sennett) he discovered the sped tempo proper to screen comedy when a green cameraman, trying to save money, cranked too slow.* Realizing the tremendous drumlike power of mere motion to exhilarate, he gave inanimate objects a mischievous life of their own, broke every law of nature the tricked camera would serve him for and made the screen dance like a witches' Sabbath. The thing one is surest of all to remember is how toward the end of nearly every Sennett comedy, a chase (usually called the "rally") built up such a majestic trajectory of pure anarchic motion that bathing girls, cops, comics, dogs, cats, babies, automobiles, locomotives, innocent bystanders, sometimes what seemed like a whole city, an entire civilization, were hauled along head over heels in the wake of that energy like dry leaves following an express train.

"Nice" people, who shunned all movies in the early days, condemned the Sennett comedies as vulgar and naive. But millions of less pretentious people loved their sincerity and sweetness, their wild-animal innocence and glorious vitality. They could not put these feelings into words, but they flocked to the silents. The reader who gets back deep enough into that world will probably even remember the theater: the barefaced honky-tonk and the waltzes by Waldteufel, slammed out on a mechanical piano; the searing redolence of peanuts and demirep perfumery, tobacco and feet and sweat; the laughter of unrespectable people having a hell of a fine time, laughter as violent and steady and deafening as standing under a waterfall.

Sennett wheedled his first financing out of a couple of ex-book-

*Silent comedy was shot at 12 to 16 frames per second and was speeded up by being shown at 16 frames per second, the usual rate of theater projectors at that time. Theater projectors today run at 24, which makes modern film taken at the same speed seem smooth and natural. But it makes silent movies fast and jerky.

ies to whom he was already in debt. He took his comics out of music halls, burlesque, vaudeville, circuses and limbo, and through them he tapped in on that great pipeline of horsing and miming which runs back unbroken through the fairs of the Middle Ages at least to ancient Greece. He added all that he himself had learned about the large and spurious gesture, the late decadence of the Grand Manner, as a stage-struck boy in East Berlin, Connecticut and as a frustrated opera singer and actor. The only thing he claims to have invented is the pie in the face, and he insists, "Anyone who tells you he has discovered something new is a fool or a liar or both."

The silent-comedy studio was about the best training school the movies have ever known, and the Sennett studio was about as free and easy and as fecund of talent as they came. All the major comedians we will mention worked there, at least briefly. So did some of the major stars of the twenties and since—notably Gloria Swanson, Phyllis Haver, Wallace Beery, Marie Dressler and Carole Lombard. Directors Frank Capra, Leo McCarey and George Stevens also got their start in silent comedy; much that remains most flexible, spontaneous and visually alive in sound movies can be traced, through them and others, to this silent apprenticeship. Everybody did pretty much as he pleased on the Sennett lot, and everybody's ideas were welcome. Sennett posted no rules, and the only thing he strictly forbade was liquor. A Sennett story conference was a most informal affair. During the early years, at least, only the most important scenario might be jotted on the back of an envelope. Mainly Sennett's men thrashed out a few primary ideas and carried them in their heads, sure the better stuff would turn up while they were shooting, in the heat of physical action. This put quite a load on the prop man; he had to have the most improbable apparatus on hand—bombs, trick telephones, what not—to implement whatever idea might suddenly turn up. All kinds of things did—and were recklessly used. Once a low-comedy auto got out of control and killed the cameraman, but he was not visible in the shot, which was thrilling and undamaged; the audience never knew the difference.

Sennett used to hire a "wild man" to sit in on his gag conferences, whose whole job was to think up "wildies." Usually he was an all but brainless, speechless man, scarcely able to communicate his idea; but he had a totally uninhibited imagination. He might say nothing for an hour; then he'd mutter "You take . . ." and all the relatively rational others would shut up and wait. "You take this cloud . . ." he would get out, sketching vague shapes in the air. Often he could get no further; but thanks to some kind of thought-transference, saner men would take this cloud and make something of it. The wild man seems in fact to have functioned as the group's subconscious mind, the source of all creative energy. His ideas were so weird and amorphous that Sennett can no longer remember a one of them, or even how it turned out after rational processing. But a fair equivalent might be one of the best comic sequences in a Laurel and Hardy picture. It is simple enough—simple and real, in fact, as a nightmare. Laurel and Hardy are trying to move a piano across a narrow suspension bridge. The bridge is slung over a sickening chasm, between a couple of Alps. Midway they meet a gorilla.

Had he done nothing else, Sennett would be remembered for giving a start to three of the four comedians who now began to apply their sharp individual talents to this newborn language. The one whom he did not train (he was on the lot briefly but Sennett barely remembers seeing him around) wore glasses, smiled a great deal and looked like the sort of eager young man who might have quit divinity school to hustle brushes. That was Harold Lloyd. The others were grotesque and poetic in their screen characters in degrees which appear to be impossible when the magic of silence is broken. One, who never smiled, carried a face as still and sad as a daguerreotype through some of the most preposterously ingenious and visually satisfying physical comedy ever invented. That was Buster Keaton. One looked like an elderly baby and, at times, a baby dope fiend; he could do more with less than any other comedian. That was Harry Langdon. One looked like Charlie Chaplin, and he was the first man to give the silent language a soul.

When Charlie Chaplin started to work for Sennett he had chiefly to reckon with Ford Sterling, the reigning comedian. Their first picture together amounted to a duel before the assembled professionals. Sterling, by no means untalented, was a big man with a florid Teutonic style which, under this special pressure, he turned on full blast. Chaplin defeated him within a few minutes with a wink of the mustache, a hitch of the trousers, a quirk of the little finger.

With *Tillie's Punctured Romance,* in 1914, he became a major star. Soon after, he left Sennett when Sennett refused to start a landslide among the other comedians by meeting the raise Chaplin demanded. Sennett is understandably wry about it in retrospect, but he still says, "I was right at the time." Of Chaplin he says simply, "Oh well, he's just the greatest artist that ever lived." None of Chaplin's former rivals rate him much lower than that; they speak of him no more jealously than they might of God. We will try here only to suggest the essence of his supremacy. Of all comedians he worked most deeply and most shrewdly within a realization of what a human being is, and is up against. The Tramp is as centrally representative of humanity, as manysided and as mysterious, as Hamlet, and it seems unlikely that any dancer or actor can ever have excelled him in eloquence, variety or poignancy of motion. As for pure motion, even if he had never gone on to make his magnificent feature-length comedies, Chaplin would have made his period in movies a great one singlehanded even if he had made nothing except *The Cure,* or *One A.M.* In the latter, barring one immobile taxi driver, Chaplin plays alone, as a drunk trying to get upstairs and into bed. It is a sort of inspired elaboration on a soft-shoe dance, involving an angry stuffed wildcat, small rugs on slippery floors, a Lazy Susan table, exquisite footwork on a flight of stairs, a contretemps with a huge, ferocious pendulum and the funniest and most perverse Murphy bed in movie history—and, always made physically lucid, the delicately weird mental processes of a man ethereally sozzled.

Before Chaplin came to pictures people were content with a couple of gags per comedy; he got some kind of laugh every second. The minute he began to work he set standards—and continually forced them higher. Anyone who saw Chaplin eating a boiled shoe like brook trout in *The Gold Rush,* or embarrassed by a swallowed whistle in *City Lights,* has seen perfection. Most of the time, however, Chaplin got his laughter less from the gags, or from milking them in any ordinary sense, than through his genius for what may be called *inflection*—the perfect, changeful shading of his physical and emotional attitudes toward the gag. Funny as his bout with the Murphy bed is, the glances of awe, expostulation and helpless, almost whimpering desire for vengeance which he darts at this infernal machine are even better.

A painful and frequent error among tyros is breaking the comic line with a too-big laugh, then a letdown; or with a laugh which is out of key or irrelevant. The masters could ornament the main line beautifully; they never addled it. In *A Night Out* Chaplin, passed out, is hauled along the sidewalk by the scruff of his coat by staggering Ben Turpin. His toes trail; he is as supine as a sled. Turpin himself is so drunk he can hardly drag him. Chaplin comes quietly to, realizes how well he is being served by his struggling pal, and with a royally delicate gesture plucks and savors a flower.

The finest pantomime, the deepest emotion, the richest and most poignant poetry were in Chaplin's work. He could probably pantomime Bryce's *The American Commonwealth* without ever blurring a syllable and make it paralyzingly funny into the bargain. At the end of *City Lights* the blind girl who has regained her sight, thanks to the Tramp, sees him for the first time. She has imagined and anticipated him as princely, to say the least; and it has never seriously occurred to him that he is inadequate. She recognizes who he must be by his shy, confident, shining joy as he comes silently toward her. And he recognizes himself, for the first time, through the terrible changes in her face. The camera just exchanges a few quiet close-ups of the emotions which shift and intensify in each face. It is enough to shrivel the heart to see, and it is the greatest piece of acting and the highest moment in movies.

Harold Lloyd worked only a little while with Sennett. During most of his career he acted for another major comedy producer, Hal Roach. He tried at first to offset Chaplin's influence and establish his own individuality by playing Chaplin's exact opposite, a character named Lonesome Luke who wore clothes much too small for him and whose gestures were likewise as unChaplinesque as possible. But he soon realized that an opposite in itself was a kind of slavishness. He discovered his own comic identity when he saw a movie about a fighting parson: a hero who wore glasses. He began to think about those glasses day and night. He decided on horn rims because they were youthful, ultravisible on the screen and on the verge of becoming fashionable (he was to make them so). Around these large lensless horn rims he began to develop a new character, nothing grotesque or eccentric, but a fresh, believable young man who could fit into a wide variety of stories.

Lloyd depended more on story and situation than any of the other major comedians (he kept the best stable of gagmen in Hollywood, at one time hiring six); but unlike most "story" comedians he was also a very funny man from inside. He had, as he has written, "an unusually large comic vocabulary." More particularly he had an expertly expressive body and even more expressive teeth, and out of his thesaurus of smiles he could at a moment's notice blend prissiness, breeziness and asininity, and still remain tremendously likable. His movies were more extroverted and closer to ordinary life than any others of the best comedies: the vicissitudes of a New York taxi driver; the unaccepted college boy who, by desperate courage and inspired ineptitude, wins the Big Game. He was especially good at putting a very timid, spoiled or brassy young fellow through devastating embarrassments. He went through one of his most uproarious Gethsemanes as a shy country youth courting the nicest girl in town in *Grandma's Boy.* He arrived dressed "strictly up to date for the Spring of 1862," as a subtitle observed, and found that the ancient colored butler wore a similar flowered waistcoat and moldering cutaway. He got one wandering, nervous forefinger dreadfully stuck in a fancy little vase. The girl began cheerfully to try to identify that queer smell which dilated from him; Grandpa's best suit was rife with mothballs. A tenacious litter of kittens feasted off the goose grease on his home-shined shoes.

Lloyd was even better at the comedy of thrills. In *Safety Last,* as a rank amateur, he is forced to substitute for a human fly and to climb a medium-sized skyscraper. Dozens of awful things happen to him. He gets fouled up in a tennis net. Popcorn falls on him from a window above, and the local pigeons treat him like a cross between a lunch wagon and St. Francis of Assisi. A mouse runs up his britches-leg, and the crowd below salutes his desperate dance on the window ledge with wild applause of the daredevil. A good deal of this full-length picture hangs thus by its eyelashes along the face of a building. Each new floor is like a new stanza in a poem; and the higher and more horrifying it gets, the funnier it gets.

In this movie Lloyd demonstrates beautifully his ability to do more than merely milk a gag, but to top it. (In an old, simple example of topping, an incredible number of tall men get, one by one, out of a small closed auto. After as many have clambered out as the joke will bear, one more steps out: a midget. That tops the gag. Then the auto collapses. That tops the topper.) In *Safety Last* Lloyd is driven out to the dirty end of a flagpole by a furious dog; the pole breaks and he falls, just managing to grab the minute hand of a huge clock. His weight promptly pulls the hand down from IX to VI. That would be more than enough for any ordinary comedian, but there is further logic in the situation. Now, hideously, the whole clockface pulls loose and slants from its trembling springs above the street. Getting out of difficulty with the clock, he makes still further use of the instrument by getting one foot caught in one of these obstinate springs.

A proper delaying of the ultrapredictable can of course be just as funny as a properly timed explosion of the unexpected. As Lloyd approaches the end of his horrible hegira up the side of the building in *Safety Last,* it becomes clear to the audience, but not to him, that if he raises his head another couple of inches he is going to get murderously conked by one of the four arms of a revolving wind gauge. He delays the evil moment almost interminably, with one distraction and another, and every delay is a suspense-tightening laugh; he also gets his foot nicely entangled in a rope, so that when he does get hit, the payoff of one gag sends him careening head downward through the abyss into another. Lloyd was outstanding even among the master craftsmen at setting up a gag clearly, culminating and getting out of it deftly, and linking it smoothly to the next. Harsh experience also taught him a deep and fundamental rule: never try to get "above" the audience.

Lloyd tried it in *The Freshman.* He was to wear an unfinished, basted-together tuxedo to a college party, and it would gradually fall apart as he danced. Lloyd decided to skip the pants, a low-comedy cliché, and lose just the coat. His gagmen warned him. A preview proved how right they were. Lloyd had to reshoot the whole expensive sequence, build it around defective pants and climax it with the inevitable. It was one of the funniest things he ever did.

When Lloyd was still a very young man he lost about half his right hand (and nearly lost his sight) when a comedy bomb exploded prematurely. But in spite of his artificially built-out hand he continued to do his own dirty work, like all of the best comedians. The side of the building he climbed in *Safety Last* did not overhang the street, as it appears to. But the nearest landing place was a roof three floors below him, as he approached the top, and he did everything, of course, the hard way, that is, the comic way, keeping his bottom stuck well out, his shoulders hunched, his hands and feet skidding over perdition.

If great comedy must involve something beyond laughter, Lloyd was not a great comedian. If plain laughter is any criterion—and it is a healthy counterbalance to the other—few people have equaled him, and nobody has ever beaten him.

Chaplin and Keaton and Lloyd were all more like each other, in one important way, than Harry Langdon was like any of them. Whatever else the others might be doing, they all used more or less elaborate physical comedy; Langdon showed how little of that one might use and still be a great silent-screen comedian. In his screen character he symbolized something as deeply and centrally human, though by no means as rangily so, as the Tramp. There was, of course, an immense difference in inventiveness and range of virtuosity. It seemed as if Chaplin could do literally anything, on any instrument in the orchestra. Langdon had one queerly toned, unique little reed. But out of it he could get incredible melodies.

Like Chaplin, Langdon wore a coat which buttoned on his wishbone and swung out wide below, but the effect was very different: he seemed like an outsized baby who had begun to outgrow his clothes. The crown of his hat was rounded and the brim was turned up all around, like a little boy's hat, and he looked as if he wore diapers under his pants. His walk was that of a child which has just gotten sure on its feet, and his body and hands fitted that age. His face was kept pale to show off, with the simplicity of a nursery-school drawing, the bright, ignorant, gentle eyes and the little twirling mouth. He had big moon cheeks, with dimples, and a Napoleonic forelock of mousy hair; the round, docile head seemed large in ratio to the cream-puff body. Twitchings of his face were signals of tiny discomforts too slowly registered by a tinier brain; quick, squirty little smiles showed his almost prehuman pleasures, his incurably premature trustfulness. He was a virtuoso of hesitations and of delicately indecisive motions, and he was particularly fine in a high wind, rounding a corner with a kind of skittering toddle, both hands nursing his hatbrim.

He was as remarkable a master as Chaplin of subtle emotional and mental process and operated much more at leisure. He once got a good three hundred feet of continuously bigger laughs out of rubbing his chest, in a crowded vehicle, with Limburger cheese, under the misapprehension that it was a cold salve. In another long scene, watching a brazen showgirl change her clothes, he sat motionless, back to the camera, and registered the whole lexicon of lost innocence, shock, disapproval and disgust, with the back of his neck. His scenes with women were nearly always something special. Once a lady spy did everything in her power (under the Hays Office) to seduce him. Harry was polite, willing, even flirtatious in his little way. The only trouble was that he couldn't imagine what in the world she was leering and pawing at him for, and that he was terribly ticklish. The Mata Hari wound up foaming at the mouth.

There was also a sinister flicker of depravity about the Langdon character, all the more disturbing because babies are premoral. He had an instinct for bringing his actual adulthood and figurative babyishness into frictions as crawly as a fingernail on a slate blackboard, and he wandered into areas of strangeness which were beyond the other comedians. In a nightmare in one movie he was forced to fight a large, muscular young man; the girl Harry loved was the prize. The young man was a good boxer; Harry could scarcely lift his gloves. The contest took place in a fiercely lighted prize ring, in a prodigious pitch-dark arena. The only spectator was the girl, and she was rooting against Harry. As the fight went on, her eyes glittered ever more brightly with blood lust and, with glittering teeth, she tore her big straw hat to shreds.

Langdon came to Sennett from a vaudeville act in which he had fought a losing battle with a recalcitrant automobile. The minute Frank Capra saw him he begged Sennett to let him work with him. Langdon was almost as childlike as the character he played. He had only a vague idea of his story or even of each scene as he played it; each time he went before the camera Capra would brief him on the general situation and then, as this finest of intuitive improvisers once tried to explain his work, "I'd go into my routine." The whole tragedy of the coming of dialogue, as far as these comedians were concerned—and one reason for the increasing rigidity of comedy every since—can be epitomized in the mere thought of Harry Langdon confronted with a script.

Langdon's magic was in his innocence, and Capra took beautiful care not to meddle with it. The key to the proper use of Langdon, Capra always knew, was "the principle of the brick." "If there was a rule for writing Langdon material," he explains, "it was this: his only ally was God. Langdon might be saved by the brick falling on the cop, but it was *verboten* that he in any way motivate the brick's fall." Langdon became quickly and fantastically popular with three pictures, *Tramp, Tramp, Tramp, The Strong Man* and *Long Pants;* from then on he went downhill even faster. "The trouble was," Capra says, "that high-brow critics came around to explain his art to him. Also he developed an interest in dames. It was a pretty high life for such a little fellow." Langdon made two more pictures with high-brow writers, one of which *(Three's A Crowd)* had some wonderful passages in it, including the prize-ring nightmare; then First National canceled his contract. He was reduced to mediocre roles and two-reelers which were more rehashes of his old gags; this time around they no longer seemed funny. "He never did really understand what hit him," says Capra. "He died broke [in 1944]. And he died of a broken heart. He was the most tragic figure I ever came across in show business."

Buster Keaton started work at the age of three and one-half with his parents in one of the roughest acts in vaudeville ("The Three Keatons"); Harry Houdini gave the child the name Buster in admiration for a fall he took down a flight of stairs. In his first movies Keaton teamed with Fatty Arbuckle under Sennett. He went on to become one of Metro's biggest stars and earners; a Keaton feature cost about $200,000 to make and reliably grossed $2,000,000. Very early in his movie career friends asked him why he never smiled on the screen. He didn't realize he didn't. He had got the dead-pan habit in variety; on the screen he had merely been so hard at work it had never occurred to him there was anything to smile about. Now he tried it just once and never again. He was by his whole style and nature so much the most deeply "silent" of the silent comedians that even a smile was as deafeningly out of key as a yell. In a way his pictures are like a transcendent juggling act in which it seems that the whole universe is in exquisite flying motion and the one point of repose is the juggler's effortless, uninterested face.

Keaton's face ranked almost with Lincoln's as an early American archetype; it was haunting, handsome, almost beautiful, yet it was irreducibly funny; he improved matters by topping it off with a deadly horizontal hat, as flat and thin as a phonograph record. One can never forget Keaton wearing it, standing erect at the prow as his little boat is being launched. The boat goes grandly down the skids and, just as grandly, straight on to the bottom. Keaton never budges. The last you see of him, the water lifts the hat off the stoic head and it floats away.

No other comedian could do as much with the dead pan. He used this great, sad, motionless face to suggest various related things: a one-track mind near the track's end of pure insanity; mulish imperturbability under the wildest of circumstances; how dead a human being can get and still be alive; an awe-inspiring sort of patience and power to endure, proper to granite but uncanny in flesh and blood. Everything that he was and did bore out this rigid face and played laughs against it. When he moved his eyes, it was like seeing them move in a statue. His short-legged body was all sudden, machinelike angles, governed by a daft aplomb. When he swept a semaphorelike arm to point, you could almost hear the electrical impulse in the signal block. When he ran from a cop his transitions from accelerating walk to easy jogtrot to brisk canter to headlong gallop to flogged-piston sprint—always floating, above this frenzy, the untroubled, untouchable face—were as distinct and as soberly in order as an automatic gearshift.

Keaton was a wonderfully resourceful inventor of mechanistic gags (he still spends much of his time fooling with Erector sets); as he ran afoul of locomotives, steamships, prefabricated and over-electrified houses, he put himself through some of the hardest and cleverest punishment ever designed for laughs. In *Sherlock Jr.,* boiling along on the handlebars of a motorcycle quite unaware that he has lost his driver, Keaton whips through city traffic, breaks up a tug-of-war, gets a shovelful of dirt in the face from each of a long line of Rockette-timed ditch-diggers, approaches a log at high speed which is hinged open by dynamite precisely soon enough to let him through and, hitting an obstruction, leaves the handlebars like an arrow leaving a bow, whams through the window of a shack in which the heroine is about to be violated, and hits the heavy feet-first, knocking him through the opposite wall. The whole sequence is as clean in motion as the trajectory of a bullet.

Much of the charm and edge of Keaton's comedy, however, lay in the subtle leverages of expression he could work against his nominal dead pan. Trapped in the side-wheel of a ferryboat, saving himself from drowning only by walking, then desperately running, inside the accelerating wheel like a squirrel in a cage, his only real concern was, obviously, to keep his hat on. Confronted by Love, he was not as dead-pan as he was cracked up to be, either; there was an odd, abrupt motion of his head which suggested a horse nipping after a sugar lump.

Keaton worked strictly for laughs, but his work came from so far inside a curious and original spirit that he achieved a great deal besides, especially in his feature-length comedies. (For plain hard laughter his nineteen short comedies—the negatives of which have been lost—were even better.) He was the only major comedian who kept sentiment almost entirely out of his work, and he brought pure physical comedy to its greatest heights. Beneath his lack of emotion he was also uninsistently sardonic; deep below that, giving a disturbing tension and grandeur to the foolishness, for those who sensed it, there was in his comedy a freezing whisper not of pathos but of melancholia. With the humor, the craftsmanship and the action there was often, besides, a fine, still and sometimes dreamlike beauty. Much of his Civil War picture *The General* is within hailing distance of Mathew Brady. And there is a ghostly, unforgettable moment in *The Navigator* when, on a deserted, softly rolling ship, all the pale doors along a deck swing open as one behind Keaton and, as one, slam shut, in a hair-raising illusion of noise.

Perhaps because "dry" comedy is so much more rare and odd than "dry" wit, there are people who never much cared for Keaton. Those who do cannot care mildly.

As soon as the screen began to talk, silent comedy was pretty well finished. The hardy and prolific Mack Sennett made the transfer; he was the first man to put Bing Crosby and W. C. Fields on the screen. But he was essentially a silent-picture man, and by the time the Academy awarded him a special Oscar for his "lasting contribution to the comedy technique of the screen" (in 1938), he was no longer active. As for the comedians we have spoken of in particular, they were as badly off as fine dancers suddenly required to appear in plays.

Harold Lloyd, whose work was most nearly realistic, naturally coped least unhappily with the added realism of speech; he made several talking comedies. But good as the best were, they were not so good as his silent work, and by the late thirties he quit acting. A few years ago he returned to play the lead (and play it beautifully) in Preston Sturges's *The Sin of Harold Diddlebock,* but this exceptional picture—which opened, brilliantly, with the closing reel of Lloyd's *The Freshman*—has not yet been generally released.

Like Chaplin, Lloyd was careful of his money; he is still rich and active. Last June, in the presence of President Truman, he became Imperial Potentate of the A.A.O.N.M.S. (Shriners). Harry Langdon, as we have said, was a broken man when sound came in.

Up to the middle thirties Buster Keaton made several feature-length pictures (with such players as Jimmy Durante, Wallace Beery and Robert Montgomery); he also made a couple of dozen talking shorts. Now and again he managed to get loose into motion, without having to talk, and for a moment or so the screen would start singing again. But his dark, dead voice, though it was in keeping with the visual character, tore his intensely silent style to bits and destroyed the illusion within which he worked. He gallantly and correctly refuses to regard himself as "retired." Besides occasional bits, spots and minor roles in Hollywood pictures, he has worked on summer stages, made talking comedies in France and Mexico and clowned in a French circus. This summer he has played the straw hats in *Three Men on a Horse.* He is planning a television program. He also has a working agreement with Metro. One of his jobs there is to construct comedy sequences for Red Skelton.

The only man who really survived the flood was Chaplin, the only one who was rich, proud and popular enough to afford to stay silent. He brought out two of his greatest nontalking comedies, *City Lights* and *Modern Times,* in the middle of an avalanche of talk, spoke gibberish and, in the closing moments, plain English in *The Great Dictator,* and at last made an all-talking picture, *Monsieur Verdoux,* creating for that purpose an entirely new character who might properly talk a blue streak. *Verdoux* is the greatest of talking comedies, though so cold and savage that it had to find its public in grimly experienced Europe.

Good comedy, and some that was better than good, outlived silence, but there has been less and less of it. The talkies brought one great comedian, the late, majestically lethargic W. C. Fields, who could not possibly have worked as well in silence; he was the toughest and the most warmly human of all screen comedians, and *It's A Gift* and *The Bank Dick,* fiendishly funny and incisive white-collar comedies, rank high among the best comedies (and best movies) ever made. Laurel and Hardy, the only comedians who managed to preserve much of the large, low style of silence and who began to explore the comedy of sound, have made nothing since 1945. Walt Disney, at his best an inspired comic inventor and teller of fairy stories, lost his stride during the war and has since regained it only at moments. Preston Sturges has made brilliant, satirical comedies, but his pictures are smart, nervous comedy-dramas merely italicized with slapstick. The Marx Brothers were side-splitters but they made their best comedies years ago. Jimmy Durante is mainly a nightclub genius; Abbott and Costello are semiskilled laborers, at best; Bob Hope is a good radio comedian with a pleasing presence, but not much more, on the screen.

There is no hope that screen comedy will get much better than it is without new, gifted young comedians who really belong in movies, and without freedom for their experiments. For everyone who may appear we have one last, invidious comparison to offer as a guidepost.

One of the most popular recent comedies is Bob Hope's *The*

Paleface. We take no pleasure in blackening *The Paleface;* we single it out, rather, because it is as good as we've got. Anything that is said of it here could be said, with interest, of other comedies of our time. Most of the laughs in *The Paleface* are verbal. Bob Hope is very adroit with his lines and now and then, when the words don't get in the way, he makes a good beginning as a visual comedian. But only the beginning, never the middle or the end. He is funny, for instance, reacting to a shot of violent whisky. But he does not know how to get still funnier (*i.e.,* how to build and milk) or how to be funniest last (*i.e.,* how to top or cap his gag). The camera has to fade out on the same old face he started with.

One sequence is promisingly set up for visual comedy. In it, Hope and a lethal local boy stalk each other all over a cow town through streets which have been emptied in fear of their duel. The gag here is that through accident and stupidity they keep just failing to find each other. Some of it is quite funny. But the fun slackens between laughs like a weak clothesline, and by all the logic of humor (which is ruthlessly logical) the biggest laugh should come at the moment, and through the way, they finally spot each other. The sequence is so weakly thought out that at that crucial moment the camera can't afford to watch them; it switches to Jane Russell.

Now we turn to a masterpiece. In *The Navigator* Buster Keaton works with practically the same gag as Hope's duel. Adrift on a ship which he believes is otherwise empty, he drops a lighted cigarette. A girl finds it. She calls out and he hears her; each then tries to find the other. First each walks purposefully down the long, vacant starboard deck, the girl, then Keaton, turning the corner just in time not to see each other. Next time around each of them is trotting briskly, very much in earnest; going at the same pace, they miss each other just the same. Next time around each of them is going like a bat out of hell. Again they miss. Then the camera withdraws to a point of vantage at the stern, leans its chin in its hand and just watches the whole intricate superstructure of the ship as the protagonists stroll, steal and scuttle from level to level, up, down and sidewise, always managing to miss each other by hair's-breadths, in an enchantingly neat and elaborate piece of timing. There are no subsidiary gags to get laughs in this sequence and there is little loud laughter; merely a quiet and steadily increasing kind of delight. When Keaton has got all he can out of this fine modification of the movie chase he invents a fine device to bring the two together: the girl, thoroughly winded, sits down for a breather, indoors, on a plank which workmen have left across sawhorses. Keaton pauses on an upper deck, equally winded and puzzled. What follows happens in a couple of seconds at most: air suction whips his silk topper backward down a ventilator; grabbing frantically for it, he backs against the lip of the ventilator, jacknifes and falls in backward. Instantly the camera cuts back to the girl. A topper falls through the ceiling and lands tidily, right side up, on the plank beside her. Before she can look more than startled, its owner follows, head between his knees, crushes the topper, breaks the plank with the point of his spine and proceeds to the floor. The breaking of the plank smacks Boy and Girl together.

It is only fair to remember that the silent comedians would have as hard a time playing a talking scene as Hope has playing his visual ones, and that writing and directing are as accountable for the failure as Hope himself. But not even the humblest journeymen of the silent years would have let themselves off so easily. Like the masters, they knew, and sweated to obey, the laws of their craft.

THE WESTERNER (1954)

By Robert Warshow

> They that have power to hurt and will do none,
> That do not do the thing they most do show,
> Who, moving others, are themselves as stone,
> Unmoved, cold, and to temptation slow;
> They rightly do inherit heaven's graces,
> And husband nature's riches from expense;
> They are the lords and owners of their faces,
> Others but stewards of their excellence.

The two most successful creations of American movies are the gangster and the Westerner: men with guns. Guns as physical objects, and the postures associated with their use, form the visual and emotional center of both types of films. I suppose this reflects the importance of guns in the fantasy life of Americans; but that is a less illuminating point than it appears to be.

The gangster movie, which no longer exists in its "classical" form, is a story of enterprise and success ending in precipitate failure. Success is conceived as an increasing power to work injury, it belongs to the city, and it is of course a form of evil (though the gangster's death, presented usually as "punishment," is perceived simply as defeat). The peculiarity of the gangster is his unceasing, nervous activity. The exact nature of his enterprises may remain vague, but his commitment to enterprise is always clear, and all the more clear because he operates outside the field of utility. He is without culture, without manners, without leisure, or at any rate his leisure is likely to be spent in debauchery so compulsively aggressive as to seem only another aspect of his "work." But he is graceful, moving like a dancer among the crowded dangers of the city.

Like other tycoons, the gangster is crude in conceiving his ends but by no means inarticulate; on the contrary, he is usually expansive and noisy (the introspective gangster is a fairly recent development), and can state definitely what he wants: to take over the North Side, to own a hundred suits, to be Number One. But new "frontiers" will present themselves infinitely, and by a rigid convention it is understood that as soon as he wishes to rest on his gains, he is on the way to destruction.

The gangster is lonely and melancholy, and can give the impression of a profound worldly wisdom. He appeals most to adolescents with their impatience and their feeling of being outsiders, but more generally he appeals to that side of all of us which refuses to believe in the "normal" possibilities of happiness and achievement; the gangster is the "no" to that great American "yes" which is stamped so big over our official culture and yet has so little to do with the way we really feel about our lives. But the gangster's loneliness and melancholy are not "authentic"; like everything else that belongs to him, they are not honestly come by: he is lonely and melancholy not because life ultimately demands such feelings but because he has put himself in a position where everybody wants to kill him and eventually somebody will. He is wide open and defenseless, incomplete because unable to accept any limits or come to terms with his own nature, fearful, loveless. And the story of his career is a nightmare inversion of the values of ambition and opportunity. From the window of Scarface's bulletproof apartment can be seen an electric sign proclaiming, "The World Is Yours," and, if I remember, this sign is the last thing we see after Scarface lies dead in the street. In the end it is the gangster's weakness as much as his power and freedom that appeals to us; the world is not ours, but it is not his either, and in his death he "pays" for our fantasies, releasing us momentarily both from the concept of success, which he denies by caricaturing it, and from the need to succeed, which he shows to be dangerous.

The Western hero, by contrast, is a figure of repose. He resembles the gangster in being lonely and to some degree melancholy. But his melancholy comes from the "simple" recognition that life is unavoidably serious, not from the disproportions of his own temperament. And his loneliness is organic, not imposed on him by his situation but belonging to him intimately and testifying to his completeness. The gangster must reject others violently or draw them violently to him. The Westerner is not thus compelled to seek love; he is prepared to accept it, perhaps, but he never asks of it more than it can give, and we see him constantly in situations where love is at best an irrelevance. If there is a woman he loves, she is usually unable to understand his motives; she is against killing and being killed, and he finds it impossible to explain to her that there is no point in being "against" these things: they belong to his world.

Very often this woman is from the East and her failure to understand represents a clash of cultures. In the American mind, refinement, virtue, civilization, Christianity itself, are seen as feminine, and therefore women are often portrayed as possessing some kind of deeper wisdom, while the men, for all their apparent self-assurance, are fundamentally childish. But the West, lacking the graces of civilization, is the place "where men are men"; in Western movies, men have the deeper wisdom and the women are children. Those women in the Western movies who share the hero's understanding of life are prostitutes (or, as they are usually presented, barroom entertainers) —women, that is, who have come to understand in the most practical way how love can be an irrelevance, and therefore "fallen" women. The gangster, too, associates with prostitutes, but for him the important things about a prostitute are her passive availability and her costliness; she is part of his winnings. In Western movies, the important thing about a prostitute is her quasi-masculine independence: nobody owns her, nothing has to be explained to her, and she is not, like a virtuous woman, a "value" that demands to be protected. When the Westerner leaves the prostitute for a virtuous woman—for love—he is in fact forsaking a way of life, though the point of the choice is often obscured by having the prostitute killed by getting into the line of fire.

The Westerner is par excellence a man of leisure. Even when he wears the badge of a marshal or, more rarely, owns a ranch, he appears to be unemployed. We see him standing at a bar, or playing poker—a game which expresses perfectly his talent for remaining relaxed in the midst of tension—or perhaps camping out on the plains on some extraordinary errand. If he does own a ranch, it is in the background; we are not actually aware that he owns anything except his horse, his guns, and the one worn suit of clothing which is likely to remain unchanged all through the movie. It comes as a surprise to see him take money from his pocket or an extra shirt from his saddlebags. As a rule we do not even know where he sleeps at night and don't think of asking. Yet it never occurs to us that he is a poor man. There is no poverty in Western movies, and really no wealth either; those great cattle domains and shipments of gold which figure so largely in the plots are moral and not material quantities, not the objects of contention but only its occasion. Possessions too are irrelevant.

Employment of some kind—usually unproductive—is always open to the Westerner, but when he accepts it, it is not because he needs to make a living, much less from any idea of "getting ahead." Where could he want to "get ahead" to? By the time we see him, he is already "there"; he can ride a horse faultlessly, keep his countenance in the face of death, and draw his gun a little faster and shoot it a little straighter than anyone he is likely to meet. These are sharply defined acquirements, giving to the figure of the Westerner an apparent moral clarity which corresponds to the clarity of his physical image against his bare landscape; initially, at any rate, the Western movie presents itself as being without mystery, its whole universe comprehended in what we see on the screen.

Much of this apparent simplicity arises directly from those "cinematic" elements which have long been understood to give the Western theme its special appropriateness for the movies: the wide expanses of land, the free movement of men on horses. As guns constitute the visible moral center of the Western movie, suggesting continually the possibility of violence, so land and horses represent the movie's material basis, its sphere of action. But the land and the horses have also a moral significance; the physical freedom they represent belongs to the moral "openness" of the West—corresponding to the fact that guns are carried where they can be seen. (And, as we shall see, the character of land and horses changes as the Western film becomes more complex.)

The gangster's world is less open, and his arts not so easily identifiable as the Westerner's. Perhaps he too can keep his countenance, but the mask he wears is really no mask; its purpose is precisely to make evident the fact that he desperately wants to "get ahead" and will stop at nothing. Where the Westerner imposes himself by the appearance of unshakable control, the gangster's pre-eminence lies in the suggestion that he may at any moment lose control; his strength is not in being able to shoot faster or straighter than others, but in being more willing to shoot. "Do it first," says Scarface, expounding his mode of operation, "and keep on doing it!" With the Westerner, it is a crucial point of honor *not* to "do it first"; his gun remains in its holster until the moment of combat.

There is no suggestion, however, that he draws the gun reluctantly. The Westerner could not fulfill himself if the moment did not finally come when he can shoot his enemy down. But because that moment is so thoroughly the expression of his being, it must be kept pure. He will not violate the accepted forms of combat though by doing so he could save a city. And he can wait. "When you call me that—smile!"—the villain smiles weakly, soon he is laughing with horrible joviality, and the crisis is past. But it is allowed to pass because it must come again; sooner or later Trampas will "make his play," and the Virginian will be ready for him.

What does the Westerner fight for? We know he is on the side of justice and order, and of course it can be said he fights for these things. But such broad aims never correspond exactly to his real motives; they only offer him his opportunity. The Westerner himself, when an explanation is asked of him (usually by a woman), is likely to say that he does what he "has to do." If justice and order did not continually demand his protection, he would be without a calling. Indeed, we come upon him often in just that situation, as the reign of law settles over the West and he is forced to see that his day is over; those are the pictures which end with his death or with his departure for some more remote frontier. What he defends, at bottom, is the purity of his own image—in fact his honor. This is what makes him invulnerable. When the gangster is killed, his whole life is shown to have been a mistake, but the image the Westerner seeks to maintain can be presented as clearly in defeat as in victory: he fights not for advantage and not for the right, but to state what he is, and he must live in a world which permits that statement. The Westerner is the last gentleman, and the movies which over and over again tell his story are probably the last art form in which the concept of honor retains its strength.

Of course I do not mean to say that ideas of virtue and justice and courage have gone out of culture. Honor is more than these things; it is a style, concerned with harmonious appearances as much as with desirable consequences, and tending therefore toward the denial of life in favor of art. "Who hath it? he that died o'Wednesday." On the whole, a world that leans to Falstaff's view is a more civilized and even, finally, a more graceful world. It is just the march of civilization that forces the Westerner to move on; and if we actually had to confront the question it might turn out that the woman who refuses to understand him is right as often as she is wrong. But we do not confront the question. Where the Westerner lives it is always about 1870—not the real 1870, either, or the real West—and he is killed or goes away when his position becomes problematical. The fact that he continues to hold our attention is evidence enough that, in his proper frame, he presents an image of personal nobility that is still real for us.

Clearly, this image easily becomes ridiculous; we need only look at William S. Hart or Tom Mix, who in the wooden absoluteness of their virtue represented little that an adult could take seriously; and doubtless such figures as Gene Autry or Roy Rogers are no better, though I confess I have seen none of their movies. Some film enthusiasts claim to find in the early, unsophisticated Westerns a "cinematic purity" that has since been lost; this idea is as valid, and finally as misleading, as T. S. Eliot's statement that *Everyman* is the only play in English that stays within the limitations of art. The truth is that the Westerner comes into the field of serious art only when his moral code, without ceasing to be compelling, is seen also to be imperfect. The Westerner at his best exhibits a moral ambiguity which darkens his image and saves him from absurdity; this ambiguity arises from the fact that, whatever his justifications, he is a killer of men.

In *The Virginian,* which is an archetypal Western movie as *Scarface* or *Little Caesar* are archetypal gangster movies, there is a lynching in which the hero (Gary Cooper), as leader of a posse, must supervise the hanging of his best friend for stealing cattle. With the growth of American "social consciousness," it is no longer possible to present a lynching in the movies unless the point is the illegality and injustice of the lynching itself; *The Ox-Bow Incident,* made in 1943, explicitly puts forward the newer point of view and can be regarded as a kind of "anti-Western." But in 1929, when *The Virginian* was made, the present inhibition about lynching was not yet in force; the justice, and therefore the necessity, of the hanging is never questioned—except by the schoolteacher from the East, whose refusal to understand serves as usual to set forth more sharply the deeper seriousness of the West. The Virginian is thus in a tragic dilemma where one moral absolute conflicts with another and the choice of either must leave a moral stain. If he had chosen to save his friend, he would have violated the image of himself that he had made essential to his existence, and the movie would have had to end with his death, for only by his death could the image have been restored. Having chosen instead to sacrifice his friend to the higher demands of the "code"—the only choice worthy of him, as even the friend understands—he is none the less stained by the killing, but what is needed now to set accounts straight is not his death but the death of the villain Trampas, the leader of the cattle thieves, who had escaped the posse and abandoned the Virginian's friend to his fate. Again the woman intervenes: Why must there be *more* killing? If the hero really loved her, he would leave town, refusing Trampas' challenge. What good will it be if Trampas should kill him? But the Virginian does once more what he "has to do" and in avenging his friend's death wipes out the stain on his own honor. Yet his victory cannot be complete: no death can be paid for and no stain truly wiped out; the movie is still a tragedy, for though the hero escapes with his life, he has been forced to confront the ultimate limits of his moral ideas.

This mature sense of limitation and unavoidable guilt is what gives the Westerner a "right" to his melancholy. It is true that the gangster's story is also a tragedy—in certain formal ways more clearly a tragedy than the Westerner's—but it is a romantic tragedy, based on a hero whose defeat springs with almost mechanical inevitability from the outrageous presumption of his demands: the gangster is *bound* to go on until he is killed. The Westerner is a more classical figure, self-contained and limited to begin with, seeking not to extend his dominion but only to assert his personal value, and his tragedy lies in the fact that even his circumscribed demand cannot be fully realized. Since the Westerner is not a murderer but (most of the time) a man of virtue, and since he is always prepared for defeat, he retains his inner invulnerability and his story need not end with his death (and usually does not); but what we finally respond to is not his victory but his defeat.

Up to a point, it is plain that the deeper seriousness of the good Western films comes from the introduction of a realism, both physical and psychological, that was missing with Tom Mix and William S. Hart. As lines of age have come into Gary Cooper's face since *The Virginian,* so the outlines of the Western movie in general have become less smooth, its background more drab. The sun still beats upon the town, but the camera is likely now to take advantage of this illumination to seek out more closely the shabbiness of buildings and furniture, the loose, worn hang of clothing, the wrinkles and dirt of the faces. Once it has been discovered that the true theme of the Western movie is not the freedom and expansiveness of frontier life, but its limitations, its material bareness, the pressures of obligation, then even the landscape itself ceases to be quite the arena of free movement it once was, but becomes instead a great empty waste, cutting down more often than it exaggerates the stature of the horseman who rides across it. We are more likely now to see the Westerner struggling against the obstacles of the physical world (as in the wonderful scenes on the desert and among the rocks in *The Last Posse*) than carelessly surmounting them. Even the horses, no longer the "friends" of man or the inspired chargers of knight-errantry, have lost much of the moral significance that once seemed to belong to them in their careering across the screen. It seems to me the horses grow tired and stumble more often than they did, and that we see them less frequently at the gallop.

In *The Gunfighter,* a remarkable film of a couple of years ago, the landscape has virtually disappeared. Most of the action takes place indoors, in a cheerless saloon where a tired "bad man" (Gregory Peck) contemplates the waste of his life, to be senselessly killed at the end by a vicious youngster setting off on the same futile path. The movie is done in cold, quiet tones of gray, and every object in it—faces, clothing, a table, the hero's heavy mustache—is given an air of uncompromising authenticity, suggesting those dim photographs of the nineteenth-century West in which Wyatt Earp, say, turns out to be a blank untidy figure posing awkwardly before some uninteresting building. This "authenticity," to be sure, is only aesthetic; the chief fact about nineteenth-century photographs, to my eyes at any rate, is how stonily they refuse to yield up the truth. But that limitation is just what is needed: by preserving some hint of the rigidity of archaic photography (only in tone and *décor,* never in composition), *The Gunfighter* can permit us to feel that we are looking at a more "real" West than the one the movies have accustomed us to—harder, duller, less "romantic"—and yet without forcing us outside the boundaries which give the Western movie its validity.

We come upon the hero of *The Gunfighter* at the end of a career in which he has never upheld justice and order, and has been at times, apparently, an actual criminal; in this case, it is clear that the hero has been wrong and the woman who has rejected his way of life has been right. He is thus without any of the larger justifications and knows himself a ruined man. There can be no question of his "redeeming" himself in any socially constructive way. He is too much the victim of his own reputation to turn marshal as one of his old friends has done, and he is not offered the sentimental solution of a chance to give up his life for some good end; the whole point is that he exists outside the field of social value. Indeed, if we were once allowed to see him in the days of his "success," he might become a figure like the gangster, for his career has been aggressively "anti-social" and the practical problem he faces is the gangster's problem: there will always be somebody trying to kill him. Yet it is obviously absurd to speak of him as "antisocial," not only because we do not see him acting as a criminal, but more fundamentally because we do not see his milieu as a society. Of course it has its "social problems" and a kind of static history: civilization is always just at the point of driving out the old freedom; there are women and children to represent the possibility of a settled life; and there is the marshal, a bad man turned good, determined to keep at least his area of jurisdiction at peace. But these elements are not, in fact, a part of the film's "realism," even though they come out of the real history of the West; they belong to the conventions of the form, to that accepted framework which makes the film possible in the first place, and they exist not to provide a standard by which the gunfighter can be judged, but only to set him off. The true "civilization" of the Western movie is always embodied in an individual, good or bad is more a matter of personal bearing than of social consequences, and the conflict of good and bad is a duel between two men. Deeply troubled and obviously doomed, the gunfighter is the Western hero still, perhaps all the more because his value must express itself entirely in his own being—in his presence, the way he holds our eyes—and in contradiction to the facts. No matter what he has done, he *looks* right, and he remains invulnerable because, without acknowledging anyone else's right to judge him, he has judged his own failure and has already assimilated it, understanding—as no one else understands except the marshal and the barroom girl—that he can do nothing but play out the drama of the gun fight again and again until the time comes when it will be he who gets killed. What "redeems" him is that he no longer believes in this drama and nevertheless will continue to play his role perfectly; the pattern is all.

The proper function of realism in the Western movie can only be to deepen the lines of that pattern. It is an art form for connoisseurs, where the spectator derives his pleasure from the appreciation of minor variations within the working out of a pre-established order. One does not want too much novelty; it comes as a shock, for instance, when the hero is made to operate without a gun, as has been done in several pictures (e.g., *Destry Rides Again*), and our uneasiness is allayed only when he is finally compelled to put his "pacifism" aside. If the hero can be shown to be troubled, complex, fallible, even eccentric, or the villain given some psychological taint or, better, some evocative physical mannerism, to shade the colors of his villainy, that is all to the good. Indeed, that kind of variation is absolutely necessary to keep the type from becoming sterile; we do not want to see the same movie over and over again, only the same form. But when the impulse toward realism is extended into a "reinterpretation" of the West as a developed society, drawing our eyes away from the hero if only to the extent of showing him as the one dominant figure in a complex social order, then the pattern is broken and the West itself begins to be uninteresting. If the "social problems" of the frontier are to be the movie's chief concern, there is no longer any point in re-examining these problems twenty times a year; they have been solved, and the people for whom they once were real are dead. Moreover, the hero himself, still the film's central figure, now tends to become its one unassimilable element, since he is the most "unreal."

The Ox-Bow Incident, by denying the convention of the lynching, presents us with a modern "social drama" and evokes a corresponding response, but in doing so it almost makes the Western setting irrelevant, a mere backdrop of beautiful scenery. (It is significant that *The Ox-Bow Incident* has no hero; a hero would have to stop the lynching or be killed in trying to stop it, and then the "problem" of lynching would no longer be central.) Even in *The Gunfighter* the women and children are a little too much in evidence, threatening constantly to become a real focus of concern instead of simply part of the given framework, and the young tough who kills the hero has too much the air of juvenile criminality; the hero himself could never have been like that, and the idea of a cycle being repeated therefore loses its sharpness. But the most striking example of the confusion created by a too conscientious "social" realism is in the celebrated *High Noon.*

In *High Noon* we find Gary Cooper still the upholder of order that he was in *The Virginian,* but twenty-four years older, stooped, slower moving, awkward, his face lined, the flesh sagging, a less beautiful and weaker figure, but with the suggestion of greater depth that belongs almost automatically to age. Like the hero of *The Gunfighter,* he no longer has to assert his character and is no longer interested in the drama of combat; it is hard to imagine that he might once have been so youthful as to say, "When you call me that—smile!" In fact, when we come upon him he is hanging up his guns and his marshal's badge in order to begin a new, peaceful life with his bride, who is a Quaker. But then the news comes that a man he sent to prison has been pardoned and will get to town on the noon train; three friends of this man have come to wait for him at the station, and when the freed convict arrives the four of them will come to kill the marshal. He is thus trapped; the bride will object, the hero himself will waver much more than he would have done twenty-four years ago, but in the end he will play out the drama because it is what he "has to do." All this belongs to the established form (there is even the "fallen woman" who understands the marshal's position as his wife does not). Leaving aside the crudity of building up suspense by means of the clock, the actual Western drama of *High Noon* is well handled and forms a good companion piece to *The Virginian,* showing in both conception and technique the ways in which the Western movie has naturally developed.

But there is a second drama along with the first. As the marshal sets out to find deputies to help him deal with the four gunmen, we are taken through the various social strata of the town, each group in turn refusing its assistance out of cowardice, malice, irresponsibility, or venality. With this we are in the field of "social drama"—of a very low order, incidentally, altogether unconvincing and displaying a vulgar antipopulism that has marred some other movies of Stanley Kramer's. But the falsity of the "social drama" is less important than the fact that it does not belong in the movie to begin with. The technical problem was to make it necessary for the marshal to face his enemies alone; to explain *why* the other townspeople are not at his side is to raise a question which does not exist in the proper frame of the Western movie, where the hero is "naturally" alone and it is only necessary to contrive the physical absence of those who might be his allies, if any contrivance is needed at all. In addition, though the hero of *High Noon* proves himself a better man than all around him, the actual effect of this contrast is to lessen his stature: he becomes only a rejected man of virtue. In our final glimpse of him, as he rides away through the town where he has spent most of his life without really imposing himself on it, he is a pathetic rather than a tragic figure. And his departure has another meaning as well; the "social drama" has no place for him.

But there is also a different way of violating the Western form. This is to yield entirely to its static quality as legend and to the "cinematic" temptations of its landscape, the horses, the quiet men. John Ford's famous *Stagecoach* (1938) had much of this unhappy preoccupation with style, and the same director's *My Darling Clementine* (1946), a soft and beautiful movie about Wyatt Earp, goes further along the same path, offering indeed a superficial accuracy of historical reconstruction, but so loving in execution as to destroy the outlines of the Western legend, assimilating it to the more sentimental legend of rural America and making the hero a more dangerous Mr. Deeds. (*Powder River,* a recent "routine" Western shamelessly copied from *My Darling Clementine,* is in most ways a better film; lacking the benefit of a serious director, it is necessarily more concerned with drama than with style.)

The highest expression of this aestheticizing tendency is in George Stevens' *Shane,* where the legend of the West is virtually reduced to its essentials and then fixed in the dreamy clarity of a fairy tale. There never was so broad and bare and lovely a landscape as Stevens puts before us, or so unimaginably comfortless a "town" as the little group of buildings on the prairie to which the settlers must come for their supplies and to buy a drink. The mere physical progress of the film, following the style of *A Place in the Sun,* is so deliberately graceful that everything seems to be happening at the bottom of a clear lake. The hero (Alan Ladd) is hardly a man at all, but something like the Spirit of the West, beautiful in fringed buckskins. He emerges mysteriously from the plains, breathing sweetness and a melancholy which is no longer simply the Westerner's natural response to experience but has taken on spirituality; and when he has accomplished his mission, meeting and destroying in the black figure of Jack Palance a Spirit of Evil just as metaphysical as his own embodiment of virtue, he fades away again into the more distant West, a man whose "day is over," leaving behind the wondering little boy who might have imagined the whole story. The choice of Alan Ladd to play the leading role is alone an indication of this film's tendency. Actors like Gary Cooper or Gregory Peck are in themselves, as material objects, "realistic," seeming to bear in their bodies and their faces mortality, limitation, the knowledge of good and evil. Ladd is a more "aesthetic" object, with some of the "universality" of a piece of sculpture; his special quality is in his physical smoothness and serenity, unworldly and yet not innocent, but suggesting that no experience can really touch him. Stevens has tried to freeze the Western myth once and for all in the immobility of Alan Ladd's countenance. If *Shane* were "right," and fully successful, it might be possible to say there was no point in making any more Western movies; once the hero is apotheosized, variation and development are closed off.

Shane is not "right," but it is still true that the possibilities of fruitful variation in the Western movie are limited. The form can keep its freshness through endless repetitions only because of the special character of the film medium, where the physical difference between one object and another—above all, between one actor and another—is of such enormous importance, serving the function that is served by the variety of language in the perpetuation of literary types. In this sense, the "vocabulary" of films is much larger than that of literature and falls more readily into pleasing and significant arrangements. (That may explain why the middle levels of excellence are more easily reached in the movies than in literary forms, and perhaps also why the status of the movies as art is constantly being called into question.) But the advantage of this almost automatic particularity belongs to all films alike. Why does the Western movie especially have such a hold on our imagination?

Chiefly, I think, because it offers a serious orientation to the problem of violence such as can be found almost nowhere else in our culture. One of the well-known peculiarities of modern civilized opinion is its refusal to acknowledge the value of violence. This refusal is a virtue, but like many virtues it involves a certain willful blindness and it encourages hypocrisy. We train ourselves to be shocked or bored by cultural images of violence, and our very concept of heroism tends to be a passive one: we are less drawn to the brave young men who kill large numbers of our enemies than to the heroic prisoners who endure torture without capitulating. In art, though we may still be able to understand and participate in the values of the *Iliad,* a modern writer like Ernest Hemingway we find somewhat embarrassing: there is no doubt that he stirs us, but we cannot help recognizing also that he is a little childish. And in the criticism of popular culture, where the educated observer is usually under the illusion that he has nothing at stake, the presence of images of violence is often assumed to be in itself a sufficient ground for condemnation.

These attitudes, however, have not reduced the element of violence in our culture but, if anything, have helped to free it from moral control by letting it take on the aura of "emancipation." The celebration of acts of violence is left more and more to the irresponsible—on the higher cultural levels to writers like Céline, and lower down to Mickey Spillane or Horace McCoy, or to the comic books, television, and the movies. The gangster movie, with its numerous variations, belongs to this cultural "underground" which sets forth the attractions of violence in the face of all our higher social attitudes. It is a more "modern" genre than the Western, perhaps even more profound, because it confronts industrial society on its own ground—the city—and because, like much of our advanced art, it gains its effects by a gross insistence on its own narrow logic. But it is antisocial, resting on fantasies of irresponsible freedom. If we are brought finally to acquiesce in the denial of these fantasies, it is only because they have been shown to be dangerous, not because they have given way to a better vision of behavior.[1]

[1]I am not concerned here with the actual social consequences of gangster movies, though I suspect they could not have been so pernicious as they were thought to be. Some of the compromises introduced to avoid the supposed bad effects of the old

In war movies, to be sure, it is possible to present the uses of violence within a framework of responsibility. But there is the disadvantage that modern war is a co-operative enterprise; its violence is largely impersonal, and heroism belongs to the group more than to the individual. The hero of a war movie is most often simply a leader, and his superiority is likely to be expressed in a denial of the heroic: you are not supposed to be brave, you are supposed to get the job done and stay alive (this too, of course, is a kind of heroic posture, but a new—and "practical"—one). At its best, the war movie may represent a more civilized point of view than the Western, and if it were not continually marred by ideological sentimentality we might hope to find it developing into a higher form of drama. But it cannot supply the values we seek in the Western.

Those values are in the image of a single man who wears a gun on his thigh. The gun tells us that he lives in a world of violence, and even that he "believes in violence." But the drama is one of self-restraint: the moment of violence must come in its own time and according to its special laws, or else it is valueless. There is little cruelty in Western movies, and little sentimentality; our eyes are not focused on the sufferings of the defeated but on the deportment of the hero. Really, it is not violence at all which is the "point" of the Western movie, but a certain *image of man,* a style, which expresses itself most clearly in violence. Watch a child with his toy guns and you will see: what most interests him is not (as we so much fear) the fantasy of hurting others, but to work out how a man might look when he shoots or is shot. A hero is one who looks like a hero.

Whatever the limitations of such an idea in experience, it has always been valid in art and has a special validity in an art where appearances are everything. The Western hero is necessarily an archaic figure; we do not really believe in him and would not have him step out of his rigidly conventionalized background. But his archaicism does not take away from his power; on the contrary, it adds to it by keeping him just a little beyond the reach both of common sense and of absolutized emotion, the two usual impulses of our art. And he has, after all, his own kind of relevance. He is there

---

gangster movies may be, if anything, more dangerous, for the sadistic violence that once belonged only to the gangster is now commonly enlisted on the side of the law and thus goes undefeated, allowing us (if we wish) to find in the movies a sort of "confirmation" of our fantasies.

to remind us of the possibility of style in an age which has put on itself the burden of pretending that style has no meaning, and, in the midst of our anxieties over the problem of violence, to suggest that even in killing or being killed we are not freed from the necessity of establishing satisfactory modes of behavior. Above all, the movies in which the Westerner plays out his role preserve for us the pleasures of a complete and self-contained drama—and one which still effortlessly crosses the boundaries which divide our culture—in a time when other, more consciously serious art forms are increasingly complex, uncertain, and ill-defined.

THE IMAGINATION OF DISASTER (1967)

By Susan Sontag

The typical science fiction film has a form as predictable as a Western, and is made up of elements which, to a practiced eye, are as classic as the saloon brawl, the blonde schoolteacher from the East, and the gun duel on the deserted main street.

One model scenario proceeds through five phases.

(1) The arrival of the thing. (Emergence of the monsters, landing of the alien spaceship, etc.) This is usually witnessed or suspected by just one person, a young scientist on a field trip. Nobody, neither his neighbors nor his colleagues, will believe him for some time. The hero is not married, but has a sympathetic though also incredulous girl friend.

(2) Confirmation of the hero's report by a host of witnesses to a great act of destruction. (If the invaders are beings from another planet, a fruitless attempt to parley with them and get them to leave peacefully.) The local police are summoned to deal with the situation and massacred.

(3) In the capital of the country, conferences between scientists and the military take place, with the hero lecturing before a chart, map, or blackboard. A national emergency is declared. Reports of further destruction. Authorities from other countries arrive in black limousines. All international tensions are suspended in view of the planetary emergency. This stage often includes a rapid montage of news broadcasts in various languages, a meeting at the UN, and more conferences between the military and the scientists. Plans are made for destroying the enemy.

(4) Further atrocities. At some point the hero's girl friend is in grave danger. Massive counter-attacks by international forces, with brilliant displays of rocketry, rays, and other advanced weapons, are all unsuccessful. Enormous military casualties, usually by incineration. Cities are destroyed and/or evacuated. There is an obligatory scene here of panicked crowds stampeding along a highway or a big bridge, being waved on by numerous policemen who, if the film is Japanese, are immaculately white-gloved, preternaturally calm, and call out in dubbed English, "Keep moving. There is no need to be alarmed."

(5) More conferences, whose motif is: "They must be vulnerable to something." Throughout the hero has been working in his lab to this end. The final strategy, upon which all hopes depend, is drawn up; the ultimate weapon—often a super-powerful, as yet untested, nuclear device—is mounted. Countdown. Final repulse of the monster or invaders. Mutual congratulations, while the hero and girl friend embrace cheek to cheek and scan the skies sturdily. "But have we seen the last of them?"

The film I have just described should be in color and on a wide screen. Another typical scenario, which follows, is simpler and suited to black-and-white films with a lower budget. It has four phases.

(1) The hero (usually, but not always, a scientist) and his girl friend, or his wife and two children, are disporting themselves in some innocent ultra-normal middle-class surroundings—their house in a small town, or on vacation (camping, boating). Suddenly, someone starts behaving strangely; or some innocent form of vegetation becomes monstrously enlarged and ambulatory. If a character is pictured driving an automobile, something gruesome looms up in the middle of the road. If it is night, strange lights hurtle across the sky.

(2) After following the thing's tracks, or determining that It is radioactive, or poking around a huge crater—in short, conducting

some sort of crude investigation—the hero tries to warn the local authorities, without effect; nobody believes anything is amiss. The hero knows better. If the thing is tangible, the house is elaborately barricaded. If the invading alien is an invisible parasite, a doctor or friend is called in, who is himself rather quickly killed or "taken possession of" by the thing.

(3) The advice of whoever further is consulted proves useless. Meanwhile, It continues to claim other victims in the town, which remains implausibly isolated from the rest of the world. General helplessness.

(4) One of two possibilities. Either the hero prepares to do battle alone, accidentally discovers the thing's one vulnerable point, and destroys it. Or, he somehow manages to get out of town and succeeds in laying his case before competent authorities. They, along the lines of the first script but abridged, deploy a complex technology which (after initial setbacks) finally prevails against the invaders.

Another version of the second script opens with the scientist-hero in his laboratory, which is located in the basement or on the grounds of his tasteful, prosperous house. Through his experiments, he unwittingly causes a frightful metamorphosis in some class of plants or animals which turn carnivorous and go on a rampage. Or else, his experiments have caused him to be injured (sometimes irrevocably) or "invaded" himself. Perhaps he has been experimenting with radiation, or has built a machine to communicate with beings from other planets or transport him to other places or times.

Another version of the first script involves the discovery of some fundamental alteration in the conditions of existence of our planet, brought about by nuclear testing, which will lead to the extinction in a few months of all human life. For example: the temperature of the earth is becoming too high or too low to support life, or the earth is cracking in two, or it is gradually being blanketed by lethal fallout.

A third script, somewhat but not altogether different from the first two, concerns a journey through space—to the moon, or some other planet. What the space-voyagers discover commonly is that the alien terrain is in a state of dire emergency, itself threatened by extra-planetary invaders or nearing extinction through the practice of nuclear warfare. The terminal dramas of the first and second scripts are played out there, to which is added the problem of getting away from the doomed and/or hostile planet and back to Earth.

I am aware, of course, that there are thousands of science fiction novels (their heyday was the late 1940s), not to mention the transcriptions of science fiction themes which, more and more, provide the principal subject-matter of comic books. But I propose to discuss science fiction films (the present period began in 1950 and continues, considerably abated, to this day) as an independent subgenre, without reference to other media—and, most particularly, without reference to the novels from which, in many cases, they were adapted. For, while novel and film may share the same plot, the fundamental difference between the resources of the novel and the film makes them quite dissimilar.

Certainly, compared with the science fiction novels, their film counterparts have unique strengths, one of which is the immediate representation of the extraordinary: physical deformity and mutation, missile and rocket combat, toppling skyscrapers. The movies are, naturally, weak just where the science fiction novels (some of them) are strong—on science. But in place of an intellectual workout, they can supply something the novels can never provide—sensuous elaboration. In the films it is by means of images and sounds, not words that have to be translated by the imagination, that one can participate in the fantasy of living through one's own death and more, the death of cities, the destruction of humanity itself.

Science fiction films are not about science. They are about disaster, which is one of the oldest subjects of art. In science fiction films disaster is rarely viewed intensively; it is always extensive. It is a matter of quantity and ingenuity. If you will, it is a question of scale. But the scale, particularly in the wide-screen color films (of which the ones by the Japanese director Inoshiro Honda and the American director George Pal are technically the most convincing and visually the most exciting), does raise the matter to another level.

Thus, the science fiction film (like that of a very different contemporary genre, the Happening) is concerned with the aesthetics of destruction, with the peculiar beauties to be found in wreaking havoc, making a mess. And it is in the imagery of destruction that the core of a good science fiction film lies. Hence, the disadvantage of the cheap film—in which the monster appears or the rocket lands in a small dull-looking town. (Hollywood budget needs usually dictate that the town be in the Arizona or California desert. In *The Thing from Another World* [1951] the rather sleazy and confined set is supposed to be an encampment near the North Pole.) Still, good black-and-white science fiction films have been made. But a bigger budget, which usually means color, allows a much greater play back and forth among several model environments. There is the populous city. There is the lavish but ascetic interior of the spaceship—either the invaders' or ours—replete with streamlined chromium fixtures and dials and machines whose complexity is indicated by the number of colored lights they flash and strange noises they emit. There is the laboratory crowded with formidable boxes and scientific apparatus. There is a comparatively old-fashioned-looking conference room, where the scientists unfurl charts to explain the desperate state of things to the military. And each of these standard locales or backgrounds is subject to two modalities—intact and destroyed. We may, if we are lucky, be treated to a panorama of melting tanks, flying bodies, crashing walls, awesome craters and fissures in the earth, plummeting spacecraft, colorful deadly rays; and to a symphony of screams, weird electronic signals, the noisiest military hardware going, and the leaden tones of the laconic denizens of alien planets and their subjugated earthlings.

Certain of the primitive gratifications of science fiction films—for instance, the depiction of urban disaster on a colossally magnified scale—are shared with other types of films. Visually there is little difference between mass havoc as represented in the old horror and monster films and what we find in science fiction films, except (again) scale. In the old monster films, the monster always headed for the great city, where he had to do a fair bit of rampaging, hurling busses off bridges, crumpling trains in his bare hands, toppling buildings, and so forth. The archetype is King Kong, in Schoedsack and Cooper's great film of 1933, running amok, first in the native village (trampling babies, a bit of footage excised from most prints), then in New York. This is really no different in spirit from the scene in Inoshiro Honda's *Rodan* (1957) in which two giant reptiles—with a wingspan of 500 feet and supersonic speeds—by flapping their wings whip up a cyclone that blows most of Tokyo to smithereens. Or the destruction of half of Japan by the gigantic robot with the great incinerating ray that shoots forth from his eyes, at the beginning of Honda's *The Mysterians* (1959). Or, the devastation by the rays from a fleet of flying saucers of New York, Paris, and Tokyo, in *Battle in Outer Space* (1960). Or, the inundation of New York in *When Worlds Collide* (1951). Or, the end of London in 1966 depicted in George Pal's *The Time Machine* (1960). Neither do these sequences differ in aesthetic intention from the destruction scenes in the big sword, sandal, and orgy color spectaculars set in Biblical and Roman times—the end of Sodom in Aldrich's *Sodom and Gomorrah,* of Gaza in De Mille's *Samson and Delilah,* of Rhodes in *The Colossus of Rhodes,* and of Rome in a dozen Nero movies. Griffith began it with the Babylon sequence in *Intolerance,* and to this day there is nothing like the thrill of watching all those expensive sets come tumbling down.

In other respects as well, the science fiction films of the 1950s take up familiar themes. The famous 1930s movie serials and comics of the adventures of Flash Gordon and Buck Rogers, as well as the more recent spate of comic book super-heroes with extraterrestrial origins (the most famous is Superman, a foundling from the planet Krypton, currently described as having been exploded by a nuclear blast), share motifs with more recent science fiction movies. But there is an important difference. The old science fiction films, and most of the comics, still have an essentially innocent relation to disaster. Mainly they offer new versions of the oldest romance of all —of the strong invulnerable hero with a mysterious lineage come to do battle on behalf of good and against evil. Recent science fiction films have a decided grimness, bolstered by their much greater degree of visual credibility, which contrasts strongly with the older films. Modern historical reality has greatly enlarged the imagination of disaster, and the protagonists—perhaps by the very nature of what is visited upon them—no longer seem wholly innocent.

The lure of such generalized disaster as a fantasy is that it releases one from normal obligations. The trump card of the end-of-the-world movies—like *The Day the Earth Caught Fire* (1962)—is that great scene with New York or London or Tokyo discovered empty, its entire population annihilated. Or, as in *The World, The Flesh, and The Devil* (1957), the whole movie can be devoted to the fantasy of occupying the deserted metropolis and starting all over again, a world Robinson Crusoe.

Another kind of satisfaction these films supply is extreme moral simplification—that is to say, a morally acceptable fantasy where one can give outlet to cruel or at least amoral feelings. In this respect, science fiction films partly overlap with horror films. This is the undeniable pleasure we derive from looking at freaks, beings excluded from the category of the human. The sense of superiority over the freak conjoined in varying proportions with the titillation of fear and aversion makes it possible for moral scruples to be lifted, for cruelty to be enjoyed. The same thing happens in science fiction films. In the figure of the monster from outer space, the freakish, the ugly, and the predatory all converge—and provide a fantasy target for righteous bellicosity to discharge itself, and for the aesthetic enjoyment of suffering and disaster. Science fiction films are one of the purest forms of spectacle; that is, we are rarely inside anyone's feelings. (An exception is Jack Arnold's *The Incredible Shrinking Man* [1957].) We are merely spectators; we watch.

But in science fiction films, unlike horror films, there is not much horror. Suspense, shocks, surprises are mostly abjured in favor of a steady, inexorable plot. Science fiction films invite a dispassionate, aesthetic view of destruction and violence—a *technological* view. Things, objects, machinery play a major role in these films. A greater range of ethical values is embodied in the décor of these films than in the people. Things, rather than the helpless humans, are the locus of values because we experience them, rather than people, as the sources of power. According to science fiction films, man is naked without his artifacts. *They* stand for different values, they are potent, they are what get destroyed, and they are the indispensable tools for the repulse of the alien invaders or the repair of the damaged environment.

The science fiction films are strongly moralistic. The standard message is the one about the proper, or humane, use of science, versus the mad, obsessional use of science. This message the science fiction films share in common with the classic horror films of the 1930s, like *Frankenstein, The Mummy, Island of Lost Souls, Dr. Jekyll and Mr. Hyde.* (Georges Franju's brilliant *Les Yeux Sans Visage* [1959], called here *The Horror Chamber of Doctor Faustus,* is a more recent example.) In the horror films, we have the mad or obsessed or misguided scientist who pursues his experiments against good advice to the contrary, creates a monster or monsters, and is himself destroyed—often recognizing his folly himself, and dying in the successful effort to destroy his own creation. One science fiction equivalent of this is the scientist, usually a member of a team, who defects to the planetary invaders because "their" science is more advanced than "ours."

This is the case in *The Mysterians,* and, true to form, the renegade sees his error in the end, and from within the Mysterian space ship destroys it and himself. In *This Island Earth* (1955), the inhabitants of the beleaguered planet Metaluna propose to conquer earth, but their project is foiled by a Metalunan scientist named Exeter who, having lived on earth a while and learned to love Mozart, cannot abide such viciousness. Exeter plunges his spaceship into the ocean after returning a glamorous pair (male and female) of American physicists to earth. Metaluna dies. In *The Fly* (1958), the hero, engrossed in his basement-laboratory experiments on a matter-transmitting machine, uses himself as a subject, exchanges head and one arm with a housefly which had accidentally gotten into the machine, becomes a monster, and with his last shred of human will destroys his laboratory and orders his wife to kill him. His discovery, for the good of mankind, is lost.

Being a clearly labeled species of intellectual, scientists in science fiction films are always liable to crack up or go off the deep end. In *Conquest of Space* (1955), the scientist-commander of an international expedition to Mars suddenly acquires scruples about the blasphemy involved in the undertaking, and begins reading the Bible mid-journey instead of attending to his duties. The commander's son, who is his junior officer and always addresses his father as "General," is forced to kill the old man when he tries to prevent the ship from landing on Mars. In this film, both sides of the ambivalence toward scientists are given voice. Generally, for a scientific enterprise to be treated entirely sympathetically in these films, it needs the certificate of utility. Science, viewed without ambivalence, means an efficacious response to danger. Disinterested intellectual curiosity rarely appears in any form other than caricature, as a maniacal dementia that cuts one off from normal human relations. But this suspicion is usually directed at the scientist rather than his work. The creative scientist may become a martyr to his own discovery, through an accident or by pushing things too far. But the implication remains that other men, less imaginative—in short, technicians—could have administered the same discovery better and more safely. The most ingrained contemporary mistrust of the intellect is visited, in these movies, upon the scientist-as-intellectual.

The message that the scientist is one who releases forces which, if not controlled for good, could destroy man himself seems innocuous enough. One of the oldest images of the scientist is Shakespeare's Prospero, the overdetached scholar forcibly retired from society to a desert island, only partly in control of the magic forces in which he dabbles. Equally classic is the figure of the scientist as satanist

(*Doctor Faustus,* and stories of Poe and Hawthorne). Science is magic, and man has always known that there is black magic as well as white. But it is not enough to remark that contemporary attitudes —as reflected in science fiction films—remain ambivalent, that the scientist is treated as both satanist and savior. The proportions have changed, because of the new context in which the old admiration and fear of the scientist are located. For his sphere of influence is no longer local, himself or his immediate community. It is planetary, cosmic.

One gets the feeling, particularly in the Japanese films but not only there, that a mass trauma exists over the use of nuclear weapons and the possibility of future nuclear wars. Most of the science fiction films bear witness to this trauma, and, in a way, attempt to exorcise it.

The accidental awakening of the super-destructive monster who has slept in the earth since prehistory is, often, an obvious metaphor for the Bomb. But there are many explicit references as well. In *The Mysterians,* a probe ship from the planet Mysteroid has landed on earth, near Tokyo. Nuclear warfare having been practiced on Mysteroid for centuries (their civilization is "more advanced than ours"), ninety percent of those now born on the planet have to be destroyed at birth, because of defects caused by the huge amounts of Strontium 90 in their diet. The Mysterians have come to earth to marry earth women, and possibly to take over our relatively uncontaminated planet . . . In *The Incredible Shrinking Man,* the John Doe hero is the victim of a gust of radiation which blows over the water, while he is out boating with his wife; the radiation causes him to grow smaller and smaller, until at the end of the movie he steps through the fine mesh of a window screen to become "the infinitely small." . . . In *Rodan,* a horde of monstrous carnivorous prehistoric insects, and finally a pair of giant flying reptiles (the prehistoric Archeopteryx), are hatched from dormant eggs in the depths of a mine shaft by the impact of nuclear test explosions, and go on to destroy a good part of the world before they are felled by the molten lava of a volcanic eruption. . . . In the English film, *The Day the Earth Caught Fire,* two simultaneous hydrogen bomb tests by the United States and Russia change by 11 degrees the tilt of the earth on its axis and alter the earth's orbit so that it begins to approach the sun.

Radiation casualties—ultimately, the conception of the whole world as a casualty of nuclear testing and nuclear warfare—is the most ominous of all the notions with which science fiction films deal. Universes become expendable. Worlds become contaminated, burnt out, exhausted, obsolete. In *Rocketship X-M* (1950) explorers from the earth land on Mars, where they learn that atomic warfare has destroyed Martian civilization. In George Pal's *The War of the Worlds* (1953), reddish spindly alligator-skinned creatures from Mars invade the earth because their planet is becoming too cold to be inhabitable. In *This Island Earth,* also American, the planet Metaluna, whose population has long ago been driven underground by warfare, is dying under the missile attacks of an enemy planet. Stocks of uranium, which power the force field shielding Metaluna, have been used up; and an unsuccessful expedition is sent to earth to enlist earth scientists to devise new sources for nuclear power. In Joseph Losey's *The Damned* (1961), nine icy-cold radioactive children are being reared by a fanatical scientist in a dark cave on the English coast to be the only survivors of the inevitable nuclear Armageddon.

There is a vast amount of wishful thinking in science fiction films, some of it touching, some of it depressing. Again and again, one detects the hunger for a "good war," which poses no moral problems, admits of no moral qualifications. The imagery of science fiction films will satisfy the most bellicose addict of war films, for a lot of the satisfactions of war films pass, untransformed, into science fiction films. Examples: the dogfights between earth "fighter rockets" and alien spacecraft in the *Battle in Outer Space* (1960); the escalating firepower in the successive assaults upon the invaders in *The Mysterians,* which Dan Talbot correctly described as a non-stop holocaust; the spectacular bombardment of the underground fortress of Metaluna in *This Island Earth.*

Yet at the same time the bellicosity of science fiction films is neatly channeled into the yearning for peace, or for at least peaceful coexistence. Some scientist generally takes sententious note of the fact that it took the planetary invasion to make the warring nations of the earth come to their senses and suspend their own conflicts. One of the main themes of many science fiction films—the color ones usually, because they have the budget and resources to develop the military spectacle—is this UN fantasy, a fantasy of united warfare. (The same wishful UN theme cropped up in a recent spectacular which is not science fiction, *Fifty-Five Days in Peking* [1963]. There, topically enough, the Chinese, the Boxers, play the role of Martian invaders who unite the earthmen, in this case the United States, England, Russia, France, Germany, Italy, and Japan.) A great enough disaster cancels all enmities and calls upon the utmost concentration of earth resources.

Science—technology—is conceived of as the great unifier. Thus the science fiction films also project a Utopian fantasy. In the classic models of Utopian thinking—Plato's Republic, Campanella's City of the Sun, More's Utopia, Swift's land of the Houyhnhnms, Voltaire's Eldorado—society had worked out a perfect consensus. In these societies reasonableness had achieved an unbreakable supremacy over the emotions. Since no disagreement or social conflict was intellectually plausible, none was possible. As in Melville's *Typee,* "they all think the same." The universal rule of reason meant universal agreement. It is interesting, too, that societies in which reason was pictured as totally ascendant were also traditionally pictured as having an ascetic or materially frugal and economically simple mode of life. But in the Utopian world community projected by science fiction films, totally pacified and ruled by scientific consensus, the demand for simplicity of material existence would be absurd.

Yet alongside the hopeful fantasy of moral simplification and international unity embodied in the science fiction films lurk the deepest anxieties about contemporary existence. I don't mean only the very real trauma of the Bomb—that it has been used, that there are enough now to kill everyone on earth many times over, that those new bombs may very well be used. Besides these new anxieties about physical disaster, the prospect of universal mutilation and even annihilation, the science fiction films reflect powerful anxieties about the condition of the individual psyche.

For science fiction films may also be described as a popular mythology for the contemporary *negative* imagination about the impersonal. The other-world creatures that seek to take "us" over are an "it," not a "they." The planetary invaders are usually zombie-like. Their movements are either cool, mechanical, or lumbering, blobby. But it amounts to the same thing. If they are non-human in form, they proceed with an absolutely regular, unalterable movement (unalterable save by destruction). If they are human in form—dressed in space suits, etc.—then they obey the most rigid military discipline, and display no personal characteristics whatsoever. And it is this regime of emotionlessness, of impersonality, of regimentation, which they will impose on the earth if they are successful. "No more love, no more beauty, no more pain," boasts a converted earthling in *The Invasion of the Body Snatchers* (1956). The half-earthling, half-alien children in *The Children of the Damned* (1960) are absolutely emotionless, move as a group and understand each others' thoughts, and are all prodigious intellects. They are the wave of the future, man in his next stage of development.

These alien invaders practice a crime which is worse than murder. They do not simply kill the person. They obliterate him. In *The War of the Worlds,* the ray which issues from the rocket ship disintegrates all persons and objects in its path, leaving no trace of them but a light ash. In Honda's *The H-Man* (1959), the creeping blob melts all flesh with which it comes in contact. If the blob, which looks like a huge hunk of red Jello and can crawl across floors and up and down walls, so much as touches your bare foot, all that is left of you is a heap of clothes on the floor. (A more articulated, size-multiplying blob is the villain in the English film *The Creeping Unknown* [1956].) In another version of this fantasy, the body is preserved but the person is entirely reconstituted as the automatized servant or agent of the alien powers. This is, of course, the vampire fantasy in new dress. The person is really dead, but he doesn't know it. He is "undead," he has become an "unperson." It happens to a whole California town in *The Invasion of the Body Snatchers,* to several earth scientists in *This Island Earth,* and to assorted innocents in *It Came From Outer Space, Attack of the Puppet People* (1958), and *The Brain Eaters* (1958). As the victim always backs away from the vampire's horrifying embrace, so in science fiction films the person always fights being "taken over"; he wants to retain his humanity. But once the deed has been done, the victim is eminently satisfied with his condition. He has not been converted from human amiability to monstrous "animal" bloodlust (a metaphoric exaggeration of sexual desire), as in the old vampire fantasy. No, he has simply become far more efficient—the very model of technocratic man, purged of emotions, volitionless, tranquil, obedient to all orders. (The dark secret behind human nature used to be the upsurge of the animal—as in *King Kong.* The threat to man, his availability to dehumanization, lay in his own animality. Now the danger is understood as residing in man's ability to be turned into a machine.)

The rule, of course, is that this horrible and irremediable form of murder can strike anyone in the film except the hero. The hero and his family, while greatly threatened, always escape this fate and by the end of the film the invaders have been repulsed or destroyed. I know of only one exception, *The Day That Mars Invaded Earth* (1963), in which after all the standard struggles the scientist-hero, his wife, and their two children are "taken over" by the alien invaders —and that's that. (The last minutes of the film show them being incinerated by the Martians' rays and their ash silhouettes flushed down their empty swimming pool, while their simulacra drive off in the family car.) Another variant but upbeat switch on the rule occurs in *The Creation of the Humanoids* (1964), where the hero discovers at the end of the film that he, too, has been turned into a metal robot, complete with highly efficient and virtually indestructible mechanical insides, although he didn't know it and detected no difference in himself. He learns, however, that he will shortly be upgraded into a "humanoid" having all the properties of a real man.

Of all the standard motifs of science fiction films, this theme of dehumanization is perhaps the most fascinating. For, as I have indicated, it is scarcely a black-and-white situation, as in the old vampire films. The attitude of the science fiction films toward depersonalization is mixed. On the one hand, they deplore it as the ultimate horror. On the other hand, certain characteristics of the dehumanized invaders, modulated and disguised—such as the ascendancy of reason over feelings, the idealization of teamwork and the consensus-creating activities of science, a marked degree of moral simplification—are precisely traits of the savior-scientist. It is interesting that when the scientist in these films is treated negatively, it is usually done through the portrayal of an individual scientist who holes up in his laboratory and neglects his fiancée or his loving wife and children, obsessed by his daring and dangerous experiments. The scientist as a loyal member of a team, and therefore considerably less individualized, is treated quite respectfully.

There is absolutely no social criticism, of even the most implicit kind, in science fiction films. No criticism, for example, of the conditions of our society which create the impersonality and dehumanization which science fiction fantasies displace onto the influence of an alien It. Also, the notion of science as a social activity, interlocking with social and political interests, is unacknowledged. Science is simply either adventure (for good or evil) or a technical response to danger. And, typically, when the fear of science is paramount—

when science is conceived of as black magic rather than white—the evil has no attribution beyond that of the perverse will of an individual scientist. In science fiction films the antithesis of black magic and white is drawn as a split between technology, which is beneficent, and the errant individual will of a lone intellectual.

Thus, science fiction films can be looked at as thematically central allegory, replete with standard modern attitudes. The theme of depersonalization (being "taken over") which I have been talking about is a new allegory reflecting the age-old awareness of man that, sane, he is always perilously close to insanity and unreason. But there is something more here than just a recent, popular image which expresses man's perennial, but largely unconscious, anxiety about his sanity. The image derives most of its power from a supplementary and historical anxiety, also not experienced consciously by most people, about the depersonalizing conditions of modern urban life. Similarly, it is not enough to note that science fiction allegories are one of the new myths about—that is, one of the ways of accommodating to and negating—the perennial human anxiety about death. (Myths of heaven and hell, and of ghosts, had the same function.) For, again, there is a historically specifiable twist which intensifies the anxiety. I mean, the trauma suffered by everyone in the middle of the 20th century when it became clear that, from now on to the end of human history, every person would spend his individual life under the threat not only of individual death, which is certain, but of something almost insupportable psychologically—collective incineration and extinction which could come at any time, virtually without warning.

From a psychological point of view, the imagination of disaster does not greatly differ from one period in history to another. But from a political and moral point of view, it does. The expectation of the apocalypse may be the occasion for a radical disaffiliation from society, as when thousands of Eastern European Jews in the 17th century, hearing that Sabbatai Zevi had been proclaimed the Messiah and that the end of the world was imminent, gave up their homes and businesses and began the trek to Palestine. But people take the news of their doom in diverse ways. It is reported that in 1945 the populace of Berlin received without great agitation the news that Hitler had decided to kill them all, before the Allies arrived, because they had not been worthy enough to win the war. We are, alas, more in the position of the Berliners of 1945 than of the Jews of 17th-century Eastern Europe; and our response is closer to theirs, too. What I am suggesting is that the imagery of disaster in science fiction is above all the emblem of an *inadequate response.* I don't mean to bear down on the films for this. They themselves are only a sampling, stripped of sophistication, of the inadequacy of most people's response to the unassimilable terrors that infect their consciousness. The interest of the films, aside from their considerable amount of cinematic charm, consists in this intersection between a naïve and largely debased commercial art product and the most profound dilemmas of the contemporary situation.

Ours is indeed an age of extremity. For we live under continual threat of two equally fearful, but seemingly opposed, destinies: unremitting banality and inconceivable terror. It is fantasy, served out in large rations by the popular arts, which allows most people to cope with these twin specters. For one job that fantasy can do is to lift us out of the unbearably humdrum and to distract us from terrors—real or anticipated—by an escape into exotic, dangerous situations which have last-minute happy endings. But another of the things that fantasy can do is to normalize what is psychologically unbearable, thereby inuring us to it. In one case, fantasy beautifies the world. In the other, it neutralizes it.

The fantasy in science fiction films does both jobs. The films reflect world-wide anxieties, and they serve to allay them. They inculcate a strange apathy concerning the processes of radiation, contamination, and destruction which I for one find haunting and depressing. The naïve level of the films neatly tempers the sense of otherness, of alien-ness, with the grossly familiar. In particular, the dialogue of most science fiction films, which is of a monumental but often touching banality, makes them wonderfully, unintentionally funny. Lines like "Come quickly, there's a monster in my bathtub," "We must do something about this," "Wait, Professor. There's someone on the telephone," "But that's incredible," and the old American stand-by, "I hope it works!" are hilarious in the context of picturesque and deafening holocaust. Yet the films also contain something that is painful and in deadly earnest.

There is a sense in which all these movies are in complicity with the abhorrent. They neutralize it, as I have said. It is no more, perhaps, than the way all art draws its audience into a circle of complicity with the thing represented. But in these films we have to do with things which are (quite literally) unthinkable. Here, "thinking about the unthinkable"—not in the way of Herman Kahn, as a subject for calculation, but as a subject for fantasy—becomes, however inadvertently, itself a somewhat questionable act from a moral point of view. The films perpetuate clichés about identity, volition, power, knowledge, happiness, social consensus, guilt, responsibility which are, to say the least, not serviceable in our present extremity. But collective nightmares cannot be banished by demonstrating that they are, intellectually and morally, fallacious. This nightmare—the one reflected, in various registers, in the science fiction films—is too close to our reality.

NOTES ON FILM NOIR (1972)

By Paul Schrader

In 1946 French critics, seeing the American films they had missed during the war, noticed the new mood of cynicism, pessimism and darkness which had crept into the American cinema. The darkening stain was most evident in routine crime thrillers, but was also apparent in prestigious melodramas.

The French cineastes soon realized they had seen only the tip of the iceberg: as the years went by, Hollywood lighting grew darker, characters more corrupt, themes more fatalistic and the tone more hopeless. By 1949 American movies were in the throes of their deepest and most creative funk. Never before had films dared to take such a harsh uncomplimentary look at American life, and they would not dare to do so again for twenty years.

Hollywood's *film noir* has recently become the subject of renewed interest among moviegoers and critics. The fascination *film noir* holds for today's young filmgoers and film students reflects recent trends in American cinema: American movies are again taking a look at the underside of the American character, but compared to such relentlessly cynical *films noirs* as *Kiss Me Deadly* or *Kiss Tomorrow Goodbye,* the new self-hate cinema of *Easy Rider* and *Medium Cool* seems naïve and romantic. As the current political mood hardens, filmgoers and filmmakers will find the *film noir* of the late Forties increasingly attractive. The Forties may be to the Seventies what the Thirties were to the Sixties.

Film noir is equally interesting to critics. It offers writers a cache of excellent, little-known films (*film noir* is oddly both one of Hollywood's best periods and least known), and gives *auteur*-weary critics an opportunity to apply themselves to the newer questions of classification and transdirectorial style. After all, what is a *film noir?*

Film noir is not a genre (as Raymond Durgnat has helpfully pointed out over the objections of Higham and Greenberg's *Hollywood in the Forties*). It is not defined, as are the western and gangster genres, by conventions of setting and conflict, but rather by the more subtle qualities of tone and mood. It is a *film "noir,"* as opposed to the possible variants of film gray or film off-white.

Film noir is also a specific period of film history, like German Expressionism or the French New Wave. In general, *film noir* refers to those Hollywood films of the Forties and early Fifties which portrayed the world of dark, slick city streets, crime and corruption.

Film noir is an extremely unwieldy period. It harks back to many previous periods: Warner's Thirties gangster films, the French "poetic realism" of Carné and Duvivier, Sternbergian melodrama, and, farthest back, German Expressionist crime films (Lang's *Mabuse* cycle). *Film noir* can stretch at its outer limits from *The Maltese Falcon* (1941) to *Touch of Evil* (1958), and most every dramatic Hollywood film from 1941 to 1953 contains some *noir* elements. There are also foreign offshoots of *film noir,* such as *The Third Man, Breathless* and *Le Doulos.*

Almost every critic has his own definition of *film noir,* and a personal list of film titles and dates to back it up. Personal and descriptive definitions, however, can get a bit sticky. A film of urban nightlife is not necessarily a *film noir,* and a *film noir* need not necessarily concern crime and corruption. Since *film noir* is defined by tone rather than genre, it is almost impossible to argue one critic's descriptive definition against another's. How many *noir* elements does it take to make a *film noir noir?*

Rather than haggle definitions, I would rather attempt to reduce *film noir* to its primary colors (all shades of black), those cultural and stylistic elements to which any definition must return.

At the risk of sounding like Arthur Knight, I would suggest that there were four conditions in Hollywood in the Forties which brought about the *film noir.* (The danger of Knight's *Liveliest Art* method is that it makes film history less a matter of structural analysis, and more a case of artistic and social forces magically interacting and coalescing.) Each of the following four catalytic elements, however, can define the *film noir;* the distinctly *noir* tonality draws from each of these elements.

War and post-war disillusionment. The acute downer which hit the U.S. after the Second World War was, in fact, a delayed reaction to the Thirties. All through the Depression, movies were needed to keep people's spirits up, and, for the most part, they did. The crime films of this period were Horatio Algerish and socially conscious. Toward the end of the Thirties a darker crime film began to appear *(You Only Live Once, The Roaring Twenties)* and, were it not for the War, *film noir* would have been at full steam by the early Forties.

The need to produce Allied propaganda abroad and promote patriotism at home blunted the fledgling moves toward a dark cinema, and the *film noir* thrashed about in the studio system, not quite able to come into full prominence. During the War the first uniquely *film noir* appeared: *The Maltese Falcon, The Glass Key, This Gun for Hire, Laura,* but these films lacked the distinctly *noir* bite the end of the War would bring.

As soon as the War was over, however, American films became markedly more sardonic—and there was a boom in the crime film. For fifteen years the pressures against America's amelioristic cinema had been building up, and, given the freedom, audiences and artists were now eager to take a less optimistic view of things. The disillusionment many soldiers, small businessmen and housewife/factory employees felt in returning to a peacetime economy was directly mirrored in the sordidness of the urban crime film.

This immediate post-war disillusionment was directly demonstrated in films like *Cornered, The Blue Dahlia, Dead Reckoning* and *Ride a Pink Horse,* in which a serviceman returns from the war to find his sweetheart unfaithful or dead, or his business partner cheating him, or the whole society something less than worth fighting for. The war continues, but now the antagonism turns with a new viciousness toward the American society itself.

Post-war realism. Shortly after the War every film-producing country had a resurgence of realism. In America it first took the form of films by such producers as Louis de Rochemont *(House on 92nd Street, Call Northside 777)* and Mark Hellinger *(The Killers, Brute Force),* and directors like Henry Hathaway and Jules Dassin. "Every scene was film on the actual location depicted," the 1947 de Rochemont-Hathaway *Kiss of Death* proudly proclaimed. Even after de Rochemont's particular "March of Time" authenticity fell from vogue, realistic exteriors remained a permanent fixture of *film noir.*

The realistic movement also suited America's post-war mood; the public's desire for a more honest and harsh view of America would not be satisfied by the same studio streets they had been watching for a dozen years. The post-war realistic trend succeeded in breaking *film noir* away from the domain of the high-class melodrama, placing it where it more properly belonged, in the streets with everyday people. In retrospect, the pre-de Rochemont *film noir* looks definitely tamer than the post-War realistic films. The studio look of films like *The Big Sleep* and *The Mask of Dimitrios* blunts their sting, making them seem polite and conventional in contrast to their later, more realistic counterparts.

The German influence. Hollywood played host to an influx of German expatriates in the Twenties and Thirties, and these filmmakers and technicians had, for the most part, integrated themselves into the American film establishment. Hollywood never experienced the "Germanization" some civic-minded natives feared, and there is a danger of over-emphasizing the German influence in Hollywood.

But when, in the late Forties, Hollywood decided to paint it black, there were no greater masters of chiaroscuro than the Germans. The influence of expressionist lighting has always been just beneath the surface of Hollywood films, and it is not surprising, in *film noir,* to find it bursting out full bloom. Neither is it surprising to find a larger number of Germans and East Europeans working in *film noir:* Fritz Lang, Robert Siodmak, Billy Wilder, Franz Waxman, Otto Preminger, John Brahm, Anatole Litvak, Karl Freund, Max Ophuls, John Alton, Douglas Sirk, Fred Zinnemann, William Dieterle, Max Steiner, Edgar G. Ulmer, Curtis Bernhardt, Rudolph Maté.

On the surface the German expressionist influence, with its reliance on artificial studio lighting, seems incompatible with post-war realism, with its harsh unadorned exteriors; but it is the unique quality of *film noir* that it was able to weld seemingly contradictory elements into a uniform style. The best *noir* technicians simply made all the world a sound stage, directing unnatural and expressionistic lighting onto realistic settings. In films like *Union Station, They Live by Night, The Killers* there is an uneasy, exhilarating combination of realism and expressionism.

Perhaps the greatest master of *noir* was Hungarian-born John Alton, an expressionist cinematographer who could relight Times Square at noon if necessary. No cinematographer better adapted the old expressionist techniques to the new desire for realism, and his black-and-white photography in such gritty *film noir* as *T-Men, Raw Deal, I the Jury, The Big Combo* equals that of such German expressionist masters as Fritz Wagner and Karl Freund.

The hard-boiled tradition. Another stylistic influence waiting in the wings was the "hard-boiled" school of writers. In the Thirties, authors such as Ernest Hemingway, Dashiell Hammett, Raymond Chandler, James M. Cain, Horace McCoy and John O'Hara created the "tough," a cynical way of acting and thinking which separated one from the world of everyday emotions—romanticism with a protective shell. The hard-boiled writers had their roots in pulp fiction or journalism, and their protagonists lived out a narcissistic, defeatist code. The hard-boiled hero was, in reality, a soft egg compared to his existential counterpart (Camus is said to have based *The Stranger* on McCoy), but he was a good deal tougher than anything American fiction had seen.

When the movies of the Forties turned to the American "tough" moral understrata, the hard-boiled school was waiting with present conventions of heroes, minor characters, plots, dialogue and themes. Like the German expatriates, the hard-boiled writers had a style made to order for *film noir;* and, in turn, they influenced *noir* screenwriting as much as the Germans influenced *noir* cinematography.

The most hard-boiled of Hollywood's writers was Raymond Chandler himself, whose script of *Double Indemnity* (from a James M. Cain story) was the best written and most characteristically *noir* of the period. *Double Indemnity* was the first film which played *film noir* for what it essentially was: small-time, unredeemed, unheroic; it made a break from the romantic *noir* cinema of *Mildred Pierce* and *The Big Sleep.*

(In its final stages, however, *film noir* adapted and then bypassed the hard-boiled school. Manic, neurotic post-1948 films such as *Kiss Tomorrow Goodbye, D.O.A., Where the Sidewalk*

Ends, White Heat, and *The Big Heat* are all post-hard-boiled: the air in these regions was even too thin for old-time cynics like Chandler.)

STYLISTICS. There is not yet a study of the stylistics of *film noir,* and the task is certainly too large to be attempted here. Like all film movements *film noir* drew upon a reservoir of film techniques, and given the time one could correlate its techniques, themes and causal elements into a stylistic schema. For the present, however, I'd like to point out some of *film noir's* recurring techniques.

• The majority of scenes are lit for night. Gangsters sit in the offices at midday with the shades pulled and the lights off. Ceiling lights are hung low and floor lamps are seldom more than five feet high. One always has the suspicion that if the lights were all suddenly flipped on the characters would shriek and shrink from the scene like Count Dracula at sunrise.

• As in German expressionism, oblique and vertical lines are preferred to horizontal. Obliquity adheres to the choreography of the city, and is in direct opposition to the horizontal American tradition of Griffith and Ford. Oblique lines tend to splinter a screen, making it restless and unstable. Light enters the dingy rooms of *film noir* in such odd shapes—jagged trapezoids, obtuse triangles, vertical slits—that one suspects the windows were cut out with a pen knife. No character can speak authoritatively from a space which is being continually cut into ribbons of light. The Anthony Mann/John Alton *T-Men* is the most dramatic but far from the only example of oblique *noir* choreography.

• The actors and setting are often given equal lighting emphasis. An actor is often hidden in the realistic tableau of the city at night, and, more obviously, his face is often blacked out by shadow as he speaks. These shadow effects are unlike the famous Warner Brothers lighting of the Thirties in which the central character was accentuated by a heavy shadow; in *film noir,* the central character is likely to be standing *in* the shadow. When the environment is given an equal or greater weight than the actor, it, of course, creates a fatalistic, hopeless mood. There is nothing the protagonist can do; the city will outlast and negate even his best efforts.

• Compositional tension is preferred to physical action. A typical *film noir* would rather move the scene cinematographically around the actor than have the actor control the scene by physical action.

The beating of Robert Ryan in *The Set-Up,* the gunning down of Farley Granger in *They Live by Night,* the execution of the taxi driver in *The Enforcer* and of Brian Donlevy in *The Big Combo* are all marked by measured pacing, restrained anger and oppressive compositions, and seem much closer to the *film noir* spirit than the rat-tat-tat and screeching tires of *Scarface* twenty years before or the violent, expressive actions of *Underworld U.S.A.* ten years later.

• There seems to be an almost Freudian attachment to water. The empty *noir* streets are almost always glistening with fresh evening rain (even in Los Angeles), and the rainfall tends to increase in direct proportion to the drama. Docks and piers are second only to alleyways as the most popular rendezvous points.

• There is a love of romantic narration. In such films as *The Postman Always Rings Twice, Laura, Double Indemnity, The Lady from Shanghai, Out of the Past* and *Sunset Boulevard* the narration creates a mood of *temps perdu:* an irretrievable past, a predetermined fate and an all-enveloping hopelessness. In *Out of the Past* Robert Mitchum relates his history with such pathetic relish that it is obvious there is no hope for any future: one can only take pleasure in reliving a doomed past.

• A complex chronological order is frequently used to reinforce the feelings of hopelessness and lost time. Such films as *The Enforcer, The Killers, Mildred Pierce, The Dark Past, Chicago Deadline, Out of the Past* and *The Killing* use a convoluted time sequence to emerse the viewer in a time-disoriented but highly stylized world. The manipulation of time, whether slight or complex, is often used to reinforce a *noir* principle: the how is always more important than the what.

THEMES. Raymond Durgnat has delineated the themes of *film noir* in an excellent article in the British *Cinema* magazine ("The Family Tree of *Film Noir,*" August, 1970), and it would be foolish for me to attempt to redo his thorough work in this short space. Durgnat divides *film noir* into eleven thematic categories, and although one might criticize some of his specific groupings, he does cover the whole gamut of *noir* production (thematically categorizing over 300 films).

In each of Durgnat's *noir* themes (whether Black Widow, killers-on-the-run, *dopplegängers)* one finds that the upwardly mobile forces of the Thirties have halted; frontierism has turned to paranoia and claustrophobia. The small-time gangster has now made it big and sits in the mayor's chair, the private eye has quit the police force in disgust, and the young heroine, sick of going along for the ride, is taking others for a ride.

Durgnat, however, does not touch upon what is perhaps the over-riding *noir* theme: a passion for the past and present, but also a fear of the future. The *noir* hero dreads to look ahead, but instead tries to survive by the day, and if unsuccessful at that, he retreats to the past. Thus *film noir's* techniques emphasize loss, nostalgia, lack of clear priorities, insecurity; then submerge these self-doubts in mannerism and style. In such a world style becomes paramount; it is all that separates one from meaninglessness. Chandler described this fundamental *noir* theme when he described his own fictional world: "It is not a very fragrant world, but it is the world you live in, and certain writers with tough minds and a cool spirit of detachment can make very interesting patterns out of it."

Film noir can be subdivided into three broad phases. The first, the wartime period, 1941–46 approximately, was the phase of the private eye and the lone wolf, of Chandler, Hammett and Greene, of Bogart and Bacall, Ladd and Lake, classy directors like Curtiz and Garnett, studio sets, and, in general, more talk than action. The studio look of this period was reflected in such pictures as *The Maltese Falcon, Casablanca, Gaslight, This Gun for Hire, The Lodger, The Woman in the Window, Mildred Pierce, Spellbound, The Big Sleep, Laura, The Lost Weekend, The Strange Love of Martha Ivers, To Have and Have Not, Fallen Angel, Gilda, Murder My Sweet, The Postman Always Rings Twice, Dark Waters, Scarlet Street, So Dark the Night, The Glass Key, The Mask of Dimitrios,* and *The Dark Mirror.*

The Wilder/Chandler *Double Indemnity* provided a bridge to the post-War phase of *film noir.* The unflinching *noir* vision of *Double Indemnity* came as a shock in 1944, and the film was almost blocked by the combined efforts of Paramount, the Hays Office and star Fred MacMurray. Three years later, however, *Double Indemnitys* were dropping off the studio assembly lines.

The second phase was the post-War realistic period from 1945–49 (the dates overlap and so do the films; these are all approximate phases for which there are many exceptions). These films tended more toward the problems of crime in the streets, political corruption and police routine. Less romantic heroes like Richard

Conte, Burt Lancaster and Charles McGraw were more suited to this period, as were proletarian directors like Hathaway, Dassin and Kazan. The realistic urban look of this phase is seen in such films as *The House on 92nd Street, The Killers, Raw Deal, Act of Violence, Union Station, Kiss of Death, Johnny O'Clock, Force of Evil, Dead Reckoning, Ride the Pink Horse, Dark Passage, Cry of the City, The Set-Up, T-Men, Call Northside 777, Brute Force, The Big Clock, Thieves' Highway, Ruthless, Pitfall, Boomerang!,* and *The Naked City.*

The third and final phase of *film noir,* from 1949–53, was the period of psychotic action and suicidal impulse. The *noir* hero, seemingly under the weight of ten years of despair, started to go bananas. The psychotic killer, who had in the first period been a subject worthy of study (Olivia de Havilland in *The Dark Mirror*), in the second a fringe threat (Richard Widmark in *Kiss of Death*), now became the active protagonist (James Cagney in *Kiss Tomorrow Goodbye*). There were no excuses given for the psychopathy in *Gun Crazy*—it was just "crazy." James Cagney made a neurotic comeback and his instability was matched by that of younger actors like Robert Ryan and Lee Marvin. This was the phase of the "B" *noir* film, and of psychoanalytically-inclined directors like Ray and Walsh. The forces of personal disintegration are reflected in such films as *White Heat, Gun Crazy, D.O.A., Caught, They Live By Night, Where the Sidewalk Ends, Kiss Tomorrow Goodbye, Detective Story, In a Lonely Place, I the Jury, Ace in the Hole, Panic in the Streets, The Big Heat, On Dangerous Ground,* and *Sunset Boulevard.*

This third phase is the cream of the *film noir* period. Some critics may prefer the early "gray" melodramas, others the post-War "street" films, but *film noir's* final phase was the most aesthetically and sociologically piercing. After ten years of steadily shedding romantic conventions, the later *noir* films finally got down to the root causes of the period: the loss of public honor, heroic conventions, personal integrity, and, finally, psychic stability. The third-phase films were painfully self-aware; they seemed to know they stood at the end of a long tradition based on despair and disintegration and did not shy away from that fact. The best and most characteristically *noir* films—*Gun Crazy, White Heat, Out of the Past, Kiss Tomorrow Goodbye, D.O.A., They Live by Night,* and *The Big Heat*—stand at the end of the period and are the results of self-awareness. The third phase is rife with end-of-the-line *noir* heroes: *The Big Heat* and

Where the Sidewalk Ends are the last stops for the urban cop, *Ace in the Hole* for the newspaper man, the Victor Saville-produced Spillane series *(I the Jury, The Long Wait, Kiss Me Deadly)* for the private eye, *Sunset Boulevard* for the Black Widow, *White Heat* and *Kiss Tomorrow Goodbye* for the gangster, *D.O.A.* for the John Doe American.

Appropriately, the masterpiece of *film noir* was a straggler, *Kiss Me Deadly,* produced in 1955. Its time delay gives it a sense of detachment and thoroughgoing seediness—it stands at the end of a long sleazy tradition. The private eye hero, Mike Hammer, undergoes the final stages of degradation. He is a small-time "bedroom dick," and makes no qualms about it because the world around him isn't much better. Ralph Meeker, in his best performance, plays Hammer, a midget among dwarfs. Robert Aldrich's teasing direction carries *noir* to its sleaziest and most perversely erotic. Hammer overturns the underworld in search of the "great whatsit," and when he finally finds it, it turns out to be—joke of jokes—an exploding atomic bomb. The inhumanity and meaninglessness of the hero are small matters in a world in which The Bomb has the final say.

By the middle Fifties *film noir* had ground to a halt. There were a few notable stragglers, *Kiss Me Deadly,* the Lewis/Alton *The Big Combo,* and *film noir*'s epitaph, *Touch of Evil,* but for the most part a new style of crime film had become popular.

As the rise of McCarthy and Eisenhower demonstrated, Americans were eager to see a more bourgeois view of themselves. Crime had to move to the suburbs. The criminal put on a grey flannel suit and the footsore cop was replaced by the "mobile unit" careening down the expressway. Any attempt at social criticism had to be cloaked in ludicrous affirmations of the American way of life. Technically, television, with its demand for full lighting and close-ups, gradually undercut the German influence, and color cinematography was, of course, the final blow to the *"noir"* look.

New directors like Seigel, Fleischer, Karlson and Fuller, and TV shows like *Dragnet, M-Squad, Lineup* and *Highway Patrol* stepped in to create the new crime drama. This transition can be seen in Samuel Fuller's 1953 *Pickup on South Street,* a film which blends the black look with the red scare. The waterfront scenes with Richard Widmark and Jean Peters are in the best *noir* tradition, but a later, dynamic fight in the subway marks Fuller as a director who would be better suited to the crime school of the middle and late Fifties.

Film noir was an immensely creative period—probably the most creative in Hollywood's history—at least, if this creativity is measured not by its peaks but by its median level of artistry. Picked at random, a *film noir* is likely to be a better made film than a randomly selected silent comedy, musical, western and so on. (A Joseph H. Lewis "B" *film noir* is better than a Lewis "B" western, for example.) Taken as a whole period, *film noir* achieved an unusually high level of artistry.

Film noir seemed to bring out the best in everyone: directors, cameramen, screenwriters, actors. Again and again, a *film noir* will make the high point on an artist's career graph. Some directors, for example, did their best work in *film noir* (Stuart Heisler, Robert Siodmak, Gordon Douglas, Edward Dmytryk, John Brahm, John Cromwell, Raoul Walsh, Henry Hathaway); other directors began in *film noir* and, it seems to me, never regained their original heights (Otto Preminger, Rudolph Maté, Nicholas Ray, Robert Wise, Jules Dassin, Richard Fleischer, John Huston, Andre de Toth, and Robert Aldrich); and other directors who made great films in other molds also made great *film noir* (Orson Welles, Max Ophuls, Fritz Lang, Elia Kazan, Howard Hawks, Robert Rossen, Anthony Mann, Joseph Losey, Alfred Hitchcock, and Stanley Kubrick). Whether or not one agrees with this particular schema, its message is irrefutable: *film noir* was good for practically every director's career. (Two interesting exceptions to prove the case are King Vidor and Jean Renoir.)

Film noir seems to have been a creative release for everyone involved. It gave artists a chance to work with previously forbidden themes, yet had conventions strong enough to protect the mediocre. Cinematographers were allowed to become highly mannered, and actors were sheltered by the cinematographers. It was not until years later that critics were able to distinguish between great directors and great *noir* directors.

Film noir's remarkable creativity makes its longtime neglect the more baffling. The French, of course, have been students of the period for some time (Borde and Chaumenton's *Panorama du Film Noir* was published in 1955), but American critics until recently have preferred the western, the musical or the gangster film to the *film noir*.

Some of the reasons for this neglect are superficial; others strike to the heart of the *noir* style. For a long time *film noir,* with its emphasis on corruption and despair, was considered an aberation of the American character. The western, with its moral primitivism, and the gangster film, with its Horatio Alger values, were considered more American than the *film noir.*

This prejudice was reinforced by the fact that *film noir* was ideally suited to the low budget "B" film, and many of the best *noir* films were "B" films. This odd sort of economic snobbery still lingers on in some critical circles: high-budget trash is considered more worthy of attention than low-budget trash, and to praise a "B" film is somehow to slight (often intentionally) an "A" film.

There has been a critical revival in the U.S. over the last ten years, but *film noir* lost out on that too. The revival was *auteur* (director) oriented, and *film noir* wasn't. *Auteur* criticism is interested in how directors are different; *film noir* criticism is concerned with what they have in common.

The fundamental reason for *film noir*'s neglect, however, is the fact that it depends more on choreography than sociology, and American critics have always been slow on the uptake when it comes to visual style. Like its protagonists, *film noir* is more interested in style than theme, whereas American critics have been traditionally more interested in theme than style.

American film critics have always been sociologists first and scientists second: film is important as it relates to large masses, and if a film goes awry it is often because the theme has been somehow "violated" by the style. *Film noir* operates on opposite principles: the theme is hidden in the style, and bogus themes are often flaunted ("middle-class values are best") which contradict the style. Although, I believe, style determines the theme in *every* film, it was easier for sociological critics to discuss the themes of the western and gangster film apart from stylistic analysis than it was to do for *film noir.*

Not surprisingly it was the gangster film, not the *film noir,* which was canonized in *The Partisan Review* in 1948 by Robert Warshow's famous essay, "The Gangster as Tragic Hero." Although Warshow could be an aesthetic as well as a sociological critic, in this case he was interested in the western and gangster film as "popular" art rather than as style. This sociological orientation blinded Warshow, as it has many subsequent critics, to an aesthetically more important development in the gangster film—*film noir.*

The irony of this neglect is that in retrospect the gangster films Warshow wrote about are inferior to *film noir.* The Thirties gangster was primarily a reflection of what was happening in the country, and

Warshow analyzed this. The *film noir,* although it was also a sociological reflection, went further than the gangster film. Toward the end *film noir* was engaged in a life-and-death struggle with the materials it reflected; it tried to make America accept a moral vision of life based on style. That very contradiction—promoting style in a culture which valued themes—forced *film noir* into artistically invigorating twists and turns. *Film noir* attacked and interpreted its sociological conditions, and, by the close of the *noir* period, created a new artistic world which went beyond a simple sociological reflection, a nightmarish world of American mannerism which was by far more a creation than a reflection.

Because *film noir* was first of all a style, because it worked out its conflicts visually rather than thematically, because it was aware of its own identity, it was able to create artistic solutions to sociological problems. And for these reasons films like *Kiss Me Deadly, Kiss Tomorrow Goodbye* and *Gun Crazy* can be works of art in a way that gangster films like *Scarface, Public Enemy* and *Little Caesar* can never be.

DIRECTORS

Kenneth Tynan once defined a critic as a man who knows the way but cannot drive the car. There's an assumption in Tynan's remark that critics want to drive the car. Actually, I suspect that many are quite content to remain in the back seat admiring the view and shouting advice at the driver. In these pieces on directors, which are perhaps the most personal in the book, there is an emotional element in the critic's tone, not envy exactly, but a rush of excited admiration for the kind of risks a director takes.

The shadow of Agee's doubt falls across the final pages of his enchanting account of John Huston's stormy early days. I suppose that these doubts have proved partially correct when focused on Huston's career as a whole, but the piece remains exciting in its romantic-aesthetic idealism; for Agee, a great director is essentially a man of *courage.* In his piece on Preston Sturges (written with William S. Poster) Manny Farber also celebrates sheer energy and bravado; the fascination of Sturges, this most manic of American artists, lies in the way his anarchic temperament both expressed and fought against the lingering Victorianism of American taste. Sturges was a man who burnt himself out quickly, and Farber's piece has gained a special pathos over the years as a premature valedictory.

Something of the same melancholy fate may befall Pauline Kael's notes on the extraordinarily talented Sam Peckinpah. In the case of this exemplary modern artist, special qualities of aesthetic temperament are inseparable from self-destructive drives: One searches unhappily for anything *sustaining* in Peckinpah's convoluted machismo. John Ford is a very different case. Andrew Sarris's piece on Ford and *The Grapes of Wrath* celebrates a long-enduring artist of powerfully conservative tendency. Ford's effortless self-assurance as a director allowed him to transform Steinbeck's vision of social oppression into a celebration of rural order and family feeling without destroying the anger and excitement of the book.—*Ed.*

UNDIRECTABLE DIRECTOR: JOHN HUSTON (1950)

By James Agee

The ant, as every sluggard knows, is a model citizen. His eye is fixed unwaveringly upon Security and Success, and he gets where he is going. The grasshopper, as every maiden ant delights in pointing out, is his reprehensible opposite number: a hedonistic jazz-baby, tangoing along primrose paths to a disreputable end. The late Walter Huston's son John, one of the ranking grasshoppers of the Western Hemisphere, is living proof of what a lot of nonsense that can be. He has beaten the ants at their own game and then some, and he has managed that blindfolded, by accident, and largely just for the hell of it. John was well into his twenties before anyone could imagine he would ever amount to more than an awfully nice guy to get drunk with. He wandered into his vocation as a writer of movie scripts to prove to a girl he wanted to marry that he amounted to more than a likable bum. He stumbled into his still deeper vocation as a writer-director only when he got sick of seeing what the professional directors did to his scripts. But during the ten subsequent years he has won both Security aplenty (currently $3,000 a week with MGM and a partnership in Horizon Pictures with his friend Sam Spiegel) and Success aplenty (two Oscars, a One World Award and such lesser prizes as the Screen Directors' Guild quarterly award which he received for his *Asphalt Jungle*).

Yet these are merely incidental attainments. The first movie he directed, *The Maltese Falcon,* is the best private-eye melodrama ever made. *San Pietro,* his microcosm of the meaning of war in terms of the fight for one hill town, is generally conceded to be the finest of war documentaries. *Treasure of Sierra Madre,* which he developed from B. Traven's sardonic adventure-fable about the corrosive effect of gold on character, is the clearest proof in perhaps twenty years that first-rate work can come out of the big commercial studios.

Most of the really good popular art produced anywhere comes from Hollywood, and much of it bears Huston's name. To put it conservatively, there is nobody under fifty at work in movies, here or abroad, who can excel Huston in talent, inventiveness, intransigence, achievement or promise. Yet it is a fair bet that neither money, nor acclaim, nor a sense of dedication to the greatest art medium of his century have much to do with Huston's staying at his job: he stays at it because there is nothing else he enjoys so much. It is this tireless enjoyment that gives his work a unique vitality and makes every foot of film he works on unmistakably his.

Huston seems to have acquired this priceless quality many years ago at the time of what, in his opinion, was probably the most crucial incident in his life. When he was about twelve years old he was so delicate he was hardly expected to live. It was interminably dinned into him that he could never possibly be quite careful enough, and for even closer protection he was put into a sanitarium where every bite he ate and breath he drew could be professionally policed. As a result he became virtually paralyzed by timidity; "I haven't the slightest doubt," he still says, "that if things had gone on like that I'd have died inside a few more months." His only weapon was a blind desperation of instinct, and by day not even that was any use. Nights, however, when everyone was asleep, he used to sneak out, strip, dive into a stream which sped across the grounds and ride it down quite a steep and stony waterfall, over and over and over. "The first few times," he recalls, "it scared the living hell out of me, but I realized—instinctively anyhow—it was exactly fear I had to get over." He kept at it until it was the one joy in his life. When they first caught him at this primordial autotherapy the goons were of course aghast; but on maturer thought they decided he might live after all.

The traits revealed in this incident are central and permanent in Huston's character. Risk, not to say recklessness, are virtual reflexes in him. Action, and the most vivid possible use of the immediate present, were his personal salvation; they have remained lifelong habits. Because action also is the natural language of the screen and the instant present is its tense, Huston is a born popular artist. In his life, his dealings and his work as an artist he operates largely by instinct, unencumbered by much reflectiveness or abstract thinking, or any serious self-doubt. Incapable of yesing, apple-polishing or boot-licking, he instantly catches fire in resistance to authority.

Nobody in movies can beat Huston's record for trying to get away with more than the traffic will bear. *San Pietro* was regarded with horror by some gentlemen of the upper brass as "an antiwar picture" and was cut from five reels to three. *Treasure,* which broke practically every box-office law in the game and won three Oscars, was made over the virtually dead bodies of the top men at Warners and was advertised as a Western. *The Asphalt Jungle* suggests that in some respects big-town crime operates remarkably like free enterprise. Huston seldom tries to "lick" the problem imposed by censorship, commercial queasiness or tradition; he has learned that nothing is so likely to settle an argument as to turn up with the accomplished fact, accomplished well, plus a bland lack of alternative film shots. And yet after innumerable large and small fights and a fair share of defeats he can still say of his movie career, "I've never had any trouble." Probably the whitest magic that protects him is that he really means it.

Nonetheless his life began with trouble—decorated with the best that his Irish imagination, and his father's, could add to it. He was born John Marcellus Huston on August 5, 1906 in Nevada, Missouri, a hamlet which his grandfather, a professional gambler, had by the most ambitious version of the family legend acquired in a poker game. John's father, a retired actor, was in charge of power and light and was learning his job, while he earned, via a correspondence course. Before the postman had taught him how to handle such a delicate situation, a fire broke out in town, Walter overstrained the valves in his effort to satisfy the fire department, and the Hustons decided it would be prudent to leave what was left of Nevada before morning. They did not let their shirttails touch their rumps until they hit Weatherford, Texas, another of Grandfather's jackpots. After a breather they moved on to St. Louis (without, however, repeating the scorched-earth policy), and Walter settled down to engineering in dead earnest until a solid man clapped him on the shoulder and told him that with enough stick-to-itiveness he might well become a top-notch engineer, a regular crackerjack. Horrified, Walter instantly returned to the stage. A few years later he and his wife were divorced. From there on out the child's life lacked the stability of those early years.

John divided his time between his father and mother. With his father, who was still some years short of eminence or even solvency, he shared that bleakly glamorous continuum of three-a-days, scabrous fleabags and the cindery, ambling day coaches between, which used to be so much of the essence of the American theater.

John's mother was a newspaperwoman with a mania for travel and horses (she was later to marry a vice-president of the Northern Pacific), and she and her son once pooled their last ten dollars on a 100-to-1 shot—which came in. Now and then she stuck the boy in one school or another, but mostly they traveled—well off the beaten paths.

After his defeat of death by sliding down the waterfall, there was no holding John. In his teens he became amateur lightweight boxing champion of California. A high-school marriage lasted only briefly. He won twenty-three out of twenty-five fights, many in the professional ring, but he abandoned this promise of a career to join another of his mother's eccentric grand tours. He spent two years in the Mexican cavalry, emerging at twenty-one as a lieutenant. In Mexico he wrote a book, a puppet play about Frankie and Johnny. Receiving, to his astonishment, a $500 advance from a publisher, he promptly entrained for the crap tables of Saratoga where, in one evening, he ran it up to $11,000, which he soon spent or gambled away.

After that Huston took quite a friendly interest in writing. He wrote a short story which his father showed to his friend Ring Lardner, who showed it to his friend H. L. Mencken, who ran it in the *Mercury*. He wrote several other stories about horses and boxers before the vein ran out. It was through these stories, with his father's help that he got his first job as a movie writer. He scripted *A House Divided,* starring his father, for William Wyler. But movies, at this extravagant stage of Huston's career, were just an incident. At other stages he worked for the New York *Graphic* ("I was the world's lousiest reporter"), broke ribs riding steeplechase, studied painting in Paris, knocked around with international Bohemians in London and went on the bum in that city when his money ran out and he was too proud to wire his father. At length he beat his way back to New York where, for a time, he tried editing the *Midweek Pictorial.* He was playing Abraham Lincoln in a Chicago WPA production when he met an Irish girl named Leslie Black and within fifteen minutes after their meeting asked her to marry him. When she hesitated he hotfooted it to Hollywood and settled down to earn a solid living as fast as possible. Marrying Leslie was probably the best thing that ever happened to him, in the opinion of Huston's wise friend and studio protector during the years at Warner Brothers, the producer Henry Blanke. Blanke remembers him vividly during the bachelor interlude: "Just a drunken boy; hopelessly immature. You'd see him at every party, wearing bangs, with a monkey on his shoulder. Charming. Very talented but without an ounce of discipline in his make-up." Leslie Huston, Blanke is convinced, set her husband the standards and incentives which brought his abilities into focus. They were divorced in 1945, but in relation to his work he has never lost the stability she helped him gain.

At forty-four Huston still has a monkey and a chimpanzee as well, but he doesn't escort them to parties. His gray-sleeted hair still treats his scalp like Liberty Hall and occasionally slithers into bangs, but they can no longer be mistaken for a Bohemian compensation. He roughly suggests a jerked-venison version of his father, or a highly intelligent cowboy. A little over six feet tall, quite lean, he carries himself in a perpetual gangling-graceful slouch. The forehead is monkeyishly puckered, the ears look as clipped as a show dog's; the eyes, too, are curiously animal, an opaque red-brown. The nose was broken in the prize ring. The mouth is large, mobile and gap-toothed. The voice which comes out of this leatheriness is surprisingly rich, gentle and cultivated. The vocabulary ranges with the careless ease of a mountain goat between words of eight syllables and of four letters.

Some friends believe he is essentially a deep introvert using every outside means available as a form of flight from self-recognition—in other words, he is forever sliding down the waterfall and instinctively fears to stop. The same friends suspect his work is all that keeps him from flying apart. He is wonderful company, almost anytime, for those who can stand the pace. Loving completely unrestrained and fantastic play, he is particularly happy with animals, roughousers and children; a friend who owns three of the latter describes him as "a blend of Santa Claus and the Pied Piper." His friendships range from high in the Social Register to low in the animal kingdom, but pretty certainly the friend he liked best in the world was his father, and that was thoroughly reciprocated. It was a rare and heart-warming thing, in this Freud-ridden era, to see a father and son so irrepressibly pleased with each other's company and skill.

He has an indestructible kind of youthfulness, enjoys his enthusiasms with all his might and has the prompt appetite for new knowledge of a man whose intelligence has not been cloyed by much formal education. He regrets that nowadays he can read only two or three books a week. His favorite writers are Joyce, his friend Hemingway (perhaps his closest literary equivalent) and, above all,

O'Neill; it was one of the deepest disappointments of his career when movie commitments prevented his staging the new O'Neill play *The Iceman Cometh.* His other enjoyments take many forms. He still paints occasionally. He is a very good shot and a superlative horseman; he has some very promising runners of his own. He likes money for the fun it can bring him, is extremely generous with it and particularly loves to gamble. He generally does well at the races and siphons it off at the crap tables. He is a hard drinker (Scotch) but no lush, and a heavy smoker. Often as not he forgets to eat. He has a reputation for being attractive to women, and rough on them. His fourth wife is the dancer, Ricky Soma; their son Walter was born last spring. He makes most of his important decisions on impulse; it was thus he adopted his son Pablo in Mexico. The way he and his third wife, Evelyn Keyes, got married is a good example of Huston in action. He suggested they marry one evening in Romanoff's a week after they met, borrowed a pocketful of money from the prince, tore out of his house to pick up a wedding ring a guest had mislaid in the swimming pool and chartered Paul Mantz to fly them to Las Vegas where they were married that night.

Huston's courage verges on the absolute, or on simple obliviousness to danger. In Italy during the shooting of *San Pietro,* his simian curiosity about literally everything made him the beau ideal of the contrivers of booby traps; time and again he was spared an arm, leg or skull only by the grace of God and the horrified vigilance of his friend Lieutenant Jules Buck. He sauntered through mine fields where plain man feared to tread. He is quick to get mad and as quick to get over it. Once in Italy he sprinted up five flights of headquarters stairs in order to sock a frustrating superior officer; arriving at the top he was so winded he could hardly stand. Time enough to catch his breath was time enough to cool off; he just wobbled downstairs again.

Huston is swiftly stirred by anything which appeals to his sense of justice, magnanimity or courage: he was among the first men to stand up for Lew Ayres as a conscientious objector, he flew to the Washington hearings on Hollywood (which he refers to as "an obscenity") and sponsored Henry Wallace (though he voted for Truman) in the 1948 campaign. Some people think of him, accordingly, as a fellow traveler. Actually he is a political man chiefly in an emotional sense: "I'm against *anybody,*" he says, "who tries to tell anybody else what to do." The mere sight or thought of a cop can get him sore. He is in short rather less of a Communist than the most ultramontane Republican, for like perhaps five out of seven good artists who ever lived he is—to lapse into technical jargon—a natural-born antiauthoritarian individualistic libertarian anarchist, without portfolio.

A very good screen writer, Huston is an even better director. H has a feeling about telling a story on a screen which sets him apart from most other movie artists and from all nonmovie writers and artists. "On paper," he says, "all you can do is say something happened, and if you say it well enough the reader believes you. In pictures, if you do it right, *the thing happens, right there on the screen."*

This means more than it may seem to. Most movies are like predigested food because they are mere reenactments of something that happened (if ever) back in the scripting stage. At the time of shooting the sense of the present is not strong, and such creative energy as may be on hand is used to give the event finish, in every sense of the word, rather than beginning and life. Huston's work has a unique tension and vitality because the maximum of all contributing creative energies converge at the one moment that counts most in a movie—the continuing moment of committing the story to film. At his best he makes the story tell itself, makes it seem to happen for the first and last time at the moment of recording. It is almost magically hard to get this to happen. In the *Treasure* scene in which the bandits kill Bogart, Huston wanted it to be quiet and mock-casual up to its final burst of violence. He told two of his three killers—one a professional actor, the other two professional criminals—only to stay quiet and close to the ground, and always to move when Bogart moved, to keep him surrounded. Then he had everyone play it through, over and over, until they should get the feel of it. At length one of them did a quick scuttling slide down a bank on his bottom and his busy little hands and feet. A motion as innocent as a child's and as frightening as a centipede's, it makes clear for the first time in the scene that death is absolutely inescapable, and very near. "When he did that slide," Huston says, "I knew they had the feel of it." He shot it accordingly.

Paradoxically in this hyperactive artist of action, the living, breathing texture of his best work is the result of a working method which relies on the utmost possible passiveness. Most serious-minded directors direct too much: "Now on this word," Huston has heard one tell an actor, "I want your voice to break." Actors accustomed to that kind of "help" are often uneasy when they start to work with Huston. "Shall I sit down here?" one asked, interrupting a rehearsal. "*I* dunno," Huston replied. "You tired?" When Claire Trevor, starting work in *Key Largo,* asked for a few pointers, he told her, "You're the kind of drunken dame whose elbows are always a little too big, your voice is a little too loud, you're a little too polite. You're very sad, very resigned. Like this," he said, for short, and leaned against the bar with a peculiarly heavy, gentle disconsolateness. It was the leaning she caught onto (though she also used everything he said); without further instruction of any kind, she took an Oscar for her performance. His only advice to his father was a whispered, "Dad, that was a little too much like Walter Huston." Often he works with actors as if he were gentling animals; and although Bogart says without total injustice that "as an actor he stinks," he has more than enough mimetic ability to get his ideas across. Sometimes he discards instruction altogether: to get a desired expression from Lauren Bacall, he simply twisted her arm.

Even on disastrously thin ice Huston has the peculiar kind of well-earned luck which Heaven reserves exclusively for the intuitive and the intrepid. One of the most important roles in *Treasure* is that of the bandit leader, a primordial criminal psychopath about whom the most fascinating and terrifying thing is his unpredictability. It is impossible to know what he will do next because it is impossible to be sure what strange piece of glare-ice in his nature will cause a sudden skid. Too late for a change, it turned out that the man who played this role, though visually ideal for it, couldn't act for shucks. Worried as he was, Huston had a hunch it would turn out all right. It worked because this inadequate actor was trying so hard, was so unsure of what he was doing and was so painfully confused and angered by Huston's cryptic passivity. These several kinds of strain and uncertainty, sprung against the context of the story, made a living image of the almost unactable, real thing; and that had been Huston's hunch.

In placing and moving his characters within a shot Huston is nearly always concerned above all else to be simple and spontaneous rather than merely "dramatic" or visually effective. Just as he feels that the story belongs to the characters, he feels that the actors should as fully as possible belong to themselves. It is only because the actors are so free that their several individualities, converging in a scene, can so often knock the kinds of sparks off each other which cannot be asked for or invented or foreseen. All that can be foreseen is that this can happen only under favorable circumstances; Huston is a master at creating such circumstances.

Each of Huston's pictures has a visual tone and style of its own, dictated to his camera by the story's essential content and spirit. In *Treasure* the camera is generally static and at a middle distance from the action (as Huston says, "It's impersonal, it just looks on and lets them stew in their own juice"); the composition is—superficially—informal, the light cruel and clean, like noon sun on quartz and bone. Most of the action in *Key Largo* takes place inside a small Florida hotel. The problems are to convey heat, suspense, enclosedness, the illusion of some eighteen hours of continuous action in two hours' playing time, with only one time lapse. The lighting is stickily fungoid. The camera is sneakily "personal"; working close and in almost continuous motion, it enlarges the ambiguous suspensefulness of almost every human move. In *Strangers* the main pressures are inside a home and beneath it, where conspirators dig a tunnel. Here Huston's chief keys are lighting contrasts. Underground the players move in and out of shadow like trout; upstairs the light is mainly the luminous pallor of marble without sunlight: a cemetery, a bank interior, a great outdoor staircase.

Much that is best in Huston's work comes of his sense of what is natural to the eye and his delicate, simple feeling for space relationships: his camera huddles close to those who huddle to talk, leans back a proportionate distance, relaxing, if they talk casually. He loathes camera rhetoric and the shot-for-shot's-sake; but because he takes each moment catch-as-catch-can and is so deeply absorbed in doing the best possible thing with it he has made any number of unforgettable shots. He can make an unexpected close-up reverberate like a gong. The first shot of Edward G. Robinson in *Key Largo,* mouthing a cigar and sweltering naked in a tub of cold water ("I wanted to get a look at the animal with its shell off") is one of the most powerful and efficient "first entrances" of a character on record. Other great shots come through the kind of candor which causes some people to stare when others look away: the stripped, raw-sound scenes of psychiatric interviews in *Let There Be Light.* Others come through simple discretion in relating word and image. In *San Pietro,* as the camera starts moving along a line of children and babies, the commentator (Huston) remarks that in a few years they'll have forgotten there ever was a war; then he shuts up. As the camera continues in silence along the terrible frieze of shock and starvation, one realizes the remark was not the inane optimism it seemed: they, forgetting, are fodder for the next war.

Sometimes the shot is just a spark—a brief glint of extra imagination and perception. During the robbery sequence in *Asphalt Jungle* there is a quick glimpse of the downtown midnight street at the moment when people have just begun to hear the burglar alarms. Unsure, still, where the trouble is, the people merely hesitate a trifle in their ways of walking, and it is like the first stirrings of metal filings before the magnet beneath the paper pulls them into pattern. Very often the fine shot comes because Huston, working to please himself without fear of his audience, sharply condenses his storytelling. Early in *Strangers* a student is machine-gunned on the steps of Havana's university. A scene follows which is breath-taking in its surprise and beauty, but storytelling, not beauty, brings it: what seems to be hundreds of young men and women, all in summery whites, throw themselves flat on the marble stairs in a wavelike motion as graceful as the sudden close swooping of so many doves. The shot is already off the screen before one can realize its full meaning. By their trained, quiet unison in falling, these students are used to this. They expect it any average morning. And that suffices, with great efficiency, to suggest the Cuban tyranny.

Within the prevailing style of a picture, Huston works many and extreme changes and conflicts between the "active" camera, which takes its moment of the story by the scruff of the neck and "tells" it, and the "passive" camera, whose business is transparency, to receive a moment of action purely and record it. But whether active or passive, each shot contains no more than is absolutely necessary to make its point and is cut off sharp at that instant. The shots are cantilevered, sprung together in electric arcs, rather than buttered together. A given scene is apt to be composed of highly unconventional alternations of rhythm and patterns of exchange between long and medium and close shots and the standing, swinging and dollying camera. The rhythm and contour are very powerful but very irregular, like the rhythm of good prose rather than of good verse; and it is this rangy, leaping, thrusting kind of nervous vitality which binds the whole picture together. Within this vitality he can bring about moments as thoroughly revealing as those in great writing. As an average sample of that, *Treasure's* intruder is killed by bandits; the three prospectors come to identify the man they themselves were on the verge of shooting. Bogart, the would-be tough guy, cocks one foot up on a rock and tries to look at the corpse as casually as if it were fresh-killed game. Tim Holt, the essentially decent young man, comes past behind him and, innocent and unaware of it, clasps his hands as he looks down, in the respectful manner of a boy who used to go to church. Walter Huston, the experienced old man, steps quietly behind both, leans to the dead man as professionally as a doctor to a patient and gently rifles him for papers. By such simplicity Huston can draw the eye so deep into the screen that time and again he can make important points in medium shots, by motions as small as the twitching of an eyelid, for which most directors would require a close-up or even a line of dialogue.

Most movies are made in the evident assumption that the audience is passive and wants to remain passive; every effort is made to do all the work—the seeing, the explaining, the understanding, even the feeling. Huston is one of the few movie artists who, without thinking twice about it, honors his audience. His pictures are not acts of seduction or of benign enslavement but of liberation, and they require, of anyone who enjoys them, the responsibilities of liberty. They continually open the eye and require it to work vigorously; and through the eye they awaken curiosity and intelligence. That, by any virile standard, is essential to good entertainment. It is unquestionably essential to good art.

The most inventive director of his generation, Huston has done more to extend, invigorate and purify the essential idiom of American movies, the truly visual telling of stories, than anyone since the prime of D. W. Griffith. To date, however, his work as a whole is not on the level with the finest and most deeply imaginative work that has been done in movies—the work of Chaplin, Dovzhenko, Eisenstein, Griffith, the late Jean Vigo. For an artist of such conscience and caliber, his range is surprisingly narrow, both in subject matter and technique. In general he is leery of emotion—of the "feminine" aspects of art—and if he explored it with more assurance, with his taste and equipment, he might show himself to be a much more sensitive artist. With only one early exception, his movies have centered on men under pressure, have usually involved violence and have occasionally verged on a kind of romanticism about danger. Though he uses sound and dialogue more intelligently than most directors, he has not shown much interest in exploring the tremendous possibilities of the former or in solving the crippling problems of the latter. While his cutting is astute, terse, thoroughly appropriate to his kind of work, yet compared with that of Eisenstein, who regarded cutting as the essence of the art of movies, it seems distinctly unadventurous. In his studio pictures, Huston is apt to be tired and bored by the time the stages of ultrarefinement in cutting are reached, so that some of his scenes have been given perfection, others somewhat impaired, by film editors other than Huston. This is consistent with much that is free and improvisatory in his work and in his nature, but it is a startling irresponsibility in so good an artist.

During his past few pictures Huston does appear to have become more of a "camera" man, and not all of this has been to the good. The camera sometimes imposes on the story; the lighting sometimes becomes elaborately studioish or even verges on the arty; the screen at times becomes rigid, overstylized. This has been happening, moreover, at a time when another of Huston's liabilities has been growing: thanks to what Henry Blanke calls his "amazing capacity for belief," he can fall for, and lose himself in, relatively mediocre material. Sometimes—as in *Asphalt Jungle*—he makes a silk purse out of sow's ear, but sometimes—as in parts of *Strangers* and *Key Largo*—the result is neither silk nor sow.

Conceivably Huston lacks that deepest kind of creative impulse and that intense self-critical skepticism without which the stature of a great artist is rarely achieved. A brilliant adapter, he has yet to do a Huston "original," barring the war documentaries. He is probably too much at the mercy of his immediate surroundings. When the surroundings are right for him there is no need to talk about mercy: during the war and just after he was as hard as a rock and made his three finest pictures in a row. Since then the pictures, for all their excellence, are, like the surroundings, relatively softened and blurred. Unfortunately no man in Hollywood can be sufficiently his own master or move in a direct line to personally selected goals. After *Treasure,* Huston was unable to proceed to *Moby Dick* as he wanted to; he still is awaiting the opportunity to make Dreiser's *Jennie Gerhardt* and Dostoevski's *The Idiot* although he is at last shooting Stephen Crane's *The Red Badge of Courage,* which he has wanted to make for years. "This has got to be a masterpiece," he recently told friends, "or it's nothing."

There is no reason to expect less of it than his finest picture yet, for the better his starting material, the better he functions as an artist:

he is one of the very few men in the world of movies who has shown himself to be worthy of the best. He has, in abundance, many of the human qualities which most men of talent lack. He is magnanimous, disinterested and fearless. Whatever his job, he always makes a noble and rewarding fight of it. If it should occur to him to fight for his life—his life as the consistently great artist he evidently might become—he would stand a much better chance of winning than most people. For besides having talent and fighting ability, he has nothing to lose but his hide, and he has never set a very high value on that.

PRESTON STURGES: SUCCESS IN THE MOVIES (1954)

By Manny Farber (with W. S. Poster)

By all odds, the most outstanding example of a successful director with a flamboyant unkillable personality to emerge in Hollywood during the last two decades has been that of Preston Sturges, who flashed into the cinema capital in 1939, wrote, produced, and directed an unprecedented series of hits and now seems to be leaping into relative obscurity. Hollywood destiny has caught up with Sturges in a left-handed fashion; most whiz-bang directors of the Sturges type remain successes while their individuality wanes. Sturges seems to have been so riddled by the complexities, conflicts, and opposed ambitions that came together to enrich his early work that he could not be forced into a mold. Instead of succumbing to successful conformity, Sturges has all but ceased to operate in the high-powered, smash-hit manner expected of him.

It is a peculiarly ironic fate, because Sturges is the last person in the world it is possible to think of as a failure. Skeptical and cynical, Sturges, whose hobbies include running restaurants and marketing profitable Rube Goldberg inventions, has never publicly acknowledged any other goal but success. He believes it is easily and quickly achieved in America, particularly by persons of his own demoniac energy, mercurial brain, and gimmick-a-minute intensiveness. During the time it takes the average American to figure out how to save $3 on his income tax, Sturges is liable to have invented "a vibrationless Diesel engine," a "home exerciser," the "first nonsmear lipstick," opened up a new-style eatery, written a Broadway musical, given one of his discouraged actors his special lecture on happiness, and figured out a new way to increase his own superhuman productiveness and efficiency.

In fact, Sturges can best be understood as an extreme embodiment of the American success dream, an expression of it as a pure idea in his person, an instance of it in his career, and its generalizer in his films. In Sturges, the concept of success operates with purity, clogging the ideology of ambition so that it becomes an esthetic credo, backfiring on itself, baffling critics, and creeping in as a point of view in pictures which are supposed to have none. The image of success stalks every Sturges movie like an unlaid ghost, coloring the plots and supplying the fillip to his funniest scenes. His madly confused lovers, idealists, and outraged fathers appear to neglect it, but it invariably turns up dumping pots of money on their unsuspecting heads or snatching away million-dollar prizes. Even in a picture like *The Miracle of Morgan's Creek,* which deals with small-town, humble people, it is inevitable that bouncing Betty Hutton should end up with sextuplets and become a national institution. The very names of Sturges's best-known movies seem to evoke a hashisheater's vision of beatific American splendor: *The Great McGinty, The Power and the Glory, The Miracle of Morgan's Creek, Hail the Conquering Hero, The Great Moment, Christmas in July* reveal the facets of a single preoccupation.

Nearly everyone who has written about Sturges expresses great admiration for his intelligence and talent, total confusion about his pictures, and an absolute certainty that Sturges should be almost anything but what he nakedly and palpably is—an inventive American who believes that good picture-making consists in grinding out ten thousand feet of undiluted, chaos-producing energy. It is not too difficult to perceive that even Sturges's most appreciative critics were fundamentally unsympathetic toward him. Throughout his career, in one way or another, Sturges has been pilloried for refusing to conform to the fixed prescriptions for artists. Thus, according to René Clair, "Preston is like a man from the Italian Renaissance: he wants to do everything at once. If he could slow down, he would be great; he has an enormous gift, and he should be one of our leading creators. I wish he would be a little more selfish and worry about his reputation."

What Clair is suggesting is that Sturges would be considerably improved if he annihilated himself. Similarly, Siegried Kracauer has scolded him for not being the consistent, socially-minded satirist of the rich, defender of the poor, and portrayer of the evils of modern life which he regards as the qualifying characteristics of all moviemakers admissible to his private pantheon. The more popular critics have condemned Sturges for not liking America enough; the advanced critics for liking it too much. He has also been accused of espousing a snob point of view and sentimentally favoring the common man.

Essentially Sturges, probably the most spectacular manipulator of sheer humor since Mark Twain, is a very modern artist or entertainer, difficult to classify because of the intense effort he has made to keep his work outside conventional categories. The high-muzzle velocity of his films is due to the anarchic energy generated as they constantly shake themselves free of attitudes that threaten to slow them down. Sturges's pictures maintain this freedom from ideology through his sophisticated assumption of the role of the ruthless showman deliberately rejecting all notions of esthetic weight and responsibility. It is most easy to explain Sturges's highly self-conscious philosophy of the hack as a kind of cynical morality functioning in reverse. Since there is so much self-inflation, false piety, and artiness in the arts, it was, he probably felt, less morally confusing to jumble slapstick and genuine humor, the original and the derivative together, and express oneself through the audacity and skill by which they are combined. It is also probable that he found the consistency of serious art, its demand that everything be resolved in terms of a logic of a single mood, repugnant to his temperament and false to life.

"There is nothing like a deep-dish movie to drive you out in the open," a Sturges character remarks, and, besides being a typical Sturges line, the sentence tells you a great deal about his moviemaking. His resourcefulness, intelligence, Barnum-and-Bailey showmanship and dislike of fixed purposes often make the typical Sturges movie seem like a uniquely irritating pastiche. A story that opens with what appears to be a bitingly satirical exposition of American life is apt to end in a jelly of cheap sentiment. In *Hail the Conquering Hero,* for example, Eddie Bracken plays an earnest, small-town boy trying to follow in the footsteps of his dead father, a World War I hero. Discharged because of hay fever, Bracken is picked up by six Marines who talk him into posing as a Guadalcanal veteran and returning home as a hero to please his mother. The pretense snowballs, the town goes wild, and Bracken's antics become more complicated and tormenting with every scene. After he has been pushed into running for Mayor, he breaks down and confesses the hoax. Instead of tarring and feathering him, the townspeople melt with admiration for his candor and courage.

This ending has been attacked by critics who claim that it reveals Sturges compromising his beliefs and dulling the edge of his satire. "At his beginning," Mr. Kracauer writes, referring to *The Great McGinty,* "Sturges insisted that honesty does not pay. Now he wants us to believe that the world yields to candor." Such criticism is about as relevant as it would be to say that Cubists were primarily interested in showing all sides of a bottle at once. To begin with, it should be obvious to anyone who has seen two Sturges pictures that he does not give a tinker's dam whether the world does or does not yield to candor. Indeed his pictures at no time evince the slightest interest on his part as to the truth or falsity of his direct representation of society. His neat, contrived plots are unimportant per se and developed chiefly to provide him with the kind of movements and appearances he wants, with crowds of queer, animated individuals, with juxtapositions of unusual actions and faces. These are then organized, as items are in any art which does not boil down to mere sociology, to evoke *feelings* about society and life which cannot be reduced to doctrine or judged by flea-hopping from the work of art to society in the manner of someone checking a portrait against the features of the original.

What little satire there is in a film is as likely to be directed at satire as it is at society. The supposedly sentimental ending of *Hail the Conquering Hero,* for example, starts off as a tongue-in-cheek affair as much designed to bamboozle the critics as anything else. It goes out of hand and develops into a series of oddly placed shots of the six Marines, shots which are indeed so free of any kind of attitude as to create an effect of pained ambiguous humanity, frozen in a moment of time, so grimly at one with life that they seem to be utterly beyond any one human emotion, let alone sentiment. The entire picture is, indeed, remarkable for the manner in which sequences are directed away from the surface mood to create a sustained, powerful, and lifelike pattern of dissonance. The most moving scene in it —Pangborn's monumentally heartfelt reactions to Bracken's confession—is the product of straight comic pantomime. The Marine with an exaggerated mother-complex sets up a hulking, ominous image as the camera prolongs a view of his casual walk down the aisle of the election hall. The Gargantuan mugging and gesturing of the conscience-stricken Bracken provokes not only laughter but the sense that he is suffering from some mysterious muscular ailment.

Such sequences, however, though integral to Sturges's best work, do not set its tone. The delightfulness, the exhilarating quality that usually prevails is due to the fact that the relation to life of most of the characters is deliberately kept weak and weightless. The foibles of a millionaire, the ugliness of a frump are all projected by similar devices and exploited in a like manner. They exist in themselves only for a moment and function chiefly as bits in the tumultuous design of the whole. Yet this design offers a truer equivalent of American society than can be supplied by any realism or satire that cannot cope with the tongue-in-cheek self-consciousness and irreverence toward its own fluctuating institutions that is the very hallmark of American society—that befuddles foreign observers and makes American mores well-nigh impervious to any kind of satire.

Satire requires a stationary society, one that seriously believes in the enduring value of the features providing its identity. But what is there to satirize in a country so much at the mercy of time and commerce as to be profoundly aware that all its traits—its beauties, blemishes, wealth, poverty, prejudices, and aspirations—are equally the merchandise of the moment, easily manufactured and trembling on the verge of destruction from the moment of production? The only American quality that can conceivably offer a focus for satire, as the early moviemakers and Sturges, alone among the contemporaries, have realized, is speed. Some of the great early comic films, those of Buster Keaton, for example, were scarcely comic at all but pure and very bitter satires, exhausting in endless combinations of all possible tortures produced as a consequence of the *naif* belief in speed. Mack Sennett was less the satirist of American speed-mania than its Diaghilev. Strip away the comic webbing, and your eye comes upon the preternatural poetic world created by an instinctive impresario of graceful accelerations. Keystone cops and bathing beauties mingle and separate in a buoyant, immensely varied ballet, conceived at the speed of mind but with camera velocity rather than the human body as its limit. Sturges was the only legitimate heir of the early American film, combining its various methods, adding new perspectives and developing the whole in a form suitable to a talking picture.

Since Sturges thought more synoptically than his predecessors, he presented a speed-ridden society through a multiple focus rather than the single, stationary lens of the pioneers. While achieving a more intense identification of the audience with the actors than in the earlier films (but less than the current talking pictures, which strive for complete audience identification with the hero), Sturges fragmented action, so that each scene blends into the next before it comes to rest, and created an illusion of relative motions. Basically, a Sturges film is executed to give one the delighted sensation of a person moving on a smoothly traveling vehicle going at high speed through fields, towns, homes, and even through other vehicles. The vehicle in which the spectator is traveling never stops but seems to be moving in a circle, making its journey again and again in an ascending, narrowing spiral until it diminishes into nothingness. One of his characters calls society a "cockeyed caravan," and Sturges, himself, is less a settled, bona fide resident of America than a hurried, Argus-eyed traveler through its shifting scenes, a nomad in space observing a society nomadic in time and projecting his sensations in uniquely computed terms.

This modern cinematic perspective of mobility seen by a mobile observer comes easily to Sturges because of his strange family background and broken-up youth. He was the son of a normal, sports-loving, successful father and a fantastic culture-bug mother who wanted him to be a genius and kept him in Paris from the age of eight to about fifteen. "She dragged me through every goddam museum on the continent," he has rancorously remarked. Glutted, at an early age, by an overrich diet of esthetic dancing, high-hatted opera audiences, and impressionist painting, Sturges still shows the marks of his youthful trauma. The most obvious result of his experience has been a violent reaction against all estheticism. He has also expressed fervent admiration for his father's business ability and a desire to emulate him. The fact that he did not, however, indicates that his early training provoked more than a merely negative reaction in him and made him a logical candidate for Hollywood, whose entire importance in the history of culture resides in its unprecedented effort to merge art and big business.

As a moviemaker, the businessman side of Sturges was superficially dominant. He seems to have begun his career with the intention of giving Hollywood a lesson in turning out quick, cheap, popular pictures. He whipped together his scripts in record-breaking time, cast his pictures with unknowns, and shot them faster than anyone dreamed possible. He was enabled to do this through a native aptitude for finding brilliant technical shortcuts. Sturges tore Hollywood comedy loose from the slick gentility of pictures like *It Happened One Night* by shattering the realistic mold and the logical build-up and taking the quickest, least plausible route to the nerves of the audience. There are no preparations for the fantastic situations on which his pictures are based and no transitions between their numberless pratfalls, orgies of noise, and furniture-smashing. A Capra, Wilder, or Wellman takes half a movie to get a plot to the point where the audience accepts it and it comes to cinematic life. Sturges often accomplishes as much in the first two minutes, throwing an audience immediately into what is generally the most climactic and revelatory moment of other films.

The beginning of *Sullivan's Travels* is characteristic for its easy handling of multiple cinematic meanings. The picture opens abruptly on a struggle between a bum and a railroad employee on top of a hurtling train. After a few feet of a fight that is at once a sterling bit of action movie and a subtle commentary on action movies, it develops that you are in a projection studio, watching a film made by Sullivan, a famous director, and that the struggle symbolizes the conflict of capital and labor. As Sullivan and the moguls discuss the film's values and box-office possibilities, Sturges makes them all sound delightfully foolish by pointing up the naïve humanity of everyone involved. "Who wants to see that stuff? It gives me the creeps!" is the producer's reaction to the film. When Sullivan mentions a five-week run at the Music Hall, the producer explodes with magnificent improbability: "Who goes to the Music Hall? Communists!" Thus, in five minutes of quick-moving cinema and surprise-packed dialogue, a complex situation has been set forth and Sullivan is catapulted on his journey to learn about the moods of America in the depression.

The witty economy of his movies is maintained by his gifted

exploitation of the non sequitur and the perversely unexpected. In nearly every case, he manages to bring out some hidden appropriateness from what seems like willful irrelevance. In *The Miracle of Morgan's Creek,* a plug-ugly sergeant mouths heavy psychiatric phrases in an unbelievable way that ends by sinking him doubly deep into the realm of the psychotic. With nihilistic sophistication, Sturges makes a Hollywood director keep wondering "Who is Lubitsch?" till you are not sure if it is simply fun or a weird way of expressing pretentiousness and ignorance. Similarly, in *The Conquering Hero,* the small-town citizens are given a happy ending and a hero to worship, but they are paraded through the streets and photographed in such a way that they resemble a lynch mob—a device which flattens out success and failure with more gruesome immediacy than Babbittlike satires.

What made Sturges a viciously alive artist capable of discovering new means of expressiveness in a convention-ridden medium was the frenetic, split sensibility that kept him reacting to and away from the opposite sides of his heredity. These two sides are, in fact, the magnetic poles of American society. Accepting, in exaggerated fashion, the businessman approach to films, he nevertheless brought to his work intelligence, taste, and a careful study of the more estimable movies of the past. He also took care to disappoint rigid-minded esthetes and reviewers. Although it has been axiomatic among advanced movie students that the modern film talks too much and moves too little, Sturges perversely thought up a new type of dialogue by which the audience is fairly showered with words. The result was paradoxically to speed up his movies rather than to slow them down, because he concocted a special, jerky, spluttering form of talk that is the analogue of the old, silent-picture firecracker tempo. Partly this was accomplished by a wholesale use of "hooks" —spoken lines cast as questions, absurd statements, or explosive criticisms, which yank immediate responses from the listener.

Sturges's free-wheeling dialogue is his most original contribution to films and accomplishes, among other things, the destruction of the common image of Americans as tight-lipped Hemingwayan creatures who converse in grating monosyllables and chopped sentences. Sturges tries to create the equally American image of a wrangle of conflicting, overemotional citizens who talk as though they were forever arguing or testifying before a small-town jury. They speak as if to a vast, intent audience rather than to each other, but the main thing is that they unburden themselves passionately and without difficulty—even during siesta moments on the front porch: "I'm perfectly calm. I'm as—as cool as ice, then I start to figure maybe they won't take me and some cold sweat runs down the middle of my back and my head begins to buzz and everything in the middle of the room begins to swim—and I get black spots in front of my eyes and they say I've got high blood pressure . . ."

As the words sluice out of the actors' mouths, the impression is that they teeter on the edge of a social, economic, or psychological cliff and that they are under some wild compulsion to set the record straight before plunging out of the picture. Their speech is common in language and phrasing, but Sturges makes it effervesce with trick words ("whackos" for "whack"), by pumping it full of outraged energy or inserting a daft idea like the Music Hall gag. All of this liberated talk turns a picture into a kind of open forum where everyone down to the cross-eyed bit player gets a chance to try out his oratorical ability. A nice word-festival, very democratic, totally unlike the tight, gagged-up speech that movies inherited from vaudeville, radio, and the hard-boiled novel.

Paradoxically, too, his showman's approach enabled Sturges to be the only Hollywood talking-picture director to apply to films the key principles of the "modern" revolutions in poetry, painting, and music: namely, beginning a work of art at the climax and continuing from there. Just as the modern painter eschews narrative and representational elements to make his canvas a continuum of the keenest excitement natural to painting, or the poet minimizes whatever takes his poem out of the realm of purely verbal values, so Sturges eliminated from his movies the sedulous realism that has kept talking pictures essentially anchored to a rotting nineteenth-century esthetic. In this and other ways, Sturges revealed that his youth spent "caroming around in High-Bohemian Europe" had not been without a positive effect on his work. Its basic textures, forms, and methods ultimately derive from post-Impressionist painting, Russian ballet, and the early scores of Stravinsky, Hindemith, et al. The presence of Dada and Surrealism is continuously alive in its subsurface attitudes or obvious in the handling of specific scenes. Sturges's fat Moon Mullins-type female, playing a hot tail-gate trombone at a village dance, is the exact equivalent in distortion of one of Picasso's lymphatic women posed as Greek statues.

Sturges's cinematic transpositions of American life reveal the outsider's ability to seize salient aspects of our national existence plus the insider's knowledge of their real meaning. But the two are erratically fused by the sensibility of the nostalgic, dislocated semi-exile that Sturges essentially remains. The first impression one gets from a Sturges movie is that of the inside of a Ford assembly line smashed together and operating during a total war crisis. The characters, all exuding jaundice, cynicism, and anxiety, work feverishly as every moment brings them the fear that their lives are going to pieces, that they are going to be fired, murdered, emasculated, or trapped in such ridiculous situations that headlines will scream about them to a hooting nation for the rest of their lives. They seem to be haunted by the specters of such nationally famous boneheads as Wrong-Way Corrigan, Roy Riegels, who ran backward in a Rose Bowl game, or Fred Merkle, who forgot to touch second base in a crucial play-off game, living incarnations of the great American nightmare that some monstrous error can drive individuals clean out of society into a forlorn no man's land, to be the lonely objects of an eternity of scorn, derision, and self-humiliation. This nightmare is of course the reverse side of the uncontrolled American success impulse, which would set individuals apart in an apparently different but really similar and equally frightening manner.

Nearly all the Sturges comedies were centered with a sure instinct on this basic drive with all its complex concomitants. Using a stock company of players (all of a queer, unstandard, and almost aboriginal Americanism), Sturges managed to give his harrowing fables of success-failure an intimate, small-town setting that captured both the moony desire of every American to return to the small world of his youth and that innocent world itself as it is ravaged by a rampant, high-speed industrialism. The resultant events are used to obtain the comic release that is, indeed, almost the only kind possible in American life: the savage humor of absolute failure or success. Sturges's funniest scenes result from exploding booby traps that set free bonanzas of unsuspected wealth. In one episode, for example, two automat employees fight and trip open all the levers behind the windows; the spouts pour, the windows open, and a fantastic, illicit treasure trove of food spills out upon a rioting, delightfully greedy mob of bums, dowagers, and clerks. In *The Palm Beach Story,* members of the "Ale and Quail" club—a drunken, good-humored bunch of eccentric millionaires—shoot up a train and lead yapping hounds through Pullmans in a privileged orgy of destruction. This would seem the deeply desired, much fantasied reward of a people that endures the unbelievably tormented existence Sturges depicts elsewhere—a people whose semicomic suffering arises from the disparity between the wild lusts generated by American society and the severity of its repressions.

Sturges's faults are legion and have been pretty well gone over during his most successful period. Masterful with noisy crowds, he is liable to let a quiet spot in the script provoke him to burden the screen with "slapstick the size of a whale bone." A good businessman believes that any article can be sold if presented with eardrum-smashing loudness and brain-numbing certitude. From a similar approach, Sturges will represent hilarity by activating a crew of convicts as though he were trying to get Siberia to witness their gleeful shrieks. To communicate the bawdy wit of a fast blonde, he will show the tough owner of a lunch wagon doubled up like a suburban teenager hearing his first dirty joke. The comic chaos of a small-town reception must be evoked by the use of no less than four discordant bands. Sturges has been accused of writing down to his audience, but it is more probable that there is too much of the businessman actually in his make-up to expect him to function in any other way. The best of his humor must come in a brash flurry of effects, all more or less oversold because there is nothing in his background that points to a more quiet, reasonable approach to life.

But even these vices are mitigated somewhat by the fact that they provide an escape from the plight of many intelligent, sensibility-ridden artists or entertainers of his period whose very intelligence and taste have turned against them, choking off their vitality and driving them into silence or reduced productivity. The result is that artistic ebullience and spontaneity have all but drained down to the very lowest levels of American entertainment. Even in the movies these days, one is confronted by slow-moving, premeditated affairs—not so much works of art or entertainments aimed by the intelligence at the glands, blood, and viscera of the audience as exercises in mutual criticism and good taste. The nervous tantrums of slapstick in a Sturges movie, the thoughtless, attention-getting antics combined with their genuine cleverness give them an improvised, blatant immediacy that is preferable to excesses of calculation and is, in the long run, healthier for the artists themselves.

As a maker of pictures in the primary sense of the term, Sturges shows little of the daring and variety that characterize him as a writer and, on the whole, as a director. He runs to middle shots, symmetrical groupings, and an evenly lit screen either of the bright modern variety or with a deliberately aged, grey period-finish. His composition rarely takes on definite form because he is constantly shooting a scene for ambivalent effects. The love scenes in *The Lady Eve,* for example, are shot, grouped, and lit in such a way as to throw a moderate infusion of sex and sentiment into a fast-moving, brittle comedy without slowing it down. The average director is compelled to use more dramatic composition because the moods are episodic, a completely comic sequence alternating with a completely sentimental scene. Sturges's treatment is fundamentally more cinematic, but he has not found a technique equal to it. Fluent as a whole, his pictures are often clumsy and static in detail, and he has not learned how to get people to use their bodies so that there is excitement merely in watching them move. In a picture like Howard Hawks's *His Girl Friday,* Cary Grant uses legs, arms, trick hat, and facial muscles to create a pixyish ballet that would do credit to a Massine. But, when Sturges selects an equally gifted exponent of stylized movement, Henry Fonda, he is unable to extract comparable values from a series of falls, chases, listings to portside, and shuddering comas. Stray items—Demarest's spikey hair, Stanwyck's quasi-Roman nose—clutter up his foreground like blocks of wood. Even dogs, horses, and lions seem to turn into stuffed props when the Sturges camera focuses on them.

The discrepancies in Sturges's films are due largely to the peculiar discontinuities that afflict his sensibility, although such affliction is also a general phenomenon in a country where whole eras and cultures in different stages of development exist side by side, where history along one route seems to skip over decades only to fly backward over another route and begin over again in still a different period. What Sturges presents with nervous simultaneity is the skyrocketing modern world of high-speed pleasures and actions (money-making, vote-getting, barroom sex, and deluxe transportation) in conflict with a whole Victorian world of sentiment, glamour, baroque appearance, and static individuality in a state of advanced decay. In all probability, his years spent abroad prevented his finding a bridge between the two worlds or even a slim principle of relating them in any other way than through dissonance. A whole era of American life with its accompaniment of visual styles is skimped in his work, the essential problems thus created being neatly bypassed rather than solved.

But his very deficiencies enabled Sturges to present, as no one else has, the final decay of the bloated Victorian world, which, though seemingly attached to nothing modern and destined to vanish with scarcely a trace, has nevertheless its place in the human heart if only for its visual splendors, its luxurious, impractical graces, and all too human excesses. From McGinty to Harold Diddlebock, Sturges gives us a crowded parade of courtly, pompous, speechifying, queerly dressed personages caught as they slowly dissolve with an era. His young millionaires—Hickenlooper III (Rudy Vallee), Pike (Henry Fonda), and rich movie director Sullivan (Joel McCrea)—a similar type of being—are like heavily ornamented bugs, born out of an Oliver Twist world into a sad-faced, senile youth as moldy with leisure and tradition as an old cheese. Incapable of action, his obsolete multimillionaires gaze out into a world that has passed them by but to which they are firmly anchored by their wealth.

A pathetic creature in the last stages of futility, Vallee's sole occupation consists of recording, in a little black book, minute expenditures which are never totaled—as though he were the gently demented statistician of an era that has fallen to pieces for no special reason and has therefore escaped attention. Fonda as Pike, the heir of a brewery fortune *(The Ale That Won for Yale),* is the last word in marooned uselessness. A wistful, vague, young, scholarly ophiologist nicknamed Hoppsey, Pike's sole business in life consists of feeding four flies, a glass of milk, and one piece of white bread to a rare, pampered snake. In between, he can be seen glumly staring at a horde of predatory females, uncooperatively being seduced, getting in and out of suits too modern for him, sadly doing the oldest card trick in the world, and pathetically apologizing for not liking beer or ale. Oddly enough, his supposed opposite, a fast, upper-class cardsharp (Barbara Stanwyck) is no less Victorian, issuing as she does from a group of obsolete card Houdinis with an oldfashioned code of honor among thieves and courtly old-world manners and titles.

If Sturges has accomplished nothing else, he has brought to consciousness the fact that we are still living among the last convulsions of the Victorian world, that, indeed, our entire emotional life is still heavily involved in its death. These final agonies (though they have gone on so long as to make them almost painless), which only Sturges has recorded, can be glimpsed daily, in the strange, gentle expiration of figures like Shaw, Hearst, Jolson, Ford; the somewhat sad explosion of fervor over MacArthur's return (a Sturges picture by itself, with, if the fading hero had been made baseball czar, a pat

Sturges ending); and the Old World pomp, unctuousness, and rural religiosity of the American political scene.

Nowhere did Sturges reveal his Victorian affinities more than by his belief in, use, and love of a horde of broken, warped, walked-over, rejected, seamy, old character actors. Some of these crafty bit players, like Walburn, Bridge, Tannen, made up his stock company, while others like Coburn, Pangborn, Kennedy, and Blore appear only in single pictures. They were never questioned by critics, although they seemed as out of place in a film about modern times as a bevy of Floradora girls. They appear as monstrously funny people who have gone through a period of maniacal adjustment to capitalist society by exaggerating a single feature of their character: meekness, excessive guile, splenetic aggressiveness, bureaucratic windiness, or venal pessimism. They seem inordinately toughened by experience, but they are, one is aware, not really tough at all, because they are complete fakers—life made it inevitable. They are very much part of the world of Micawber and Scrooge but later developments—weaker, more perfect, bloated, and subtle caricatures—giving off a fantastic odor of rotten purity and the embalmed cheerfulness of puppets.

They all appear to be too perfectly adjusted to life to require minds, and, in place of hearts, they seem to contain an old scratch sheet, a glob of tobacco juice, or a brown banana. The reason their faces—each of which is a succulent worm's festival, bulbous with sheer living—seem to have nothing in common with the rest of the human race is precisely because they are so eternally, agelessly human, oversocialized to the point where any normal animal component has vanished. They seem to be made up not of features but a collage of spare parts, most of them as useless as the vermiform appendix.

Merely gazing at them gives the audience a tremendous lift, as if it were witnessing all the drudgery of daily life undergoing a reckless transmutation. It is as if human nature, beaten to the ground by necessity, out of sheer defiance had decided to produce utterly useless extravaganzas like Pangborn's bobbling cheeks, Bridge's scrounging, scraping voice, or Walburn's evil beetle eyes and mustache like a Fuller brush that has decided to live an independent life. It is all one can do to repress a maniac shriek at the mere sight of Harold Lloyd's companion in *Mad Wednesday.* His body looks like that of a desiccated 200-year-old locust weighed down by an enormous copper hat. Or Pat Moran's wrecked jeep of a face, and his voice that sounds as if its owner had just been smashed in the Adam's apple by Joe Louis. These aged, senile rejects from the human race are put through a routine that has, in one minute, the effect of a long, sad tone poem and, after an hour, gives a movie a peculiar, hallucinatory quality, as if reality had been slightly tilted and robbed of significant pieces.

No one has delineated sheer indolence as Sturges has with these characters. When one appears on the screen, it looks as if he had wandered into the film by mistake and, once there, had been abandoned by the makers. When a second one of these *lumpen* shows up, the audience begins to sit on the edge of its seat and to feel that the picture is going to pieces, that the director has stopped working or the producer is making a monkey out of it. After a few minutes of lacerated nothingness, it becomes obvious that the two creatures are fated to meet; considerable tension is generated, as the audience wonders what build-up will be used to enable them to make each other's acquaintance. To everybody's horror, there is no build-up at all; the creatures link arms as the result of some gruesome asocial understanding and simply walk off. In *Mad Wednesday,* this technique yields a kind of ultimate in grisly, dilapidated humor, particularly in the long episode which begins with Harold Lloyd meeting the locustlike creature on the greasiest looking sidewalk every photographed. The two repair to a bar presided over by Edgar Kennedy, who slowly and insanely mixes for Lloyd his first alcoholic potion. This entire, elaborate ritual is a weirder, cinematic version of the kind of "study in decrepit life" for which e. e. cummings is famed; certainly it is at least comparable in merit and effectiveness.

Sturges may not be the greatest director of the last two decades; in fact, it can be argued that a certain thinness in his work—his lack of a fully formed, solid, orthodox moviemaker's technique—prevents him from being included among the first few. He is, however, the most original movie talent produced in recent years: the most complex and puzzling. The emotional and intellectual structure of his work has so little in common with the work of other artists of our time that it seems to be the result of a unique development. Yet it is sufficiently logical and coherent to give it a special relevance to the contemporary American psyche—of precisely the kind that is found in some modern American poetry and painting, and almost nowhere else. Nothing is more indicative of the ineptitude of present-day Hollywood than its failure to keep Sturges producing at his former clip.

JOHN FORD: THE GRAPES OF WRATH (1973)

By Andrew Sarris

Who is the actual (or even predominant) author of a film? This question had perplexed film scholars long before auteurism added a new dimension to the debate. (*Vide* the voluminous briefs filed in the expressionistic-camera case of Murnau vs. Mayer.) Even when we stipulate multiple authorship in a collaborative art form, we find that the problem has not been solved. Certainly *The Grapes of Wrath* could not have become a motion picture if Darryl F. Zanuck or some other producer had not willed it into being by purchasing the rights to John Steinbeck's novel. The next-in-command after Zanuck was associate producer-scenarist Nunnally Johnson, who adapted the novel into a screenplay for John Ford to direct. Ford, in turn, worked very closely with Gregg Toland on the camera set-ups, but there was a great deal of second-unit work as well, and the final editing was very much a studio operation. But even if we could imagine a single ego which encompassed all the creative and productive functions represented by the names Steinbeck, Zanuck, Johnson, Ford, Toland, *et al.,* we would still be confronted with the autonomous assertions of the players on the screen, not only on the stellar level of Henry Fonda's Tom Joad nor on the archetypal level of Jane Darwell's Ma Joad, nor on the grizzled grandeur level of Charles Grapewin's Grampa Joad, nor on the messianic level of John Carradine's Casey, but down also to such cameo gems as Paul Guilfoyle's wry-mouthed born-troublemaker and Grant Mitchell's benignly tut-tutting New Deal bureaucrat.

We would be confronted also with the vast area of affecting accident recorded by the camera for display on a canvas which extends in both space and time. Even the constituent viewer elements of the editorial "we" would provide a bewildering diversity of viewpoints and associations, and the passage of time would actually alter the "look," "sound," and "feel" of the film. When *The Grapes of Wrath* was screened for students at a Yale seminar I gave in 1970, the hostile reaction baffled me at first, but then I realized that what had seemed unusually courageous in 1940 seemed unduly contrived in 1970. And what had once seemed the last word in "realism" now seemed strangely stylized. Besides, the New Dealish optimism which had initially inspired the project had evaporated over the years with the swings to the Right of McCarthyism, Eisenhowerism, the Nixonism, and with the growing realization that the original Okies of *The Grapes of Wrath* were destined to become the staunchest supporters of Ronald Reagan in California.

Rebecca Pulliam provides a thoughtfully radical critique of *The Grapes of Wrath* in the *Velvet Light Trap No. 2* (August 1971), and concludes: "As with the Protestant ethic and New Dealism, John Ford à la 1940 stays within certain safe limits of expression and does not assault the confines of its preconceptions any more than he penetrates the political organization. Certainly, a man cannot be blamed for the shortness of vision of his times. But the makers of this movie were unfortunately caught without a new vision—between decades and between myths."

Of course, one can argue that few movies of any decade or any country can be said to be genuinely radical in opposition to the social substance upon which they feed. Eisenstein dutifully excluded Trotsky from the October Revolution in *October,* and one would search in vain for any signs of Hollywood pacifism between Pearl Harbor and Hiroshima. Even so, Ford's conservative evolution in the fifties and sixties has misled modern film historians into theorizing about a conservative conspiracy back in 1940 to subvert Steinbeck's scathing critique of American society by substituting New Dealish homilies. It all depends upon one's frame of reference. Compared with other Hollywood movies of 1940, *The Grapes of Wrath* doesn't seem conservative at all. But compared with the writings of Che Guevara, Pablo Neruda, and Eldridge Cleaver, *The Grapes of Wrath* seems more like a hymn to honky capitalism and rugged individualism. Even so, it would be a mistake to view the alleged betrayal of a sacred literary source in purely ideological terms. Steinbeck's "choric interludes" which Ms. Pulliam considers crucial to the novelist's cosmic conception of suffering humanity would have loaded down the screen with a kind of rhetorical bombast reminiscent of D. W. Griffith's universal-brotherhood superimpositions in *Birth of a Nation,* and his recurring refrain of Lillian Gish's (and Walt Whitman's) "Cradle Endlessly Rocking" in *Intolerance.* Indeed, Steinbeck's "choric interludes" seem today only to increase the novelist's biological distance from his protagonists, who, by absorption into the mass of abstract mankind, became a small detachment of lowly marchers in a veritable army of avenging ants on the picnic blankets of the bourgeoisie. A very pitying expression of liberal guilt, to be sure, but hardly the heady stuff of which revolutions are made. It is perhaps more than a coincidence that both Steinbeck and John Dos Passos, from whose "newsreel" and "camera eye" in *U.S.A.* Steinbeck had borrowed his "choric interludes," turned conservative in their later years, thus reflecting the ultimate rupture between the New Deal–Old Left of one generation and the New Left of another.

Back in 1940, however, the problem of adapting Steinbeck's novel to the screen must have been one more of poetics than of politics. We are a long way from Theodore Dreiser's ideological commitment to Eisenstein over Sternberg for the film version of *An American Tragedy.* Still, even Eisenstein with all his clickety-clackety montage never demonstrated how a long novel could be faithfully adapted into a short movie. As it is, *The Grapes of Wrath* runs for 129 minutes, not too long by the one-shot standard of *Gone With the Wind,* but appreciably longer than the slightly under ninety-one-minute average running time of Ford's twenty-six features in the thirties. Ford, especially, had become a legend on the set for replacing precious literary lines with eloquent silences. The trick was to find the visual equivalents for wordy plots. Don't tell 'em, show 'em. Indeed, most critics had been brainwashed by high-brow aestheticians into believing that talk was the mortal enemy of cinema as an art form. Hence, the process of reducing and simplifying a novel for the screen enjoyed the highest aesthetic sanction.

Modernistic film aestheticians like Jean-Luc Godard and Roland Barthes can debate the contrasting ideologies of words and images, but in the forties there was very little critical precedent for examining the tensions between word and image, screenwriter and director, content and form, substance and style. There could be a disparity of effectiveness, but not a disparity of meaning. Thus critics could applaud John Ford's stylistic contribution to *The Grapes of Wrath* without suggesting in any way that he was undermining the thematic thrust of John Steinbeck's novel and Nunnally Johnson's screenplay. That there could be an ideological contradiction between the beautiful pictures of Ford and Toland and the angry words of Steinbeck and Johnson would have seemed as strange a notion in 1940 as any similar critique of the stylistic beauties of the neorealistic films would have seemed a decade later. At the very least, Ford and Toland could be charged by a retroactively revolutionary tribunal with diminishing the urgency of this enterprise with their eye-catching compositions of light and shadow on windswept fields and weather-beaten faces. There is even a ceiling (of a diner) photographed a full year before *Citizen Kane,* and a novelistic flashback shortly before *Rebecca* and a year before *How Green Was My Valley.* Thus, another film classic turns out to be more expressionistic than its realistic reputation would indicate. The term used to circumvent this stylistic contradiction is "poetic realism."

Only long after the event has it become possible to conclude that Ford's personal concerns were particularly inimical to Steinbeck's biological conception of his characters. Whereas Steinbeck depicted oppression by dehumanizing his characters into creatures of abject necessity, Ford evoked nostalgia by humanizing Steinbeck's economic insects into heroic champions of an agrarian order of family and community. But both Steinbeck and Ford share a kind of half-baked faith in the verities of outhouse existence and a sentimental mistrust of machinery. Neither Steinbeck nor Ford would have fitted very comfortably in the Soviet scheme of things with its worship of industrialization. However, the early forties were years of Popular Front sentimentality once the temporary embarrassment of the Nazi-Soviet pact had been forgotten and forgiven, and in this ecumenical era it did not seem too farfetched to link the rural evangelism in *The Grapes of Wrath* with world revolution. After all, more seemed to be at stake than a crass studio's desire to make money from a downbeat project. The minds and hearts of the moviegoing masses were thought to be hanging in the balance. Why depress and alienate these masses needlessly by reproducing Steinbeck's vision of existence as a dung-hill of despair? In hindsight, we might note that only a Luis Buñuel at his most outrageous would be capable of rendering all the gruesome horror of Steinbeck's saga on the relatively squeamish screen. But what would Buñuel have evoked with his lurid fidelity to Steinbeck, tacticians of the time might have asked, beyond the nervous laughter of the sophisticates and the revulsion of the general public? By contrast, the strategy tacitly agreed upon by Zanuck, Johnson, and Ford enabled the audience to identify itself with the sufferings of the characters, partly by making these characters active rather than passive, partly by stressing their coherence as a family though not as a class, and partly by offering hope in the future through Jane Darwell's concluding we-the-people speech, in its own way almost as controversial as Charles Chaplin's world-peace speech in *The Great Dictator.* Still, it is worth remembering that Odetsian audiences in Manhattan balconies cheered wildly in the forties when Ma Joad dispensed her populist manifesto: "Rich fellas come up an' they die, an' their kids ain't no good, an' they die out. But we keep a-comin'. We're the people that live. Can't nobody wipe us out. Can't nobody lick us. We'll go on forever."

Resounding rhetoric aside, *The Grapes of Wrath* is graced with subtler virtues than its dated "message" would indicate. After being overrated in its time as a social testament, it is now underrated both as a Hollywood movie (not glossily mythic enough) and as a Ford memento (not purely personal enough). What *does* stand up to every test of time, however, is Henry Fonda's gritty incarnation of Tom Joad, a volatile mixture of the prairie sincerity of *Young Mr. Lincoln* with the snarling paranoia of Fritz Lang's *You Only Live Once.* Once more, Fonda was passed over for top acting honors by both the Academy and the New York Film Critics. Possibly, his was too unsettling a performance for facile audience identification. Fonda-Joad's physical and spiritual stature is not that of the little man as victim, but of the tall man as troublemaker. His explosive anger has a short fuse, and we have only his word for it that he is tough without being mean. Indeed, it is mainly his awkwardness in motion that suggests his vulnerability whereas there is a tendency in the devious blankness of his expression to make him seem more sullen than he has any right or motivation to be. Consequently, his putatively proletarian hero becomes ominously menacing in the shadowy crossroads where social justice intersects with personal vengeance. Fonda's Joad is no Job, and as much as his mouth spouts slogans of equality, his hands are always reaching for a club or a rock or a wrench as an equalizer against the social forces massed against him. His is ultimately the one-man revolution of the ex-con with whom society can never be reconciled. By contrast, Jane Darwell's Ma Joad is the pacifier and unifier and high priestess of liberal reform at the altar of the sacred family.

Even within the Joad family, however, the significantly generational conflict between Charley Grapewin's Grampa Joad and Jane Darwell's Ma Joad is generally misunderstood and misinterpreted as the affectionate squabbling of rural types. But what is actually transpiring is nothing less than the transformation of the Joad family from a patriarchy rooted in the earth to a matriarchy uprooted on the road.

It is no accident that, even in the casting, Charley Grapewin's Grampa dominates Zeffie Tilbury's Grandma Joad as completely as Jane Darwell's Ma Joad dominates Russell Simpson's Pa Joad. Once on the road, the men have a tendency to wander and finally run away altogether either via drink or via distance. The women of the family must then hold the fort and save the children as poverty and unemployment destroy the authority of the paterfamilias.

Ford's own feelings are so powerfully patriarchal that when Grampa dies, something in the movie seems to die with him. Hence, the complaint of many critics that the first third of *The Grapes of Wrath* is superior to the final two-thirds. Parker Tyler noted astutely that even the surface of the screen seemed to change from lyrical dustiness to an antiseptic enamel finish. Ford's concern with the sacraments of the soil is expressed in the poetically sifting hands of John Qualen's maddened Muley and Grampa himself, and it is this primal property gesture through which we sense the conservative commitment of Ford's feelings to the dirt shriveled by the wind into dust, but still drenched in all its dryness with the blood, sweat, and tears of generations. Later, in *They Were Expendable,* Ford even redeems Russell Simpson (who is so diminished in *The Grapes of Wrath*) by casting him as Dad, chief of the shipyard, and a haunting hold-out who sits on his porch with his rifle perched on his lap, and his dog poised by his side, waiting, waiting, waiting for the invading Japanese. As doggedly loyal-to-the-land Dad, Russell Simpson revives the patriarchy which disappeared in *The Grapes of Wrath* somewhere on the road between Oklahoma and California.

NOTES ON THE NIHILIST POETRY OF SAM PECKINPAH (1976)

By Pauline Kael

Sam Peckinpah is a great "personal" filmmaker; he's an artist who can work as an artist only on his own terms. When he does a job for hire, he must transform the script and make it his own or it turns into convictionless self-parody (like *The Getaway*). Peckinpah likes to say that he's a good whore who goes where he's kicked. The truth is he's a very bad whore: he can't turn out a routine piece of craftsmanship—he can't use his skills to improve somebody else's conception. That's why he has always had trouble. And trouble, plus that most difficult to define of all gifts—a film sense—is the basis of his legend.

Most movie directors have short wings; few of them are driven to realize their own vision. But Peckinpah's vision has become so scabrous, theatrical, and obsessive that it is now controlling him. His new film, *The Killer Elite,* is set so far inside his fantasy-morality world that it goes beyond personal filmmaking into private filmmaking. The story, which is about killers employed by a company with C.I.A. connections, is used as a mere framework for a compressed, almost abstract fantasy on the subject of selling yourself yet trying to hang on to a piece of yourself. Peckinpah turned fifty while he was preparing this picture, and, what with booze, illnesses, and a mean, self-destructive streak, in recent years he has looked as if his body were giving out. This picture is about survival.

There are so many elisions in *The Killer Elite* that it hardly exists on a narrative level, but its poetic vision is all of a piece. Unlike Peckinpah's earlier, spacious movies, with Lucien Ballard's light-blue, open-air vistas, this film is intensely, claustrophobically exciting, with combat scenes of martial-arts teams photographed in slow motion and then edited in such brief cuts that the fighting is nightmarishly concentrated—almost subliminal. Shot by Phil Lathrop in cold, five-o'clock-shadow green-blue tones, the film is airless—an involuted, cork-screw vision of a tight, modern world. In its obsessiveness, with the links between sequences a matter of irrational, poetic connections, *The Killer Elite* is closer to *The Blood of a Poet* than it is to a conventional thriller made on the C.I.A.-assassins subject, such as *Three Days of the Condor.* And, despite the script by Marc Norman and Stirling Silliphant that United Artists paid for, the film isn't about C.I.A.-sponsored assassinations—it's about the blood of a poet.

With his long history of butchered films and films released without publicity, of being fired and blacklisted for insubordination, of getting ornerier and ornerier, Peckinpah has lost a lot of blood. Even *The Wild Bunch,* a great imagist epic in which Peckinpah, by a supreme burst of filmmaking energy, was able to convert chaotic romanticism into exaltation—a film comparable in scale and sheer poetic force to Kurosawa's *The Seven Samurai*—was cut in its American release, and has not yet been restored. And Peckinpah was forced to trim *The Killer Elite* to change its R rating to a PG. Why would anybody want a PG-rated Peckinpah film? The answer is that United Artists, having no confidence in the picture, grabbed the chance to place it in four hundred and thirty-five theaters for the Christmas trade; many of those theaters wouldn't have taken it if it had an R and the kids couldn't go by themselves. The film was flung into those neighborhood houses for a quick profit, without benefit of advance press screenings or the ad campaign that goes with a first-run showing. Peckinpah's career is becoming a dirty, bitter game of I-dump-on-you-because-you-dump-on-me. Increasingly, his films have reflected his war with the producers and distributors, and in *The Killer Elite* this war takes its most single-minded form.

Peckinpah's roots are in the theater as much as they're in the West; he loves the theatricality of Tennessee Williams (early on, he directed three different stage productions of *The Glass Menagerie*), and, personally, he has the soft-spoken grandness of a Southerner in a string tie—when he talks of the way California used to be, it is in the reverent tone that Southerners use for the Old South. The hokum runs thick in him, and his years of television work—writing dozens of "Gunsmoke" episodes, "creating" the two series "The Rifleman" and "The Westerner"—pushed his thinking into good-guys-vs.-bad-guys formats. The tenderness he felt for Tennessee Williams' emotional poetry he could also feel for a line of dialogue that defined a Westerner's plain principles. He loves actors, and he enjoyed the TV-Western make-believe, but that moment when the routine Western script gave way to a memorably "honest" emotion became for him what it was all about. When Peckinpah reminisces about "a great Western," it sometimes comes down to one flourish that for him "said everything." And Peckinpah lives by and for heroic flourishes; they're his idea of the real thing, and in his movies he has invested them with such nostalgic passion that a viewer can be torn between emotional assent and utter confusion as to what, exactly, he's assenting to.

As the losing battles with the moneymen have gone on, year after year, Peckinpah has—only partly sardonically, I think—begun to see the world in terms of the bad guys (the studio executives who have betrayed him or chickened out on him) and the people he likes (generally actors), who are the ones smart enough to see what the process is all about, the ones who haven't betrayed him yet. Hatred of the bad guys—the total mercenaries—has become practically the only sustaining emotion in his work, and his movies have become fables about striking back.

Many of the things that Peckinpah says in conversation began to seep into his last film, *Bring Me the Head of Alfredo Garcia* (1974), turning it into a time-machine foul-up, with modern, airborne killers functioning in the romanticized Mexico of an earlier movie era. Essentially the same assassins dominate the stylized, darkened San Francisco of *The Killer Elite.* In a *Playboy* interview with William Murray in 1972, Peckinpah was referring to movie producers when he said, "The woods are full of killers, all sizes, all colors. . . . A director has to deal with a whole world absolutely teeming with mediocrities, jackals, hangers-on, and just plain killers. The attrition is terrific. It can kill you. The saying is that they can kill you but not eat you. That's nonsense. I've had them eating on me while I was still walking around." Sam Peckinpah looks and behaves as if he were never free of their gnawing. He carries it with him, fantasizes it, provokes it, makes it true again and again. He romanticizes himself as one of the walking wounded, which is no doubt among the reasons he wanted to direct *Play It As It Lays.* (He was rejected by the businessmen as being strictly an action director.) In that Murray interview, he was referring to the making of movies when he said, "When you're dealing in millions, you're dealing with people at their meanest. Christ, a showdown in the old West is nothing compared with the infighting that goes on over money."

Peckinpah swallowed Robert Ardrey whole; it suited his emotional needs—he *wants* to believe that all men are whores and killers. He was talking to Murray about what the bosses had done to him and to his films when he said, "There are people all over the place, dozens of them, I'd like to kill, quite literally kill." He's dramatizing, but I've known Sam Peckinpah for over ten years (and, for all his ceremonial exhibitionism, his power plays, and his baloney, or maybe because of them, there is a total, physical elation in his work and in his own relation to it that makes me feel closer to him than I do to any other director except Jean Renoir) and I'm convinced that he actually feels that demonic hatred. I think Sam Peckinpah feels everything that he dramatizes—he allows himself to. He's a ham: he doesn't feel what he doesn't dramatize.

Peckinpah has been simplifying and falsifying his own terrors as an artist by putting them into melodramatic formulas. He's a major artist who has worked so long in penny-dreadful forms that when he is finally in a position where he's famous enough to fight for his freedom—and maybe win—he can't free himself from the fear of working outside those forms, or from the festering desire for revenge. He is the killer-élite hero played by James Caan in this hallucinatory thriller, in which the hirelings turn against their employers. James Caan's Mike, a No. 1 professional, is mutilated by his closest friend, George Hansen (Robert Duvall), at the order of Cap Collis (Arthur Hill), a defector within the company—Communications Integrity Associates—that they all work for. Mike rehabilitates himself, however, by a long, painful struggle, regaining the use of his body so that he can revenge himself. He comes back more determined than ever, and his enemies—Hansen and Cap Collis—are both shot. But when the wearily cynical top man in the company (Gig Young) offers Mike a regional directorship—Cap Collis's newly vacated position—he rejects it. Instead, he sails—literally—into unknown seas with his loyal friend the gunman-mechanic Mac (Burt Young).

There's no way to make sense of what has been going on in Peckinpah's recent films if one looks only at their surface stories. Whether consciously or, as I think, part unconsciously, he's been destroying the surface content. In this new film, there aren't any of the ordinary kinds of introductions to the characters, and the events aren't prepared for. The political purposes of the double-crosses are shrouded in a dark fog, and the company itself makes no economic sense. There are remnants of a plot involving a political leader from Taiwan (he sounds off about democratic principles in the manner of

Paul Henreid's Victor Laszlo in *Casablanca*), but that fog covers all the specific plot points. Peckinpah can explain this disintegration to himself in terms of how contemptible the material actually is—the fragmented story indicates how he feels about what the bosses buy and what they degrade him with. He agrees to do these properties, to be "a good whore," and then he can't help turning them into revenge fantasies. His whole way of making movies has become a revenge fantasy: he screws the bosses, he screws the picture, he screws himself.

The physical rehabilitation of the hero in *The Killer Elite* (his refusal to accept the company's decision that he's finished) is an almost childishly transparent disguise for Peckinpah's own determination to show Hollywood that he's not dead yet—that, despite the tabloid views of him, frail and falling-down drunk, he's got the will to make great movies. He's trying to pick up the pieces of his career. Amazingly, Peckinpah does rehabilitate himself; his technique here is dazzling. In the moments just before violence explodes, Peckinpah's work is at its most subtly theatrical: he savors the feeling of power as he ticks off the seconds before the suppressed rage will take form. When it does, it's often voluptuously horrifying (and that is what has given Peckinpah a dubious reputation—what has made him Bloody Sam), but this time it isn't gory and yet it's more daring than ever. He has never before made the violence itself so surreally, fluidly abstract; several sequences are edited with a magical speed—a new refinement. In *Alfredo Garcia,* the director seemed to have run out of energy after a virtuoso opening, and there was a scene, when the two leads (Warren Oates and Isela Vega) were sitting by the side of a road, that was so scrappily patched together, with closeups that didn't match, that Peckinpah appeared to have run out of zest for filmmaking. Maybe it was just that in *Alfredo Garcia* his old obsessions had lost their urgency and his new one—his metaphoric view of modern corporate business, represented by the dapper, errand-boy killers (Gig Young and Robert Webber as mirror-image lovers)—had thrown him off balance. He didn't seem to know why he was making the movie, and Warren Oates, who has fine shadings in character roles, was colorless in the central role (as he was also in the title role of John Milius's *Dillinger*). Oates is a man who's used to not being noticed, and his body shows it. When he tried to be a star by taking over Peckinpah's glasses and mustache and manner, he was imitating the outside of a dangerous person—

the inside was still meek. And, of course, Peckinpah, with his feelers (he's a man who gives the impression of never missing anything going on in a room), knew the truth: that the actor in *Alfredo Garcia* who was like him, without trying at all, was Gig Young, with his weary pale eyes. In *The Killer Elite,* James Caan is the hero who acts out Peckinpah's dream of salvation, but it's Gig Young's face that haunts the film. Gig Young represents Peckinpah's idea of what he will become if he doesn't screw them all and sail away.

Peckinpah is surely one of the most histrionic men who have ever lived: his movies (and his life, by now) are all gesture. He thinks like an actor, in terms of the effect, and the special bits he responds to in Westerns are actors' gestures—corniness transcended by the hint of nobility in the actors themselves. Like Gig Young, he has the face of a ravaged juvenile, a face that magnetizes because of the suggestion that the person understands more than he wants to. It's a fake, this look, but Peckinpah cultivates the whore-of-whores pose. He plays with the idea of being the best of men and, when inevitably betrayed, the worst of men. (He's got to be both the best and the worst.) Gig Young has the same air of gentleness that Peckinpah has, and the dissolute quality of an actor whose talents have been wasted. Gig Young's face seems large for his body now, in a way that suggests that it has carried a lot of makeup in its time; he looks rubbery-faced, like an old song-and-dance man. Joel McCrea, with his humane strength, may have been Peckinpah's idealized hero in *Ride the High Country,* and William Holden may have represented a real man to him in *The Wild Bunch,* but Gig Young, who represents what taking orders from the bosses—being used—does to *a man of feeling,* is the one Peckinpah shows the most affection for now. Gig Young can play the top whore in *The Killer Elite* because his sad eyes suggest that he has no expectations and no illusions left about anything. And Peckinpah can identify with this character because of the element of pain in Gig Young, who seems to be the most naked of actors—an actor with nowhere to hide. (Peckinpah's own eyes are saintly-sly, and he's actually the most devious of men.) Peckinpah could never for an instant identify with the faceless corporate killer played by Arthur Hill. When you see Arthur Hill as Cap Collis, the sellout, you know that it didn't cost Collis anything to sell out. He's a gutless wonder, something that crawled out of the woodwork. Arthur Hill's unremarkable, company-man face and lean, tall body are already abstractions; he's a corporate entity in himself. In Peckinpah's iconography, he's a walking cipher, a man who wasn't born of woman but was cast in a mold—a man whose existence is a defeat for men of feeling.

James Caan goes through the athletic motions of heroism and acts intelligently, but he doesn't bring the right presence to the role. His stoicism lacks homicidal undercurrents, and he doesn't have the raw-nerved awareness that seems needed. The face that suggests some of what Peckinpah is trying to express—the residual humanity in killers—is that of Burt Young, as the devoted Mac. The swarthy, solid, yet sensitive face of Burt Young (he played the man looking at pictures of his faithless wife at the beginning of *Chinatown*) shows the weight of feelings. Mac's warm, gravelly croak and his almost grotesque simpleness link him to the members of the Wild Bunch. His is a face with substance, capable of dread on a friend's account. In *The Killer Elite,* his is the face that shows the feelings that have been burnt out of Gig Young's.

Peckinpah has become wryly sentimental about his own cynicism. When the Taiwanese leader's young daughter pompously tells the hero that she's a virgin, and he does a variation on Rhett Butler, saying, "To tell you the truth, I really don't give a shit," the director's contempt for innocence is too self-conscious, and it sticks out. Peckinpah wants to be honored for the punishment he's taken, as if it were battle scars. The doctor who patches up the hero says, "The scar looks beautiful"—which, in context, is a sleek joke. But when the hero's braced leg fails him and he falls helplessly on his face on a restaurant floor, Sam Peckinpah may be pushing for sympathy for his own travail. From the outside, it's clear that even his battle scars aren't all honorable—that a lot of the time he wasn't fighting to protect his vision, he was fighting for tortuous reasons. He doesn't start a picture with a vision; he starts a picture as a job and then perversely—in spite of his deal to sell out—he turns into an artist.

Much of what Peckinpah is trying to express in *The Killer Elite* is probably inaccessible to audiences, his moral judgments being based less on what his characters do than on what they wouldn't stoop to do. (In Hollywood, people take more pride in what they've said no to than in what they've done.) Yet by going so far into his own hostile, edgily funny myth—in being the maimed victim who rises to smite his enemies—he found a ferocious unity, an Old Testament righteousness that connects with the audience in ways his last few pictures didn't. At the beginning of *The Killer Elite,* the lack of sunlight is repellent; the lividness looks cheap and pulpy—were those four hundred and thirty-five prints processed in a sewer? But by the end a viewer stares fixedly, not quite believing he's seeing what he's seeing: a nightmare ballet. In the freeform murderous finale, with guns, Samurai swords, and lethal skills one has never heard of before, there are troops of Oriental assassins scurrying over the phantom fleet of Second World War ships maintained in Suisun Bay, north of San Francisco. Wrapped up in their cult garb so we can't tell one from another, the darting killers, seen in those slow-motion fast cuts, are exactly like Peckinpah's descriptions of the teeming mediocrities, jackals, hangers-on, and just plain killers that Hollywood is full of.

The film is so cleanly made that Peckinpah may have wrapped up this obsession. When James Caan and Burt Young sail away at the end, it's Sam Peckinpah turning his back on Hollywood. He has gone to Europe, with commitments that will keep him there for at least two years. It would be too simple to say that he has been driven out of the American movie industry, but it's more than half true. No one is Peckinpah's master as a director of individual sequences; no one else gets such beauty out of movement and hard grain and silence. He doesn't do the expected, and so, scene by scene, he creates his own actor-director's suspense. The images in *The Killer Elite* are charged, and you have the feeling that not one is wasted. What they all add up to is something else—but one could say the same of "The Pisan Cantos." Peckinpah has become so nihilistic that filmmaking itself seems to be the only thing he believes in. He's crowing in *The Killer Elite* saying, "No matter what you do to me, look at the way I can make a movie." The bedevilled bastard's got a right to crow

PERFORMERS

For a great many moviegoers, educated and uneducated, sophisticated and naïve, the central appeal of the movies remains the actors, the stars. And it's not the art of acting that excites most viewers, but the faces, bodies, voices—the stylized physical *being*—of individual performers. Film, the most sensual of the arts, combining movement, music, and imagery, enters the mainstream of our waking fantasies with an overpowering stimulus—fully formed images of our physical ideals. The physical side of performance—the erotics of cinema—is something that is often left out of aesthetic theory and expositions of film "language."* For instance, an admirable recent collection of essays on film aesthetics contained exactly eight pages (out of 639) on film acting—two short articles on Garbo, the most obvious example of transcendent physical presence in the history of film. The best critics have been openly aware that the face and body of an actor (*all* actors, ordinary as well as "divine"), are themselves key elements in the "language" of cinema; and they've been unafraid of sounding naïve, of responding, at times, in much the same excited, star-gazing fashion as everybody else. A critic who can't do this has probably forgotten what drew him to the movies in the first place.

I've made a rather arbitrary selection here of pieces by critics who write well on performers. (See also, in other sections of the book, Agee on the silent comedians, Warshow on the stance of the Western actor, Kael on W. C. Fields and Mae West, etc.) In the first part of his review of *Something to Sing About*

*A recent exception to these generalizations is Leo Braudy's work on film aesthetics, *The World in a Frame* (Anchor Press/Doubleday, 1976), which has many interesting observations on acting.

(I've cut out the review proper) Otis Ferguson praises James Cagney for breaking through the stuffy, stage-bound conventions of proper diction and deportment that temporarily ruled the American cinema in the early sound period. Cagney established the new convention of easy, colloquial intimacy with the audience that we now recognize as the classic style of American film acting.

Cagney commanded his own space, set his own tempo; his dominating presence made him both actor and *auteur.* Writing some twenty years later, Manny Farber laments the decline of this kind of autonomy and also the disappearance of the small "character" performance that enlivened so many big-studio productions in the thirties and forties. According to Farber, some of the key movies of the sixties were paralyzed by pretentious, overly centralized conceptions—visual or thematic—which foisted on the actor a style of performance and a significance (symbolic, metaphysical, etc.) that was a violation of his natural temperament and rhythm.

In his voluminous writings on film (he also wrote art criticism and poetry), the late Parker Tyler devoted many pages of affectionate analysis, often with wickedly funny results, to the erotic substratum of film imagery. No matter how obscure or vague Tyler's ideas occasionally became, he never forgot that a film was an erotic event, an exchange of fantasies, both individual and collective, between audience and performers. Tyler wrote particularly well about actresses (he gets rather lyrically imprecise about male performers). In this short, ironic essay on the "sex goddess," Tyler traces the decline of the type from "authentic" myth to camp parody.

I conclude the section with two female critics writing about men. Penelope Gilliatt is a critic who moves in close to the object. Her specialty is detailed, almost microscopic notation of gesture and expression which she then elaborates into full-scale delineation of spiritual style. I've chosen her piece on Langdon, probably the least well-known of the great silent comedians. Molly Haskell, an excellent general critic, is a feminist with a vigorous distaste for the clichés of feminist discourse. She has consistently opened film criticism to a broad variety of general ideas—social, sexual, psychological—thereby enriching its resources and language. In these two selections from her nine-part series on Marlon Brando, which appeared in the *Village Voice* in the summer of 1973, Haskell mixes biography and criticism, idolatry and iconoclasm, in an attempt to understand the mystique of the most physical (and the most ambivalently physical) actor of them all.—*Ed.*

CAGNEY: GREAT GUY (1937)

By Otis Ferguson

It was just four years ago, when I hadn't been going to the movies very much, that I stopped around to see *Footlight Parade* and made the happy discovery of James Cagney. He had been known to almost everybody else before that in heavier roles (*Public Enemy,* for instance), and before he was well known at all he had been doing bits in pictures. But in this one he happened to be cast as the original Cagney, the hoofer and general vaudeville knockabout. The story had him drilling a line of girls, stomping out the routines and cracking around like the end of a whip, and even the presence of Dick Powell could not dim that vitality and flow of motion, and a grace before the camera that puts him in the company of the few who seem born for pictures.

It was a sunny introduction: seeing him you couldn't help feeling better about the industry—or the state of the nation for that matter. Because through this countrywide medium and in spite of whatever its story was about, this half-pint of East Side Irish somehow managed to be a lot of what a typical American might be, nobody's fool and nobody's clever ape, quick and cocky but not too wise for his own goodness, frankly vulgar in the best sense, with the dignity of the genuine worn as easily as his skin.

Since that time it has come out plainly that his character was no delusion of the flickers, that there was conscious purpose behind it. Once he was a star, Cagney used a star's privilege to tell them what was in character and what wasn't—gently, though, and with tactful stratagems, for he is no sea-lawyer (you will remember from the screen his trick of speaking more softly the more violent he gets). They wanted him to enounce with measure and dignity, now that he's got to be a star on them; so he had to explain that the characters he was portraying never knew anything about this enounce, measure, etc.; and an actor should be in character, shouldn't he? So they finally had to skip that. For *Jimmy the Gent* he got his head shaved and reported for work. The director was scared to death of shooting him that way (Ah, he kept saying with a slight accent, my main love interest should open with a head like a pig's knuckle?); and lord knows what the office would do. But Cagney gentled them and squared it with everybody—and anyway they couldn't hold up work while his hair grew—and managed to bring out a story about a thug who chased ambulances or sneaked up on dead horses or something, giving it the works. And if this wasn't the fastest little whirlwind of true life on the raw fringe, then I missed the other. When the picture *Here Comes the Navy* came out, the New York heavy lads naturally placed it for an incentive to imperialist war—Cagney had been so neat on his feet that only the common citizens got the obvious point of this bantamweight taking his blithe falls out of the stooge tradition of the United States Navy itself.

In such seemingly little ways he has managed to ad-lib, shift emphasis, and bring out his own relief. But behind that is the basic appeal he has for the audience as a person—under all that tough surface and fast talk people glimpse a sweet clarity of nature, a fellow feeling and rightness and transparent personal honesty. It makes all the difference in the world, and when he rips out a statement you sense without stopping to question that it is the living truth spoken through him, and not a line rehearsed and spoken on the set any longer. His screen life is not a natural autobiography, not something he just fell into. He is not a mug but one of the intelligent few; he isn't a perpetual handspring but a man with a troubling illness; his conversation is more a subdued questioning than a bright explosion of syllables; and while he swings all the punches in his stories he has been taking plenty on the chin in all these actual years, from down-under to up-on-top (no one can help wondering if the ship isn't sinking when Jimmie Fiddler creeps over ratguards to write a patronizing Open Letter from awfully safe ground). Don't think because he didn't produce *Hamlet* on Broadway last year that Cagney is automatically himself; and therefore no actor. His art is in an intense projection of those qualities within himself which he feels to be honestly representative of something, and in the fact that while all that rapid fire and assurance and open charm are enough to take the audience anywhere he wants to go, he has a guiding notion of where he's going.

THE DECLINE OF THE ACTOR (1966)
By Manny Farber

The strange evolution of movies in the last ten years—with the remaining studios ever more desperate, ever more coordinated—has brought about the disappearance of something that reviewers and film theorists have never seemed to miss: those tiny, mysterious interactions between the actor and the scene that make up the memorable moments in any good film. These have nothing to do with the plot, "superb performance," or even the character being portrayed. They are moments of peripheral distraction, bemusement, fretfulness, mere flickerings of skeptical interest: Margaret Sheridan's congested whinny as a career woman sparring with Kenneth Tobey (Christian Nyby's *The Thing*); Bogart's prissy sign language to a bespectacled glamour girl through the bookstore window (Howard Hawks's *The Big Sleep*); or Richard Barthelmess's tiredly defiant dissolute slouch when he enters the *cabaña* in *Only Angels Have Wings* (also by Hawks). Such tingling moments liberate the imagination of both actors and audience: they are simply curiosity flexing itself, spoofing, making connections to a new situation.

Even so-called photographed plays—for instance, George Cukor's *Dinner at Eight*—could once be made to produce that endless unreeling of divergence, asides, visual lilts which produce a vitality unique to the movies. With the setting and story of a Waldorf operetta, Cukor was able to get inflections and tones from the departments that professional cinematicians always class as uncinematic: make-up, setting, costumes, voices. Marie Dressler's matronly bulldog face and Lee Tracy's scarecrow, gigolo features and body are almost like separate characters interchangeable with the hotel corridors and bathtubs and gardens of Cukor's ritzy and resilient imagination. Cukor, a lighter, less sentiment-logged Ernst Lubitsch, could convert an obsession or peculiarity like Jean Harlow's nasal sexuality, or Wallace Beery's line-chewing, into a quick and animating caricature—much as Disney used mice and pigs in his thirties' cartoons.

Lately, however, in one inert film after another, by the time the actor moves into position, the screen has been congealed in the manner of a painting by Pollock, every point filled with maximum pungency, leaving no room for a full-regalia performance. No matter what the individuality of the actor may be—an apprehensive grandstander (Jeanne Moreau) with two expressions: starved and less starved; an ironing board (Gregory Peck) who becomes effective in scenes that have been grayed, flattened, made listless with some domesticity; a defensively humble actress (Anne Bancroft) who overvalues her humanism and eloquence—and no matter how fine the director's instincts may be, the result is invariably almost the same. In a situation where what counts is opulence and prestige—a gross in the millions, winner of the Critics' Award, Best Actor at a film festival—the actor has to be fitted into a production whose elements have all been assembled, controlled, related, like so many notes in a symphony. As a full-blooded, big-wheel performer rolling at top speed, the actor would subvert this beautiful construction, and so the full-blooded, big-wheel performance has become an anachronism.

Item: David Lean's *Lawrence of Arabia* is almost a comedy of overdesign, misshapen with spectaclelike obtrusions: the camera frozen about ten feet in front of a speeding cyclist, which, though it catches nice immediate details of his face, primarily shows him fronted on screen for minutes as a huge gargoylish figure; the camels, by far the most exciting shapes in the movie, photograph too large in the "cineramic" desert views; an actor walking off into fading twilight becomes the small papery figure of an illustrational painting; Jack Hawkins's General Allenby, so overweighted with British army beef, suggests a toy version of a Buckingham Palace guard. While the other technicians are walloping away, the actors, stuck like thumbtacks into a maplike event, are allowed—and then only for a fraction of the time—to contribute a declamatory, school-pageant bit of acting.

Item: Another prime example of this sort of thing is Serge Bourguignon's *Sundays and Cybele,* whose two leading players are made to resemble walking receptacles for the production crew. The story (Patricia Gozzi, a twelve-year-old, goes on little outings to the park with Hardy Kruger, an amnesiac) is made into a rite of style consisting mainly of layer-on-layer compositions in which the actors become reflected, blurred, compartmented, speckled, through some special relation with apparatus, scenery, a horse's body, windshield wipers. Such things as the tilt of a head or a face reflected in a drinking glass become so heightened, so stretched, that they appear to go on echoing, as if making their effect inside a vacuum. Yet all this is in the service of the kind of role that consists of little more than being delightful with a sniffle or looking transported while walking through trees carrying a child who is cutely imitating a corpse.

The new actor is, in fact, an estranged figure merely jiggling around inside the role. Sometimes he seems to be standing at the bottom of a dark pit, a shiny spot on his pomaded hair being the chief effect of his acting. Or he may be a literate fellow riffling the clutter on his desk. But, in either case, performance is invariably a charade: the actor seldom makes his own sense. He is no longer supposed to act as close to credible as possible; he is a grace note or a trill; he is a dab of two-dimensional form floating on the film surface for photogenic purposes.

Item: Keir Dullea's acting of the psychotic student in Frank Perry's *David and Lisa* is broad, swingy, without a moment that suggests either curiosity or the macabre homeliness, jaggedness, that might be expected in a disturbed kid. The set-piece handling of each scene usually finds Dullea's Frank Merriwellish, chalk-white face in the empty stillness, holding to an emotion for an unconscionable time. His tantrum when a doctor pats him on the back takes so long in evolving that the performance of it (crying, a face rigid with intensity, a stiff-handed wiping at his clothes to get rid of germs) seems to be going backward in slow motion.

The only good acting in recent films has been lavished on the role of the eternal sideliner, as played by John Wayne (the role of the homesteader in John Ford's *The Man Who Shot Liberty Valance*) or by George Hamilton (as the liquescent juvenile in Vincente Minnelli's *Two Weeks in Another Town*). These actors salvage the idea of independent intelligence and character by pitting themselves against the rest of the film. Standing at a tangent to the story and appraising the tide in which their fellow actors are floating or drowning, they serve as stabilizers—and as a critique of the movie. Mickey Rooney's murderously gloomy, suspicious acting in Ralph Nelson's *Requiem for a Heavyweight* is another case of superior sidelining, this time among the lunatic effects of apartment scenes that are pitch black except for a 40-

watt bulb, a huge hotel sign blinking on and off, actors photographed as eucalyptus trees being ogled from the ground by tourists.

While today's actor is the only thing in the film that is identifiably real, his responses are exploited in a peculiar way. His gaucheries and half-hitches and miscalculations are never allowed their own momentum but are used self-consciously to make a point—so that they become as inanimate and depressing as the ceaseless inventories in Robbe-Grillet novels. Jean-Paul Belmondo, the cool cat car thief in Jean-Luc Godard's *Breathless,* is seen standing before the stills at a theater entrance, doing a smeary Bogart imitation that leans on false innocence instead of developing spontaneously. Monica Vitti, a frightened erotic drifter in Antonioni's *Eclipse,* does a scene-hog's cheerful reaction to a dog's trick walk, full of "meaning" that upstages the characterization.

Falling out of the film along with the actor as performer are other related devices that once had their value. Compare, for example, the heavy, weighted masks of the actors in *Lawrence* with the cariactured features of William Powell, Cary Grant, or Edgar Kennedy, features that served to offset and counterpoint what might otherwise have been precious, sour, or effete about them. Powell, an artist in dreadful films, would first use his satchel underchin to pull the dialogue into the image, then punctuate with his nose the stops for each chin movement. He and Edgar Kennedy, who operated primarily with the upper torso, were basically conductors, composing the film into linear movement as it went along.

Another loss is the idea of character that is styled and constructed from vocation. In Kurosawa's *Yojimbo* (a bowdlerized version of Dashiell Hammett's *Red Harvest,* with a bossless vagabond who depopulates a town of rival leaders, outlaws, and fake heroes), the whole superstructure of Hammett's feudal small town is dissolved into an inchoate mass of Goyalike extras whose swarmings and mouthings are composed with naïve pictorialism. Swarming, moreover, seems to be the full-time occupation; you never see interiors, work, or any evidence of everyday life. The exposition of character through vocation has completely evaporated and been replaced by a shorthand of the character's daily habit, jotted into a corner of the role by set-designer, costumer, author. Jean Seberg's journalistic career is merely wedged into appropriate notches of *Breathless:* a *Herald Tribune* sweat shirt, a quick question to a celebrity novelist at the airport. The source of Monica Vitti's well-tended existence in *Eclipse* is snagged in a one-line footnote about her translator's work. The idea of vocations is slipped into the spectator's acceptance without further development.

The idea of movement per se has also lost its attraction to moviemakers. The actor now enters a scene not as a person, but like a Macy's Thanksgiving balloon, a gaudy exhibitionistic fact. Most of those appurtenances that could provide him with some means of animation have been glazed over. The direct use of his face as an extension of the performance has become a technique for hardening and flattening; and the more elliptical use of his face, for showing intermediate states or refining or attenuating a scene, has vanished, become extinct. In fact, the actor's face has been completely incapacitated; teeth—once taken for granted—or an eyeball, or a hairdo, have all become key operators. They front the screen like balustrades, the now disinherited face behind.

The moving body, too, in its present state of neglect has become a burden—particularly on foreign directors, who seem to realize that their actors might be mistaken for oxen, pillars, or extensions of a chaise longue and, so, give each of their films a kind of late, sudden, jolt. Toshiro Mifune suddenly comes alive toward the end of *Yojimbo,* throwing daggers into the floor of his hideout. Before this, he could usually be seen in one of those compositions Kurosawa prizes of three heads sticking out of their respective potato bags watching one another's faces while waiting for the lunch whistle to blow and break up the photography. *Eclipse* has a parody, very exciting, of people using their arms and hands in a stock exchange scene; most of the time these actors working on telephones, sandwiches, penciling, seem to be trying to fling their hands away. The *Lawrence* ensemble travels over literally half a continent with almost no evidence that any legs have been used. No actor is ever trusted with more than a few moves: a thin path having been cleared for him to make his walk down a dune, or to pontificate around porch furniture, he is then choreographed so that each motion, each bit of costume creaks into place.

Item: The lack of athleticism in *Requiem for a Heavyweight* is, under the circumstances, peculiarly comical. The cast seems made up of huge monolithic characters being held in place, incapable of a natural movement—particularly the overrated Anthony Quinn.

Walking down a lonely street sparring at the sky or mumbling while he puts on a shirt and tie, Quinn plays the role as though the ground were soft tapioca, his body purchased from an Army-Navy store that specialized in odd sizes.

The late work of certain important directors—Cukor's *The Chapman Report,* Huston's films since *The Roots of Heaven,* Truffaut's *The 400 Blows*—shows a drastic change into the new propulsive style. Every element of the film has been forced into serving a single central preoccupation, whether of character (gelatinous frigidity), a metaphysic (elephants are the largeness and mystery of life), or situation (the kid as misunderstood delinquent). A key, symbolic feature of the new style is the transformation of dialogue into a thick curtain dropped between the actor and the audience. The words spoken by Alec Guinness in *Lawrence* (prissily elocutionary), by Montgomery Clift in Huston's *Freud* (mashed, faintly quivery), by Laurence Harvey's Washington journalist in John Frankenheimer's *The Manchurian Candidate* (girlish, whispering) sound like valedictory speeches coached by Archibald MacLeish or the way Indians talk on TV Westerns. The peculiar thing is that each word has been created, worked over by a sound engineer who intercepts the dialogue before it hits the audience. There is no longer the feeling of being close to the actor.

Joan Crawford—despite the fact that each of her roles was played as if it were that of the same dim-witted file clerk with a bulldozer voice—always seemed hooked up to a self-driving sense of form which supplemented exactly what the movie couldn't give her. The current population of actors must probably be said to have more real skills than Crawford, but they don't come off as authentically. Geraldine Page, for instance, an actress of far greater sensibility and aplomb, must go through an entire glossary of mouth-shifting, sinus-clearing, and eye-blinking to make her character in *Sweet Bird of Youth* identifiable as anything. The difference between Crawford's tart in *Grand Hotel* and Page's obsessed ex-star is as great as that between George Kelly and William Inge. The effect of Miss Page's increased power and leisure, which expects no resistance from the movie, is to eviscerate the entire film. The same is true of Gregory Peck's pious Lincoln impersonation in *To Kill a Mockingbird* and of Angela Lansbury's helicopterlike performance in *The Manchurian Candidate,* in which every sentence begins and ends with a vertical drop.

The first sign of the actor's displacement could be seen in a 1952 Japanese film whose implications were not made clear until the New Wave, Antonioni, and others incorporated them into that special blend of modern-art cliché and Madison Avenue chic that now makes such good business. Just about every film aimed at American art theaters has come to be a pretentious, misshapen memory of *Ikiru* that plays on the double effect of the image in which there is simultaneously a powerful infatuation with style and with its opposite—vivid, unstoppable actuality. The fantastic clutter and depression of a petty government office; mouthed-in tepid talk that dribbles endlessly (as in John O'Hara's fiction, where dialogue now devours structure, motive, people, explanation, everything); the poor ghosts who crawl in trying to push a request for a playground in their spot of a slum—each of these items in *Ikiru* seems overrun by a virus of creativity without concern for its direction, everything steaming together into an indictment of drudgery that finally muffles the actors.

The same funguslike creativity and narcissistic style appear in an almost dead-handed way in *Freud, Lawrence of Arabia,* and *Eclipse.* Here the actors show up as rugs, or an entire battle scene is converted by artful lighting into an elongated shadowy smear. Just as *Ikiru* moves from a white emptied abstract death ceremony to a jammed city scene, *Lawrence* employs the split between desert and crowded Cairo to accent the peculiar density of each, and Antonioni juxtaposes the frenzied stock exchange with inarticulate lovers in emptied streets. Even in the crudely constructed *Divorce, Italian Style,* a din of diverse technical energy moves over streets, trains, the very bodies of the acting team. Mastroianni's face, sleep-drenched and melancholic, stares out of a dining car at the flat, parched Sicilian fields; and few actors have looked so contaminated by sleaziness, a draggy kind of living: it is the whole movie that is sitting on him. *Divorce, Italian Style* is like a parody of the realism in *Ikiru;* there is nothing to touch this unfunny farce for the sheer jarring effect of eager-beaver technicians charging into one another, trying to put in *more*—more funny stuff, more realistic stuff, more any kind of stuff.

Most directors have been pushing Kurosawa's invention to the extreme of treating actors with everything from the fancy tinker-toy construction of *Lawrence of Arabia* to the pure sadism of *The Manchurian Candidate.* One of the wildest films in its treatment of actors, *The Manchurian Candidate* is straight jazz all the way through—from the men who are supposed to be brainwashed to the normal ones in army intelligence. When Sinatra, for instance, moves in a fight, his body starts from concrete encasement, and his face looks as though it were being slowly thrown at his Korean houseboy opponent, another freak whose metallic skin and kewpie-doll eyes were borrowed from a Max Factor cosmetic kit. Janet Leigh seems first to have been skinned and stretched on a steel armature, and then compelled to do over and over again with hands and voice things supposed to be exquisitely sexual. The audience is made to feel unclean, like a Peeping Tom, at this queer directional gamboling over bodies. And Sinatra's romantic scenes with Miss Leigh are a Chinese torture: he, pinned against the Pullman door as though having been buried standing up, and she, nothing moving on her body, drilling holes with her eyes into his screw-on head.

In one advanced film after another, we find an actor being used for various purposes external to him—as a mistake, a pitifulobject, a circus sight. The most troublesome aspect of Peter O'Toole's Lawrence is that the story moves faster and further than the actor, who is not unlike the Tin Woodsman of Oz (O'Toole starts with a springing outward movement, to walk over the world, and then turns into a pair of stilts walking in quick, short strides). Consider also the squashy ineffectual performance by Peter Ustinov in *Billy Budd* (which he himself directed) or the pitiful ones by Jeanne Moreau in Orson Welles's *The Trial* and Truffaut's *Jules et Jim*. A frightened actress, Miss Moreau is never there with enough speed, sureness, or grace, but her directors realize that her inadequacies can be exploited photogenically. Watching her stretch out in a sexy bed pose, or teeter on a diving board, or climb up on a bridge abutment, stand poised, and then leap off, you get the feeling that her feeble creaking is intentionally being underlined as something to sorrow over.

What we have, then, is a schizoid situation that can destroy the best actor: he must stay alive as a character while preserving the film's contrived style. Thanks to this bind, there are roughly only two kinds of acting today. With the first, and the least interesting, type, the actor is hardly more than a spot: as in Antonioni's films, where he becomes only a slight bulge in the glossy photography; or, as in the endless gray stretches of Truffaut's, where his face becomes a mask painted over with sexual fatigue, inert agony, erosion, while his body skitters around weightlessly like a paper doll. Huston's work, too, has moved in a progression from the great acting of, say, Bogart and Mary Astor in *Across the Pacific* to no acting at all: in *Freud,* the actors do not escape for one moment from the spaces Huston has hacked out of the screen for them in order to make an elegant composition.

The second style of acting turns up in fairly interesting films. Here the actor does a movie-full of intricate acting by turning his back to the camera. He piles a ferocious energy and style into sorrowful characters who have lived through dismal orphanages, or alcoholism, or life membership in Alcatraz—precisely the characters who should have nothing in common with his kind of joy in performing, happy animal spirit, all-out vigor. The result is that there is no communication at all between the setting—which is flat and impressively accurate—and the actor, who splatters every second with a mixture of style and improvisation. Blake Edwards's *Days of Wine and Roses* drags unbelievably while Jack Lemmon kicks in a liquor store door or stares drunkenly at the dirty sea water. Lemmon in this movie is a blur of pantomimic skill, though with enough cynicism in his performance to cut the mechanical writing of the role. However, inside all the style, the actor seems to be static, waiting around sourly while the outer masquerade drags on.

There has, finally, never been worse acting nor more mistakes made by actors being given impossible things to do. A fan's memory gets clouded by these weird performances: a jilted intellectual (Francisco Rabal in *Eclipse*), who goes through an entrance gate as though he had learned to walk by studying an airplane taking off; a U.S. Senator imitating Lincoln at a costume ball (James Gregory in *The Manchurian Candidate*), picking up his didactic acting from several garbage heaps left over from the worst propaganda films of World War II. The poor actor today stands freezing, undone, a slab of beef exposed to public glare as never before. Clift's Freud may be hidden behind a beard, buried in a tomb (his walk to the cemetery must be pulled by earthmovers), but he is still unmercifully revealed as an unused performer. Some actors, like Jackie Gleason in *Requiem for a Heavyweight,* haven't yet moved into their act. And Kirk Douglas, as a gesticulating, angry ex-actor in *Two Weeks in Another Town,* is a body on display, one now shrinking in middle age while the mind of his employer is fixed on other things. Criticism of acting has always been quick to cover a performance with a blanket word, but trying to consider today's actors as auxiliaries of the story in the pre-fifties' sense is like analyzing post-Jackson Pollock painting with an esthetic yardstick that esteems modeling.

THE AWFUL FATE OF THE SEX GODDESS (1968)

By Parker Tyler

What, by virtue of the movies, is a sex goddess? It is easy to point, say, to Sophia Loren, imagine her quite naked (as may be done without the camera's assistance) and have the right answer. But Miss Loren's case is relatively simple and unaffected. The matter, with regard to the movies' history of sex, is too complex for mere pointing. The sex goddess's mutation, starting with the celebrated Vampire, is something to arrest and fascinate movie buffs and other susceptible scholars. Its ups and downs, turnabouts and triumphs, take on cosmic dimensions. Going in as straight a line as possible from Theda Bara to Greta Garbo, one's wits are staggered by so vast a change visible in one stroke of the imagination—and that stroke takes us only to 1941 . . . Technically, Garbo is a direct descendant of her distant Hollywood predecessor: the fatal Queen of Love and Ruler of Man which a sex goddess is—or was—supposed to be.

I change the tense and *there's* the rub. For whatever reasons, a sharp decline of divine dimensions in nominal sex goddesses has come about; it is as if "sex" and "goddess" were terms that, idiomatically, no longer agreed. Take the case of one who bore a notable physical resemblance to Sophia Loren, Jane Russell, a goddess ephemeral and now long extinct. Miss Russell was two great breasts mounted upon a human pedestal with a doll's head to top it off. Besides being no actress at all (which Loren, after all, *is*), Russell was hardly a sound recipe for a sex goddess. Her peculiar weakness may have lain in the very fact that a California judge, passing on the claim that her film, *The Outlaw,* was obscene owing largely to her salient and partly exposed mammary equipment, decided that anything God-given, such as breasts, could not be "obscene." Goddesses, by definition, *are* beyond the law. But voluptuous breasts are but the window-dressing of sex divinity. Jane represented one of the last historic efforts to invent a great personality on the basis of sex-appeal alone.

Plausibly, the physical dimensions of sex goddesses first tended to be ample. Theda Bara had a maternal figure. She was, in fact, remarkably like a suburban housewife circa World War I, bitten by the glamor bug into imagining herself supreme seductress of men, and by some weird turn of fate succeeding at it. Today, an Elizabeth Taylor also succeeds though *her* proportions and personality start by being those of the reigning office minx, from whom neither president of the company nor errand boy is safe. By another weird turn of fate we get instead, in this actress, a universal Miss Sexpot—for a sex goddess, one is obliged to call that a comedown. Nowadays sex-goddessing is more a trade than something, as it were, acquired by divine privilege. Another Italian star, Gina Lollobrigida, oddly resembles Miss Taylor although she is better-looking. Lollobrigida is simply Sophia Loren seen a few paces further off: a sort of reproduction in minor scale. But big and beautiful as La Loren is, we must face the fact that sheer majesty in the female body has become, historically, badly compromised as a glamor asset. Being a sex goddess has nothing whatever to do with the sexual act as such. Getting laid is a strictly human, quite unglamorous occupation.

Mediating between Bara and Garbo, Mae West turned up as an eccentric, utterly unexpected manifestation of sex divinity. Like the old gods of the Greek plays, she appeared with the primal authority of "Here I am!" Part of the majesty of Mae's corseted figure, hefty of hip and bosom, was its anachronism: she duplicated the physical image of the late 19th-century stage, where even chorus girls were girthy. The very pathos of distance helped make West a goddess, and historic. I confess to having been, in 1944, the first to describe what her style owed to the female impersonator: just about everything basic. A true parody of sex divinity, Mae was the opposite of the classic Vampire because she aimed at being both funny and good-natured: qualities more plebeian than royal or divine.

The movie canon of the teens and twenties had it that personified sex-appeal was a destroyer of men. Hence the Vampire embodied irresistible sexual evil. She was no laughing matter till time gave us the modern perspective, in which she's little *but* that. Vintage eroticism, regally portrayed by beautiful ladies throughout the twenties, automatically evokes titters when seen today. Mae West's sudden greatness was to have introduced a *deliberately* comic parody of the sex goddess. Her unique blend of sexiness and vulgar comedy, in other words, was the screen's first sterling brand of conscious sex camp. Other brands developed but these were the cynical farcing of tired-out actresses who had never quite believed in their own eroticism. Mae *did* believe in hers. That was the wonder of the spectacle she made. Few others actually did—probably not even her leading men! What her public believed in was the raw, happy camp of it. That incredible nasality, that incredible accent!

Garbo is virtually unique among the remoter goddesses because, even in some of her earlier roles (such as that in *Romance*), she can still be taken seriously. And yet even Garbo is not foolproof against the sensibility of what once a very few called, and now the world calls, camp. (Camp, one must note, is a proved culture virus affecting non-deviates as well as deviates.) Seeing Greta gotten up as an innocent country girl in *The Torrent,* one understands better that creeping parody of passion that meant her downfall in *Two-Faced Woman,* her last picture. The "two-faced" was painfully exact. A split personality may have suited the being termed by Robert Graves the Triple Goddess of archaic times on earth. But for our times, even one extra personality makes *The Divine Woman* (the title of a Garbo film) into a schizophrenic with professional delusion-of-grandeur. Film myths of the making and unmaking of a star began to appear as early as the thirties and their climax, in the sixties, was explicitly labelled *The Goddess.*

The sex goddess, supposedly, satisfies a basic human need: she would and should be the sanctified, superhuman symbol of bedroom pleasure, and bedroom pleasure as such seems here to stay. Europe, however, held a more tangible appreciation of sex as sex. Thus, a Brigitte Bardot came as no surprise at all. This legitimate goddess, after fifteen years' hard labor, has faded. Yet while she was at her international peak (somewhat pre-Loren), she had the simplicity and stark presence natural to erotic greatness. B.B., with canonic plenitude up front, facile nudity and long, tumbling blonde hair, was an impressive paradox: a cheerful Magdalene. Repentance and guilt were alien to her if only because her assets (like Jane Russell's before her) were so unmistakably God-given. Unworldly innocence imparted to B.B.'s sexiness a gay pathos; worldly sophistication imparted to Mae West's a more complex gaiety, a more complex pathos. B.B. was a symbol that implied nothing but reality, Mae a reality that implied nothing but a symbol . . .

When the self-farcing tendency began overtaking stars and films in the late fifties and sixties, even bouncy B.B. began parodying her rather down-to-earth divinity. As of now, screen nudity (to take sex at its simplest) has begun to be so proliferant as to look common. Arty, self-conscious, coyly denuding camera shots of the sexual clutch (one has had to creep up on body-candor in the movies) has become, by 1969, a cliché. Sex goddesses inevitably were victimized by the big breakthrough toward sexual realism. Currently, we are down to the nitty-gritty of the postures, the paintings, the in-plain-view of sex—down, in other words, to its profanity, including the garniture of those four-letter words. The sex goddesses have become sitting ducks for the exploding peephole of a film frame. In *La Dolce Vita* (1960), Fellini's genius for casting cannily registered the fatal downwardness then true of sex-goddessing. We found a perfect big-blonde-goddess type, Anita Ekberg, playing a parody movie star with a bust like a titaness, a baby voice and the courage of Minnie Mouse.

Sexy even so? Well, yes. Fellini pressed some delicate poetry no less than some satire from the combination of Miss Ekberg's shape, poundage and sweet, naïve femininity. Yet when, in the film, her husband whacks her for moonlighting with Mastroianni and she slinks off to bed, La Ekberg is just another silly woman—and "divine" only as a young man's midnight fancy. Even when she had answered in kind to the baying of neighborhood dogs, it was more a chorus than a command: the gorgeous bitch fled in an auto when the baying became serious. Fellini thereby branded the explicit profession of sex goddess a benignly comic fraud. Why ever should sex goddesses have fallen so low as to be "caught out" like that? The way they were caught out is clear enough: their regal posture was shown as an imposture: a fabricated illusion based on physical pretensions and almost nothing else. The method was to expose the base fleshly mechanism behind a grand illusion. In Hollywood, both sex goddesses and other stars were, it seemed, manufactured. Essentially, the goddesses had been lovely hoaxes foisted upon a naïve, gullible and dated public of both sexes: the gaga identifiers (female) and the gasping adorers (male).

It is a pause-giving irony that the truly great among sex goddesses were the first to show glaring symptoms of the decline and fall of the movie line. Was there something too *façade-like* about the Very Greats? Gazing back, one can detect one of the handsomest, Nita Naldi (who played opposite Valentino in *Blood and Sand*), unable to be anything from head to foot but a striking mask. In the teens and early twenties, statuesque feminine fulsomeness was still bona fide; it was the sweet and pure star actresses who were petite. Today, like Bara, Naldi must seem a rather puffy anachronism; if not downright absurd, at least strangely pathetic—a period clotheshorse, stunning but quite without humor. And take Mae West as a "mask" rather than a comedienne: physically she seems made from a mold, as if her whole body were a layer of simulated flesh about an inch thick, with nothing whatever inside. It took wit, humor and an interesting face to make La West a real "divine woman."

Historically, humor came into Hollywood supersex with the later twenties in the personnel of Flaming Youth: chiefly the "It Girl," Clara Bow. And then, of course, came Jean Harlow, who created a totally new standard for sex goddesses. Jean was a sacred-whore type whose unabashed vulgarity (even as West's) was integral with the spell she cast. Yet a few veils of illusion had been brutally torn off: evidently the sex goddess was no lady if, as Harlow, she could be a downright slut. Nobody sensed it then, I think, but a great symbol was being debunked. There could be no question about *Harlow's* real fleshliness, all over and through and through, if only because nothing seemed to exist between her and her filmy dresses but a little perspiration.

Like Mae, Jean was funny—more professionally and seriously so than Clara Bow, who was only a rampaging teenager with sex-appeal; essentially, that is, Clara was *decent.* Both West and Harlow let a certain middle-class decency (allied with basic chastity) simply go by the board. Both gloried in being, at least potentially, unchaste. They weren't exactly prostitutes (or but rarely) yet that they exploited sex professionally hit one between the eyes. They were Gimme Girls as much as Glamour Girls and quite beyond morality in those vocations. It would be humanly unnatural should beautiful ladies, every bare inch of them, cease to be darlings of the camera's eyes. But capitalized Lust is either a mad holiday or a deadly sin. Once, being a sex goddess was to skip all mundane considerations and assume that Lust meant Glorious Aphrodite. In the movies' advanced age (they are well over seventy), sex and other sorts of violence keep the film cameras grinding. But make no mistake: the goddessing of movie sex, subtly and brutally too, has met an awful fate.

In West, parody was a divine she-clown act; in Harlow, sex bloomed miraculously, nakedly, gaudily from the gutter. *The Queen,* a documentary about classy transvestites competing for the title of Miss All-American, offers (at the moment I write) the most eloquent evidence anywhere that sex-goddessing can still be taken seriously. Yet among those to whom queendom is synonymous with homosexuality, the divinity of sex as a public symbol carries a necessary irony and a necessary narrowness. "Harlow" has become a sort of trade name among professional transvestites. The winner of the contest in *The Queen* calls himself just Harlow, and one of Andy Warhol's home-made films is titled *Harlot* because it features an Underground transvestite's camp act in a blonde wig.

This "superstar," Mario Montez, has attached the name of a minor sex goddess (extinct) who was lately honored with an Underground cult: Maria Montez. The camp symbolism of the Warhol film, whose action takes place entirely on and about a couch where four people are grouped—two young men, a "lesbian" and "Harlow"—is to have Montez extract first one banana than another from various caches and munch them deliberately, in voluptuous leisure, for about an hour. This is the principal "action." Get the picture? If you do, you qualify for the Underground sex scene. It's this way: one is to imagine a camp queen of sex, even when genuinely female, not with an adoring male crawling up her knees, but an adored male with *her* crawling up *his* knees. In her early days, Garbo herself used to slither over her men like a starved python. But she was only combatting Old Man Morality: her erotic power, and its authenticity, were never in question.

Today everything is in question about the sex goddess but the blunt mechanism any woman offers a man. Personally, I find the progressive demoralization of the s.g. in females rather desperately saddening. Two acting celebrities, Bette Davis and Tallulah Bankhead (while neither was ever a sex goddess), have parodied neurotic and unconsciously funny females so often and so emphatically that they represent an historic attack on high feminine seductiveness. Sex-parody became, rather early, an integral part of Miss Davis' style till it exploded in her 100 per cent camp films, *Whatever Happened to Baby Jane?* and *Hush, Hush, Sweet Charlotte.* The aging Miss Bankhead's failure as a serious actress was suavely turned into success on the radio as a bass-voiced caricature. In the movies, finally, Bankhead followed suit to *Hush, Hush, Sweet Charlotte* with *Die, Die, My Darling* (Ugh!). Yet she (a handsome woman in her own right) had once in her career, if transiently, vied with Garbo.

We find a rich clue to the fate of the sex goddesses if we look at the way classic beauty currently serves movie sex. If the physical proportions and personalities of Sophia Loren and Anita Ekberg lend themselves easily to light sex-comedy with a wedge of farce and satire, the face and figure of Ursula Andress (taken in themselves) have a pure, invulnerable classic beauty. In the 19th century and the first quarter of the 20th, Ursula would have been destined as a sex goddess of real if removed divinity, surrounded with protocol and awe, a queen of fashion as of sex. On looks and style alone, Andress would do as well in society as in the acting profession. But what, alas! was her fate? To be an ultra-classy foil for a James Bond—a lesbian-like Pussy Galore! A "destroyer of men," by all means, but stamped with the comicstrip sensibility (see *Modesty Blaise,* et al.) that informs all Pop versions of camp sex.

The newest archetype of the sex goddess, robbing her of her former dignity and classic authority, inhabits the comic strip itself, where Barbarella (played by Jane Fonda) has been enshrined as the supreme Vinyl Girl of sex-appeal. Fundamentally, she is the oldtime serial queen, *rediviva.* Remember that serials (take *The Perils of Pauline*) were always animated comic strips with real performers. Even more significantly, there has been the completely nude Phoebe Zeit-Geist, the comicstrip heroine introduced by the *Evergreen Review.* Like a metaphysical idea, Phoebe seemed not to know what clothes are. Her sole function, naked and attractive as she was, was to be camp sacrificial victim *in perpetuo* for the historic villains and most grandiose, come-lately freaks of comicstripdom (for more clarification on this theme, consult the well-thumbed dictionary of sadomasochism at your local library).

Maybe no fate is really awful so long as, like Phoebe's, it's also fun. Yet the point is erotically disputable. To those tending to think the female sex represents a supreme power, like antiquity's Ruler of Men, the latterday Pop versions of sex goddesses partake more of existential gloom than existential fun. The "fun" is slightly sick.

Shouldn't the put-it-on-the-line psychology of sex-presentation be left for the hardcore geeks in the audience? Actually the transvestites, with their delusions of reincarnating extinct sex goddesses, are truer queens of beauty and sex than Ursula Andress—who looks more and more as if she had been cut out of cardboard and achieved her classic volumes by courtesy of 3-D (flesh-tones by Technicolor). I, for one, think it an awful fate that the grand profession of sex-goddessing should have sunk to the petty profession of sex-shoddessing. The robotizing trend of female charms (against which only that cartoon pair of *Playboy* tits seems holding out) must not be underrated. Think, ladies and gentlemen! The supreme goal of male propulsion, as foreseen in *2001: a Space Odyssey,* is a geometric black slab with unproved sexual capacities. Theda Bara would, tacitly, be more negotiable than that; and shapelier.

Come to think of it, Marilyn Monroe came along in those fidgety 'fifties and altered the whole set-up. There was something genuine about her, and really pathetic, as if she were all too human to exercise the great craft of queening it for the tradition. We know what finally happened to her. Maybe she was the last "goddess" actually seeming to be made out of flesh rather than foamrubber: something to sleep *with,* not *on.* And that was probably her fatal mistake. Goddesses are to be slept *about.*

LANGDON (1971)

By Penelope Gilliatt

Keaton, Chaplin, Lloyd, Langdon; and the unsung of these is Langdon. A lot of his silent films are beautifully funny.

If Harold Lloyd looks like a schoolboy who is hitting the awkward age and who is also a bit of a swot, Harry Langdon looks like a small girl with high hopes of one day being eight. The exquisite

Bessie Love face is hung with panniers of puppy fat. The make-up, which weirdly manages not to seem androgynous, gives him the likeness of a child who has been mooning for hours in front of a looking glass with its mother's lipstick and mascara. The mouth looks babyish and jammy, and the eye-black has been put on in a state of trance; the whole face has then been dreamily smothered in talcum powder. When Langdon gazes into the distance in a film—when he is playing a soldier looking for his regiment in country too hard for him—his lineless, unpanicked face is the mask not of a mind hard at work, like Keaton's, but of a mind gently lolling at anchor, like a punt. He seems to be contemplating not a problem but his own reflection, with an interest too infantile to be called vanity. Any intrusions of thought would be perilous, like noises that could make a sleepwalker break an ankle. The face exudes great sweetness and placidity. When cunning takes over, it is the response of someone before morality. He is very much an only child, and it has made him a duffer at games. As a 1914–1918 private in *The Strong Man*—the only private in the whole Army who might easily fail someday to absorb the fact that the war is over—he takes abstracted aim at a tin can and then at a German officer's helmet, using Army biscuits slung from a catapult. Only a girl would find such a rotten form of bullet, and only a girl would be so thrilled and surprised to get a hit: a girl with aspirations not to be a butterfingers, but doomed in the hope, and solitary. Langdon automatically goes his own way, without troubling himself to get in touch with the rest of the world. The position seems to be shared by all the great cinema comedians; the movies' double acts, the fables about alliance, derive from the stage, and never seem to be as glorious on screen as they can be in music hall.

When Langdon is in mufti—when he isn't being a soldier, or isn't dressed up in a morning coat to marry some scheming, avaricious bride—he generally wears a hat with the brim turned up all the way round, an outgrown jacket of which only the top buttons will fasten, baggy trousers, and large, amoebic boots. He stands with his feet in the first position of ballet, toes out, again like a girl without much of a clue. There can never have been such a spry comedian who gave such an impression of unathleticism. He looks as if he couldn't run for toffee. The best of his films—including some that he directed himself—reflect his schoolgirl torpor and move along with a beautiful dumbbell liquidity. He has a child's blitheness in egoism, a child's greed and hope and other-world criminality, and if the characterization ever slips into a moment of adult, this-world proneness to wounds, the film falters. Keaton is entirely grown up, stoic, decisive, ancient; Langdon seems most himself when he is unformed and seraphically naïve. He is a virtuoso of infant twitches that signal some tiny, fleeting worry, and a master of the beguilingly fatuous motions of beings who are still at the stage of experimenting to find their muscles. He can be especially splendid when he is working at a slant, trudging around the precipitous floor of a shack in a cyclone as if he had only just learned to walk.

The girls in his films are filthy grownups, treacherous and not very pretty. There is a terrible harridan in *The Strong Man* who cons him into thinking that she was the flower-faced girl who was his pen pal at the front; back home in America, she slips a stolen wad of bills into his pocket to offload detection by a dick behind her, and then faints massively outside her choice of mansion. Langdon is told severely by a servant that one can't leave one's women lying around like that. He lugs her inside as if she were a very large roll of carpet, keeling under her weight and avoiding several nasty blows from her *diamanté* jewelry. Her neck looks like a boxer's. Langdon staggers, sees the immense curving staircase that she wants to be carried up, and staggers some more. Starting the long haul, he gets his foot stuck in a flowerpot. There is a joyful moment when the overdressed burden, who is still pretending to be in a swoon, has to be propped on the marble banisters for an instant and then slides all the way down on her stomach. Langdon anxiously begins over again, sitting down on the stairs and carting the woman up step by step on his lap. He has indoctrinated himself so sternly into making the taxed movement that he plugs on with it, still backward, up a stepladder at the head of the stairs, right to the top of the ladder, and then beyond and over. It is a marvelous passage of mime. Maybe inflexibility, automatism, abstractedness and unsociability are great staples of funniness; Langdon's films sometimes have them all.

Unlike Chaplin and Harold Lloyd, he doesn't wheedle. We might as well not be there. He is subject to attacks of entirely private petulance, and doesn't give a damn that they're dopey. He will kick a cannon, or throw things irritably, and with a girl's aim, at a cyclone. In one celebrated set piece in, again, *The Strong Man,* he has a cold and attends devotedly to curing himself with stinking remedies in a crowded vehicle. The other passengers object, especially when he rubs his chest with Limburger cheese instead of liniment. A fusspot on his left is incensed. Langdon, hampered by feeling lousy, gives him an effete punch and also managers to spatter cough syrup over his dandyish enemy. His revenges are always serene and his movements oddly meditative. As with the business of lugging the hefty woman thief upstairs, his physical gags often come out of the old vaudeville-comedy discipline of repeating a movement mechanically after the need for it has gone. In *Tramp, Tramp, Tramp,* he somehow gets himself into and out of a prisoners' work camp in the middle of a cross-America walking race; he has grown entirely accustomed to walking with a ball and chain when he rejoins the race, and when a train happens (never mind how) to run over the chain and cut it loose he picks up the ball gamely and carries it as if it were a given of life. Sometimes he will stoop to pull up the iron links around his legs because they have drooped like sock garters. You can see that the things have given him pins and needles. He rubs the circulation back. Comedy is to swallow a camel and strain at a gnat.

Comedy is also to be tenacious in pursuit of hermetically peculiar tasks. In *Long Pants,* Langdon tries desperately to train a ventriloquist's dummy to run, doing demonstration sprints again and again, and coming back each time to see if the lesson has taken. He is fine with props, and a great punster with objects. Planning radiantly to murder his prospective bride in a wood, he drops his pistol into the undergrowth and retrieves in its stead a pistol-shaped branch, which he carries on with for a while. The historic team of the Goons used to do this sort of thing in their great days at the BBC. Spike Milligan would suddenly pick up a passing banana in the recording studio and plant it in his ear as a telephone receiver for an improvised call to Peter Sellers, blandly ignoring the fact that they were doing radio, not television.

Harry Langdon was born in 1884—child of two Salvation Army officers, which was a start. He worked as a cartoonist, a prop boy, a barber, and a performer in a patent-medicine show, and then in vaudeville for twenty years before he went to Mack Sennett. It was Frank Capra, a Sennett gag writer at the time, who invented *Tramp, Tramp, Tramp* for him. Capra apparently understood Langdon's comic personality perfectly, and begged to be allowed to work with him. (Later on, it was Capra who directed the two films that are probably Langdon's best—*The Strong Man* and *Long Pants.*). In *Tramp, Tramp, Tramp,* Capra correctly shows him coming out on top, as infants do, and winning the cross-continental marathon in spite of the ball and chain and in spite of infatuation with a girl played by Joan Crawford. The spiritual load for Langdon of loving Joan Crawford is inspired.

In Langdon's most characteristic films, the girls tend to be armor-plated. While he slips them love notes, they are likely to be immersed in some manly correspondence with other criminals about loot and dope. His attitude toward them is distant and spiked with decorum. He may sleep with a framed poster of the beloved's face in his bed, but this is as far as he will go. The strapping lady thief in *The Strong Man* tries to seduce him; though he is perfectly polite, the occasion is beyond his experience, and all he knows is that it tickles. There are some Langdon pictures in which the misogyny becomes delicately surreal. In *Three's a Crowd,* which he directed, he has a nightmare about having to fight in a brightly lit boxing ring, with his girl rooting against him, eyes hard as quartz; in the end, loopy with bloodlust, she bites her straw hat to pieces. Girls are never much help to Langdon. His best friend is providence—some fall of a stone in the nick of time, some Old Testament collapse of a saloon filled with stronger enemies. There is one cast list in which the characters include "His Bride," "His Downfall," "His Finish"; all three, predictably, are girls. Nonetheless, he is chivalrous. There are standards to be kept up. Sometimes he will explain these standards in a subtitle. They have a charming impatience and oddness: "Can't you see, Pa, when your sweetheart's in distress you can't go around marrying other women?" His love letters have the same straightforward idiosyncrasy: "I love you, I love you, I love you, I love you, and hope you are the same. Harry."

The America of his films is grounded in the twenties. It is a world of marathons and patent medicines and bootlegging, of religion that has a thunderous edge to it, of wedding rings in hock, of keeping one's end up. There is an out-of-work strong man who wears a brocade waistcoat for bravado; he boasts, to maintain his spirits, "I lift the heaviest weights in the world, and when I shoot myself from a cannon to a trapeze it's a sensation." Sometimes Langdon's films movingly catch the desperate, squalid courage of the epoch. His father in *Tramp, Tramp, Tramp* is a small-time cobbler on his way out because of the coming of mass production. "I can't battle those big shoe manufacturers," Pop says tremulously from, of course, a wheelchair. The sentimentality about crafts and private enterprise also belongs to the times; it seems half-mock, but meant, too. The great silent comedians demonstrate a philosophy of me-against-the-world, of small-town decency against metropolitan mayhem, of the loner against the propertied. Greed whirls over the landscape in a dark cone, drawing with it everyone except the tramp comedian and his kin. But though the tramp doesn't have a bean, he has benedictive luck. In one of Langdon's famous stunt sequences, he has leaped over the fence of a yard enticingly labeled "Private, Keep Out," to be saved on the other side only by a nail from falling down a cliff face. Whoever wrote that notice had a satanic passion for property and no great feeling for the lives of natural daredevils. Langdon's belt catches on the nail, and so does his sweater. He removes the sweater from the nail carefully and starts to unbuckle the belt. Then he sees the drop below him, absorbs it gravely, and does up the buckle, going on to cover up the sight of it with his sweater, in one of my favorite hopeless moments in silent comedy. Langdon did the stunt himself. "There was no one else to do it," he told a friend later, after the talkies had come in and his career had hit bankruptcy, "so I had no alternative." He was apparently deeply worried at the time because there wasn't a titter from the crew as he hung there. He didn't allow for their being fond of him; he thought it meant the sequence wouldn't be funny.

MARLON BRANDO (1973)

By Molly Haskell*

THE WOMAN IN THE "ALL-MAN" LEGEND

Spoiled by a rapid celebrity turnover, a fickle public must be reminded of its prior loyalties, and besides, who among us can resist forever the lure of publicity? This is the season for cinema's most

**Editor's note:* These are the second and fifth parts of a nine-part study of Marlon Brando that appeared in the summer of 1973. Brando had recently rejected the Academy Award for best actor in protest against Hollywood's "degrading" treatment of American Indians. He then appeared on the "Dick Cavett Show" on TV to defend the Indians' cause. The intervening and concluding sections of Molly Haskell's series mix biographical information with analysis of individual performances.

fashionable recluses to come down from their eyries and renew their lifeline with the public. After Ingmar Bergman at Cannes, and Brando on the Dick Cavett Show, it only remains for Garbo to choose her time and place—a guest appearance, say, on "Not for Women Only."

But Brando has never been one for talk shows and, unlike Bergman, is not—as far as we know—planning to make a movie with Barbra Streisand (although he was seen lunching with her in some desert oasis). Brando's first television appearance was to have been, according to an announcement he himself made back in 1955, on the Edward R. Murrow show, an honorable intention that somehow went agley. Instead it was as a guest of Faye Emerson on that pioneering, monumentally but endearingly inconsequential talk show that he made his debut, and it was, according to one eyewitness observer, a charming encounter. Brando was attired, characteristically, in Stanley Kowalski sloppy shirt and jeans, and Faye was attired, also characteristically, in an exceedingly low-cut gown. As she was talking, a slip of paper fell from her lap to the floor.

"Oh, Marlon," she said, pleadingly, turning to her guest. "I daren't."

"Daren't you?" Brando replied, smiling, as he leaned over and retrieved the paper. This was a side of Marlon, urbane and quick-witted, that was rarely allowed to surface and finally seems to have been permanently squashed under the combined weight of stardom and the white man's burden.

Why, after so successfully avoiding the limelight, should Brando decide to go on the Cavett show and promote the Indian cause? No doubt to restore his missionary credibility, the credibility that Sasheen, with a flap of her Little Feathers, had reduced to the ashes of her own meteoric rise and brief stint in celebrity heaven.

Brando, competing with Watergate, went on the Cavett show to explain that he hadn't gone to Wounded Knee because it would have looked like a "plot" to grab headlines. To remove the tincture of ego-tripping, Brando brings with him three Indians and a quote unquote non-Indian economic adviser to the Lumi tribe from Washington. The Brando delegation reminds me of the way Godard used to drag Gorin everywhere in the early days of their alliance, a symbol of that collective entity into which Godard had supposedly submerged his own despised Individuality. And indeed, this dual front did have the effect of politicalizing, and depersonalizing, every exchange.

Brando belittles acting with a choice of expression—"a craft, like plumbing"—that reduces it, typically, to the elemental-physiological level. And he babbles on about Indian rights, supported by "facts and figures," with the kind of hard sell—leaving out such ticklish subjects as the rights of the original inhabitants of Wounded Knee, or the conflict between different Indian factions—that detergent and drug advertisers might find a little too onesided.

He concedes that movies have given him a "good living." But it is not the good living or the plumber-like execution of his craft that enables him to command the attention of television land for an hour-and-a-half lecture on the Indians, and a few insults besides. (In referring sneeringly to "beer-drinkers" Brando instinctively avoids insulting his true followers who are more likely to be on wine, whiskey, or hash.) It is, rather, the legend.

What is the legend, and how has it managed to stay alive through all these years of dubious achievements? It is written in a word. BRANDO. Like Garbo. An animal, a force of nature, an element; not a human being who must as a member of society distinguish himself from other members with a Christian name and an initial as well as a surname. There is only one Brando the actor, even as he plays his favorite role, that of serious, socially-conscious anti-star. One of the five or six greatest actors—some would say *the* greatest—the cinema has yet produced. And yet how few great films have gone into the formation of that reputation!

He exploded onto the screen, after he had made a name for himself in the theatre, in the early fifties: *The Men* (1950), *A Streetcar Named Desire* (1951), *Viva Zapata!* (1952), *The Wild One* (1954), and *On the Waterfront* (1954).

The superlatives flew. Pauline Kael called his performance in *On the Waterfront* "the finest we have had in American films since Vivien Leigh's Blanche duBois," saying he "makes contact with previously untapped areas in American social and psychological experience."

Stanley Kauffmann said of him, "His future has the farthest artistic horizon of any American film actor—indeed of *any* English speaking actor . . . except Christopher Plummer and Colleen Dewhurst."

But hardly had the ink dried on the favorable reviews than the critics were complaining of the waste of a great talent, of the subversion of genius by American-Hollywood commercialism. This was the period of scandal and setbacks, of poor decisions, altercations with directors, of walking off sets and being walked over by the press. The films ranged from commercial hits (*The Teahouse of the August Moon,* 1956; *Sayonara,* 1957; *The Young Lions,* 1958; *Mutiny on the Bounty,* 1962), to moderate critical hits (*Guys and Dolls,* 1955; *Julius Caesar,* 1953; *One-Eyed Jacks,* 1961; *Reflections in a Golden Eye,* 1967), to a great many near- and total-disasters, including *The Fugitive Kind,* 1960; *The Ugly American,* 1963; *Bedtime Story,* 1964; *Morituri,* 1965; *The Chase,* 1966; *The Appaloosa,* 1966; *Candy,* 1968; *The Night of the Following Day,* 1969; *The Night Comers,* 1971. Two, *The Countess from Hong Kong* (1967) and *Burn!* 1970, though not hits, had their followers. But for the most part it was a period of unfulfillment, and the mystery is not how Brando fell so low, but how he fell so low and remained so high! For all the while the man was dividing his time between politics and Tahiti, and the actor was squandering his creative resources on unworthy projects, the legend was alive and blazing. Whatever Marlon Brando might be doing or not doing, *Brando* was still a name whose potency was undiminished, a name to excite, to ignite, to conjure with.

As with Garbo's career, you can count on one hand the great movies, and yet you wouldn't miss one if your life depended on it, if you had to see it in Spanish on a double bill, or miss dinner, or spend your last dollar. And no matter how bad it was (and every one of them has its champions), you'd wait breathlessly for the next one. Indeed, the similarities between the careers, and the myths, of the two stars are too striking to overlook. First, as you bemoan the scarcity of good films, you begin to wonder if there wasn't something in each of them that kept them from achieving a great, rounded oeuvre on the scale of the work produced by great artists in other fields—or even other film personalities who were perhaps more modest in their ambitions and/or talent. The actor is dependent on others for the realization of his potential, and yet, if he is a genius or feels "complete" in his own right, he has trouble submitting to a higher authority. Brando's difficulties with directors attest to this, and neither he nor Garbo worked often, or repeatedly, with film-makers of the first order. Brando did his best work—understandably—for Elia Kazan, an "actor's director" who, especially in his early work, was more inclined to accommodate the actor as a creative force on his own, rather than a director-surrogate or one element in a grand, directorial design. (Kazan's films became increasingly autobiographical, and it is interesting to note that Brando bowed out of *The Arrangement* for "political reasons," and the part of the protagonist, a Kazan-surrogate, was played by Kirk Douglas.)

In addition to their problems with directors, neither Brando nor Garbo ever seemed adequately matched in their co-stars and surrounding players. Their leading ladies and leading men were almost never remarkable or vivid in their own right, but were generally torch-bearers at the altar of the idol. Was this sheer coincidence, or was there something in the Brando-Garbo constitution, in their peculiar incandescence, that filled the space and left little room for other sources of light in the same sphere? Was it, perhaps, not just that they dominated members of the opposite sex, but that they contained ingredients of the other sex within them; was it not their androgyny, as much as their brilliance, that made their partners superfluous?

This is not unusual. Certain stars, like certain people, seem to reconcile sexual opposites. Chaplin and Mae West, Dietrich and Mick Jagger, are only the most obvious ones. And Garbo and Brando. They understand, intuitively, what it is to be "feminine" and "masculine," and they explore these qualities while remaining just within the boundaries of their sex, i. e., without being "gay" or "butch." Chaplin can be delicate, flirtatious, and coy, while Mae West is never less than forthright. Garbo is fearless in the transactions of love, while Brando hesitates in vulnerable self-defense. He is more sensitive than the women he loves, while Garbo makes the men to whom she devotes herself look indecisive and weak. Physically, too, they unite or borrow opposite sexual characteristics. Garbo and West are large-boned and lanky, while Chaplin and Brando are small and agile. Mae West's voice, stride, and lechery are masculine, while Brando's high-pitched "feminine" voice has been a determining factor in his career, preventing him from playing straight romantic leads in conventional love stories.

In movies as in real life, Brando's female opposites have never been his "equals"—active or emancipated women with some claim to autonomy outside their Brando-bound destiny. Nor have they been, except for Magnani, full-bodied, sensual women with an appetite for life (and even Magnani, in *The Fugitive Kind,* was the Older Woman, more to be pitied than feared for her sexual appetite).

Rather, Brando's partners have been virgins or romantic slaves who, from the pedestal or the ground, focused attention on him and happily accepted his dominance.

In both personal and fictional romances, an unusually large number were foreign or foreign-type women: Lotus Blossom (Machiko Kyo) in *Teahouse;* Hana-Ogi (Miiko Taka) in *Sayonara;* Josefa (Jean Peters) in *Viva Zapata!;* Louisa (Pina Pellicer) in *One-Eyed Jacks;* Trini (Anjanette Comer) in *The Appaloosa;* the blonde (Rita Moreno) in *The Night of the Following Day;* and, in real life: Anna Kashfi, to whom he was married from 1957–59; Movita, his wife from 1960–61; Rita Moreno as friend and occasional girlfriend; Josiane-Mariani Berenger, his one-time fiancée; and Tarita, whom he met during the shooting of *Mutiny on the Bounty.*

Then there were the films with no women *(The Young Lions, Mutiny on the Bounty, The Ugly American, Morituri, Julius Caesar, Burn!)* or films with women he wasn't interested in: Teresa Wright as the wife, in an eviscerated part, in *The Men;* Vivien Leigh in *Streetcar;* Joanne Woodward in *The Fugitive Kind;* Elizabeth Taylor in *Reflections in a Golden Eye.*

And finally, the pure, undefiled virgins, the princesses on the pedestals who could never fully appreciate the intricate agonies of their all-too-human lover. Mary Murphy in *The Wild One,* Eva Marie Saint in *On the Waterfront,* and Jean Simmons in *Guys and Dolls* are all dolls, china dolls, who are even more remote from "life" than their dark-skinned counterparts. Just as his chattel-mistresses are dependent on Brando to bear the burden of life, they are dependent on him to initiate them into its mysteries. They are buds who will blossom at his touch, or (in Magnani's case) a withered husk who can be revitalized. But Brando is always the center of gravity, a man that is more "man" than any of his women will ever know and yet, in his sensitivity, more "woman" than they are.

For Brando fans, the absence of a strong or interesting woman opposite him works to his, and their, advantage. Because his leading ladies are weak, transparent, unobtrusive, audiences can respond to him directly. Just as the male spectators of soft-core porn movies preferred all-female lovemaking scenes, where they could enter directly into the fantasy without the obstacle of a (competing) male figure, Brandolaters would prefer to have their sightline unobstructed. As he unites the characteristics of both sexes, he also appeals to both men and women. He is at once tough and vulnerable, the former a poor attempt to conceal the latter. He sees through the sham of sexual role-playing—particularly pernicious in the fifties—but seems powerless to change it. Protecting himself on one side while exposing the other, he dances around like a prize-fighter, tries to break through, to reach the other person on a deeper, true level of communication, but he is usually blocked by the forces of convention. Eventually, he is sorry: the person turns out to be not unlike the rest, a little better, perhaps, but unwilling to take the risk to stand against society. And so he, Brando, is generally left alone, the rebel, the outsider, the outlaw, the artist, man against society, man-woman against men and women, actor-genius against the Hollywood film.

Everything contributes to the legend; even the failures of his career feed the idea of an actor too "large" for any one role. There is more of him than can be contained or expressed in one part, and consequently when he is bad or outrageous, it is somehow the film's fault for trying to reduce him to the lineaments of a mere mortal. Like the wheelchair paraplegic in Fred Zinnemann's *The Men*—an unfortunate metaphor for Brando's whole career—he is a dynamo being restrained by forces outside his control. Because all but the best roles are too confining, he is constantly bursting their seams, exciting our imagination but throwing the movie out of line.

His essence is contradiction, conflicts, that can never come to rest in resolution, and he will therefore frustrate and disappoint all those who travel society's single tracks. His coarse language and brute force are not the impulses of a boor but the masque of a poet, the cry of rage against the imprisoning niceties of civilization. And because of this side, he doesn't belong with the pure roughnecks either, the toughs and delinquents who are genuinely coarse and unfeeling.

"You're a fake," Mary Murphy tells Johnny of *The Wild One*. Meaning you don't belong with these hyenas and apes who run around scaring old men anymore than you belong to the straights, the parents and sheriffs and "squares." But in her heart, like a good, sweet, obnoxious fifties girl, she hopes she can reconcile him to that world. In making the effort she betrays the integrity of their love, and loses it. By this time, the motorcycle gang is long gone, and so Johnny rides off alone, halfway between gangster and straight society. And

Brando, the man-myth who has not yet found his Indian delegation, is a rebel in search of a cause, but one who is destined never to unite successfully with a revolution because it is all within him, because the moment he thinks he is fighting shoulder-to-shoulder with the underdog he will find himself on opposite shores of his own inner self.

SUBMERGED IN THE STANLEY* PERSONA

It's a toss-up as to whether Brando brought more of himself to his roles, or vice versa. The role of Stanley was like an emotional bank account: what he invested nightly in terms of intuition, feeling, personality traits, he drew on daily as a dungaree-wearing bohemian living in New York. He rode a motorcycle, played the bongos, and was a friend of waifs and winos—outcasts he would find on the street and bring back to the apartment he shared with his old school friend, Wally Cox. Tales told of these early years, Brando's freest in terms of the relative anonymity he enjoyed at the threshhold of his movie career, all contain a note of self-dramatization, of a man playing out a part, or practicing for a new one. The friend of the people was perhaps rehearsing for *Viva Zapata!* The guy who went to pick up a blind date on a motorcycle (and, according to Maurice Zolotow, told her, as they were whipping around Central Park, that he could do even better if he had his glasses) was revving up for *The Wild One.* As the years went on, lines from scripts, which he had no doubt inspired if not actually written, turned up in interviews. But can a man plagiarize himself?

He was completely submerged in the Stanley persona when he first went to Hollywood; no doubt as a safeguard against any claims it might try to make on him. The film he had chosen for his debut was Fred Zinnemann's *The Men* (1950), a study of the problems of adjustment of paraplegic veterans after World War II, and the furthest thing from Hollywood fluff. With one suit and tie in his suitcase, and wearing jeans and a T-shirt, he went to live with his aunt and uncle in a two-room bungalow where, coming and going at odd hours, he tried to maintain the low standard of living to which he was accustomed.

The "problem film" was the justification for going to Hollywood, a category in which *The Men* slipped more easily than some

*The character Stanley Kowalski, in *A Streetcar Named Desire.*

of Brando's other films. These could be justified as socially conscious only by stretching the definition of the term—or the message of the film. *The Wild One* was a study of the delinquent mentality; *Teahouse of the August Moon* a dissection of Sino-American relations; *The Godfather* a parable of American capitalism.

But for being the most ostensibly high-minded of them all, *The Men* made greater compromises. A Stanley Kramer production, with a screenplay by Carl Foreman and a subject that would make up in heavenly rewards what it lost in mere commercial ones, it was drowning in good intentions. After a brief battle-scene prologue (the only "action" in the film), the rest of the picture dealt with the return home of a group of wounded GI's. They try to pick up the pieces—Brando his life and his fiancee played by Teresa Wright, Jack Webb the girl he meets in the army hospital—only to have the pieces break into smaller pieces.

In preparation for his role as a paralytic (his first, but not his last), Brando went to live at the veterans' hospital where the film would be shot. (This was the occasion of some relief to his aunt and uncle who, as much as they loved him, were beginning to feel cramped in their shared quarters and disconcerted by nephew's life style.)

Brando caught, with tense eloquence, the sudden change of moods, the raging bitterness, despair, and hope, of the disabled man. He rages inwardly and outwardly at his impotence, and his oscillations from boyish helplessness to demonic fury key the film's emotional temperature. But the other half of his "problem"—the effect of his disability on his wife, and her conflicting reactions, are barely considered. The only other performance of any significance is that of Jack Webb in the sub-plot.

In Miss Wright's reduced role lies a story, a parable that illuminates our own morality tale concerning the real or imagined battle between Art and Commerce. Miss Wright, according to a confession she made several years ago, was tired of the way her career was going at Paramount, and agreed to take a salary cut to do *The Men* because it promised to be a worthwhile project. After shooting several scenes in which she is courted by a man in love with her and tempted to divorce her difficult husband, she complained to the director and producer that the actor was utterly untalented and impossible to work with. They more or less agreed, but informed her that he was the son of a man who was financing the picture and therefore a non-negotiable condition of the picture. Filming continued with the newcomer and the picture was completed, but he made such a poor showing that all of his scenes had to be cut in order to release the film, with the result that Teresa Wright's part was virtually cut in half. In the name of art, she became a reflector of Brando's misery rather than a human being with decisions to make, and a life and alternatives of her own.

A Streetcar Named Desire came out in 1951, with the same director (Elia Kazan) and the same cast—Brando, Karl Malden, Kim Hunter—as the Broadway play, except with Viven Leigh playing the Jessica Tandy part. The only important change—an unfortunate but no doubt necessary concession to Production Code morality—was the punitive unhappy ending in which Stella and Stanley are forced to separate.

Blanche and Stanley, the perfervid creations of a homosexual playwright writing in a period of repression, look outrageous today—several successful productions of the play notwithstanding. Sexually speaking the fifties were a time of too much and too little, homosexuals halfway out of the closet, baroque fantasies masquerading as realism. Even then, the realism of *Streetcar* did not lie in the sex or psychology of the characters but in a basic tribal struggle, a competition among in-laws, as Mary McCarthy suggested when she dubbed the play, which she called a comic epic, *The Struggle for the Bathroom.* (Not that the humor was unintentional, and this is what we give Williams too little credit for, perhaps because he himself has denied it in his Neil Simonish determination to be profound.) The idea governing the in-law interpretation is to concentrate on the domestic territorial imperative—to see Blanche as the Older Sister (or, metaphorically, the Widowed Mother) who disapproves of her relative's marriage and at the same time resents her happiness. She is the archetypal threat to marriage (a role that can also encompass the "homosexual experience from Stanley's past"), and as instinctively as she is bent on destroying Stanley (and as instinctively as Stella is intimidated into deferring to her own blood) Stanley is bent on saving himself—hence the justification of his cruelty to Blanche.

But just as Blanche's plantation fantasies keep intruding on the senses like cheap incense, so Williams's homosexual distortions keep impinging on the authenticity of the domestic melodrama. They are all close to caricature: Stanley, an "ethnic" before his time who doesn't really belong in this environment to begin with and is obviously a homosexual pin-up, a male sex object, while Blanche's pinched-but-sensitive spinster is the traditional cover for the aging homosexual. The endlessly-glorified "animal" relationship of Stanley and Stella is the ideal of a homosexual view of the world in which sex occupies the supreme, central place. The difference between Henry James and Tennessee Williams, two writers with a "feminine sensibility" who identify with women (aside, but perhaps not separate, from the difference between a greater and a lesser talent), is that for James the mind and spirit are supreme (and in this he is truer to the nature of women) while for Williams, sex is uppermost and thus he is untrue to the women with whom he identifies.

Williams pours himself indiscriminately into all the characters, and contradictions naturally arise: Blanche is a self-deluded, thoroughly disruptive force (cut off from her "animal nature") until suddenly she redeems herself by becoming the votary of art. Stanley is a slob, and yet he has a feminine intelligence, nerve ends that are as delicate and acute as Blanche's own.

And yet, Brando and Leigh manage to bring it off. They make us accept these characters, become involved with them, even as we realize their essential hokiness. They deemphasize the contradictions by establishing a magic circle of their own, an equilibrium created not out of the naturalism, the "reality" they bring to the parts but, on the contrary, out of the equal degrees of unreality they both possess. To a far greater degree than Magnani (which may have been one reason why he didn't want to play with her), Brando and Leigh are creatures of fantasy. Kazan knew instinctively how to deal with this, how to channel their larger-than-life voltage into something at once mystical and pseudo-real, and to turn contradictions into paradox. Who else could get away with the scene in which Brando, as elemental beer-drinking male, wails for his woman at the bottom of the stairs as Kim Hunter descends!

As Stanley, Brando was the American counterpart of the proletarian Angry Young Man in British kitchen-sink drama. His violence and destructiveness are both terrifying and curiously liberating. If he is cruel to Blanche, it is because the only way he can preserve his integrity in an emasculating situation is by never conceding an inch to her, by never participating, with so much as a gallant gesture, in the rituals of a social code by which she will always retain the upper hand. And reciprocally, as the angel of sensibility, she "gets to" him, shakes his male complacency and brings out the feminine side of his nature.

ENTERTAINMENT

In this final group of pieces, a few critics get a chance to relax and show off their skill at comic banter. Mary McCarthy once referred to some prominent dramatic critics as "wits indentured to the theater." I doubt whether any movie critic would characterize his work as forced labor (the critic's life is usually very pleasant), but wit is certainly an essential attribute for the long haul. The critic sits through dozens of unspeakable movies every year; without an occasional outburst of violence or adolescent joking he would turn gray from self-suppression. James Agee, I feel sure, was able to sustain his lofty and judicious tone for seven years (1942–48) only because he allowed himself a wild swing now and then. In honor of the irresponsible side of our official Humanist Critic, I've chosen a few of his funny short reviews (the movies are of no consequence), plus one of his virtuoso round-up pieces (from 1948), in which he managed to say something witty or intriguing about twenty different movies in no more than a sentence or two per movie (the last review, perhaps the shortest in movie history, is exactly four words). Somehow I doubt that Joan McCracken, in *Good News,* really reminded Agee of a "libidinous peanut" and Mel Torme of "something in a jar," but I'm grateful Agee was occasionally frivolous enough to write that way.

Otis Ferguson may have been a little unfair to the talented Soviet filmmaker Dziga Vertov in his parody of "montage" in Vertov's *Three Songs about Lenin,* but I find the piece hard to resist. At the time (1934), montage was still a sacred truth for "serious" moviegoers; now that respect for montage as a method has declined, Ferguson's brazenly sophomoric tone seems to have grown in authority (although it's still brazen). No one *could* have been fair to the bloated, archaic biblical monstrosities that followed one another, like elephants lumbering through the gates of Babylon, in the TV-jaded, spectacle-hungry fifties and sixties. Sometimes a sitting duck deserves what it gets. What makes Dwight Macdonald's hatchet job on *The Greatest Story Ever Told* such fine comedy is the fierce display of unnecessary rigor —the "rules" and categories and Concern for Accuracy, all obviously contrived in order to be violated by a helpless movie.

Unlike most critics, who need the stimulus of scorn to get the jokes moving, Pauline Kael can be very funny when praising a movie or performer. But perhaps she is best when her feelings are crossed between affection and doubt, as in these three samples from the many film "notes" she has written over the years.—*Ed.*

ARTISTS AMONG THE FLICKERS (1934)

By Otis Ferguson

In Vertov's *Three Songs about Lenin* the Soviets come forward to bury the great leader in Westminster Abbey, with something of the atmosphere of Patriots' Day. Objectively, it is an attempt to idolize, not so much a man as his concepts; it is thus rather limited in appeal. Washington in boats with his ragged army, Lincoln freeing the slaves —these things could be dramatized in some fashion. But when Lenin tots up a column of figures to give some of the Eastern peoples economic freedom, what are you going to do about it in terms of pictures? Near the end of the film there is a moving section of Lenin's Russia today, with men working, tractors, forges, the dams, etc.; but on the whole it seems poorly melted newsreel material with a poetic cast. I would not have brought it up except that it has gone the way of many foreign films in its reception here, and got its most honorable citation on the grounds of its being pure cinema.

And this suggests the subject of film criticism in general, which is really the subject of this piece. The appreciation of pictures is much like all other forms; but there is the sad fact of its having thus far got so little intelligent consideration that intelligence, when it appears, tends to become the high priest guarding marvels. Everyone goes to the movies, to laugh or to delight his heart; they are a part of common experience—and very common at that, usually. Now and then one is good, but in thinking of it we do not think of art. It's just a movie; we only went for the fun. So when someone comes along and says down his nose, Art in the cinema is largely in the hands of artists in cinematographic experimentation, we think, Mm, fancy such a thing, I wonder what *that* is like. When someone, almost holding his breath, says, Well, there is surely no better *montage* (or *régisseur*) than this *montage* (or *régisseur*), we are apt to be discouraged: Oh damn, I missed it again, all I saw was a story with people and action. And when someone says of *Three Songs about Lenin,* This is pure cinema, implying that you couldn't say more for it, we think, Well, well, can't miss that surely.

The pay-off is that *régisseurs* are in ordinary life directors, that *montage* is simply the day-in-day-out (in Hollywood) business of cutting: all you need, except for the higher technical reaches, is a pair of shears and a good sense of timing. As for pure cinema, we would not praise a novel (in which field by this time you must, to be intelligent, be intelligible, or perish) by saying merely that it was pure *roman.* I do not wish to pull rabbits out of the hat, but here is a fact: you too can make pure cinema.

Given the proper facilities and scientific advice, anyone can, me for instance. Out of my window I can see a rather mean-looking tenement. Doors, windows, a sidewalk. Just above it, rising over it, is a tall very recent building, elevator apts, electrolux, 1, 2, 3, 4, 5 rooms, etc., but wait, we'll not open there. We will catch the meanness of the mean street by opening on pages 18–19 of *The New York Times* for last week, dirty and blowing along the mean sidewalk in the morning wind. Dust, desolation. The paper blowing and on the sound-track a high piccolo note—wheeeeeeee—and the street empty, deserted, it is morning. Now (take the shots separately; cut and paste them together afterward): the sky (gray), the house (sleeping), the paper, the sky, the house, the paper (whee). Follow the paper down to, suddenly, the wheel of a milk truck (Ha! truck—life, the city stirs; throw in a tympani under the piccolo for the city stirring) which goes down to the mean house, stops, the driver gets out: follow him with one bottle of Grade B up three flights of mean stairs to a mean door where—stop.

Down in the street the driver comes out, yawns. Up the house front slowly to a top-floor window where a man, touseled, yawns. As the truck drives off its wheels turn, gain speed, and suddenly there are other wheels (the city awakes): trucks pounding down the Concourse, the subway, the "El," streetcars and the trucks pounding, the "Els," the subways, and now (on the sound-track, the piccolo goes a fifth higher) you cut in the big dynamo wheels, all the wheels, all the power houses, wheels and wheels, Rah, *montage.* Then from the dynamo out (space, motion, speed) to—what do you think? An electric grill in the big stinking apartment house, with a colored servant in white, frying bacon and looking at the dumbwaiter. Title: WHERE ALL IS THAT MILKMAN NOHOW. Now down to the milkman, taking in a bottle of heavy cream (flash: SERVANTS' ENTRANCE) to the dumbwaiter; now back to the poor house, and out over the city and up over the high, proud bulge of the apartment house to the high gray clouds, over the city, over the rich and poor getting up, getting their separate service from the milkman. And on into a great dither of wheels, clouds, gaping windows, yawns, men walking—into plush elevators, on the hard, mean sidewalk, faster, faster, everybody getting into motion, the same city, the same sky, the two remote worlds rich and poor. For special effect, let us say, a kid coming out of the door of the mean house, with pennies for a loaf of whole-wheat, and running past the feet and in front of the wheels, and tripping on the broken cement, falling, smack. Close-up of the head showing a splash of blood spreading on the mean stones, and flash to the apartment house, up, up, to a window, in through the window to the cream being poured into the coffee, being drunk in bed, in silk pyjamas, spilling, a splash of coffee spreading on the silk pyjamas.

Any good? I'm afraid not. But it is pure cinema. Pure cinema can be anything: the important thing always is whether it is done well, whether you can pile one thing on another in a clear beautiful moving line. The wonderful and humbling thing about the movies in general is the skill and sure judgment behind this mechanical transfer of images to strips of celluloid, of a certain number of feet of celluloid into a moving series of images that will have a certain effect on those who watch. It doesn't matter whether the result is a story of a Significant Experiment: what we have got to single out is the difference between a picture that catches you up in its own movement, and a picture that stammers, stands doubtfully, hammers at a few obvious meanings, and leaves you with a feeling of all the mechanism used to capture emotion, without the emotion. *Three Songs about Lenin* may have been attacked with a new attack, may be an awesome experiment. My point is that it is not a good picture, and my quarrel with movie criticism is simply that if it was, those who thought so have not done one thing to show why, in so many simple honest words.

THREE SHORT REVIEWS (1945–48)
By James Agee

(1945)

In *God Is My Co-Pilot* the Flying Tiger hero, Dennis Morgan, tells a priest, Alan Hale, that he has killed a hundred men that day; he obviously feels deeply troubled by the fact, and is asking for spiritual advice. Since the priest does not answer him in any way about that, but pretends to by commenting comfortably on a quite different and much easier perplexity—*every* death makes a difference to God—it is regrettable, not to say nauseating, that they bothered to bring up the problem at all. Aside from these religious conversations, any one of which would serve to unite atheists and religious men in intense distaste for the lodgers in the abyss which separates them, there is a good deal of air combat on process screens, obstructed by the customary close-ups of pilots smiling grimly as they give or take death in a studio, for considerably more than soldiers' pay, a yard above the ground. The picture is not as bad, I must admit, as I'm making it sound; but it is not good enough to make me feel particularly sorry about that. God is my best pal and severest critic, but when He asked for this touching March afternoon off, I didn't have it in my heart to refuse Him.

(1946)

Till the Clouds Roll By is a little like sitting down to a soda-fountain de luxe atomic special of maple walnut on vanilla on burnt almond on strawberry on butter pecan on coffee on raspberry sherbet on tutti frutti with hot fudge, butterscotch, marshmallow, filberts, pistachios, shredded pineapple, and rainbow sprills on top, go double on the whipped cream. Some of the nuts, it turns out, are a little stale, and wandering throughout the confection is a long bleached-golden hair, probably all right in its place but, here, just a little more than you can swallow. This hair, in the difficult technical language of certain members of the Screen Writers' Guild who exult in my nonprofessionalism—political as well as cinematic—would, I suppose, be called the "story-line." The story is enough of the life and not very hard times of the late Jerome Kern to make you want either not to hear any of it at all or to get the real story instead. Besides the story, however, the picture contains something over twenty stars and featured players, many of them nice people, and they sing no less than twenty-two of Kern's songs. If, as I do, you like a good deal of his graceful, nacreous music, the picture is pleasantly, if rather stupefyingly, worth all the bother. The songs are nearly all sung with care and affection, though not one that I have heard before is done here quite as well as I have heard it elsewhere. The most surprising defection is the failure twice around to give "Old Man River" any of the pulse and momentum which go so far toward making it Kern's best song. Both Sinatra and a colored singer do it, instead, with all misplaced reverence, as if they were retranslating at sight, out of Tacitus, the Emancipation Proclamation. This I realize is called *feeling* the music; for that kind of feeling I prefer W. C. Fields's cadenza on the zither, which was rendered in sparring-gloves.

(1947)

Carnegie Hall is about the thickest and sourest mess of musical mulligatawny I have yet had to sit down to, a sort of aural compromise between the Johnstown flood and the Black Hole of Calcutta. I have an idea that some of the music was well done, but I was so exhausted by suffering and rage that I can't possibly be sure of what. However, as a gnarled mirror of American musical taste at its worst, and as a record of what various prominent musicians look like under strange professional circumstances, it is a permanently fascinating and valuable show. There is, for a single instance, the protracted spectacle of Stokowsky—shot from the floor—who seems to be undergoing for the public benefit an experience, while conducting a portion of Tschaikowsky's Fifth Symphony, which men of coarser clay wish exclusively on women, or perhaps on albums of prefabricated trade-union folk songs. I am sorry to be writing this way about *Carnegie Hall,* for I can't avoid feeling that some rather good intentions were involved in it. But then I can't doubt that Hitler had good intentions. He and I just didn't see eye to eye.

Midwinter Clearance (1948)

Albuquerque. An actor, shot at, grabs his kneecap and falls downstairs. Within a few seconds he is able to explain, in a politely stoical voice, that he isn't badly hurt—just hit in the leg. This is a fair measure of how intimately most movies are acquainted with even the most rudimentary realities of experience. A good excruciating crack on every kneecap that needs it might be enough to revolutionize Hollywood. Even if it didn't, it would be a pleasure to deliver.

A Lover's Return. Louis Jouvet, in charge of a ballet troupe, gets back to Lyon after twenty years and torments the bourgeois types who did him dirt. The story is essentially sub-Montherlant trash, but it is acutely understood, easily filmed, and nicely played. Pleasant ballet stuff, backstage and on.

An Ideal Husband. Vincent Korda's sets are good, Cecil Beaton's costumes are mouth-watering, and most of the players are visually right. The composing and cutting of this fine raw material is seldom above medium grade. Wilde's lines are unevenly and in general too slowly and patiently delivered, and the whole production is too slow and realistic.

A Woman's Vengeance. Aldous Huxley's screen play of his *Gioconda Smile.* A rather literary movie, but most movies aren't even that; much less are they real movies. Sensitively directed by Zoltan Korda and generally well played, above all by Jessica Tandy.

Bush Christmas. Australian children hound horse thieves through some beautiful wilderness. A child's-eye movie, not imaginative enough, but simple and likable.

Captain from Castile. The first few reels have flow and a kind of boys'-book splendor; the rest is locomotor ataxia. The costumes of Montezuma's emissaries are as magnificent as any I have ever seen. They are utilized, for movie purposes, about as appreciatively as so many sack suits.

Furia. An Italian farmer's wife plays around with a Cornel Wilde-ish groom. This is filmed with a carnal and psychological frankness I am happy to see—and to thank the censors for saving a good deal of—and the picture is essentially sincere rather than pornographic. It is also rather childish in conception and inept as art. Good work by the two most prominent women in the cast.

Golden Earrings. Dietrich as a gipsy, Ray Milland as a British agent. Dreary comedy-melodrama; a good bit by Reinhold Schunzel.

Good News. I like the tunes and June Allyson. Joan McCracken makes me think of a libidinous peanut; Mel Torme reminds me of something in a jar but is, unfortunately, less quiet. If they had used the old George Olson arrangements on the tunes and had had any real feelings for the late twenties, this could have been a beauty.

If Winter Comes. In its essence this tearjerker is much better than the determinedly tearproof allow themselves to realize. From there on out it is pretty awful. Rather well played; an overdone but promising performance by Janet Leigh.

I Walk Alone. Good performances by Wendell Corey and Kirk Douglas; a sharp scene about an old-fashioned gangster's helplessness against modern business methods. Some better than ordinary night-club atmosphere. Otherwise the picture deserves, like four out of five other movies, to walk alone, tinkle a little bell, and cry "Unclean, unclean."

Mourning Becomes Electra. In my opinion a badly mistaken play; so, a bad mistake to turn into a movie, especially a reverential movie. Within its own terms of mistaken reverence it seems to me a good, straight, deliberately unimaginative production.

The Paradine Case. Hitchcock uses a lot of skill over a lot of nothing. Some very experienced work by Laughton and Leo G. Carroll; better work by Ann Todd and Joan Tetzel, who is at moments very beautiful. Valli is something to look at, too. The picture never for an instant comes to life. This is the wordiest script since the death of Edmund Burke.

The Road to Rio. Hope, Crosby, Lamour. Enough laughs to pass the time easily and to remind you how completely, since sound came in, the American genius for movie comedy has disintegrated.

The Secret Beyond the Door. Because he thought his mother didn't love him, the poor fellow developed a terrible, but of course forgivable, compulsion to kill women. Fritz Lang gets a few wood-silky highlights out of this sow's ear, but it is a hopeless job and a worthless movie.

The Senator Was Indiscreet. Kaufman, MacArthur, and Nunnally Johnson put William Powell through some loosely adjusted political wringers. Most of it would seem feeble in print or on stage, but because of the generally vapid state of the movies it seems quite bold and funny on the screen.

T-Man. This is being over-promoted and overrated, but it is an enjoyable and energetic semi-documentary melodrama.

This Time for Keeps. Jimmy Durante; Esther Williams; some shiny bellowing from Lauritz Melchior; an attempt at off-beat locale work in Michigan; Metro's customary brats and good-will; a lot of boring music; Technicolor. The money spent on this production might easily have kept Mozart and Schubert alive and busy to the age of sixty, with enough left over to finance five of the best movies ever made. It might even have been invested in a good movie musical.

Tycoon. Several tons of dynamite are set off in this movie; none of it under the right people.

You Were Meant for Me. That's what you think.

THE GREATEST STORY EVER TOLD (1965)

By Dwight Macdonald

It seems to be impossible for this Christain civilization to make a decent movie about the life of its founder. From De Mille's sexy-sacred epics up to the film under consideration, George Stevens's *The Greatest Story Ever Told,* they have all been, as art or as religion, indecent. Yet the rules for success, deducing them inversely from the failures, are simple enough:

(1) Use the original script.

(2) Avoid well-known performers, especially in small parts.

(3) Try to realize that the past was once a present, as everyday and confused and banal as the present present, and that Jesus and the people of his time didn't know they were picturesque any more than the builders of Chartres knew they were making Gothic architecture (though the builders of our collegiate Gothic did).

(4) Keep it small. In spirit: no dramatics, sparing use of emphatic close-ups and photography, no underlining of a story that still moves us precisely because it is not underlined; Jesus was a throw-it-away prophet, direct and unrhetorical even in a speech like the Sermon on the Mount. Also keep it small literally: no wide screen, no stereophonic sound, no swelling-sobbing mood music (maybe no music at all), no gigantic sets or vast landscapes or thousands of extras milling around with staves, palm branches and other picturesque impedimenta.

(5) The story of Jesus should be told with reverence for the text in the New Testament (taking into account historical corrections by recent scholarship), but with irreverence for the sensibilities of contemporary religious groups—Buddhist, Moslem, Taoist, Catholic or Jewish.

Of the three most recent stabs—*le mot juste,* I think—at the Christ story, Nicholas Ray's *King of Kings* is lowbrow kitsch, Pier Pasolini's *The Gospel According to St. Matthew* is highbrow kitsch, and the present work is the full middlebrow, or Hallmark Hall of Fame treatment. I must add, in fairness to Mr. Pasolini, that his was much the best try: it followed rules (1) and (2) completely, observed (3) intermittently, and systematically violated (4), which unfortunately is the most important. I must also add, in fairness to Mr. Stevens, that his movie was premiered "Under the Patronage of the President of the United States and Mrs. Johnson"; and, in fairness to myself, that even Bosley Crowther, normally a pushover for Biblical spectaculars, didn't like it.

For reasons which as usual escape me, George Stevens has long enjoyed a reputation in Hollywood as a dedicated artist. Dedicated he may be, but his films look to me overblown and pretentious, even *A Place in the Sun,* even *Shane.* Maybe it's because he takes so long —five years on *The Greatest Story.* Or perhaps it's because he takes himself very seriously—in Hollywood it's often all that is necessary. How can they tell out there, after all? Maybe the guy *is* an artist. Dismissing previous biblical films as "superficial," Mr. Stevens announced his treatment was going to be different. No clichés, he told a *New York Times* reporter, and furthermore: "The basic theme of the story is one which, unfortunately, has not always been associated with it in the past. It relates to the universality of men and how they must learn to live together. I think it is a theme of great earnestness and utmost simplicity. And I think all the usual trappings connected with Biblical productions . . . are an alarming disagreement with this simple theme. We tried, without diverging from the traditional, to think out the story anew and present it as living literature." The safety clause about not "diverging from the traditional" seems to contradict the rest, but let's be realistic: it's a $20,000,000 property.

What I saw on that wide screen was something else again. Had I not just this moment thought up my five simple rules, I might have suspected Mr. Stevens had somehow got a peek and, reasoning that whatever I like the box office wouldn't, simply inverted them.

(1) The screenplay, by Mr. Stevens and James Lee Barrett, is

"based on The Books of the Old and New Testaments, Other Ancient Writings, The Book *The Greatest Story Ever Told* by Fulton Oursler, and Other Writings by Henry Denker." Decent of them to list the New Testament and nice, if puzzling, to include the Old so nobody gets left out. The Other Ancient Writings are intriguing, as are the Other Writings, presumably non-Ancient, by Mr. Denker, an unknown writer to me. I have heard of the late Mr. Oursler but have not felt it necessary to read him. He is described in *The Reader's Encyclopedia of American Literature* as "a versatile writer . . . detective stories . . . plays and motion-picture scenarios, including *The Spider* (1927) . . . in 1944 became a senior editor of *Reader's Digest* . . . His most famous books were those on the Bible and Christianity, particularly *The Greatest Story Ever Told* (1951). Oursler had a great gift for popularization." His religious career was eclectic: "In his early years Oursler was a Baptist, for a while he was an agnostic, in his later years a devout Catholic." Just the man for a biblical movie. There was one more litterateur involved. "Produced in Creative Association with Carl Sandburg," the titles proclaim—a job as vague as it was elevated. Mr. Sandburg seems to have been a kind of cinematic Holy Ghost. The script that emerged from this olio of writers and Other Writings teeters between the vapid and the punchy, every line destroying whatever illusion of history or religion the acting, photography and direction have accidentally spared. "The party responsible is Jesus of Nazareth." "Don't lie there, Matthew, you'll catch a sickness," says Jesus, meaning a cold, but "sickness" is more Biblical. "Your majesty, if I may be so bold. . . ." "I have never liked you, Baptist," says José Ferrer (Herod Antipas) to Charlton Heston (John the Baptist) in his most sneering tone, which is plenty. Later they have a spirited exchange: "I've heard things about you, Baptist." "And I've heard many things about *you,* Herod [pause], all bad!" "How shall I be saved?" Herod asks, trying to change the subject—you can tell by Ferrer's expression he doesn't really mean it, just cynical and effete. His father, Herod the Great, alias Claude Rains, is even more cynical, in that world-weary style on which Mr. Rains took out a patent in 1927. But Baptist-Heston, who is neither cynical nor effete, replies with simple dignity: "By standing in the next line when you meet him—this side of Hell!" I prefer the original dialogue by Matthew, Mark, Luke and John.

(2) Max Von Sydow—who must have found George Stevens an interesting contrast to his usual director, Bergman—is a gentlemanly

Christ, restrained, earnest and handsome in a Nordic way. I wonder why, incidentally, all movie Christs, from H. B. Warner on (with the exception of Pasolini's, who I'm told is a Spanish Jew, though he looked just Spanish to me), have been non-Jewish; likewise most of the disciples, except of course Judas. I also wonder why those Jewish-chauvinist groups and magazines that gave me a hard time when, in my review of *Ben-Hur,* I complained the Crucifixion was blamed entirely on the Romans, have never made a fuss about this point. Why no protests against Mr. Stevens's casting the ostentatiously Irish Dorothy McGuire as Mary? I suppose it's a tricky business: the Semiticists don't want Jews to be villains in the Christ story, but they aren't keen either to claim the heroes for their side since, despite the recent scholarly researches—with which I largely agree—proving that the Romans were more and the orthodox Jewish authorities were less responsible for sending Jesus to the Cross than the New Testament alleges, still he did preach a new religion that was—and is—in important respects opposed to Judaism. Getting back to casting, Von Sydow is not bad as Jesus; for all his lack of Semitic expressiveness, he's at least dignified and he's not so familiar as to make one think, "There's Max!" whenever he appears. But when Ed Wynn, wearing contact lenses, comes on as the blind Aram, a quaveringly ecstatic convert, I was wrenched back to the Texaco Fire Chief. I have noted the difficulty of suspending disbelief when Ferrer, Rains and Heston go through their familiar routines, also the difficulty of keeping Dorothy McGuire in focus as Mary, but I might add that Simon of Cyrene was all too obviously Sidney Poitier, ditto Van Heflin and Sal Mineo and John Wayne and Angela Lansbury in other "cameo" parts. The illusion-destroying effect was all the greater because they came on so suddenly and briefly. I never got used to them as, respectively, Bar Armand, Uriah, The Centurion, and Claudia; it was as if some nutty relative had come bursting in dressed up as Napoleon. There was also that "Woman of No Name" who pushes through the crowd as Jesus is healing the sick and, after he has grappled with her, cries out in purest Bronx, "Oi'm cured! Oi'm cured!" and turns around to run toward the camera with arms waving in triumph—and damned if it isn't Shelley Winters. A shock like that can suspend belief for quite a while.

(3) Mr. Stevens says he tried to avoid "the clichés and the usual trappings connected with Biblical productions" and to "think the story out anew and present it as living literature." His effort was

unsuccessful, one might say spectacularly so. He rushed to embrace every biblical-movie cliché and trapping in sight. Picturesque effects are unremitting, beginning with the star that guides the three wise men to the manger. It is a very large star, gleaming in the shape of a Hallmark cross in the dark-blue Panavision sky, and the wise men would have had to be extremely nearsighted to miss it. The manger is rather pictorial too, not to mention the lovely Miss McGuire ensconced there looking down with misty eyes on her miraculous babe. The wise men, like the other characters, have a tendency to get themselves photographed against the sky. I haven't seen so many skyline shots since Dassin's *He Who Must Die,* another Christ movie. It's in modern dress, but otherwise it's done in the same spirit.

(4) The scale is bigger than in any biblical film I've seen, which is a large statement. Not just a Panavision but Ultra Panavision 70. Not just sound but stereophonic sound that comes at you from all quarters. There are lots of squalling babies, to show that Life Goes On, and once the cry came so clearly from under my seat that I looked down to see if some careless mother . . . There are also lots of screaming gulls wheeling and gliding most pictorially to show that the lower orders also reproduce themselves—the M.P.A.A. Code should blacklist seagulls as local color, except in art films. The music roars and throbs and nudges continually, more Wagnerian than Christian. For the finale of Part One, Handel's *Hallelujah Chorus* was belted out with such deafening *brio* that, what with Lazarus rising from the dead and the extras running around like grand-opera peasants, telling each other, needlessly since we and they had seen it happen, "Lazarus has risen! He's *alive!"* and Ed Wynn recovering his sight (*I think,* but there was so much confusion) and tottering up to Herod's palace to shout triumphantly up to the guards on the high Babylonian ramparts that Lazarus has risen . . . is *alive,* etc.—I then decided I had spent a reasonable amount of time, two hours, on *The Greatest Story* and that after this the Crucifixion could only be an anticlimax. So I left.

The landscape Mr. Stevens had chosen was a factor in my decision. With his customary thoroughness, he had, according to the *Times,* spent "months of research in the Holy Land." But he was disappointed: it looked worn, beat up, mingy, *small.* Not a worthy setting for the greatest story ever told. So he returned to the U.S.A. and shot the film in Utah, Nevada and California, where vistas are quite large. "Some of the landscapes around Jerusalem," he explained, "were exciting, but many had been worn down through the years by erosion and man, invaders and wars, to places of less spectacular aspect." Therefore, as one of his handouts puts it, our own West is a "far more authentic" locale for filming the life of Christ "than is the modern Holy Land." (The Forest Lawn cemetery in Los Angeles suggests in its literature that its replicas of Michelangelo's sculptures, carved by hand out of the same Carrara marble he used and by Italians just like him, are really closer to his conception than those chipped, stained, dilapidated "originals" in Florence.) So what we have is a biblical Western. Jesus and his disciples crawl like ants over the most stupendous kind of rocky terrain. The Sermon on the Mount is escalated to The Sermon on the Mountain, with Jesus on the pinnacle of a high mesa with scenery stretching for miles around him. He begins the Lord's Prayer in a meadow, then the bored camera moves off and we get some more mountain scenery and finally they camp by a broad river at the bottom of what looks like the Grand Canyon and, dramatically silhouetted against the sunset, with great black cliffs beetling over him and the wide river roiling turbulently as it catches the evening light, Jesus delivers the Lord's Prayer complete. The setting is impressive, a little too impressive. Custer's last stand or the battle of the Alamo might compete successfully with such natural grandeur. The Lord's Prayer gets lost in the scenery.

(5) All biblical movies are theologically circumspect, for obvious reasons, but this one overdoes it. The Romans are the bad goys again —though Pilate looks Jewish for some reason—and the Jews couldn't be more friendly to the founder of Christianity. Jesus-Sydow is walking with his disciples, and one says, "Look, some Pharisees!" (Like "Hey, Indians!") And there they are, those oft-denounced Pharisees: "Woe unto you . . ." And they have come to warn him about certain plots against him. Nor is the Catholic audience slighted. When Jesus asks the disciples just who they think he is, exactly, Judas hems and haws ("Er, um, you're a great leader, a teacher"); the others are more enthusiastic but also vague; finally Peter gives the right answer: "You are the Son of God, the Messiah." Jesus is pleased: "Peter, you are the rock on which my church will be founded." As a lapsed Presbyterian, I object to this building up of Peter. He didn't show up so well at Gethsemane. Jesus said unto him, "Verily I say unto thee, that this day, even in this night, before the cock crow twice, thou shalt deny me thrice." And he did. Some rock. "Do you consider wealth a

crime?" the rich Lazarus asks. "Not at all," smoothly replies Max Von Norman Vincent Peale, "but it may become a burden." One of the many things I admire about Jesus is his prejudice against the rich.

"The film moves to excite the imagination of the audience by rendering before it the beauty and the extraordinary nature of Him who represents many things, and one thing," states the vellum-paper program in that gnomic style of which Mr. Stevens is a master. "To recall, or is it to challenge, one's own image of Christ—an image derived from a word, a panel of stained glass, a Gothic lettered Christmas card, a burst of organ music, an inner exaltation, an experience."

You can get an image of Christ, it seems, from practically anything, including a Hallmark greeting card, except the writings of Matthew, Mark, Luke and John.

THREE PROGRAM NOTES (1967)

By Pauline Kael

All About Eve. This is ersatz art of a very high grade, and one of the most enjoyable movies ever made. Eve, a young actress (Anne Baxter), intrigues to take the place of an aging star (Bette Davis) on stage and in bed, and the battle is fought with tooth, claw, and a battery of epigrams. The dialogue and atmosphere are so peculiarly remote from life that they have sometimes been mistaken for art. The synthetic has qualities of its own—glib, over-explicit, self-important, the You're-sneaky-and-corrupt-but-so-am-I-We-belong-to-each-other-darling style of writing. Author-director Joseph L. Mankiewicz's bad taste; exhibited with verve, is more fun than careful, mousy, dehydrated good taste. His nonsense about "theatre" is saved by one performance that is the real thing: Bette Davis is at her most brilliant. Her actress—vain, scared, a woman who goes too far in her reactions and emotions—makes the whole thing come alive (though it's hard to believe Anne Baxter could ever be a threat to Bette Davis). With George Sanders, Celeste Holm, Gary Merrill, Thelma Ritter, Gregory Ratoff, Hugh Marlowe, and Marilyn Monroe. Academy Awards for 1950: Best Picture, Director, Screenplay, Supporting Actor (Sanders), etc.

Ecstasy (Extase). In the early sixties there was the scandalous *The Lovers,* with Jeanne Moreau as a deep-watery Madame Bovary; in 1933 it was *Ecstasy,* with Hedy Lamarr, directed by Gustav Machaty in Czechoslovakia, which was always being "banned" and released and withdrawn and reissued and all the rest of the sex/art exploitation routine. What's in these movies? Well, in *Ecstasy,* along with some explicit sequences there is symbolic erotic imagery—romantic, poetic, and despite a kind of innocent absurdity about it, sensuous and exciting. In "Reflections on Ecstasy," Henry Miller wrote, "This is a Laurencian theme, and Machaty is the one man in the movie world capable of giving adequate expression to Lawrence's ideas." There were always people around to say, "But you must see the original, complete version!" Yes, but how many original versions were there, and where were they to be seen? (One distributor I know swears he has handled prints with two different men playing the engineer.) And have people really seen what they say was in the "original" film or have they just fantasized their own particular sexual predilections onto the screen? Recently, I was held spellbound as a writer described what had gone on in the *Ecstasy* he'd seen; later I remembered that, as an undergraduate, I'd gone to the picture with him. In recent versions, someone has decided to prolong the ecstasy by printing climactic sequences over and over again. Still, whichever *Ecstasy* one sees, it's a sweeter, more tender movie than *The Lovers,* which is the planned poetry of sex.

My Little Chickadee. W. C. Fields and Mae West acted together only once, in 1940, in *My Little Chickadee*—near the end of both of their screen careers.

Fields had made his first movie in 1915 and had worked with D. W. Griffith. But it was in the talkies of the thirties that he became the familiar figure with the assertive drawl, the muttered asides, the grandiose pretensions, and the florid, obsequious flattery that was his own brand of insult. Whether playing con men or harried, henpecked, lower-middle-class husbands who schemed to escape to the barbershop-poolhall-racetrack-saloon world for a few hours, Fields was shifty, weaseling, mean-spirited, put-upon. His characters never asked for sympathy; they always expected the worst—that they would be found out. His film effusions form one big snarl of contempt for abstinence, truth, honest endeavor, respectability, and human and animal offspring. The great tosspot is essentially a man's comedian, a bulbous fixture of the man's world. Women are not easily won over to his cringing cowardice, his massive pretentiousness, his paranoia, his gloating over his secret knowledge of avarice or sin (Fields, peeking through a keyhole, mutters, "What won't they think of next?"), his vaunted prowess (Fields to Peggy Hopkins Joyce: "I shall dally in the valley and believe me I can dally"), his ambivalence (Fields to Franklin Pangborn: "Young man, if you're not very careful, you're going to lose my trade"). Groucho, with all his affront, has a pixyish charm, but Fields is a dirty, repulsive man—a man without romantic illusions. His world is divided between blue noses and red noses. No maiden escapes his lewd suggestions; no shrew escapes his foul derision; no homosexual escapes his knowing eye. In his top hat and long johns, he is American dada. For women, he is an acquired taste—like sour-mash bourbon. But then, you can't go on sipping daiquiris forever.

Mae West was a wiggling, bosom-heaving combination of permissive mama and shady lady hinting at exotic new tricks. She enraged the respectable women of America by turning sin into a joke ("I used to be Snow White but I drifted"). The primrose path might be thorny but at least it went somewhere; the gin mill might be perdition but it wasn't dull, like your small town. In movies like *She Done Him Wrong, I'm No Angel,* and *Belle of the Nineties,* Mae West celebrated the victory of experience over innocence, of talent over youth. Shifting her white flesh in her corsets, she sang good, dirty blues. And if songs like, "Where Has My Easy Rider Gone?" led to the industry's self-policing Production Code, they were worth it. We enjoyed the crime so much that we could endure even the punishment of family entertainment.

My Little Chickadee is a classic among bad movies: despite the presence of Mae West and W. C. Fields, the satire of Westerns never really gets off the ground. But the ground is such an honest mixture of dirt, manure, and corn that at times it is fairly aromatic. Mae West is rather slowed down by the censors breathing down her decolletage; but even less bawdy, and rather more grotesque than at her best, she is still overwhelming. Fields is in better form: whether cheating at cards, or kissing Miss West's hand ("What symmetrical digits!"), or spending his wedding night with a goat, he remains the scowling, snarling misanthrope. With Joseph Calleia, Margaret Hamilton, Dick Foran. Directed by Edward Cline. Fields and West, who wrote most of their own vehicles, collaborated on the script.

Fields went on a little longer. His last two comedies, *The Bank Dick* (1940) and *Never Give a Sucker an Even Break* (1941), which are just about one-man shows, are often described as "the height of his achievement." Both deal with making a movie. In *The Bank Dick* there are moviemakers and bank robbers and a great chase on a dirt road up a mountain. With Una Merkel, and, of course, Franklin Pangborn and Grady Sutton. In *Never Give a Sucker an Even Break,* the movie Fields wants to make is a large part of the film, and it's set in a kind of cuckoo-cloud Ruritania that's the damnedest thing ever seen. Up there Fields encounters the woman for him: Margaret Dumont. He gets back to some kind of earth for the chase-finale. The film has its horror: an erstwhile ingenue named Gloria Jean; you can't just shut your eyes, because she *sings.* With Leon Errol. Edward Cline directed both.

NOTES ON CONTRIBUTORS

JAMES AGEE (1909–1955) wrote on film for *The Nation* and *Time* from 1942 to 1948. Most of his criticism has been collected in *Agee on Film.* A companion volume includes his screenplays. Among his works of poetry and prose are *Let Us Now Praise Famous Men* (with Walker Evans), *A Death in the Family, The Morning Watch,* and *Permit Me Voyage.*

RICHARD CORLISS is film critic of *New Times,* editor of *Film Comment,* and the author of *Talking Pictures,* a critical study of the Hollywood screenwriter.

MANNY FARBER has written movie criticism for *The Nation, The New Republic, Artforum, Film Comment,* and other periodicals. A significant portion of his work has been collected in *Negative Space* (paperback title: *Movies*). He is also a painter, art critic, and teacher.

OTIS FERGUSON (1907–1943) wrote jazz, literary, and movie criticism for *The New Republic* from 1933 to 1942. Most of his work on movies has been collected in *The Film Criticism of Otis Ferguson.*

PENELOPE GILLIATT alternates with Pauline Kael in six-month periods as film critic of *The New Yorker* and was formerly film critic of the London *Observer.* She has written a study of film comedy *(Unholy Fools)*, a book on the work of Jean Renoir, two novels, three collections of short stories, and the screenplay for *Sunday, Bloody Sunday.*

MOLLY HASKELL is a film critic for *The Village Voice* and *Viva* and the author of a historical study, *From Reverence to Rape: The Treatment of Women in Movies.*

PAULINE KAEL alternates with Penelope Gilliatt in six-month periods as movie critic of *The New Yorker.* She was formerly movie critic of *McCall's* and *The New Republic,* and her work has been collected in *I Lost It at the Movies, Kiss Kiss Bang Bang, Going Steady, Deeper Into Movies,* and *Reeling;* her long essay, "Raising Kane," appears in *The Citizen Kane Book.* She ran revival theaters in Berkeley during the late fifties.

STANLEY KAUFFMANN is film and theater critic of *The New Republic.* His film criticism has been collected in *A World on Film, Figures of Light,* and *Living Images.* He has also written a number of novels and plays.

VACHEL LINDSAY (1870–1931) wrote *The Art of the Moving Picture* in 1915 and was movie critic for *The New Republic* in 1917. He is best known as a poet.

DWIGHT MACDONALD was film critic of *Esquire* from 1960 to 1966. Most of his work from this period, as well as a variety of earlier pieces, has been collected in *Dwight Macdonald on Movies.* His books include *Memoirs of a Revolutionist* (which includes material from *politics,* a magazine he edited from 1944 to 1949), *Against the American Grain,* and other works of social, political, and cultural criticism.

ERWIN PANOFSKY (1892–1968) is the author of *The Life and Art of Albrecht Dürer, Early Netherlandish Painting, Meaning in the Visual Arts, Studies in Iconology,* and numerous other works of art history and criticism. For many years he was associated with the Institute for Advanced Study at Princeton.

HARRY ALAN POTAMKIN (1900–1933) wrote for *Hound & Horn, Close-Up, New Masses,* and a variety of other periodicals. Some of his later pieces on film can be found in *Hound and Horn: Essays on Cinema.*

ANDREW SARRIS is film critic of *The Village Voice* and professor of Cinema Studies at Columbia. His books include *The Films of Josef Von Sternberg, Interviews with Film Directors, The American Cinema: Directors and Directions 1929–1968, Confessions of a Cultist, The Primal Screen,* and *The John Ford Movie Mystery.*

PAUL SCHRADER is author of *The Transcendental Style* (a study of Ozu, Bresson, and Dreyer) and was formerly the editor of *Cinema.* He wrote the screenplays for *The Yakuza, Taxi Driver,* and *Obsession.*

GILBERT SELDES (1893–1970) is the author of *The Seven Lively Arts, An Hour with the Movies and the Talkies, The Public Arts, The Great Audience* and other works on popular culture. He worked professionally in all aspects of radio and television production and was dean, in his later years, of the Annenberg School at the University of Pennsylvania.

JOHN SIMON is film critic of *New York* magazine and was formerly film critic of *The New Leader* and *Esquire* and drama critic of *New York*. His film criticism has been collected in *The Acid Test, Private Screenings* and *Movies Into Film* and he has written a study of Ingmar Bergman. His theater criticism has been collected in *Singularities* and *Uneasy Stages*.

SUSAN SONTAG has written essays on film, theater, photography, aesthetics, politics, and many other topics. Much of this work has been collected in *Against Interpretation* and *Styles of Radical Will*. She is also the author of two novels, *The Benefactor* and *The Death Kit,* and the director of *Duet for Cannibals, Brother Carl,* and *Promised Lands*.

WILLIAM TROY (1903–1961) reviewed movies for *The Nation* from 1933 to 1935. A portion of his literary criticism has been collected in *Selected Essays*.

PARKER TYLER (1904–1974) is the author of *The Hollywood Hallucination; Myth and Magic of the Movies; Chaplin; Sex, Psyche, Etcetera in the Film; Underground Films: A Critical History,* and other works of film aesthetics and criticism. He also wrote art criticism and poetry.

ROBERT WARSHOW (1917–1955) was managing editor of *Commentary* magazine when he died. Most of his essays on movies, literature, comics, and other aspects of popular culture were collected posthumously in *The Immediate Experience*.

ABOUT THE EDITOR

DAVID DENBY is film critic of the Boston *Phoenix,* and was film critic of *The Atlantic* from 1970 to 1973. His articles and reviews have appeared in *The New York Times, Harper's, Sight and Sound, Film Quarterly, Partisan Review,* the Boston *Real Paper* and other publications. He edited four of the yearly anthologies of articles by the National Society of Film Critics and has taught courses in film aesthetics and criticism at Stanford.